AN UNQUIET
PEDAGOGY

AN UNQUIET PEDAGOGY

Transforming Practice in the English Classroom

Eleanor Kutz

University of Massachusetts/ Boston

Hephzibah Roskelly

University of North Carolina at Greensboro

Foreword by

Paulo Freire

BOYNTON/COOK PUBLISHERS
HEINEMANN
Portsmouth, NH

Boynton/Cook Publishers, Inc.
A subsidiary of Reed Elsevier Inc.
361 Hanover Street   Portsmouth, NH 03801-3912
Offices and agents throughout the world

We are grateful to the following for permission to reprint material:

Excerpts from *The Water Is Wide* by Pat Conroy, copyright 1972, 1987 by Pat Conroy.
Reprinted by permission of Houghton Mifflin Co.

Every effort has been made to contact the copyright holders for permission to reprint
borrowed material. We regret any oversights that may have occurred and would be
happy to rectify them in future printings of this work.

Library of Congress Cataloging-in-Publication Data

Kutz, Eleanor.
    An unquiet pedagogy: transforming practice in the English classroom/Eleanor Kutz,
Hephzibah Roskelly; foreword by Paulo Freire.
        p.   cm.
    Includes bibliographical references (p.) and index.
    ISBN 0-86709-277-7
    1. English language—Study and teaching (Secondary)—United States.
    2. Language arts (Secondary)—United States.   3. Classroom environment—United
States.   4. Intercultural education—United States.   I. Roskelly, Hephzibah.
II. Title.
LB1631.K88   1991
428.0071'273—dc20
                                                                     90-24244
                                                                        CIP

Designed by Jenny Greenleaf
Printed in the United States of America
02 01   EB   11

A pedagogy is that much more critical and radical the more investigative and less certain of "certainties" it is. The more unquiet a pedagogy, the more critical it will become.

PAULO FREIRE

CONTENTS

FOREWORD

When I read *An Unquiet Pedagogy* in manuscript form, I was happy to see that Ellie Kutz and Hepsie Roskelly did not need a how-to manual for putting into practice some of the theoretical ideas and educational experiences I had had in other areas of the world, particularly in Africa and Latin America. The beautifully written chapters of *An Unquiet Pedagogy* demonstrate a profound understanding that practices and experiences can be neither imported nor exported. In essence, Kutz and Roskelly have liberated themselves from the North American culture of how-to manuals. These authors critically understand the parameters of the sociocultural and historical context and the concrete conditions that created my work and they have extracted the valid principles so they could be re-created and reinvented in the North American context.

The title, *An Unquiet Pedagogy*, reflects the critical posture that informs the entire book. In fact, an unquiet pedagogy not only should be part of any educational process that purports to be critical and emancipatory but constitutes an integral part of knowledge itself. In most respects, an unquiet pedagogy forms the essence of our very existence.

By understanding and emphasizing the role of language in cultural and multicultural literacies, Kutz and Roskelly have, in a significant way, advanced the theoretical discourse that views students' language as the only means by which they can develop their own voice. It is through their own language that they will be able to reconstruct their history and their culture, hence their position in the world. It is important, then, to comprehend the different varieties of language. It is just as important to understand that even when we speak the same language, we express ourselves in different ways. Not only is it imperative that educators understand that different language varieties involve different grammars and different syntactical and semantic representations that are conditioned and explicated by people in varying positions relative to forces of production and power, but it is critical that we understand that language is also culture. That is, language is the mediating force of knowledge, but it is also knowledge itself. *An Unquiet Pedagogy* poses this dynamic, contradictory comprehension and the dynamic, contradictory nature of education as a permanent object of curiosity on the part of learners. *An Unquiet Pedagogy* makes problematic the general simplicity as espoused by educators like E. D. Hirsch concerning the appreciation of these cultural phenomena. Unlike E. D. Hirsch, who proposes a cultural warehouse with selective Eurocentric values to be uncritically and unreflectively consumed by students, as though all had been already known and decreed by the dominant forces of our society, Kutz and Roskelly successfully demonstrate that everything that takes place at the level of culture has something to do with other discourses, such as the discourse of imagination and the discourse of production. In essence, these authors have brilliantly shown that a pedagogy will be that much more critical and radical the more investigative and less certain of "certainties" it is. The more unquiet a pedagogy, the more critical it will become.

Because an unquiet pedagogy is preoccupied with the uncertainties of the culture of the classroom, language and thought, home and school language, cultural literacy and multicultural education, reading and meaning, writing and composing, it is, by its nature, a pedagogy that requires investigation. For this reason, Kutz and Roskelly's *An Unquiet Pedagogy* is much more a pedagogy of question than a pedagogy of answer. This book should be enthusiastically read by anyone interested in education, the composing process, and multicultural literacies, and read with the same seriousness as that with which it was written.

Paulo Freire
Secretary of Education
São Paulo, Brazil

PREFACE

Long before we began writing this book or even thinking about writing it, we began to talk about what it's about. We talked with our students, and they told us of their fears as they thought about becoming teachers, of their confusion as they tried to connect their own reading and writing and learning with what they saw in classrooms, of their impatience with their courses about teaching that provided too little knowledge too late. We talked with teachers—with teachers who felt burned out and frustrated in their efforts to teach, in traditional ways, an increasingly diverse group of students; and with teachers who had renewed their commitment to their own learning and teaching through collective participation in groups like the Boston Writing Project. We talked with researchers and scholars who were focusing on questions of reading and writing—with Shirley Brice Heath, with our colleagues Ann Berthoff, Suzy Groden, Vivian Zamel—and engaged in real or imaginary conversations with many others whose names appear in this book. We talked with each other, about our own teaching and what we had learned from it, about what was missing from teacher preparation, about the roles that teachers and schools were being asked to play in our society. From all of this talk, we began to see that ours were not the isolated concerns of individuals but were common to those who were thinking about teaching, learning, and schools.

One conversation took place with Paulo Freire, when he visited UMass/Boston a few years ago. In large and small gatherings, members of the UMass community explored with him our work *as* teachers and *with* teachers. We talked of the need for teaching that encourages both teachers and learners to ask questions and examine everything critically, and of the need for learning that connects with students' real lives and builds on their social experience. And we talked about the particular context of U.S. schools, and about how pedagogy could not be transposed from one setting to another setting—from peasant collectives in Brazil to U.S. high school or college classrooms—but had to grow out of teachers and students, together, questioning their own situations. Some of that questioning will be formal, and we begin this book with structured inquiry into the real classrooms that our student teachers have entered. But much of it will begin informally, emerging in talk.

This book is about exchanging silent classrooms for talk-filled ones, about the role of language in the classroom: about teaching English. It's about how students can be encouraged to question, sys-

tematically, the ways that they use language and the ways that language
is used in their worlds and in the literature they read. It's about how
teachers can build on the language and knowledge and social experience
that their students bring to their classrooms. For it is through language
that we make sense of the world — that we make the world.

In talking together, the two of us came to understand the nature of
our own experiences as well as those of other teachers in elementary
and high school and college classrooms. In talking together, we came to
define one of our roles — that of teachers of teachers. Soon we began to
teach together and to write together as well. Over time our conversations
led to an experimental course to prepare teachers, to a collaboration
with teachers from the Boston Writing Project, and gradually to changes
in our own institutional structures.

We recognize that connections between words and action, between
learning and teaching, are not apolitical. Although we may have avoided
direct political statement in the book, the call for change is nonetheless
clear. We believe that attitudes that cause cultural difference to be seen
as deficiency must change. We believe institutional structures that
assign — and consign — people to levels of ability based on prejudicial
evaluation must be altered. Institutional change begins with individuals
in conversation — learning from one another, mutually reinforcing,
challenging, and reshaping thought and action. It's talk that nurtures
change, talk that moves outside to change the listener or the classroom
or the society and inside to change the mind. So our hope for this book
is that its readers will continue the conversation that reading it begins.

We're grateful to Paulo Freire, who has inspired many teachers like
us to form our own small culture circles, where we teach and learn,
change, and try to "stimulate the certainty of never being too certain"
in our students and in ourselves. We would like to thank Donaldo
Macedo, who translated Freire's Foreword and who continues to challenge our thinking about education. We would like to express our
appreciation to Joe Check and Peter Golden of the Boston Writing
Project for supporting the community of reflective teachers and writers
who have been models for our students. Finally, we want to thank all
of the teachers and students who have worked with us over the past
few years, but especially the teachers — Bruce Rettman and John
Welsh — whose classrooms provided examples for exploration and the
students whose critical, questioning work has helped so much to shape
this book — Pam Ahl, David Arsenault, Darrelle Boyd, Priscilla Connors,
Peter Connolly, Mark Couzens, Clare Dowling, Diane Darrigo, Diane
Eagon, Matt Evans, Sylvia Femmino, Geraldine Garten, Margaret
Gilleran, Tiana Gorham, Gwen Gray, Tracey Herbert, Sara Matson,
Tricia McCarthy, Donna Montenegro, Jeanmarie Morey, Cris Newport,
Mat Peters, Anthony Poole, Jennifer Ryan, Marie Shaw, Laraine
Sheridan, Emily Singer, Sela Skolnick, Janet Stavris, David Stokkink,

Valerie Voner, Stanley Wanucha, and Deb Wolfson. And a final thanks to the freshmen whose work over the years has helped us to learn about writers and writing, including Albert Johnson, Allison Sharkey, Aqeelah Akbar, Dana Joly, Ken Maxwell, Nancy Arguello, Winnie Chan, Peter Conrad, and Michael Mooney.

AN UNQUIET
PEDAGOGY

INTRODUCTION

A teacher who enters an English classroom in a typical public school in the United States steps into a familiar culture. It's one she remembers from her own experience as a student, one that even her parents would not find alien. Buildings have been replaced, but inside the buildings time, space, and activity are divided in much the same way they have been for generations of students. School rituals continue—the class bell, the hall pass, the late note—and even the smell of school, hard to describe but unmistakable to the educated nose, seems unaltered.

> It was strange going back to high school after all these years. I met Ms. N in her study hall in the cafeteria. How can it be that this cafeteria smells the same as my own high school cafeteria 250 miles and twenty years away? I spent more time trying to guess what they were going to serve for lunch and wondering if the menus were identical. Do they serve American Chop Suey here too? Tuna Surprise? (Matt)

Like the school, the classroom itself is predictable and familiar:

> The classroom that this twelfth grade class meets in is well lit and bright, partly because of newly installed windows. The ceilings are tall and the floors are clean and shiny. The room, however, has a sense of crowdedness about it. The desks are arranged in two groups—a group on the left and a group on the right with an aisle in between them. Each group is about 4 or 5 rows deep with 5 or 6 desks in each row. Each desk in the row, however, is pushed up against the desk next to it and the distance between each row is wide enough only to allow a student to slip in to his/her seat ... the arrangement is such that the focus is geared toward the front area where the teacher stands or sits. She does not use the blackboard in back of her desk much.
>
> The teacher's desk at the front of the room is crowded with papers and books and provides only a small working space. To the left of her desk is a student desk piled high with small, hard-covered dictionaries that look like they might topple over if anyone walked by too rapidly. The other wall has a blackboard with assignments and vocabulary words written on it for another class that uses the room.
>
> At the front of the room small handmade signs are tacked up over the blackboard pointing out the different mistakes people often make in their speaking, mistakes such as ain't, seen, mines, cuz, yous, gonna, dose. The correct usage is written beneath the mistake. Also there are posters of Shakespeare and other famous literary figures hung about the front and one side of the room. (Laraine)

The blackboard is filled with assignments for the week for the several classes—from different grades and different levels—taught in the room.

Mr. M has homeroom, studies, two junior honors classes, three general senior classes, and two SAT classes. Written on the boards are the assignments for the seniors and for the juniors.

Seniors

1. Go over vocab list #2
    Test on vocab & spelling #2 will be on Monday
2. Make sure all homework is ready
3. General topics
    "The Outstation"—Read pp. 60—78
                              Answer I, 1—4, p. 78
                                      II, Text 1—3, p. 79
                                      III, Diction 1—2, p. 78

    Spelling Words

prestige	propagate
prevalent	psychoanalysis
privilege	receive
procedure	recommendation
propaganda	referred

Juniors

1. Research paper—thesis statement
2. Poetry
    Read Robinson pp. 630, 632
        e.e.cummings p. 641
        Robinson Jeffers p. 642
        Wallace Stevens p. 650
        Edna St. Vincent Millay p. 661
        Robert Frost pp. 684—698
3. Group presentations
        Feb. 22—*Death of a Salesman*
        Feb. 23—*Grapes of Wrath*
        Feb. 24—*The Great Gatsby*
        Feb. 25—*Babbitt*
        Feb. 26—*The Old Man and the Sea*
4. Questions and answers on *Our Town* (Jeanmarie)

Honors students have a lot of reading assigned, some to be discussed in class, some to be read at home in preparation for a test or a writing assignment or a class presentation. There are likely to be essay assignments—even research papers—and students are expected to be responsible for independent topics and long-term assignments. For the "general" sections—classes where students may not be college-bound and are assumed to be less interested in school—assignments are likely to involve less reading, and the reading comes from texts with "general-interest" selections, like short stories about teenagers. Writing assignments are limited — perhaps to answering the questions about the plot that appear after a reading selection in the text — and spelling and vocabulary work are emphasized.

If the beginning teacher feels an almost disquieting sense of familiarity with the school, the classroom, and the assignments on the board, she may feel less familiar with the students who walk through the door, for they're different from her own high school peers, more racially mixed, more ethnically diverse. Still, she knows how they'll behave. Before the class begins, she watches as students cluster in small talkative groups. At the bell, they take their seats but continue to talk about school, friends, neighborhoods. The groups can be defined by race or ethnicity, but individual students call to other groups, exchanging greetings and news. Students tease and challenge each other verbally, often with sly wit. "Is that your homework, man? Where did you get the manual?" The language they use is colloquial, allusive, appropriately attuned to their listeners. They talk about problems with jobs, dates, parents; and they contribute ideas for possible solutions, argue with one another's positions, and find analogies to their own situations.

> As the bell rings students saunter around the classroom door, stalling as they hesitate to enter. They begin new conversations with friends in the hall, rush out to their lockers, and beg to go to the lavatory. Of course these attempts to waste time are denied and the disappointed students settle into class. (Darrelle)

The teacher knows from experience and tradition her own role and assumes it a little self-consciously at first perhaps, but with increasing confidence. She stands at the blackboard anticipating the bell, spends several minutes taking attendance while the students talk, and then summons their attention.

> The period-five seniors were copying examples of index cards from the board. Mr. M waits patiently, takes attendance, makes a general statement that from now on no one is to wear a hat to class. (Jeanmarie)

Over a gentle roar of student protests and paper shuffling, the teacher begins the day's work, perhaps by going over the homework from the night before. But she's often interrupted.

> An announcement comes over the loudspeaker — the students pay attention. The woman announces that two incidents of violence happened outside the front door last week. She guarantees that more security will be placed outside the school, and wants the teachers, students, and employees to know that the school places the utmost importance on their safety and peace of mind.
>
> A student in the front seat appears to be a troublemaker. He shouts, slams his books repeatedly on the desk, and says loudly to nobody in particular, "I didn't know we had a test today." Nobody pays attention. Donna announces, "Clear off your desks for the test; put your books

and things on the floor." She gives a spelling test, using words like animosity, obstinate, recklessness, and furtively. The students turn their papers over when they are finished. The boy I thought was a troublemaker turns out to be the class clown. He has the class in an uproar with his antics.

Donna doesn't threaten the class. She says quietly, "Settle down. There are too many conversations going on at once." Then she asks the class clown to act out a part of the book they are reading. He is very good and receives loud applause for his performance: he swaggers, pulls up imaginary socks, uses appropriate gestures. (Sylvia)

Although the teacher may draw a particular student into the lesson, more often communication in the classroom takes familiar forms that both teacher and students know intuitively. The teacher asks the questions, looking hopefully at the students in front of her. They give the answers, and "they" are almost always the same ones, those who seem always to raise their hands. Every once in a while, the teacher surprises somebody by calling a name, but the selected student seldom responds with much more than a mumble, and she goes back to the familiar raised hand with a sigh of relief. Some students stay on the fringes of this "discussion"; they never respond, and the teacher has learned never to call on them.

In period three, they started by going over the results of Friday's vocabulary test. The kids did very poorly, and the teacher let his anger and disappointment show. Hard to judge what effect that had on the kids, but I suspect it was negative. Again he called mainly on those who didn't seem to be paying attention, but he did recognize a raised hand. (David S)

Occasionally, a student will respond to the teacher's question with an offbeat or original remark, but the teacher knows the pressure of work to be accomplished and usually dismisses anything but the answer he has in mind. The moments of real interest in the class are inadvertent rather than planned; a student throws a wad of paper toward the basket at the front of the room and makes it, tires screech in the parking lot outside the window, the lights blink on and off. The teacher sometimes tries to use the moment; he provokes a little laughter with a joke about the student's jump shot, or the principal's driving ability, or the solvency of the school system, and then quickly pulls attention to the work at hand.

A couple of kids in each class are dressed up for Halloween, provoking some humorous banter. John joins in and jokes some before bringing the class to order. But the kids are restless today. Some discipline problems in period three. Nathaniel was toying with something and John asked him twice to put it away. Nathaniel was boldly challenging John, talking back to him, and John got sterner and sterner until Nathaniel obeyed. (David S)

There's movement in this classroom too, in spite of the generally quiet and one-sided communication. Students wander in with late passes, a representative from the office comes to collect attendance slips, and two students request lavatory permission slips. The teacher valiantly carries on through all the incidental action in the class, cheerfully determined to discuss what she has been taught is the main work of her English classroom — literature.

> One particular day the students' homework assignment was to read the "Prologue" to the *Canterbury Tales*. In class Ms. N goes over the Prologue, reading each character's passage and then at the end asks the students very specific questions. For instance, how you can tell that the Franklin likes food and drink, what he was wearing, why he was on a pilgrimage, etc. Ms. N asks specific students each question. "Eleanor," she says, "can you tell me what the Franklin loves to drink?" When the question is answered, the discussion leaps forward to another question and eventually another passage. (Sara)

The literature discussion may end or trickle out, but the teacher is prepared with an activity to use up the time remaining: seat work. It's a way for students to begin their homework, and she hopes that maybe beginning it will mean that most of them will complete it at home. Grammar exercises are good for seat work, easy to fill in, easy to grade. There's silence in the room now, except for a few complaints — "Do we really have to do *every* sentence?" — or teacher admonishments — "This adds up to be a big part of your six weeks' grade, you know." The teacher sits at the desk, recording grades, commenting on papers from other classes. Everybody is waiting for the bell ring.

If her classroom is a typical one, the teacher can count on students to be reasonably well behaved day after day as they "discuss" literature, do homework, read and write occasionally in class. She can also count on their lack of enthusiasm for any of the tasks they accomplish.

> There is absolutely no problem with discipline in this class. The students know what is expected of them and do as they are told ... there is a minimal amount of conversation among them as they come into the room and they settle down quickly and are ready to begin. More often than not they are prepared with the answers, having done their homework the night before. Almost every student when called upon to answer a question is responsive to the teacher. With the exception of two or three students, however, most of them do not volunteer but rather wait to be called upon to answer.... In fact, at times some of the students are resting their heads on their hands or are slouched over their desk tops, not exactly a posture that conveys commitment and involvement. Although the students are prepared and do respond to the teacher's questions, there is no spark or sense of real eagerness to participate. (Laraine)

The comments interspersed above are the words of English majors who are readying themselves to become teachers in high schools. They're beginning a student-teaching semester or are in a final series of courses leading to student teaching. Like the hypothetical teacher we've been characterizing, these students find much that they remember from their educational experience, much they're familiar with, some things they want to keep, some they'd like to change. Like most teachers, their ideas for their own classrooms will be challenged by their real experience. They struggle between wanting to bring innovations to their teaching and wanting to succeed in the system they're comfortable with. Often, they may make small alterations that seem to change traditional activities — creating a crossword puzzle out of vocabulary words rather than using the exercises in the vocabulary textbook, designing home-work sheets that require real writing from students, letting students work in small groups on their end-of-class grammar exercises. But the changes don't seem to affect overall structures, and the patterns of traditional instruction repeat themselves in classroom after classroom. Perhaps because the activities and traditions of school are so established, but also because their preparation for teaching has been so limited, new teachers often wonder how or even if they should change the classroom setting that everybody — students, teachers, administrators, parents, and public — knows so well.

> Mrs. Z was simply going to go over the twenty words assigned for the test and their definitions, right from their workbook. I created some crossword puzzle word games and creative sentences on mimeo-graphed sheets, so that the students would have to think, but also so that they would have something tangible to study from. My first class went okay, but I wasn't in total control. . . .
>
> Reflecting on my first week of student teaching has me feeling a little unenthusiastic, weary, hopeless, and questioning. I say all of these negatives because I am frankly *floored* by the large number of students at the high school who don't care about school. . . . I have so many ideas for the class, but I'm scared of them and failing them. (Deb)

The preparation of teachers at any level, elementary to college, is by and large woefully inadequate. College teachers have not until very recently received any instruction at all in pedagogy. And though teachers in public schools receive training in methods and educational theories, the "how" of method is never partnered with the "what" of content. From their education courses, teachers have learned about cognitive development, readability, and curriculum design. They know how to prepare the lesson plans that their school will require, how to make up tests to evaluate their students' learning of those lessons, how to manage the dynamics of a question-and-answer session. From their courses in English, they've gained some knowledge of English and American

literature that they can use to prepare background lectures and intro-
ductions to readings. They've most often learned some rhetorical structures like comparison and contrast or process analysis from their course
in freshman composition, and they can work these into the occasional
essays required in the honors curriculum, though it's hard to get students
in other sections to write more than a few error-filled sentences. But
nothing in the preparation of most teachers will help them design the
work of the classroom in ways that support the development of readers
of literature and writers of essays, to connect the reading of literature
and the writing of essays with other acts of reading and writing and
speaking, to create a coherent pedagogy for their teaching of English.

This typical training also prevents teachers from making real change
in the familiar school structures, prevents them from creating, rather
than simply replicating, a classroom. Sometimes unwillingly, sometimes gratefully, they turn to prepared curriculum guides, discussion
sections at the end of textbooks, and fill-in-the-blank worksheets. They
stand at the front of the room, behind a desk, maintaining a long-held
tradition of education, emphasizing transfer of information from teacher
to students, with the teacher at the active center, students on the passive
margin, of the work of the classroom.

In *Hard Times*, Charles Dickens describes a school and a nineteenth-
century educational system where the accumulation of information was
primary, so that teacher preparation consisted of testing how well
teachers had accumulated that information. Mr. McChoakumchild was
one of those teachers.

> He and some one hundred and forty other schoolmasters had been
> lately turned at the same time, in the same factory, on the same
> principles, like so many pianoforte legs. He had been put through an
> immense variety of paces, and had answered volumes of headbreaking
> questions. Orthography, etymology, syntax, and prosody, biography,
> astronomy, geography, and general cosmography, the sciences of
> compound proportion, algebra, land-surveying and leveling, vocal
> music and drawing from models, were all at the ends of his ten child
> fingers. He had worked his stony way into Her Majesty's most
> Honourable Privy Council's Schedule B, and had taken the bloom off
> the higher branches of mathematics and physical science, French,
> German, Latin, and Greek. He knew all about all the Water Sheds of
> all the world (whatever they are), and all the histories of all the
> peoples, and all the names of all the rivers and mountains, and all the
> productions, manners, and customs of all the countries, and all their
> boundaries and bearings on the two-and-thirty points of the compass.
> Ah, rather overdone, McChoakumchild. If he had only learnt a little
> less, how infinitely better he might have taught much more. (17)

As is true with most of Dickens' characters, McChoakumchild's
name is no coincidence. But McChoakumchild's problem with his

students is as much the fault of his learning and his society as his personality. In the newly industrialized society depicted in *Hard Times*, students were preparing to take their places in the mechanized world of the factory. Those who were being educated to positions of managers or bankers or owners would focus on the hard facts of profit and loss, not on soft concerns about human relationships and individual well-being. And so the education at McChoakumchild's Coketown school, headed by a Mr. Gradgrind, "a man of realities," provided what society demanded. "You can only form the minds of reasoning animals upon Facts," Mr. Gradgrind asserts, following his society's maxim, "nothing else will ever be of service to them."

Our society now espouses different educational goals from those in Dickens' Victorian England, and our teachers are hardly the mean-spirited autocrats of the Coketown school. But often our school structures are as authoritarian. Dickens reminds us that schools are shaped by society and by history. American education is bound by the goals of the society that surrounds us and by a history that continues to see schools and teaching in much the same way as did the Gradgrinds and McChoakumchilds in Coketown. Teacher preparation and classroom instruction that focus so exclusively on the transference of information, the passing on of convention, the unreflected maxims of society leave teachers and students with little room for creativity and growth, and little opportunity to reflect critically on their education and their society.

Our school structures, like our classroom practices, are inherited, and they too have developed in response to a variety of social and economic factors. In the typical structure, teachers remain isolated within their classrooms, with little opportunity to share ideas and strategies. The physical design of schools in blocks of separate rooms allows school systems to respond economically to fluctuations in student enrollment; if an individual teacher has responsibility for a class, new classes can be added or eliminated in a way that's not so easily allowed where a team of teachers share responsibility. In this arrangement, each individual teacher is the authority in the classroom and is responsible for the work that goes on there. Teachers who have worked only within the apparent autonomy of their own classrooms soon come to fear the self-exposure that alternative systems would require. The system is so highly and tightly structured that innovation, when it's suggested, becomes a messy annoyance: Writing workshops before school? Can't fit into the bus schedule. Team teaching with the Latin teacher? Schedules don't match. Only highly visible or easily measured results are wanted, and teachers who work well within the established system receive, after six years or so in most school systems, a lifetime tenure that encourages sameness and supports staying put intellectually as well as physically. Ironically, after tenure, the best teachers are likely to be taken out of the classroom, through promotion to administrative positions.

Institutional constraints become intellectual ones as well. Not only are teachers isolated from intellectual engagement with other teachers, they're isolated from the talk of their discipline. They might be encouraged to take more courses, but those courses often just repeat the inadequacies of the earlier preparation. Even when courses challenge their pedagogical ideas, teachers have little opportunity to bring what they're learning back to their own schools, make their new knowledge practicable in their own curricula. Teaching four or five classes with little time allotted for preparation or planning, teachers have no energy for reading or discussing current theory and practice with one another. In-service workshops set up by administrators don't feed the intellect much either. Outside presenters come to disseminate information — not to communicate with teachers who have both knowledge and experience — and themselves mirror the inadequacies of a learning scene where one knows and tells and all the others watch and wait. Teachers try to overcome their isolation — by taking on student teachers, by taking part in professional organizations, by taking more courses — but for most there's no forum anywhere that effectively integrates the study of the discipline with relevant theory and effective classroom practice. Such a forum is rarely found in schools, in professional organizations, or in the university. The skill of a few model teachers suggests that gifted individuals can master the adversities of the isolated classroom, but their success obscures the larger social/cultural context in which all teachers operate.

All these factors have shaped school culture for a long time, but new ones make the educational situation seem worse today. The school population is increasingly diverse, and that means that teachers encounter students who have problems with standard English, who come from cultures with ways of knowing and communicating different from those of the mainstream, those who, in earlier decades, would not have been in school at all. Such students enter the schools less prepared to achieve the literacy of the mainstream culture, yet they must achieve a higher level of literacy than most students in the past. Societal and cultural influences surrounding the classroom often seem more negative than in the past, even antiliterate.

Some education critics have seen these social and cultural influences as contributing to a decline in the quality of American education. In the view of critics like E. D. Hirsch, American institutions have wantonly accommodated themselves to ill-prepared, illiterate students, and the unfortunate result has been a hopelessly diluted curriculum. The solution is to be found consequently in mixing a hardier brew, a curriculum made stronger by its single vision of culture, its emphasis on facts and shared information. Within this curriculum, literate students would be identified by their use of a standard language and by their familiarity with a common cultural tradition, embodied in a finite group of terms and concepts. "Standards" of literacy must be maintained, say these critics, even if this requires a return to the fact-laden teaching of the Coketown school. They see schools as certifying agents for the dominant culture, and they blame teachers and the school systems for failing to pass on that dominant cultural tradition to their students.

We don't believe McChoakumchild had the answer for his Victorian children, and we don't believe the critics who want narrowly defined "standards" have the answer today. People like Hirsch have brought public consciousness to bear on the issue of education and literacy, but we will argue that their solutions are wrong, that a return to their view of monocultural education is not the answer. Our population is increasingly diverse and comes with a variety of cultural traditions, and we believe that teachers need to learn how to use the diversity of American cultures to create a richer school environment. We're not just making a virtue out of necessity: learning for all is enhanced when students use rather than bury their backgrounds, when a variety of perspectives contribute to the development of one. This multicultural classroom will help all students to achieve the kind of higher literacy that society now demands and it can help to create a different and more effective relationship among the cultures of the home, of the school, and of the larger society.

The aim of this book is to explore ways of making that classroom a reality in schools. We draw together the separate strands of learning that our hypothetical teacher might bring to her teaching, weaving them into a coherent understanding of what constitutes truly literate behavior, of the ways in which language, cognition, reading, and writing work together in the classroom, and of how they are affected by culture and society. The three major sections of the book follow our aim, focusing on the relationships among thought and language and culture, on the relationship between literacy and learner, and on how these relationships affect what we do in the English classroom.

Throughout the book, we use the experiences and insights of teachers and students we've worked with — prepractice and student teachers, freshman writers, graduate students learning to teach those freshman writers, innovative teachers in the public school system, participants in the Boston Writing Project — and you'll hear their voices in every chapter. We use as well our own study and research in composition and reading theory, learning theory, applied linguistics, and literature, our own teaching of English at both the high school and college levels, and our observations of public school classrooms. Drawing together all our work as teachers, learners, and scholars, the book represents not just a summary of what we know and have experienced, but our philosophy of teaching and learning.

We see teaching and learning as active, which means that teacher and learner, reader and writer, *act* rather than react in the classroom.

We see a relationship between teachers and learners as individuals and as part of culture and believe that classrooms build and expand ways of knowing by using the relationship between individual and community and culture. While we recognize the many constraints imposed by existing social structures and institutions, we see a possibility for change and growth as individuals — teachers and learners — come to know more about themselves and others in the cultural settings that shape their experiences.

What follows is designed to prepare and support English teachers at all levels in meeting the challenges they face in the classroom. Our discussion is centered on the learner, on the person good teaching is designed to reach and transform. We explore what learners bring to their studies, and we consider how to see and build on what individual learners might bring to create communities of learners. But the emphasis on the learner doesn't omit the teacher. We think of teachers as learners whose experiences shape the way they nurture learning in their students. Teachers will see themselves as learners by thinking of themselves as readers and writers, by becoming careful observers, by letting students teach them how their learning takes place, and by learning from others — researchers, teachers, theorists in a number of fields — who can help make coherent the many areas of English teaching. We use these ways of learning ourselves in this book as we observe, study, reflect, and theorize about the issues we explore. And we return frequently to the writings of those who have helped us formulate our thinking about teaching — Paulo Freire, Shirley Brice Heath, Ann Berthoff, James Britton, Mina Shaughnessy, James Moffett, and many others whose work is reflected in the pages of this book. We hope that our book will introduce readers to a wide range of thinkers and writers who can help transform pedagogy, that they will turn to them and return to this book as well at different times, engaging in a continuing dialogue about teaching and learning, writing and reading.

We've envisioned the readers of this book as teachers in all stages of learning, from students beginning to prepare for a career in teaching to experienced teachers who continue to reflect on their own practice, in a variety of settings, from middle school through college. While many of the examples in this book come from the reflections of students at the beginning of their work in teaching, their observations have led us to see more clearly our own work as teachers, and we believe their insights offer new perspectives to all teachers. Although institutional structures divide the learning of English into grades and levels, from first-grade "language arts" to a college Shakespeare course, what it means to be a reader and writer remains constant, in some important ways, throughout this schooling. And, while many examples of practice come from our own college courses in composition and literature, we believe that they illustrate ways of learning about literacy that can be adapted to any level. We hope, then, that readers in any of these settings at any stage of their teaching lives will want to share the process of observation, of study and reflection, that we and our students have engaged in and begin the process of generating theory and practice. At the end of the book, we offer a chapter entitled "Strategies for the Teacher and Learner." These strategies come from real activities in our courses for undergraduate and graduate students and represent the ways in which we approach the process of making theory into personal practice. The strategies indicate how teachers might observe students, how student teachers might look at the dynamics of talk and action in the classroom, how all readers may become more conscious of their roles as readers, writers, and learners. While they're placed at the end, they're integrally related to earlier units, and readers may find it useful to look back at them as they move through the chapters.

The "Strategies" chapter suggests that the relationship between the writers and the readers of this text is interactive. And the model of learning implied by this book involves a change in other dynamics as well, a change in relationships between students and teachers, between the classroom and the school, between the school and the world. This book intends to provoke change by showing how changes in authority and power create new authority in classrooms. The application of the understandings about thought and language and culture gained from Unit 1, about literacy and the learner gained from Unit 2, to pedagogical and curricular practice in Unit 3, will, we hope, give teachers transformative power over their own classrooms to make them into richly literate learning environments. Paulo Freire, a Brazilian educator, is one of the people whose work has been important to us as we've examined the connections among teaching, learning, and literacy. Freire argues that the transformed classroom comes about as people learn to become critical, to know how to ask questions of what surrounds them, to know that asking questions means that one never becomes too sure of answers.

Teaching must be *unquiet* in both senses of that word. There must be talk—lots of it—among administrators, parents, teachers, students, the community and the culture at large. And there must be change— true change—that comes from individuals' becoming critically aware of the many factors that shape the school. Only when pedagogy is unquiet does it have a chance to make a difference in the real lives of students and teachers alike.

UNIT 1

Language, Thought, and Culture

In the United States, education is seen as a personal affair. We tend to think of it mainly in terms of its potential for affecting the life and welfare of the individual — her capabilities, his rights and opportunities, her responses and responsibilities. Though, ideally, we try to provide the same (or an "equal") educational opportunity for everyone, we see individuals taking advantage of or passing up that opportunity, succeeding or failing in their schooling. Our rituals and structures — I.Q. and achievement tests, homogeneous "ability" groupings, academic and vocational tracks — place these individuals with others within a common school culture and lead us to attribute a student's performance to individual ability. But once the learner has been placed in an ability group or a track, the school's attention to individual characteristics ends, and too often the individual is seen only through the group label — "Oh, you can't expect that of him. He's a 9-D."

Long before students reach a high school or freshman college classroom, they have internalized the outer structures of their educational world, seeing themselves as good writers or poor readers, as honors students or 9- or 10- or 11-D's. And much of their assessment of themselves as learners and others' assessment of them as well has been based on the twin poles of ability: the ability to think and the ability to express oneself in language. But ways of thinking and knowing, and ways of using language to express what is known, are determined to a large degree by the culture of the home and community in which the student has grown up.

Learning is intimately bound up with human culture. Culture is the knowledge we pass on from one to another—our speech, beliefs, customs, ways of doing things—anything that is not wholly instinctive. We are born relatively undeveloped as compared with other mammals, and we require a long period both of physical dependence on adult caretakers and of learning survival skills that are appropriate to the context in which we live. Human survival has depended on our passing on not only ways of doing things that are focused in our immediate environment but also ways of thinking about what we do that are transferrable to other settings. The story of human learning is, then, a story of the individual learning to survive within a culture.

Our ways of knowing are aspects of our culture and are embedded in our language. We learn the names for things in our world of experience, the words that help us think and communicate those thoughts, from others around us. Adults provide children with labels—"elephant," "silly," "very"—which suggest that things are meaningful, and which help them sort out and make sense of the world around them. Language represents shared concepts that are rooted in shared experience.

Schools extend children's development of thought and language, presenting new concepts, shaped by experiences beyond those of the home, and, ideally, giving them access to other worlds and other ways. But, as humans, we never exist outside of a cultural context, and schools have a culture of their own—one that may not be continuous with the culture of the child's home. Where there's a general continuity between home and school ways of knowing and speaking, as is the case for most middle-class children, the child's "natural" (culturally learned) ways of talking and thinking are rewarded in the classroom. But even middle-class children may not be "at home" in the classroom, because they're expected, mostly, to sit silently and to use those familiar ways of talking and thinking only when the teacher calls for them. Where home and school ways of knowing and speaking are significantly different, differences in ways of using language can be perceived as representing a difference in the ability to think. To be smart is to express yourself in school ways.

Students soon come to picture themselves as thinkers and language users based on how easily they have been able to adopt those school ways. By high school, "school ways" include knowledge of a fund of specific information—history, geography, literature—information that is, to some degree, common to the culture of the educated in this country. And teachers judge students on the basis of how much of this knowledge they possess or how readily they can acquire it, and how well they can express it in school language.

But school ways are generally invisible to most of us who have spent much time, with any success, in the school culture. It's difficult to see that the school itself has a culture, that the structures of schools and classrooms represent and promote that culture, and, most crucially, that there might be alternatives to present school structures that would make school culture more diverse. Teachers need to understand the cultural environment they're asking students to enter. With this understanding, teachers can help students ease their way into the school environment, connect what they know from the world outside the classroom to what they find within it, and bring their various ways of knowing into the classroom and enrich the classroom world. And so we'll begin to consider our task as teachers by inquiring into the nature of the classroom culture and into the ways in which that culture is shaped by society and tradition as well as by individual teachers and the learners who come to their classrooms.

CHAPTER 1

The Culture of the Classroom

Our prepractice students found striking similarities in the classrooms they observed. But most teachers see their classrooms as unique, created largely out of their own efforts and ideas. In the fall, the teacher comes to his classroom armed with books and posters, with plans for positioning chairs and desks, with ideas for lesson units and strategies for teaching them. But there are many elements of the classroom already in place when he arrives, elements less tangible but no less real than dictionaries and paste. The classroom has been shaped by practices long established by tradition and experience, practices that are unconsciously at work in the minds of both students and teacher as the activities of the class begin. It's a familiar classroom culture that this chapter uncovers.

School culture as stereotype

In the classroom of Hollywood movies and the one that may exist in our own imaginations and memories, the teacher dominates—even comprises—the classroom's culture. She knows everything, and thus she's the final authority, a not-quite-human figure who asks only the questions she already knows the answers to and who doesn't answer any questions herself unless she has asked them first. This stereotypical teacher's primary responsibility is to ensure that students come away from her class privy to at least a few of the answers she possesses about her subject matter. Her classroom is a place where she holds court, dispensing knowledge from her forbidding paper-strewn desk at the front of the room, and dispensing road maps to knowledge—answer sheets, summary questions, study guides—for her students to read properly and fill in neatly and in good time. The student in this stereotypical scene is on the periphery of the action. One of many who look and act precisely alike, he sits in his chair as quietly as he is able, given his lack of interest, and tries with more or less success to figure out what the teacher wants of him.

The observations made by our student teachers and the studies by teachers and researchers across the country support this stereotype to a great degree. From their reflections and analyses, there emerges a picture of a classroom where active teachers meet passive students, where right answers are sorted out from wrong ones, and where knowledge is seen as static and quantifiable, rather than fluid and dynamic, something to be passed down but not made. Unfortunately, the training new teachers get often reinforces the stereotypical classroom by suggesting that knowledge is dispensed like a pill and that students swallow it to get educated. New teachers may be given strategies to help them communicate information — sentence combining to teach subordinate clauses, reader response theory to teach literature, puzzles to teach spelling. And they may be taught about established theories of teaching and learning. But because this knowledge, too, is dispensed, it provides no real model for a different, more active and integrated way of learning. We know that the way people learn is not by being filled with information or by learning answers but by engaging in a process of inquiry that will make them think about their own learning as well as the outcomes of that learning. Simply put, people learn by asking questions. But teachers aren't trained to ask questions about their own learning or about the classroom setting they create.

Teachers must become more than consumers of educational theory and classroom methods, just as students must be more than consumers of predigested skills. But to be creators as well as consumers, teachers have to learn to be inquirers, asking real questions about themselves as learners, as writers and readers, questions about their students, and questions about the social factors that affect learning in their classrooms. They must find out how to inquire into the culture of the classroom in order to discover its patterns of meaning and values, to see the relationship between those patterns and the ways of knowing that students bring from their homes, and to use their own questions to create scenes for real learning for their students.

Knowing and asking

All learning is related to theory making. As people learn, they ask questions to which they actively seek answers; they generate informal models of how the world works and test these models against the data of their ongoing experience in the world. They revise the model as new experiences conflict with it, and they're able to revise because they theorize about possibilities and categories. Conscious learners reflect on this process — on how they're learning — and their learning is active and constructive, not passive.

> Knowing, then, is to be seen as a form of doing. There is no simple
> sense in which we apply our knowledge in the way we apply a
> poultice to a swelling. In any confrontation, what we know must be
> reformulated in the light of what we perceive and our knowledge is
> thus forever on the move. (Britton 1970, 19)

James Britton, whose study of students' writing has reshaped British
schools, is talking here about classroom inquiry carried out by teachers.
What we know is inescapably dynamic, he believes, because it must
always *move around* to accommodate what we're only beginning to
know. Confronting new experience, something that happens continually
to a child (and should be happening continually to learners at all levels),
the learner reformulates, or shapes again, what was already known in
terms of what is newly perceived. It's the reformulation, the necessity
of examining old ideas in light of new experience, that characterizes
learning and that develops knowledge. So old teaching ideas — about
the value of instruction from grammar books or about how to set up
groups in the classroom — get reshaped and revised as teachers encounter
new experiences — learning to speak a foreign language, or circulating
among groups in first-period class.

Britton explains that new experiences not only reshape old ones,
but that the new experiences themselves are shaped by past ones: "We
face the new, therefore, not only with knowledge drawn from the past
but also with developed tendencies to interpret it in certain ways" (16).
Learners, therefore, are continually in mental motion, and they are
never neutral in any situation. The philosopher Susanne Langer argues,
like Britton, that knowledge is based on this dynamic and individual
process of learning, particularly as the knower questions her experience.
"The technique, or treatment, of a problem begins with its first expression
as a question," she says. And even more important: "The way a question is
asked limits and disposes the ways in which any answer to it — right or
wrong — may be given" (4). So when a teacher asks herself, for example,
why group work in first-period class was so successful today, she
asserts unconsciously a principle of what success in class consists of. But
she doesn't question that assumption often. Is it success for students to
remain quiet in groups, or is it success if they're noisy? Is it success if
they finish a task or if they don't? Langer stresses that any analysis of
data, any research or inquiry, can never go beyond what our questions
are able to yield. It's clearly important then for a teacher to pay attention to
the questions she asks about her students and her teaching, for her
questions expose attitudes of mind about learning and learners. If people,
teachers and students alike, don't question their questions — examine the
assumptions that lie underneath their inquiry — they won't be critical or
conscious thinkers.

Of course, teachers recognize the importance of questions. Informally
and often unconsciously, they theorize about teaching and learning, and

this theorizing follows a process of observation and abstraction. They might begin by asking themselves about events in their classrooms: "Why was Wanda so quiet today?" They invent hypotheses to explain what they see: "Maybe she didn't understand the story, or maybe something was upsetting her." They gather data to test their hypotheses: "I'll ask her a few questions about the story tomorrow." They look for larger patterns: "Actually, Joanie and John were quieter than usual too. And they always contribute. Maybe the story was too far away from everybody's experience. Maybe nobody's ever been on a farm or in the South before." They discover alternatives: "Tomorrow I'll start the discussion by asking them about what the story reminds them of." They begin to generalize the inquiry they've established: "My students seem to understand a story better when we start out with their experience. From now on, I'll begin that way."

This is inquiry of the kind that Langer and Britton describe, and it goes on in classrooms daily. But this informal process has not been conceived of as "real" research by educational theorists or even by teachers themselves, and so until recently it has been devalued as "only" practice. Even today, with greater emphasis on teachers as researchers and on the value of qualitative or narrative data in research, the kind of teacher inquiry we've described is seldom systematic enough or even conscious enough to be considered "theory making." Educational research generally remains solely the province of experts outside the classroom, and often the questions asked by these experts have assumed that learning is measurable and thus quantifiable. They have accumulated classroom data by examining separate or discrete skills — how correctly does this ninth-grade class identify clauses, define words, punctuate sentences — using standardized tests, surveys, questionnaires as devices of inquiry. This kind of research can demonstrate some useful things, of course; how one school system ranks against national norms in certain skills like vocabulary recognition; or how patterns change within one school system — what happens to vocabulary scores when basal readers are introduced into the system. But there's much that quantitative empirical research can't show. The underlying assumptions of measurability and similarity don't help teachers find answers to questions about practices in individual classrooms or various learners' experiences. Quantitative research doesn't reveal what's wrong with Wanda today.

In the last twenty-five years, there's been a proliferation of descriptive analyses of classrooms and case studies of individual students and groups of students that carry a new underlying assumption: that individual observations can yield general understanding, can even help make theories of learning. In fact, in the field of composition (as we'll see in Chapter 6), a large portion of the most provocative work in the field has emerged from such qualitative observations of students' writing. Teachers themselves have begun to undertake more deliberate and systematic inquiries in their own classrooms. A new image of the teacher, as a researcher, has begun to emerge, reflecting a deepening awareness of the importance of teachers' questions in the making of pedagogical theory.

Teacher inquiry

The first observations of students in our prepractice class demonstrate how important this process of inquiry is for the teacher who would be more than a consumer of educational practice. Our students entered English classrooms as observers and as hopeful participants, beginning their work by keeping a journal of what they encountered in the schools they visited. Their early observations and their reflections on what they saw are full of questions often expressed through frustrated remarks or admissions of fears. They haven't learned to see their questions as the beginning of an inquiry that will lead them to new understandings; they see mostly blooming, buzzing confusion in what's around them, confusion that they'll learn attends any new experience. But although their inquiry isn't systematic or even conscious, it has begun.

Here are some of those early journal entries. The questions are apparent, and the assumptions that underlie them often are too. And some of the thorniest pedagogical issues get raised.

> It's a new building, fresh paint everywhere, polished floors, desks fairly new and ungraffitied. It's so quiet. What is wrong with these kids? They don't seem to care about anything at all, even about asserting themselves to the slightest degree. How does one deal with that? (David S)

> But is a teacher supposed to *like* the human beings in her classroom? For God's sake, we can't like everyone who passes in front of our desk. Are we supposed to be good teachers in spite of the kids and in spite of ourselves? I guess so. (Gwen)

> Is it discipline or subject matter we are teaching? Both, obviously. As much of the former as is necessary to teach the latter. It is important to know why students are placed in low-level classes. I'd rather have a homogeneous motivation-problem group than one that's mixed. The techniques are so different and difficult to integrate. Somehow, the teacher of low-level kids has to convince them to learn, that the material is going to be useful. (Priscilla)

> I have never been in a school like this. There are so many discrepancies and problems. I can't even imagine being a student here. I spoke with Mr. L, the Dean of Discipline, and we discussed discipline problems that I could not begin to imagine. Inside the school there are 20 security people who carry walky talkies and handcuffs. Every day

Mr. L goes to court with at least four cases of assault, drugs, guns, knives, or gang problems. He mentioned how with a lot of these kids there is really nothing you can do with them because of their home lives. They come from broken, abusive, drug-addicted, alcoholic homes where they have to deal with stuff I will never see everyday. That is not only scary, it is terribly sad. He told me about one girl who just kept saying "I don't know" every time they asked her name, address, and schedule. They later found out she comes from a home where she is abused. There was nothing they could do to her that hadn't been done twenty times worse. Seventeen years old and she's already an old woman. How do you reach a girl like that? She hates school, her home, and life. What do you do? What can you do? It's just so awful. (Clare)

I felt a little uneasy as I was introduced to the classes I will be observing, especially since the kids seemed amused by the arrangement. In both classes, the students were very anxious to have my role clarified. "Is he going to *teach* us?" they asked uneasily. (Matt)

All of these students are asking the kinds of questions that teachers who make theory as well as initiate practice need to ask. David asks questions about who the students are who sit in the room. He's frustrated by his inability to understand the motivations of the group he's observing; their passivity bothers him. Gwen asks about herself and her own responses to her students. Priscilla looks beyond the classroom to curricular and institutional constraints that determine the relationship between teacher and student teacher, between motivated and unmotivated student, between classroom form and classroom content. Clare asks questions about outside forces that affect the institution, questions about the society and a teacher's responsibility or ability to alter educational lives when real lives seem impossible to improve. Matt finds the high school students questioning him, giving voice, perhaps, to his own questions about his role here. The comments from these prepractice students are tentative, speculative, and form the beginnings of the inquiry that teachers need to make in their classrooms. But the reflections show the many perspectives from which teachers must view the learning situation—the social, individual, cultural, institutional perspectives that intersect in the environment of a particular classroom.

Teachers beginning in any unfamiliar setting must extend the sort of inquiry represented in these questions by making their process conscious and continual. They need to learn to look at their students and ask questions about how they learn. In *The Water Is Wide*, a book on his own teaching in a small island school off the South Carolina coast, novelist Pat Conroy shows how he learns to ask important questions and to create a theory to guide his students' learning. Conroy is no green recruit in the teaching profession; he's been teaching at his hometown high school in Beaufort, but the Yamacraw Island school presents a radical change. The school has one room; its students are all black and all speakers of Gullah, a dialect that combines West African speech and English. Most of the students speak English haltingly to Conroy but speak fluently among themselves. Faced with a classroom of students, grades five through eight, whose speech he can't understand, Conroy has to improvise, to begin with the evidence at hand—often of what they can't do—to discover what his students do know and can do.

> I put Plan Number 1 into immediate effect. I asked the kids to write a paper briefly describing themselves telling me everything about themselves that they felt was important, what they liked about themselves and what they didn't like. This seemed like a fairly reasonable request to me but most of the kids stared at me as if I had ordered them to translate hieroglyphs from a pyramid. I repeated the instructions and insisted they make some attempt to follow them. So they began.
>
> As I walked around my new fiefdom, the kids earnestly applying themselves to the task at hand, I had my first moment of panic. Some of them could barely write. Half of them were incapable of expressing even the simplest thought on paper. Three quarters of them could barely spell even the most elementary words. Most of them hid their papers as I came by, ashamed for me to see they had written nothing. By not being able to tell me anything about themselves, they were telling me everything. (24–25)

Conroy begins to ask questions, tentatively, thinking of the ways people demonstrate literacy, not aware yet of the strategy he's formulating. He tries reading without success. Then he tries speaking, asking students questions about their lives. Each child repeats a safe formula that the first has stammered out. Saul tells Conroy: "I slop de hog. I feed de cow. I feed two dog. I go to Savannah on the boat." The next student replies: "I slop de hog. I feed de cow. I feed three dog. I go to Savannah on the boat." Finally, Conroy tries art, asking the children to draw him and then themselves, and he comes up with his first, speculative theory as he pins their papers on the bulletin board. "I couldn't help but notice there was some correlation between those who could not draw and those who could not write."

Conroy is dismayed by what he learns, but not overcome. His discovery of the children's ignorance begins his inquiry, leads him to larger questions about why it is so and how to change the situation. Even with this early and limited data about what his students know, he's beginning to find patterns to help him see his next steps. Over time, he builds his early improvisations into coherent teaching strategies that are shaped by his careful and respectful observation of the children's lives and language. Conroy's book provides a wonderful example of how practice and developing theory interweave, as observation and inquiry combine in the pedagogy of a sensitive teacher. We'll be referring to this book throughout this first unit, following the direction his inquiry takes and seeing how he learns to make learning meaningful to the isolated group of children he teaches.

Unlike Pat Conroy or our student teachers, Mina Shaughnessy was an experienced college teacher whose theories were established when her inquiry into student learning began. But confronted suddenly with a new group of students, her uncertainty mirrored theirs.

> I remember sitting alone in the worn urban classroom where my students had just written their first essays and where I now began to read them, hoping to be able to assess quickly the sort of task that lay ahead of us that semester. But the writing was so stunningly unskilled that I could not begin to define the task nor even sort out the difficulties. I could only sit there, reading and rereading the alien papers, wondering what had gone wrong and trying to understand what I at this eleventh hour of my students' academic lives could do about it. (Preface)

Shaughnessy taught at the City University of New York in the 1960s, when a new open-admissions policy changed the faces of the students in her classrooms. Students were no longer relatively homogeneous, relatively sophisticated, relatively well read. Instead, teachers faced a wildly various student group who came without sophisticated codes of reading and writing behavior and with a frightening level of what seemed to be irremediable illiteracy. Shaughnessy's questions about this new group and about her responsibilities as a teacher of them produced *Errors and Expectations*, her account of how she altered her own program of teaching to fit her students' strategies of learning. Like Conroy, Shaughnessy found that she had to change her perspective on literacy to reach these students; she had to reorient her way of regarding error so that she could help them progress. Shaughnessy's students were different enough, their papers alien enough, to force her to look beyond the error of their prose and toward the reasons that their writing appeared the way it did: "...the work must be informed not only by an understanding of what is missing or awry but of why this is so" (6).

From studying the data of her students' errors, Shaughnessy began to develop a theory that would explain the patterns she found. Her theory of basic writers, and hence of basic writing instruction, recognizes developmental stages in a student's learning and in a writer's process: they make mistakes "because they are beginners," and as beginners, they must be allowed to make mistakes. But because these students are also adults, Shaughnessy modifies current theories of development that center on a child's learning. Her thinking has been seminal to basic writing instruction in universities across the country, and her insistence that the basic writer be regarded as inexperienced, not deficient, remains the cornerstone of curricula at all levels of writing instruction designed to "meet student needs." Shaughnessy's book illustrates eloquently how a teacher's learning must be tied organically to her developing sense of what she sees in the classroom, to the theory she makes out of her perceptions.

In an essay in which she reflects on the process of producing *Errors and Expectations*, Shaughnessy describes stages in a teacher's development in terms of the questions the teacher asks, from "What are the consequences of flunking an entire class?" to "How do I teach these students?" to "How is it that these young men and women whom I have personally admitted to the community of learners cannot learn these simple things?" Such questions lead the teacher to "the careful observation not only of his students and their writing but of himself as writer and teacher." The final stage in the development of a teacher Shaughnessy calls "diving in," where a teacher makes "the decision to remediate himself, to become a student of new disciplines and of his students themselves. . . ." For Shaughnessy, as a teacher of writing, the new disciplines included linguistics, developmental theory, and what we would now describe as literacy theory and the ethnography of communication, fields that "examine more closely the nature of speaking and writing and divine the subtle ways in which these forms of language both support and undo each other" (1987, 74). (These are fields we too will explore in the course of this book.) Like Shaughnessy, teachers who "dive in" will learn how to look in more than one direction at once, at their students, their schools, their society, and themselves, and will recognize that the ability to look at all of these elements in the classroom culture simultaneously is integrally tied to their ability to teach effectively.

Shaughnessy's work moved outside the then-dominant model of educational research. Instead of setting up controlled experiments or designing studies based on widespread testing, it focused on the work of actual students and teachers in classrooms. And it was conducted by a teacher in her own classroom, as an inquiry into questions that had arisen for her in that context. The answers, and the ways of looking for them, would affect her own classroom practice and influence that of all others who taught "basic writers." A number of teacher-initiated studies into students' writing followed, studies by teachers who were reacting to their own classroom situations. Like our student teachers, they saw problems, asked questions, and gathered data to try to solve them. And this work provided the basis for later, more systematic inquiry in the field of composition. That systematic inquiry has been aided by theorists examining the research and methods of other fields, particularly anthropology.

Ethnographic inquiry

While composition teachers were devising ways to find answers to their own questions about student writing within their own classrooms, other researchers were turning to individual classrooms to understand more about education and how it works in our society. Anthropologists turned their attention from studying the cultures of distant societies to studying the different cultural settings that our own society comprises, and they began to study schools and classrooms as cultures — to try to understand the forms and rituals and patterns of meaning that distinguished school culture from the culture of other settings, and to determine the role it played within the larger culture of Western society. The primary method of anthropological investigation — ethnography — became the tool of a new group of educational researchers. Ethnography provided a highly systematic method of inquiry that had been used in a variety of cultural settings. Ethnographers entered schools to study the patterns that dominated in these settings, bringing new types of questions and ways of gathering data, beyond those that grew out of the teachers' own puzzlement. Ethnography is a useful tool for teachers for several reasons. It provides a way of studying learning in real contexts — real classrooms. It gives teachers a way to take on new perspectives and to question their old assumptions about how real classrooms work. And it suggests a method for making inquiry systematic, of moving beyond random observations toward the making of theory. Anthropologist Clifford Geertz has said that "all knowledge is local knowledge" (5), that all larger meanings are actually found in particular, immediate, local contexts. Looking at a particular classroom context can allow investigators to see the actual workings out of educational theory, to revise theory to fit with experience, to integrate practical and theoretical understandings.

The ethnographer attempts to provide what Geertz calls a "thick description" of a culture. The ethnographer records all possible details of the cultural setting that she observes — the objects and artifacts that are present, the terms for relationships among the people, their movements and interactions, the language they use and the ways they use it in particular contexts. Gradually, as the ethnographer accumulates these details, certain patterns begin to emerge — some roles and relationships seem to take on particular meaning within the culture while others are conspicuously absent, some uses of language are highly valued while others are discouraged. If the ethnographer is an outsider to this cultural setting, she consults with "insider" informants who can help her interpret the observations she has made and discover what meaning these things have to those who are part of the culture. In time, as she takes on a more active role in the community, she becomes not an outside observer but a participant-observer.

If the cultural setting is a familiar one, the ethnographer will bring certain assumptions about its meanings and values. But a particular classroom may support different values from those that informed the researcher's own classroom experiences, and its participants may offer a different picture of what activities mean. Prepractice students discover

these differences as they interview young informants about their classrooms. The following excerpts report on such interviews. The first is
with Ellie's daughter Karen, then a third grader, and the second is with
three high school freshmen on the soccer team coached by the interviewer. In each interview, the informants provide perspectives from
inside the classroom culture, which the interviewer then uses to reflect
on larger patterns.

> Karen did not seem to feel that the teacher was *the authority* and hence
> the "keeper" of all knowledge. In fact, there did not seem to be one
> authority, i.e. teacher, in the classroom. Karen usually spoke of people
> in pairs; X helps us with math and Y helps us with spelling and so on.
> I lost track of the number of times Karen said "help" and I thought
> how wonderful it is for students to realize that they have the capabilities
> inside themselves to do x, y, or z and must only be "helped" not "told
> how to do it." (Margaret)

By interviewing students from different classrooms, the interviewers
begin to question the assumptions underlying their inquiry into education—the assumption, for example, that the teacher must appear as
the authority in the successful classroom. The second interviewer begins
with a different assumption, that where journal writing is used in a
classroom, its goal is to foster individual thinking and self-expression.
Yet that assumption too proves false.

> In theology class, the students were asked to keep a journal. The
> problem, they said, was that the teacher gave them an assigned topic
> on which to write. The teacher then commented on the style and
> content of their entries. They were counted as an exam grade. Mary
> said, "We have to write on abortion and sex, but we have to be careful
> about relating it to the class." There seems to be a logic about this;
> religion is the class and it is a parochial high school, so the purpose is
> not really journal entries for personal expression, but more likely a
> check on the thinking of the girls to be sure that they are following
> along with the agenda being taught. Mary said, "It's easy to know
> what to say in the journals. Take notes during the class and rewrite
> them saying, 'I think.'" . . . The emphasis in reading and writing was
> on socialization and conformity. (Tiana)

Through the interviews with their informants, these researchers begin
to look in detail at a particular classroom context, learning to see the
classrooms they're studying from the perspectives of all the participants
in the classroom culture. They discover that the assumptions that have
come from their own educational experience cannot be applied to all
settings.

  One of the most significant ethnographic studies for teachers was
Ways with Words, Shirley Brice Heath's study of home and school
settings for students in the Piedmont area of North Carolina. Heath

brought to her study the systematic inquiry of the trained ethnographer. Her inquiry was prompted by the questions generated by her graduate students, many of them public school teachers, who asked whether published research on language really reflected the ways language was used in their own communities.

> As long-time residents of the area, the teachers, businessmen, and mill personnel in my classes had observed differences in the language use and general behavior patterns of children and adults from certain communities or cultural groups. They had an endless store of anecdotes about children learning to use language across and within groups of the region, and they asked why researchers did not describe children learning language as they grew up in their own community cultures. Their questions set the stage for me to encourage them to examine their own ways of using language with their children at home and to record language interactions as thoroughly and accurately as possible, without preconceived judgements about what was happening in the exchanges in which they observed and participated. (3)

Heath encouraged her students to use their questions as the starting point for their own inquiry. She shared her methods, those of the anthropologist and ethnographer of communication, so that they could carry out the sort of systematic inquiry that might lead them to answers. She went on to use their questions as a starting point for her own work as well, and spent the next ten years studying the language learning of children in these communities, at home and at school. Finally, she encouraged the teachers to share these methods of inquiry with their students, so that students could conduct their own study of their home and school language, and in the process, master school ways. Heath's work provides important understandings of home culture and language use, and we'll study it in more detail in Chapter 3.

Before Heath's study, students' language had most often been looked at from the perspective of the teacher, who represented the uses and patterns of the dominant culture. But one of the values of ethnography is that it requires the ethnographer to take on the perspectives of various participants within a culture. One well-known ethnographer of education, Frederick Erickson, maintains that the ethnographer must assume that "everybody is smart." In other words, the ethnographer cannot simply identify with one member of a culture and decide that what is important is only what is seen from that person's perspective. A student's perspective, as well as the teacher's, is crucial to an understanding of the dynamics of the classroom. Everyone sees and understands and tries to maintain an advantage within a culture, and what is "dumb" from one person's perspective may be smart from another's. For the ethnographer of the classroom, the idea that everyone is smart means, for example, that behavior which is apparently dumb, antisocial, and self-defeating may really make a lot of sense from the perspective of the person behaving. Particularly for adolescents, whose primary locus for rewards and self-esteem lies with the peer group, not the teacher, dumb behavior may come from the cleverest kids.

All people tend to see experience from their own perspectives, and thus to identify with the perspectives of those most like them. The ethnographer can never eliminate personal perspective entirely, but he can learn to use that perspective to make him more aware of others'. In fact, Erickson defines ethnography as "a deliberate inquiry process guided by a point of view," noting its interested rather than neutral perspective (51). The point of view is not a liability, but a stance that informs and empowers the researcher's intuitive understandings. Erickson calls the result "disciplined subjectivity": the ethnographer using her reactions, in a systematic and conscious way, to discover some of what is significant in a context. What generates a strong response in the ethnographer — behaviors that seem outrageous or structures that seem strange — may tell most about a setting and how it differs from traditional expectations. And sometimes when an ethnographer begins to observe a cultural setting, she can become conscious of those reactions by reflecting on her own feelings and associations and past experiences.

When Sylvia, a prepractice student, first visited the classroom she was to observe, she reacted strongly to the behavior of one student, who complained loudly about having a test and slammed his books on the desk. In a journal entry (included as part of the composite classroom portrait introducing this book), she labeled him "the class troublemaker" for his violation of her sense of what should happen in the classroom. She questioned, that day, why "the teacher makes no sign the students are unruly," implicitly criticizing the teacher for not paying enough attention to discipline in the classroom. After more looking and more writing, however, she revised her thinking and her categories and renamed the student "the class clown." Gradually, she began to see how the teacher was using the student's desire for attention in productive ways. By the end of the semester, her picture of the classroom, its students, and its teacher had shifted dramatically, as did her ideas about what constitutes discipline in the classroom. She concluded: "Donna is an excellent teacher. She has just the right balance of being a teacher and being a friend. The kids will kid around with her, but treat her with the respect she deserves." In coming to see in new ways the aspects of the classroom that troubled her the most initially, she discovered what was significant in this classroom context — the way the teacher helped the students use the behaviors and responses they brought to the classroom in constructive ways, and the cooperation and respect the teacher received from students who were "unruly" only on the surface.

Engaging in classroom inquiry

As we've been suggesting in this chapter, people's perceptions of what lies around them are shaped by knowledge and experience. Those whose experience has been mostly as students are likely to pay attention to the front of the room, where they've been conditioned to look throughout their years of schooling. They're likely to interpret action from a student's point of view, too, to feel anxious if there's a chance that they might have to perform, to feel admonished if the teacher directs a criticism at the class. Those who have been at the front of the room, who are teachers themselves, are likely to perceive from that point of view, to notice those students who respond to the teacher, to overlook those who don't. Point of view can be changed, quite literally, by a change in position: thrust back behind a student's desk, teachers may no longer be able to see as a teacher would.

Although no perception is unmediated by personal experience and personal reference points, teachers can do two things to use the subjectivity that shapes their perceptions. They can learn to recognize clearly the frame of reference they bring to the observation, the lens that focuses and filters their perceptions in this setting. And then, being aware of their subjective view, they can consciously train their eyes to take in more: trying out different points of view, and examining formal categories of experience so that they can be examined analytically. Having an established methodology to follow encourages disciplined subjectivity, as Heath's sharing of her methodology with teachers and mill personnel helped them analyze systematically what had been random perceptions and interesting anecdotes. The sorts of ethnographic data teachers might want to gather are described in the "Strategies" chapter.

Keeping a journal

One of the most valuable tools for a teacher engaged in the conscious inquiry that we promote in this book is the journal. The journal we suggest provides a record both of observations and of reflections on those observations. When you keep notes about what you see and then go back and comment on your notes, you're not only looking at the classroom; you're looking at yourself looking at the classroom, interpreting what you see and developing theories to explain it. One form the journal or notebook might take is that of the double-entry notebook, in which you systematically react to and enter into a dialogue with what you observe and read. Composition theorist Ann Berthoff has suggested this format, and it has proved useful to many learners and teachers, who find that they study not only a subject but their own path of engagement with the subject as they comment on their reactions as well as on the text. The double-entry format lets writers pay attention to how they go about making meaning when they respond to reading or when they observe the world.

> What makes this notebook different from most, perhaps, is in the notion of the double entry: on the right side reading notes, direct quotations, observational notes, fragments, lists, images — verbal and visual — are recorded; on the other (facing) side, notes about those notes, summaries, formulations, aphorisms, editorial suggestions, revisions, comment on comment are written. The reason for the double-entry format is that it provides a way for the student to conduct that "continuing audit of meaning" that is at the heart of learning to read and write critically. The facing pages are in dialogue with one another. (1981, 46)

We can see how this double-entry format allows a beginning teacher, Tricia, to link her observations of a classroom to her own experiences, creating larger understandings.

Reflections:	**Observations:**
L does not hesitate to take a lot of time on what some might consider a diverting, "fun" exercise. She, with the "cliché" lesson, has involved them in actively identifying what they, as writers, will not want in their writing and empowered *them* to choose good and bad writing rather than telling them what is not acceptable. I am reminded of a "cliché" of my own that I adopted as my motto when volunteering in Central America: "Tell me and I hear. Show me and I remember. Involve me and I *understand*."	— Talked about "public wisdom." — No clichés in writing. — "Games" picture to i.d. clichés, students work aloud and together, much laughter and talking. — Really drove home point of clichés by throwing out beginning sentences and letting them finish to "sate" them of clichés. — Exercise for final drafts.

We urge teachers, student teachers, and prepractice students to keep a journal that they use in two ways. One use is for keeping notes from a systematic observation of a classroom, and for reflecting on those observations (or providing field notes for an ethnography of the classroom). The journal also is useful for responding to and reflecting on ideas speculatively in a way that helps teachers become more conscious of themselves as knowers, drawing what they know and think and experience into a coherent pedagogy. As Tricia looks back through her journal, she traces her own progress in developing theory to support her teaching practice. She has moved from thinking that "these 'new' notions of multilanguage, multilevel, multicultural teaching were high-minded but probably unachievable," to recognizing that she had been drawing on many of the principles of such teaching in her own practice, often over the opposition of "the veteran teachers" who encouraged her to use a more traditional approach. She has also begun to connect her own student experience in a local high school with her teaching experience in Belize, to question familiar as well as distant practices and structures. And her reflections on what she has experienced and observed and read have led her to a new understanding of the basis for her own practice. Her final entry concludes:

> Veteran teachers (unwilling to change) be damned, I now have my methodology which had previously been mere instinct without rational form.... I have found the direction and formulation which has until now eluded my thoughts. Now let's hope I can put it to use.

When teachers like Tricia engage in this sort of inquiry and reflection, they often find themselves teaching in new ways. In *Through Teachers' Eyes*, an ethnographic study of writing classrooms in one large school district, Sondra Perl and Nancy Wilson present a series of portraits of teachers and of the ways in which they see their teaching. They explain the value of the questioning that goes on in the journal:

> As we observed the teachers at work, we asked ourselves what the habit of reflection contributed to teaching. In the journals we thought we could see the connection: teachers who inquired into the nature of their teaching taught writing in the same spirit of inquiry. Realizing that there was always more to see than they had originally suspected, these teachers demonstrated with their teaching what they also believed to be true about writing: that there was always more to learn, that teaching, like writing, was subject to revision. In fact, we realized that insight in teaching and writing often sprang from the same source — the questioning that required one to pause, to look closely, to think for oneself, to engage what was yet unknown." (253)

CHAPTER 2

Thought and Language

What does it mean to know something? How does knowing connect to telling? As their journals lead them into reflection and inquiry, teachers and prepractice students discover that knowing and telling, or thought and language, are issues of central importance to their ideas about teaching:

> I've been asking myself how I came to know whatever things I know and feel are worth knowing. Most of what is really valuable was not *told* to me by someone else. Then I ask, why be a teacher anyway? The best reason would be so that I can participate in the making of intelligence and thereby affect the development of society.... As a teacher, I'd like to help students discover what kind of knowledge they think is worth knowing and to help them decide what procedures they can use to find out what they want to know. (Janet)

Janet works as a teacher's aide in the Boston Public Schools and has had opportunity to observe and reflect on classrooms. She confesses that she would like to be "the sort of teacher who can initiate *thinking*," which she sees as an active process, based on discovery. Throughout her journal she voices this concern:

> Many of the students simply take orders. They know when to be quiet, when they can look around and take a break, when to copy the notes, and when questions are asked they often sit back—do not think, even when called upon to answer. It seems kind of empty to just grade a student because they've learned to be passive accepters. Maybe we need to measure success by the frequency with which they question or the frequency and conviction of the challenges to assertions made by teachers or students.

One of the major tasks of a teacher is to inquire into the relationship between what students know and what they express. The McChoakum-childs of the educational world believe that thought and language equate exactly: if you can't say it, you don't know it. Pat Conroy explored the thought-language connection from a different perspective: by giving his students lots of opportunities to tell and know, by asking them to write, to speak, to draw, he showed that telling could be accomplished in a number of ways. Mina Shaughnessy explored the connection by looking for students' underlying understandings about writing in the consistent patterns of error they produced. But typically the form of inquiry that teachers use as they examine the thought and language of students is the test, where students prove that they know and are able to tell what they've read and heard in the classroom. Tests won't provide Janet with a picture of "active" knowing and expression of ideas, and she suggests a good alternative method: paying attention to students' questions or assertions. But to uncover the relationship between what is said and what (and how it) is known, Janet needs to inquire more deeply into the nature of thought and its relationship to language. Her concerns lead us directly to the primary concern of this chapter — what it means to know, and the relationship between what we think or know and the language in which we express it to ourselves or to others.

In many of the classes that Janet has observed, knowledge seems to be something sharply defined, coming in measurable units and transferred through contact, like so many film negatives making prints on each sheet of photographic paper they touch. Learners are like those blank sheets of paper, ready to receive the exact image printed on them. They sit passively and "copy the notes." The teacher's job is to make a good photographic plate of each of the units of knowledge, to transfer the knowledge stored in texts and in his head into the heads of the students, and he knows that he has succeeded when the students can reproduce exactly what has been pressed upon them.

Obviously, quantifiable and replicable knowledge, knowledge transmitted by one and reproduced precisely by another, can be useful. It can be accessed to provide correct answers when a particular situation matches what's been learned. And, indeed, there are real-life situations where people need to reproduce knowledge exactly — the name of a medicine or the model number of an auto part or the spelling of words on a page being edited. Knowing exact information makes tasks simpler, easier to accomplish. But life provides relatively few true "matching" situations. Human survival, in fact, has always depended on the ability to learn when situations don't match: to use one situation and locate key features to compare in another, to test out possible responses and continue to modify them until a new match is made. A patient's symptoms don't follow the textbook disease, the car parts manual doesn't explain the car broken down on the highway, and the dictionary doesn't decide whether a word is appropriate for the audience. Janet, who will teach biology, is aware of how limited textbook information alone is in helping students encounter the natural world.

> The way in which science affects us today (with the advent of new diseases like AIDS, or of genetic engineering, etc.) asks us to think through and respond not only with the facts, but also to evaluate moralistic, value-type questions. Scientists have to be articulate, to develop ideas through writing from the "internal" and personal meaning. Students I have observed never get to develop their ideas about

science and its effects via writing. Reading and writing are reserved for mundane, rote learning, unfortunately.

In Janet's developing teaching theory, knowledge is not facts by themselves but the uses to which those facts can be put. To contradict Mr. Gradgrind, facts are *not* all that matters. Learners need to be engaged in *acts* of knowing — "to *do*" as well as to memorize. Knowledge, then, is a construction, something people make tentatively through attempts to act on and respond to the world, and which they revise as they go along. And knowing becomes the way the mind works to carry out this process. The teacher's role, as Janet realizes, must be to encourage the learner's thinking about and acting upon the world, his engagement in a process of generating new understandings.

"How do I know what I think till I see what I say?"

Language is an inherent part of the process of conceptualization. As humans, we not only perceive the world, but we represent it to ourselves and others, storing our knowledge of it in actions (riding a bicycle), in images (a mental picture of an old man on a bicycle in Cherokee Park), and in words ("He can ride a bicycle"). We represent as well as take in experience, and language helps us characterize — pinpoint, generalize, alter — our ideas. We can see the man riding the old Schwinn in the park; we can't see him *not* riding and it would be harder to draw a picture of the nonact. But language allows us to say, "He's not riding that bicycle because his doctor told him to quit," and we can use words like *sad, resigned, dismayed* to show how we feel about that. Language allows thinkers to restructure experience, to select elements of it and combine them, to rename and reconceptualize the act of riding a bicycle. So we use language both for naming the things of our world and for grouping and categorizing the things that we name, for comparing new things with what we've already known and named, for using what we already know to help us make sense of our world. We learn what we know by expressing it, as E. M. Forster says in his famous line above.

This process of knowing and telling is particularly clear in the language of children, whose capacities in thought far exceed their ability to express them in language: When Hepsie's niece Carrie was two, she went to the circus for the first time. She had just sat down when the elephants entered the tent. Carrie's word for dog at the time was *ga-ga* and she repeated it constantly every time she went to visit at Hepsie's house, where there was a dog in residence. As the lead elephant galumphed toward her she called out confidently, "Ga-ga." But her assurance was shaken a minute later as the elephant swayed toward her. The elephant stopped directly across from her, and Carrie turned to the adults with a question in her eyes. "*Big* ga-ga," she said finally.

Carrie was categorizing, lining up a new experience, seeing an elephant, with an experience she already had in place, *ga-ga* or *dog*, and finding mismatches between the two. She renamed the category as she recognized both similarity and difference between the elephant and ga-ga. When Hepsie renamed the "big ga-ga" as *elephant*, Carrie continued the process of making new categories using the new language she was acquiring, adding *efant* to *ga-ga* as types of animals. Language helped Carrie divide experience into the categories she needed to conceptualize it. Without her ability to make categories, Carrie would be trapped in the here and now, unable to predict and unable to think, unable to move beyond the immediate experience of the individual dog or elephant to imagine new relationships and possibilities. Language, then, allows humans to extrapolate from experience, to interpret it, and the way language orders our experience is our process of thinking.

Formal studies of children have helped us understand the complex relationship between thought and language in human learning. The work of the cognitive psychologists Jean Piaget and Lev Vygotsky, in particular, has enriched understanding of how thought and language develop in children. Piaget's early observations of his own children led him to undertake a systematic study of their development and, in turn, to posit a theory of the development of such mental processes as perceiving, remembering, reasoning. He was primarily interested in the child's development of one particular kind of thought — of logical reasoning as represented in scientific and mathematical thinking. As with any inquiry, the questions he asked determined what he saw, and what he found does not give us a complete or even accurate picture of cognitive development. But it does direct our attention to some important issues. Below are some major tenets of Piagetian theory that we'll expand on as we discuss cognition and language.

1. Children's thought and language are unique rather than deficient.

The language and thought of children are not inadequate forms of adult thought and expression, but appropriate expressions of the child's development. As such, the thought and language of a child at any point represents the cognitive development of the child within that stage. Carrie's phrase "big ga-ga" is a creative construction that appropriately represents her grasp of a new experience. It shows the power of her thought, not her lack of it.

2. Children's knowing is an active, constructive process.

The development of a child's thought is linked to her growing ability to perceive the physical world, to operate in conjunction with it, and to predict the outcome of those operations. The child develops from experience an internal model of the world. When this model comes up against the evidence of the real world, some parts of the model match that evidence, but some do not. To a point, the child is able to assimilate new evidence from the world into her model of how the world works, but where the model and evidence contradict each other dramatically, she must alter the model and accommodate the new evidence. The terms *assimilate* and *accommodate* can be applied to processes learners use all the time. Carrie assimilates the elephant into her model of "ga-ga." But she's uncertain as she does so, because that model cannot easily encompass something far larger and stranger than the dog she knew at home, and it will have to be altered to accommodate this new reality. Janet revises her prior theories of learning when she reviews the evidence of her life experience and discovers that most of what she feels is worth knowing "was not *told*" to her by someone else.

3. Children move through stages in the development of their capacities to think about the world.

As they acquire language, children begin to represent the world through symbols, and they gradually develop the ability to manipulate objects abstractly, in mental images and symbols, as well as physically. They come to recognize, for example, that operations are reversible (something that can be added can be subtracted), that objects can be classified and arranged systematically, and that quantities can remain the same despite changes in their physical appearance (as when Koolaid is poured from a tall, thin glass into a short, squat one). And, while the young child saw things only from her own perspective, egocentrically, the child in the middle years (ages six to eleven) begins to see other points of view. The Piagetian child in these early stage of development can't think systematically about difficult abstract concepts like space or time, think about larger questions from more than one perspective, imagining how all aspects would be arranged with each perspective, or think hypothetically about ways to solve a problem. These kinds of "formal operations" Piaget found to appear in adolescence, when the child could create hypotheses, logically deduce, and abstract.

Piaget's universal schema of development, with set stages taking place at set times for all children, has for both good and ill been extremely influential in educational practice as teachers have attempted to modify their instruction to the developmental stages they assumed their students to be laboring within. "We won't work with symbols until grade nine," the Piagetian math teacher might say. "These students aren't out of the concrete-operational until they're fifteen." Studies in the past few years have shown that stages of development (Piaget

named them *preoperational, concrete operational, formal operational*, emphasizing mental activity) cannot be as rigidly defined as Piaget appeared to
make them, that most children and adults, in fact, operate on different
levels in different areas of their lives and in different physical and social
and emotional contexts. Yet Piaget's theory did help to focus attention
on the fact that learning is developmental, that some thinking processes
are precursors to others, and that the growth of a learner's thinking
occurs in meaningful patterns.

Vygotsky's research with young children in postrevolutionary Russia
owed much to Piaget's work, and some of his conclusions about the
relationship of thought and language derive from his attempt to replicate
Piaget's experiments and observations. Both Piaget and Vygotsky emphasize the active role of the child in constructing an understanding of
the world, in building theories or models or schemata of how things
work, and then testing these against available evidence. For both, knowledge is something actively constructed by the learner, not a body of
information to be placed into children's empty heads by some outside
force.

But there are significant differences between the work of Piaget and
Vygotsky in the role each assigns to the social element of thought, in
the effect of social context on the way cognition develops in the role of
language. Vygotsky found, for example, that Piaget's developmental
stages were socially rather than naturally determined: "The developmental uniformities established by Piaget apply to a given milieu, under the
conditions of Piaget's study. They are not laws of nature, but are
historically and socially determined" (55). One of the major differences
between the two psychologists is the way in which each views the
world surrounding the child. Piaget focuses on the physical universe.
For Piaget, the child develops toward closer and closer approximations
of one stable reality, a real world with more or less fixed operations and
objects. He does so in stages that are universal. Essentially independent
of any social or cultural context, he assimilates and accommodates to
the world around him. Vygotsky focuses on the social environment as
well as the physical one. He shows how the child assimilates and
accommodates to the environment surrounding him in a social rather
than individual context. The child's development, he shows, takes place
in and is stimulated and altered by social context in a world that is
shifting and dynamic rather than fixed and stable. Vygotsky's provocative
ideas about the role of the social in individual development lead to three
final tenets in a theory of cognitive development.

4. *The child's development of thought and language is not just an individual but a social process, with the individual embedded in a society and culture from the first.*

The child's models of her larger world, and even the features she would notice in the physical world and the questions she would ask about it, are shaped in part by her ongoing engagement with others and by the cultural context in which such engagement takes place. Carrie's attention has been directed to the circus and its animals by the adult members of her family, who value the social activity of taking a child to the circus. And Carrie's perception of *ga-ga* as something to pet or admire rather than something to eat is shaped by her culture. It's also the culture or community that provides the language to explain the reality the child perceives, just as Carrie's conversation with Hepsie provides the term *elephant*.

5. *Language mediates between the learner and the world, shaping and extending thought. The child actively constructs a world, and language helps shape the construction.*

Piaget's child explores an individual relationship with the physical universe using speech "egocentrically," to represent ideas to himself. Only later does he use speech socially, to communicate those ideas to others. For Vygotsky's child, on the other hand, the very words the child uses as "egocentric speech," to represent his thoughts to himself, are words that are necessarily drawn from a social context. Even where the child talks to himself, he's engaged in a conversation with others who have contributed to his language, so that the individual and the world he inhabits always exist in a conversation. The internalization of social speech, of dialogue with others, Vygotsky calls "inner speech," or "thought saturated with sense," and that speech pushes and extends and contributes to thought. As Carrie internalizes her conversation with Hepsie, the term Hepsie has provided will extend her conceptual framework for thinking about animals, and she'll conduct similar conversations in her own mind. In Piaget's theory, "egocentric speech" disappears as the child becomes "socialized" to the outside world; Vygotsky's idea is that egocentric speech never disappears but "goes underground" to enhance development of social and inner speech. Even our thoughts, then, are conversations.

6. Skilled teaching not only supports the development of thought and language but enhances it.

In Piaget's theory, while language and thought develop together, language represents and supports thinking but does not directly shape it. The teacher, in Piaget's world, would offer appropriate settings in which a child could form the understandings and discover the principles appropriate to her stage of development, but the teacher could not hasten that development beyond the age-appropriate stage in the child's inborn program of cognitive development. In Vygotsky's world, the teacher has, potentially, a much larger role, and a skilled teacher not only can expose the child to situations in which he can make discoveries and form understandings but also can engage the child in dialogue and support his learning, leading him into a "zone of proximal development," Vygotsky's term for helping a child's reach always exceed his grasp.

A theory of learning that will provide important underpinnings to the work of the English classroom can be based on the six tenets we've summarized here: the uniqueness rather than the deficiency of the learner's thought and language; the active, constructive nature of learning; the existence of coherent and meaningful patterns of development; the importance of social context, and of the language it provides, to this development; and the significance of effective teaching to the learning process. In an essay entitled "State of the Child," Jerome Bruner, another cognitive psychologist, notes the importance of cognitive theory for education: "Theories of development can serve as theories of education as well. For what, after all, is educational theory but a set of canny ideas for arranging the world so that the child may reach his full powers?" (1983, 89).

Thought, language, and the writer

This whole book grows out of a Vygotskian notion of the role of the teacher in the learner's development, and so we won't spend time arguing that point specifically here. But the other five tenets of cognitive theory as we've abstracted them from the work of Piaget and Vygotsky will be helpful to keep in mind as we look at some excerpts from the work of Allison, a developing writer, who was a freshman in Ellie's Basic Writing class. The class moved through a sequence of informal and formal writing assignments that connected personal experience to a series of course readings (Marjory Shostak's anthropological study *Nisa*, *The Diary of Anne Frank*, Maya Angelou's *I Know Why the Caged Bird Sings*) that showed adolescents growing up in a variety of cultural and historical contexts. Students moved back and forth between writing

about their own experiences, listening to what classmates had written
about their experiences, reading and writing about the experiences
represented in these texts, discussing all of this, and returning to reexamine what had gone before in the light of each new part. These
excerpts represent Allison's work at three points in the semester: an in-
class "early memory" assignment on the first day of class, a section of
a midterm essay on *The Diary of Anne Frank*, and a final journal entry.

9/2—One of the first and most frightening things I remember as a
child is when my mother got sick.

first we have to start from the beginning, my mother has asthma
So I was already used to her bein sick sometimes and not being able to
breathe. But it never stopped her from doing anything, and if it did, it
didn't stop her for long.

Well the day that I remember she was very sick and had been for
about five days or so. I just thought it was another one of those times
and she would be fine in another day. What did I know I was only
about seven, well that night she got worse and I remember standing at
the bottom of the stairs and watching my brother carry my mother
down the stairs.

I couldn't believe it my mother who always could do just about
anything—was being carried down the stairs.

Well I was very confused but after a while I went to see my mother
in the hospital, and found out she would be fine and would come
home.

10/16 (excerpt)—In reading the diary of anne frank, I was impressed
at how mature she was and how she handled the changes in her life. In
one part of the book Anne talks of how she is frightened by the
bombing and she goies in and sleeps with her farther. She says in the
book that she is acting like a frightened little child. I think that just by
recognising that she was acting like a child that it showed how mature
she was. Because if you are immature than you really can't recognize
when you are acting immature, but if you are mature than you can
recognized when you are being immature.

[margin note: More thinking]

11/27—Well I am now nineteen and just recently my mother went to
the hospital for her asthma. It was quite a different situation from the
last time. This time I wasn't even home when she went to the hospital, I
was at a friends house and didn't find out that my mother had gone to
the hospital til the next day. But I remember feeling the same way as I
did when I heard about the last time. At first I was scared. But this
time I was able to understand more and I didn't have all those crazy
ideas that she would never come home or die. I knew this time that
she would be fine and the doctors would help her. Also this time I was
thinking more about her than about myself. Last time all I could think
of was, "what will I do without her." This time I thought "What can I
do for her" I feel I have matured and can look at things like this much
clearer.

[margin note: Compare & Contrast — maturity]

The tenets inherent in the work of Piaget and Vygotsky can help teachers to read student texts like Allison's in new ways.

1. Learners' language should be seen as appropriate to their stage of learning rather than as deficient.

While Allison's writing could certainly be seen as deficient in comparison to the sophisticated writing that will be a goal in her college writing classes, it's not useful for us to look first at the writing's deficiencies if we're trying to find out what it's saying. Just as Mina Shaughnessy saw in her students' errors a way to understand their present thinking about writing and its conventions, it's more productive for readers of this work to see what Allison is able to do as she writes each of these pieces, and to look at her growth as a thinker and writer forward from where she begins, rather than backward, from a final or ideal goal far in her future. Early writing assignments rooted in things that she knows about (her personal experience) and ways of thinking and talking about that experience that she already uses confidently in her daily speech (narrating and describing) allow her to build on what she knows and allow teachers to see what she's bringing to her work in our classrooms. Allison's writing is appropriate to her examination of experience, to her development within the course, and to the demands of the task. She'll be using her writing, and her feeling of freedom in producing it, as part of a larger act of interpretation, which she'll extend throughout the semester.

2. The learner's process of knowing is active and constructive.

Allison's knowledge is not fixed or static. She's actively thinking and inquiring, trying out and testing ideas, as she moves through successive course activities and assignments. Talking and writing help her do this, particularly when they allow her to focus her attention on working on ideas in process, rather than only on preparing a clean final product. And she's aware of herself as a thinker, frequently expressing this awareness with "I thought," "I think," and noticing changes in her own thinking, recognizing that now she can "look at things like this much clearer." Allison's voice also changes as she controls experience through memory and reflection.

3. The learner's development of new forms of thought and language is systematic.

Allison's thought is developing in some systematic ways. While her work doesn't reflect a particular stage of development in Piagetian terms (at eighteen her growth can't be defined in terms for children's development), it can be helpful for us to look at some features of her conceptualization. She is, for instance, attentive to issues of logical structuring: in the first piece, she thinks about chronological sequencing ("First we have to start from the beginning"); she sees relationships between events ("My mother has asthma *so* I was already used to her being sick"); she makes a beginning generalization ("One of the first and most frightening things I remember as a child"), which she backs up with the specific details of her experience. By the third entry, she systematically contrasts the events of two different time periods ("last time" versus "this time"), seeing the relationships between two whole sequences; and she not only can prove a larger point, but also can do so inductively, moving from a set of observations to a concluding generalization ("I have matured"). She's also able to interpret events and see their significance—to see that one incident can represent a whole perspective on life—and she shows that she's able not only to maintain a consistent perspective or point of view but, in the third excerpt, to contrast two different perspectives, that of the child and that of the young adult. She can also contrast two different interpretations of events—as in excerpt two where she disagrees that Anne is acting like a frightened little child, showing the logical consistency of her new interpretation and using the terms that signal those logical relationships ("*because if* you are immature *then* you really can't recognize when you're acting immature, *but if* you are mature *then* you can recognize when you are being immature."). Comparing what Allison accomplishes at any one point with what she's accomplished earlier, a teacher can see systematic development in the ways she represents her ideas. The assignments, which build on each other, facilitate Allison's reseeing her earlier work from new perspectives. (We'll talk more about this in Unit 3.)

4 and 5. The learner's conceptual development is a social process, embedded in a culture and mediated by language.

The development of language and thought can't be separated from the social/communicative context in which it occurs. Allison has talked with others, read what others have written, and drawn on words and concepts that have been constructed in the common discussion of the classroom. Her reading of Anne Frank's life gives her a new perspective on her own life. Class discussions about what it means to be mature have given her both a word and a concept to apply both to Anne's life and to her own and have pushed her to a new understanding of old events. Being mature is related to ways of seeing oneself and the world, and not only is Allison able to apply the term, but she comes to enact it, seeing herself in a new, "mature" perspective. Allison's ability to broaden her perspective does not emerge from an isolated movement into a developmental stage of formal reasoning about logical patterns, as Piaget would suggest, but from the social engagement with others — both in life and in texts — who give voice to new ways of seeing and representing things.

This process is important for learners of all ages, for the elementary school child no less than for the adult college student. For the adolescent, who is generally both intensely focused on the self and engaged in the task of moving outside it, work that makes connections to that self while moving the learner outward into new perspectives, new knowledge, and new ways of using language to represent them is particularly important to the process of development.

Language, thought, and culture

The social context that provides the language for thought is also a cultural context — one in which things are perceived and represented in special ways, laden with meaning and values. Piaget's world, the world of the Western scientist, focused on the physical universe and valued particular kinds of thinking — and this focus determined what Piaget saw. Vygotsky, in a postrevolutionary Russian society where major upheavals of class and society led to questions about how social change shaped people's thinking, added new questions to those Piaget had asked. Because he was asking different questions, Vygotsky saw much that Piaget hadn't seen.

The kind of abstract, logical reasoning that Piaget valued in the actions of the children he observed and in his assumptions about their development has long been valued in Western society and in our schools. Formal logical reasoning moves the learner farther and farther away from real or specific contexts and concerns to generalizable problems, and, while it has the important advantage of helping us see generalizations and principles that can occur across many contexts, it's not always easy for learners with real-life concerns to understand why the specific and the real have no place in the logical and formal.

In *Hard Times*, Sissy Jupe, the circus horse-trainer's daugther, has been given a home by the Gradgrinds so that she might get a "proper education" in the superiority of facts over fancy. But Sissy has trouble learning to operate within the world of decontextualized knowledge that McChoakumchild's classroom and the Gradgrind home demand. McChoakumchild reports that she is "extremely slow in the acquisition of dates, unless some pitiful incident happened to be connected therewith." And Sissy herself has come to the conclusion that she is "O so stupid" and that everything she knows is a "mistake." She responds to a question about national prosperity by saying, "I couldn't know whether it was a prosperous nation or not, and whether I was in a thriving state or not, unless I knew who had got the money, and whether any of it was mine." She knows that her thinking does not fit with the problem as presented. "But that had nothing to do with it. It was not in the figures at all." She can't focus on the correct response to an arithmetical question about proportions when the figures given are for those out of a total population who have starved to death, or about percentages when they are for those drowned or burned out of the total who went on sea voyages. Soon she gets resigned to her failure: "Although I am so anxious to learn ... I am afraid I don't like it" (62–65).

What Sissy doesn't like is learning devoid of application. And with good reason. It has nothing to do with her. What neither she nor her teacher nor the Gradgrinds can see is that unconnected learning isn't the only way of getting knowledge. Jerome Bruner, whose work has been influenced by Vygotsky, balances the logical, analytical, or "paradigmatic" mode of reasoning with another, equally important mode of knowing—one that's intuitive more than rational, and that represents its meaning in stories rather than logical syllogisms and formulae (1986, 13). This "narrative knowing" accounts for a large part of the way we make sense of our world, and we use it in our most mundane conversations as well as our most significant texts of literature, history, religion. When we select details from the flux of experience and shape them into a story, we're also engaged in naming, abstracting from, and restructuring the raw data of the physical world, and in finding its patterns of meaning. And it's in our stories—of Hepsie's niece, of the illness of Allison's mother—that we embed our understanding of more abstract concepts like categorization or maturity.

All cultures have stories, but some are especially attuned to the ways that stories represent important knowledge and meanings for the society, and they particularly value the words and the wisdom of the storyteller. In Scott Momaday's *The House Made of Dawn*, a Native American preacher, The Priest of the House of the Sun, connects the word of God with traditional tribal storymaking and shows how the story helps listeners understand:

> My grandmother was a storyteller; she knew her way around words. She never learned to read and write, but somehow she knew the good of reading and writing; she had learned how to listen and delight. She had learned that in words and in language, and there only, she could have whole and consummate being. She told stories, and she taught me how to listen. I was a child and I listened. She could neither read nor write, you see, but she taught me how to live among her words, how to listen and delight. "Storytelling; to utter and to hear ...." And the simple act of listening is crucial to the concept of language, and more crucial even than reading and writing, and language is, in turn, crucial to human society,... When she told me those old stories,

something strange and good and powerful was going on. I was a child, and that old woman was asking me to come directly into the presence of her mind and spirit; she was taking hold of my imagination, giving me to share in the great fortune of her wonder and delight. She was asking me to go with her to the confrontation of something that was sacred and eternal. (87–89)

The Priest of the House of the Sun presents a version of literacy that shows how learning comes from the power of words embedded in old stories that the child hears. He tells how the grandmother's few words, when repeated and remembered, grow in meaning, while the white man's many words — "words by the millions, an unending succession of pamphlets and papers, letters and books, bills and bulletins, commentaries and conversations" — have made him "sated and insensitive." And then he turns from preaching about the Word to bringing his listeners to understanding through the words of the grandmother's stories, using the old stories for teaching and learning, as Conroy learns to do with the children on Yamacraw Island.

Both paradigmatic and narrative knowing are found in all cultures, though the forms they take and the ways in which they are used vary. A study of schooling across cultures, by Silvia Scribner and Michael Cole, suggests that "all culture groups thus far studied have demonstrated the capacity to remember, generalize, form concepts, operate with abstractions, and reason logically" (1973, 553), but that people who have been to school tend to perform these cognitive acts in different ways from those who haven't. Those who've been to school tend to treat problems as examples of a class of problems that can be solved by a general rule, and they use language to describe the tasks they are doing and what they are doing with them, because these ways of thinking and using language are valued in schools. People who haven't been to school are likely to categorize in different ways and, like Sissy Jupe, draw on real contexts rather than abstract syllogisms in their problem solving.

There's a frequently told story about an anthropologist who put twenty items — various fruits and vegetables, kitchen implements, and farm implements — on a table in front of an illiterate farmer. When asked to put these in groups, the farmer paired each tool with the object it would be used on — so that the orange was paired with the knife, because the knife is used to cut the orange. Now, this is a standard test performed by cognitive psychologists to test someone's ability to categorize and to reason abstractly, and the "right" answer in their terms is to group things by function — e.g., all kitchen implements together. So the anthropologist kept asking the farmer whether he could do it another way, until the farmer, in exasperation, said, "Yes, you could, but this is how a smart person would do it." "Oh," said the anthropologist. "How would a dumb person do it?" And the farmer responded by grouping the items by function. So the farmer sees the anthropologist's groupings of objects by functions — "foods," "tools" — as the "dumb way." He's equally capable of categorization, but according to different principles — principles that are related to what's important for life in his society.

For a long time the particular form of abstract thinking associated with schooling in the West was seen as a consequence of literacy — of the further abstraction of moving from having words represent things to having written symbols represent those words, so that they could be manipulated far from any context in which they had originated. Historically, the Greeks "invented" the alphabet (adapting the sort of syllabary used in Hebrew and other written languages of the Mediterranean area), and that invention has been seen as allowing the development of logic, geometry, philosophy. (Here, as in other questions of the interrelationship of language and thought, it's hard to separate cause from effect, to know whether the existence of the alphabet allowed the development of more abstract thinking, as the historical anthropologists Goody and Watt have suggested, or whether the culture's interest in more abstract ways of thinking pushed it to refine existing orthography and make an alphabet that would be more explicit and thus less dependent for its meaning on the reader's knowledge of the specific context it was written in.)

Alexander Luria, another Russian psychologist and a colleague of Vygotsky's, studied changes in the thinking of illiterate and formerly illiterate Russian peasants during a period of collectivization and literacy education. Luria agreed with Vygotsky that social context contributed to the development of thought and language, and together they theorized that this period of significant social change would result in changes in the peasants' ways of thinking and of expressing their thoughts. Luria collected data that showed significant changes in the thinking of adults exposed to different work contexts and to some education, and he saw these changes as comparable to stages in children's acquisition of new modes of thought. Luria found that peasants with some schooling and experience in a collective were able to engage in cognitive processes such as generalization and abstraction, deduction and inference, and reasoning and problem solving in the ways that schooled people generally did, scoring high on tests for these processes. For example, they could reason logically within a set of given facts, even where they had no personal knowledge. The illiterate peasant, when presented with the syllogism

> In the Far North, where there is snow, all bears are white. Novaya Zemlya is in the Far North and there is always snow there. What color are the bears there?

would not answer outside personal knowledge, and the response would be, "I don't know what color the bears there are; I never saw them," or, "A person who had traveled a lot and been in cold countries and seen everything could answer; he would know what color the bears were." On the other hand, the peasant who's becoming literate and who's lived for two years on a collective farm answers, "You say that it's cold there and there's snow, so the bears there are white."

Similarly, the illiterate peasant doesn't want to imagine places he's never been or questions he might want to ask, although the workers on collective farms do this readily. And he doesn't talk about what he's like as a person or what he'd like to change or improve, except in his external circumstances. When asked about his personal shortcomings he responds: "I was a farmhand; I have a hard time and many debts." But the collective farm activist responds readily with an analysis of his personality and mental processes:

> I am neither good nor bad.... I'm an average person, though I'm weak on literacy and can't write at all; and then I'm very nasty and angry, but still I don't beat my wife. That's all I can say about myself.... I forget very fast; I walk out of a room and I forget. I also don't understand very well; yesterday I was given a long explanation, and I didn't understand anything. If I were educated, I would do everything well. I have to change this shortcoming in education. I don't want to change anything in my character; if I study it'll change by itself. (159)

Luria sees such changes representing "an internal restructuring in the consciousness of our subjects" (155). Certainly a shift from one way of life and one set of values to another has given these workers different ways of thinking about and looking at the world and themselves. Having participated in new experiences, they're more willing to speculate about the world, to think of alternatives, to imagine it in different ways. Luria's conclusion is that social change invites cognitive change:

> As the basic forms of activity change, as literacy is mastered and a new stage of social and historical practice is reached, major shifts occur in human mental activity. These are not limited simply to an expanding of man's horizons, but involve the creation of new motives for action and radically affect the structure of cognitive processes. (161)

More recent interpretation of Luria's findings suggests that these adults were not necessarily developing new capacities, as children do, but were shifting existing modes of thinking to the particular problems being posed by the new setting, seeing things from new perspectives, and changing their sense of what was a "smart way" versus a "dumb way" of thinking as they moved into new contexts and started to learn to think and talk like the psychologists who were testing them. But certainly, significant patterns of difference did appear between the two groups of peasants.

While Luria didn't assert that literacy alone, apart from other changes in experience, produced cognitive changes, his work was often cited to show that literacy per se brought about changes in thought, that teaching people to use the technology of literacy—how to write words and letters and to read them out from the page—would alter their thinking in profound ways. But a more recent study by Scribner and Cole (1981) suggests that literacy alone, apart from Western-style schooling or significant experience outside the culture of the immediate community, doesn't have this effect. Scribner and Cole studied the Vai, a group of people in Liberia who had invented their own script and passed it on, one to one, in informal settings, to other members of the community. Those people who had learned only Vai literacy did not think in ways significantly different from those who were illiterate. But those who had been to school or who had been to other communities with different perspectives, could more easily do the sorts of thinking we saw Allison developing—systematically comparing different events, recognizing different points of view, and recategorizing and restructuring what they knew. And so it seems that *either* school experience or multicultural experience helps us see that the ways we've categorized things aren't the only ways they can be categorized, and that the things we see as significant aren't the only things that can be seen this way—that there are many different ways of knowing the world and presenting its meaning.

Our school culture particularly values the ability to think and problem-solve outside the context of one's own immediate experience, and to be self-reflective and aware of one's own thinking and ways of acting. And one aim of schooling in our society may be to facilitate these sorts of changes from thinking in personal, context-based terms to thinking more abstractly, much like what we saw in Allison's writing. But we would argue that Allison was developing new ways because she was engaged in experiences that expanded what she knew and could express, and because these new ways connected with what had gone before. She didn't have to leave the context of her life and her experience behind as she entered the classroom, but could reexamine it from new perspectives gained from her reading and her class discussions, and thus come to understand it in new ways.

More abstract thinking, in itself, is not always better. We've all heard of or perhaps listened to the demagogue or smooth politician who speaks only in abstractions—*patriotism*, or *truth*—without rooting these terms in the complex details of real life and real examples. And, as we know, it's been easy to talk about "American education" without a very close look at the work of the real classrooms and students and teachers that term represents. Operating on a high plane of abstraction without grounding in rich particulars becomes especially dangerous when policy decisions are based on theoretical models that don't take into account the real impact on the real lives of people they'll affect. Janet reflects on this concern in her journal entry at the beginning of the chapter, in which she argues that biology must be taught in a human context. So our ability to learn and to engage in inquiry about the world depends on our being able to link specific details — of our lives or the lives of others or our observations of the physical world — with the more abstract concepts that can pull together these details into a larger coherent model of how things work. And the more richness of detail we bring into our model, the more we'll understand.

The attempt to encompass different ways of seeing these details and experiences — as, for example, all of the different ways that the students in Allison's class perceived their own actions and those of the characters in the books they read — necessarily moves us to create more abstract structures that can include all of the specific instances. Many specific actions could be seen as "mature," for example, so, for Allison, *mature* names a larger concept that can encompass many different examples of behavior. In the same way, *animal* will soon enter Carrie's vocabulary as a more general concept that can include the subcategories of *dog* and *elephant*. And both Carrie and Allison will continue to develop their expertise in moving back and forth between specific experiences and abstractions.

All of this leads us to recognize two things: first, that language and conceptualization are developed by experience; and second, that we expand our experience and our ways of knowing when we have the opportunity to see things from multiple perspectives — personal, cross-cultural, historical.

Sissy was not mistaken at all.

Language, thought, culture, and schooling

Despite the fact that people learn in more than one way and know things through more than one means, our schools have, by and large, allowed just one way of knowing to be developed in the classroom, an analytical and discrete way, often competitive and individualistic, highly abstract and intellectualized, and authority-centered. In such classrooms, students' ways of thinking, when they differ from this school-sponsored way, are most often seen as errors or deviations, rather than as part of a developing system of thought. There's little room for learners to explore, inquire, question, or create abstractions from their own experiences.

Janet, in reflecting back on her own learning experiences, remembers an extreme version of such a classroom:

> My memories are all of fearful days spent hoping I wouldn't get called to perform at the blackboard and hoping that I wouldn't make a mistake and she'd yell at me or call me stupid in front of the class. Not being able to make a mistake, ask questions, share ideas with peers ...

do creative things with color, movement, etc. . . . instead of being stuck to seat 3 aisle 1 for seven years. . . .

I think I started out quite bright and creative and got education "inflicted" upon me. It created intense inhibition and fear of thinking. I didn't want to "risk" at all after a while. I didn't dare ask for clarification, but just faked it, went along, kept my mouth shut and tried to "duck out," stay quiet and tucked away to avoid embarrassment.

I recall a scene once, where we were all forty of us in the class to report to the auditorium for a special event. We went and someone had brought in a record player with Irish music for us to stepdance or square dance to. The teacher literally told us where to stand and what to do, how to move . . . exactly. In the process of her explaining . . . I experienced so much fear (fear of making a mistake, not getting exactly right on the first try) that I couldn't hear her anymore, only ringing. When the music began, I got pushed and shuffled by other bodies and didn't know how or where to move. She got enraged, grabbed me, yanked me by the shirt, and slapped me in the face for not dancing correctly. This scene got played in many other similar ways, all the time, and not only to me.

Here, Janet comes to the classroom with a different sort of knowledge from that we've been talking about—a knowledge that's expressed in movement rather than in words, a knowledge of how to respond to movement, of how to dance. She may not know the correct steps, the proper positioning for the particular style of dance she's called upon to perform, but no attempt is made to connect this new style with her existing experience. So this encounter becomes, like all others of her early schooling, one where whatever she does is a mistake, and where her fear of being in error incapacitates her. She's closed down physically in the auditorium, just as she's been silenced in the classroom, and this event comes to represent her entire experience of schooling.

Many learners are silenced in their classrooms. And if this is true of mainstream children, it's often even more true for children from other cultures, who may bring ways of knowing that are radically different from the ways the educational system has promoted. Ronald and Suzanne Scollon's studies of the Athabaskans, for example, show the extent to which their strategies for understanding experiences differ from that of the Western schools they attend. The Athabaskan way, which the Scollons refer to as "bush consciousness," is not individualistic in the Western sense of valuing the isolated, abstract mental processes of the individual thinker, but rather integrated between individual and culture. While Western individualism actually leads to a highly compartmentalized concept of knowledge within the society, with each individual bearing a highly specialized portion of the society's total knowledge, among the Athabaskans, the individual must carry the understandings needed for survival. These understandings are shared among all members of the society, are taken and passed on through common experience in which all participate, so that all contribute continually to the ongoing making of the knowledge. The Athabaskan storyteller, in recounting his own experience hunting in the frozen wastes, shares with his listeners a common understanding of how to hunt and survive. The young hunter listening to him will need all of the old man's knowledge to accomplish the same task. But a way of knowing that's shared rather than competitive, communal rather than individual, relative rather than positive, experiential rather than abstract is rarely honored in Western schools, where the opposite case — learning as competitive, individual, positivist, abstract — is almost always the only learning style recognized.

The differences that the Scollons found between Native American and Western consciousness are indicative of the sorts of differences that have been found to exist, in a less marked form, among other groups of knowers within Western society. Many women have also felt out of place in the schools. In their study *Women's Ways of Knowing*, four researchers, Mary Field Belenky, Blythe McVicker Clinchy, Nancy Rule Goldberger, and Jill Mattuck Tarule, began with questions about why women were so often silent as learners. Because they started with this question, which hadn't been addressed in other studies of learning and cognition, they looked first at women's accounts of their own experience, to see what these women could tell them that cognitive psychology had not. They discovered that particular aspects of experience that women repeatedly voiced as central to "how they knew" were not accounted for in the dominant, Piagetian model of knowing. These researchers found that while women seemed to go through a number of stages in their development of ways of knowing, in the end they were not satisfied with the model of abstract, objective, rational knowing held by Western scholars; they preferred instead a way of knowing that was connected and rooted in context, integrating emotional and rational, subjective and objective, individual and collaborative. They saw question posing at the heart of "connected knowing," and they stressed the importance of really listening to others, of having empathy, of building understanding through real conversations and dialogue rather than through the often adversarial language of logical argument. (Peter Elbow, a composition theorist whose ideas we'll come across in later chapters, calls this process playing "the believing game" rather than "the doubting game.")

Belenky and her colleagues would revise the Piagetian model to allow these other ways of knowing to find a place in cognitive theory and school practice. Vygotsky's emphasis on learning through language in a communicative, social context and Bruner's model of narrative as well as paradigmatic knowing provide a basis for such a revision. In fact, if Vygotsky and Bruner are right, the findings of Belenky and her colleagues suggest that the "connected knowing" strategies they describe are part of everyone's process, not just women's. In the dominant educational model then, some part of everybody has been silenced.

Teachers will see many silenced learners — mainly because, like Janet, these learners fear making mistakes. They'll be reluctant to respond to teachers' questions in the classroom, they'll write as little as possible on any writing task so that there'll be less probability of error, they'll hesitate to take risks or to ask questions on their own. Like Conroy's students who repeated the same story over and over again when he asked them about their summers, they'll hesitate to speak, and if they do, they'll often try to mimic the words of someone else to minimize the risk of humiliation and failure. If left to their own devices, they'll pass quietly through classes, and their teachers will learn little about them. It's not easy to overcome their suspicion, to gain their trust, to bring their energy and life and curiosity back into the classroom, as Conroy found out. But it's important that teachers do so:

> Perfect classroom order and a group of students trying to supply the right answers and please the authority is dangerous nowadays, because as teachers we need to encourage students to be free thinkers, who can actively criticize and who can question and discover knowledge in an atmosphere of acceptance; it's necessary for our survival. (Janet)

A teacher's acceptance and real caring is a first step. In *I Know Why the Caged Bird Sings*, Maya Angelou tells how she's been totally silenced, not by schools, but by a physical assault. A woman from the community, Mrs. Flowers, takes her under her wing, and invites her to read and talk with her:

> Now no one is going to make you talk — possibly no one can. But bear in mind, language is man's way of communicating with his fellow man and it is language alone which separates him from the lower animals.... Your grandmother says you read a lot. Every chance you get. That's good, but not good enough. Words mean more than what is set down on paper. It takes the human voice to infuse them with the shades of deeper meaning. (82)

Mrs. Flowers gives Maya some books to read, on the condition that she read them out loud to herself. When Maya begins to use her voice again, she's asked to recite. But has a handful of books alone made this difference for Maya? No. The real issue is that a human connection was made:

> I was liked, and what a difference it made. I was respected not as Mrs. Henderson's grandchild or Bailey's sister but for just being Marguerite Johnson.
> Childhood's logic never asks to be proved (all conclusions are absolute). I didn't question why Mrs. Flowers had singled me out for attention, nor did it occur to me that Momma might have asked her to

give me a little talking to. All I cared about was that she had made tea cookies for *me* and read to *me* from her favorite book. (85)

Students who are *liked*, who feel respected, who perceive a teacher's genuine interest in them and in talking and listening to them, may find their voices, to ask their questions and express their thoughts.

When students begin to talk, teachers need to listen. Conroy's students, most of whom had been repeatedly told by their principal that they were "retarded," were reluctant to offer their own answers to Conroy's questions.

> When I asked who was the greatest man that ever lived, Mary answered, "Jesus." Everybody, of course, fervently agreed. When I asked who was the second greatest man who ever lived, her brother Lincoln answered "Jesus Christ." Once again the entire class unanimously consented to this second choice. (36)

Gradually, Conroy gets beyond the communication gap by limiting his questions and encouraging general, "tangential" talk:

> We spent the whole day talking. I told them about myself, about my mother and father, about my four brothers and two sisters, about teaching in Beaufort, about going to Europe, and about my coming to Yamacraw.... They asked me about the places I had been, and what New York looked like, and had I ever been on an airplane.
>
> They then told me about hunting on the island, and the boys became extremely animated describing the number of squirrels to be found deep in the woods and how you had to be a great shot to pick out the gray tuft of fur in the black oaks and bring it down with one shot of the .22. The further you went in the woods, they told me, the more tame the squirrels became, the closer they came, and the easier they were to kill. The girls told me in elaborate detail how to clean the squirrels. They called the process "scrinching." You slit open the belly with a sharp knife, peeled the squirrel's pelt off like the skin of a grape, then scraped the squirrel's skin until it was white and smooth. Ethel said, "A lady in Savannah won't eat squirrel cause she say after a squirrel been scrinched it look like little white baby." (36–37)

Once Conroy gives his students permission to talk about what they know, he realizes that they know a lot. As they talk, he sees that they have both thought and language that he can tap into, connect with, and build on, and that is his "theoretical" beginning. It's not just *his* thought and language that are important in the classroom; his students have both thought and language that he can learn from and that they can use to teach one another. As they begin to verbalize their thinking, they find ways to draw on their own knowledge to solve problems.

> It was strange how I marveled about their lack of knowledge concerning history and geography. On the third day, though despairing, I wondered

if they felt any pity for me for not having feasted on squirrel stew or enjoyed the simple pleasures of scrinching. (39)

When teachers listen to students, they hear evidence that will cause a shift in the model of what effective teaching and learning looks like in the classroom. Janet concludes in her journal:

> Teaching is an amazing challenge ... every day, wake up ... what am I going to have students do today? What's it good for? How do I know? Confronting students with problems, thought, is painful for the students I see who are unaccustomed to it. I've learned throughout this course, I'd like to give students the space to *think* ... because thinking is really *not* a painful process.... They need to un-learn the feeling of creativity as painful. I would like to be the sort of teacher who can initiate *thinking*.

We need to know things in particular contexts as well as through abstractions, through personal experience as well as through formal structures, through manipulating objects as well as through reading about them. When we allow multiple ways of knowing, and the language in which they're represented, into our classrooms, we'll support the developing thought and language of all of our students. How and why we should do so will be the focus of our next chapter.

CHAPTER 3

Language in Context: Home and School

As we've seen, language is inextricably bound up with learning; learners develop thought and language as they revise and expand what they already know. Because students don't sit in the classroom as empty vessels and because they don't learn by having facts poured into them, we can't get them actively involved in the making of new understandings without discovering and building upon what's already understood. What's already understood includes both what students know and the ways they come to know it. And it includes, as well, the language in which that knowledge and those ways are represented. Teachers recognize that the language their students use in the home and with their peers may be quite different from what's expected in the context of the classroom. But most schools have regarded "home" language and anything else that students carry with them — cultural differences, individual learning styles — primarily as a liability to their learning, something to be dismissed or erased before school learning can take place. Schools are accustomed to seeing what students do bring with them "from the outside" — stories, ideas, beliefs — as excess baggage rather than chests full of tools to aid their learning.

When teachers ignore what students bring to the classroom, the students may ignore what the teacher brings as well. In one urban high school classroom of mostly black students, the teacher lectures on readings from a text, *Currents in Fiction*, in which Guy de Maupassant and Pearl Buck are the most recent selections. Anthony, who observes this class, comments that "while these offerings certainly merit consideration, they do not speak to the particular cultural needs of the class." As he continues his observation, he discovers how little the concerns of the teacher and those of the students connect in this classroom.

A milieu marked by ethnicity unaddressed by the man in charge, whose mind may be elsewhere, provokes unattentiveness. The tenor of this class is stilted. One feels slightly uncomfortable as three male students talk incessantly while Mr. V begins his lecture without remonstrance. This awkwardness grows as the middle-aged white male teacher ignores the dialectic of the black males, their repartee, and their audience of black females. His attempts at wit are ambushed by his own mocking laughter and by their utter failure at responding to the ritual insults of the students. The class yearns for the chance to signify, while the teacher deems significant only properly structured discourse. No wonder Sheldon decides to pass up a chance at reading aloud when called to do so. He is thoroughly bored by a story set in China, yet continually zings his classmates with clever barbs.

If, as Vygotsky has told us, learning takes place through a process of negotiating shared meanings in a communicative, social context, little learning can go on in a classroom where there's no communication, where no connection is made between the teacher's talk and his students' talk. Whether the students are silenced by the authority of the teacher and his control of the language of the classroom or are, as in this instance, ignored by the teacher, their talk becomes a tangent to his, and the two lines of conversation pull increasingly farther apart.

In school and out of it, students are perceived as "knowers" through the language they use to represent their knowledge (though, like all of us, they certainly know things they cannot represent linguistically). But when the language students bring to the classroom is not that of their teachers, not that of the textbooks they will read from, and sometimes not even that of their peers, that language, and the knowledge it represents, is ignored, or worse, judged to be inferior or disabling, something to be overcome. And as long as the patterns and uses of language of these students remain nonstandard, they're seen as incapable of knowing, even in a passive way. They're empty until they become so filled with school language that it displaces whatever was there before.

The problem

In an essay titled "Teacher Training and Urban Language Problems," Roger Shuy cites these characteristic responses from interviews with urban teachers:

> In the program, the children come with a very meager vocabulary.... I think it's because of the background of the home and the lack of books at home, the lack of communication with the family, especially if there are only one or two children in the family. (169)

> In the inner-city, the child's vocabulary is very limited. (169)

> I can't get them to make a sentence. Even if I have them repeat after me exactly, they don't do it. They repeat in sentences they are familiar with. They're not really sentences but fragments of sentences, and they understand them. They don't realize that they aren't making a complete thought. (170)

Of the first two statements, Shuy notes: "These comments are typical in that the home situation is blamed for the limited vocabulary. Neither teacher gave any indication that the home environment might produce a different vocabulary. On the contrary, both felt that lack of school vocabulary was equivalent to a lack of overall vocabulary" (169). The third teacher comment shows the too common conclusion — that lack of school vocabulary and lack of school grammar indicate an inability to make a complete thought.

This judgment extends through all levels of education. In a recent article in *College Composition and Communication*, Thomas Farrell argues:

> Cognitive differences manifested on [I.Q.] tests grow out of differences in grammar. . . . So far as I know, everybody acknowledges that most black ghetto children do not use the standard forms of the verb "to be," which are used in storybooks and schoolbooks and other commercially published material in this country today. Many of those same black ghetto children have difficulty learning to read, and they do not score highly on measures of abstract thinking. The circumstantial evidence leads me to make the inference that they need to learn the grammar of standard English. (477)

Farrell asserts that students whose dialect doesn't include the full inflection of the verb "to be" (as in, for example, Black English Vernacular's "he going") are unable to discuss states of being rather than actions, and end up being incapable of abstract thought. In order to learn to think abstractly, he argues, they must first be successfully *drilled* in the "full deployment of the verb 'to be.'"

When their teachers and professors think this way, it's not surprising that students themselves come to believe that because they don't speak Standard English, they're stupid or can't think; they internalize the school culture's assessment of their abilities and, in too many instances, fulfill the prophecy of their own defeat. In *The Hunger of Memory*, Richard Rodriguez recounts his internal conflict as a speaker of Spanish who must learn to speak English, and the eventual silencing of his parents who felt constrained not to detract from his acquisition of English by speaking Spanish with him at home. In spite of his attempts, Rodriguez knew he hadn't succeeded, and he echoed his school's assessment of him: "I knew that I spoke English poorly. My words could not extend to form complete thoughts" (14).

These naive assumptions were given scholarly support by Basil Bernstein's early work in language (1960) that suggested there was a definable and one-to-one relationship between the language people spoke and the ideas they thought, that the sparser the language the more limited the ideas of the speaker. Bernstein used the terms *restricted codes* and *elaborated codes* to distinguish between the kinds of discourse used by two classes of people in Great Britain, the working class and the middle class. Bernstein discovered there were differences in the contexts of language that surrounded the working-class and the middle-class child. The parents of middle-class children would typically explain things in terms of larger, "universal" rules and fully stated logical propositions ("It hurts animals to have their ears pulled. And I know you don't want to hurt your cat, so you mustn't pull on her ears!" for example), while working-class parents would refer only to the immediate situation or context ("Stop pulling that cat's ears"). The more universal, less context-bound language was similar to that used in school, so children who spoke the restricted, particularistic, context-bound code were also those who failed in school tasks (as Sissy Jupe did when she was unable to consider a shipwreck as a mathematical problem instead of a human tragedy). Schools provided, in Bernstein's terms, an elaboration or extension of social identity for the middle-class child, while they forced a change of social identity for the working-class child.

Unfortunately, Bernstein's study led easily to the assumption that those who spoke a restricted code were linguistically and culturally deprived (the very word *restricted* may have had something to do with it) and even intellectually inferior (they performed more poorly on I.Q. tests that assumed elaborated codes). The study was cited often as support for early-childhood intervention programs that sometimes exacerbated the problem rather than mediating it by pulling children out of a home environment where their language was valued into an alien one where it was not. Too often these programs created a gap rather than a bridge between two linguistic worlds of home and school. Bernstein was not wholly to blame. He later stated his position on these codes more explicitly:

> That the subculture or culture through its forms of social integration generates a restricted code does not mean that the resultant speech and meaning system is linguistically or culturally deprived, that its children have nothing to offer the school, that their imaginings are not significant. It does not mean that we have to teach these children formal grammar, nor does it mean that we have to interfere with their dialect.... But if the contexts of learning, the samples, the reading books, are not contexts which are triggers for the child's imaginings — are not triggers on his curiosity and explorations in his family and community, then the child is not at home in the educational world.... If the culture of the teacher is to become part of the consciousness of the child, then the culture of the child must first be in the consciousness of the teacher. (1970, 57)

And he makes a point that is a major premise of this chapter, that the social and linguistic experience of a student should be used in school to extend the development of language that takes place in all settings:

> We should start to realize that the social experience the child already possesses is valid and significant, and that this social experience should be reflected back to him as being valid and significant. It can

only be reflected back to him if it is part of the texture of the learning experience we create. (58)

All normal language users are successful at communicating complex and subtle meanings in their home environments, whether these meanings are expressed in words alone (in elaborated, fully lexicalized language), or in a combination of words, facial expressions, and gestures that point toward features of the immediate environment. Formal schooling, in all societies, has drawn learners out of the immediate context of their daily lives, and emphasized general and universal aspects of experience. Where learners and teachers share a common language or style of language use and a common culture, learning within the school context can make conscious and explicit the sorts of things that learners already know intuitively from experience, but perhaps had never put into words. But where common ways of using language are not shared by school and learner, there's bound to be a disjunction. What schools must realize is that this disjunction does not indicate that a learner can't think: what it does indicate is that bridges haven't been made between the way a learner thinks and the way a school teaches.

To understand more about why the "restricted linguistic code/ restricted thought" arguments are wrong, to enlarge the perspective of the urban teachers Shuy worked with, to begin to see how to build on rather than condemn the linguistic and cognitive resources our students bring to our classrooms, teachers need to investigate how language itself is structured and how it's acquired.

The acquisition of language

There are two sets of rules that the child acquires with his native language: those governing structure and those governing use. The first refers to the set of syntactic structures or grammatical rules that can be described for the language. Any adult native speaker of a language can make accurate judgments of grammaticality for virtually any sentence in that language. Thus speakers of English know, without any formal study of grammar, that "The old man was wearing a hat" is grammatical in English, and that "Wearing was man old hat the" is not. Speakers know too that "The hat wore the old man" suggests the peculiar situation of the hat wearing the man. (In German, however, inflectional endings identify *hat* as the object of the verb even when it comes first in the sentence, so for the speaker of German there would be no confusion in "Den Hut trug der alte Mann.") It is this unconscious knowledge of English syntax that Lewis Carroll's poem "Jabberwocky" draws on. Even young readers have no trouble making "sense" out of its nonsense words: "And the mome raths outgrabe."

Now, while all language is governed by grammatical rules, the speakers of a language are largely unconscious of those rules, and even linguists have difficulty determining the majority of them. What we teach as school grammar — its rules and regulations — derives from the rules of Latin, somewhat wrongly applied to English. School grammar doesn't offer a very accurate description of the language and how it works. To describe English or any language as it actually functions, to locate some of the rules of a language, linguists try out sentences on native speakers. If the sentence makes sense to the speaker, the linguist sees it as grammatical — an acceptable sentence in the grammar of the language. In fact, if native speakers of a language sometimes use a construction and it makes sense to listeners, it cannot be ungrammatical. So, the fact that for a long time it was true that "*ain't* ain't in the dictionary" made no difference to the linguist, because to the linguist if a construction is used and understood, it is grammatical. *All* language as it is used for communication is grammatical, governed by regular rules that allow speakers to generate understandable sentences.

But not all constructions are acceptable in all social circumstances. While *ain't*, as a construction used frequently by native speakers of English and understood by their listeners, is entirely grammatical, it's considered unacceptable in some social contexts. And so there's a second set of rules that learners acquire about language — rules for how language gets used in varying social contexts — like what sort of greeting to give to a stranger versus a family member, or what words one shouldn't say in front of grandma; and these rules are learned by using language in those contexts.

The term *language acquisition* is used to describe the process by which a child develops competence in his native language. We know that the child is not born speaking (though this is a matter of physiological and probably cognitive as well as linguistic development), nor does he begin to speak using immediately the full structures of the language — although researchers working with young children keep pushing back, to earlier and earlier ages, the time at which a child can demonstrate some competence with complex structures such as passive verbs. The linguist Noam Chomsky believes that our brains are structured with much language competence built in, waiting to be activated through use in communication. Where similar structures appear in different languages, they appear at roughly the same time in a child's development, and from this it appears that the capacity to understand and use these structures is an innate and universal feature of the human brain. (Chomsky refers to this as "Universal Grammar".)

But while much of our potential linguistic competence may be innate, this potential is not realized unless we're actually involved, through our early years, in communication with those around us. The terrible case of Genie shows us that. The child was locked in a room in infancy, fed but not talked to, and not discovered until she was in her teens. With intensive instruction she was able, within a couple of years, to make significant gains in general cognitive functioning (as measured by standard intelligence tests), and she gained a fairly extensive vocabulary, but she was never able to acquire the full syntactic structures of the language, such as the rules for forming tenses or showing plurals or possessives. Her speech remained like that of the very young child who says "Daddy go work."

It seems, then, that we are born with an innate grammatical potential but that the potential is activated and expanded by actual use. Those structures that are part of the child's native language are activated and confirmed as others talk to the child, and they become part of the child's underlying language competence.

There's a debate about how much actual learning is involved in activating or developing this language competence. Some developmental psycholinguists have argued that the child does actively, though unconsciously, *learn* language. The child receives rich data from the social/cultural context; that is, she hears a lot of language spoken, and from this data is able to infer the rules. But Chomsky points out that the data received can never be rich enough to account for all of the language the child knows. In particular, the child has, early on, a great deal of knowledge about negative features of language — about syntactic constructions that would not be used, while having heard very few of these unacceptable constructions. The fact that the child's knowledge exceeds what she could have heard suggests to Chomsky that language is not learned wholly by deducing rules from the language data received, but that there must be some form of preexisting language mechanisms in the brain, whose parameters can be set on the basis of relatively little, selected information.

On the other hand, there is much evidence of rule-governed language development in some areas. The child of four or five moves from reproducing correct past-tense verb forms in irregular verbs — *gave*, *sang* — to overgeneralizing the fact that *ed* marks past tense, and, for several years, he produces forms like *singed* and *gived* before finally deriving the double past-tense system that has come to exist in modern English through historical accident. Such generalization and overgeneralization of rules happens naturally with all children (and with second-language learners) and, for children, it is not altered by direct instruction. Most parents have had the experience of trying to correct such a nonstandard feature, without success. The parents can repeat the statement "You *gave* the toy to Johnny" *ad nauseam*, but the child will continue to say "That's right, Mama. I gived it to him." So, while some linguistic mechanism is probably innate and determinate of the types and order of linguistic structures a child acquires, the child also draws on the rich speech data from his own environment, perceiving patterns and deducing general rules that are gradually refined to match the actual grammar of the language. And all the while, because the child is hearing real speech, in ordinary family and community contexts, he is also inferring the rules for how to actually use language in context. So the child gains both linguistic competence and communicative competence naturally and unconsciously.

A second feature of the language data the child receives from the adults around her is that it is "appropriate." That is, while the child's general language environment is rich in variety of forms and expression, some of the elements of the environment are selected and focused for the child by the adult. Studies of "motherese" or "caretaker language" highlight several important features of the adult's communication with the child: 1) the adult caretaker elicits language, in early years, by focusing on the child and on things in the immediate environment that are of interest to the child (food, toys, siblings and friends, noise, and later books and television); 2) she or he repeats and extends the child's utterances, validating them while giving new input (Child — "More milk." Adult — "You want more milk in your cup?"); 3) the focus of attention is on the meaning of an utterance rather than on its linguistic form ("Me want juice" is responded to as a request for juice, with juice given or held until after supper. The parent does not say, "Wrong. Say 'I want juice'"); and 4) these genuine conversational interactions are responded to with praise and delight in the child's expanding linguistic ability ("Daddy, did you hear what your little girl just said?" "Tell Daddy what's in your Grover cup, honey!").

The patterns of caretaker communication described here are typical of middle-class English-speaking parents in the United States. Differe-- cultures, with differing expectations of the child's participation in conversation, have different patterns of parent-child linguistic interactions. Heath, for example, found that adults in Trackton didn't often initiate conversations with young children, but that children learned to aggressively insert themselves into ongoing adult conversations. In other words, language acquisition takes place within the normal cultural/social patterns for child-adult conversational interaction within a particular community, and virtually all children grow up to be competent language users within their communities, knowing not only the grammatical structures of their dialect but also all of the complex rules for its social use. But the focus of attention in each instance is on meaningful communication as it's carried on in that community, rather than on specific reference to the linguistic code. We use our home language correctly and appropriately without being aware of its rules.

Language in its social context

Researchers who have themselves come from middle-class backgrounds with literate-style language practices often can't appreciate the complexity of the home language they hear from children of different background — if indeed they hear much of the child's language. Children intimidated by alien researchers often respond to questions with silence or a muttered "I don't know". Carl Bereiter and Siegfried Engelmann, influential designers of preschool programs for disadvantaged children, reported in their early studies that black four-year-olds "could make no statements of any kind," that their few utterances are merely "emotional cries," and so, for educational purposes, they would have to be treated "as if the children had no language at all" (Labov, 1972, 205). Some older students also say little in school, like the one who provoked the question "How do you reach a girl like that?" from our student teacher Clare in Chapter 1. The student kept responding "I don't know" to any question put to her, even to questions about her name, address, or schedule. Clare discovered in a conversation with the dean of discipline that the student was not linguistically or cognitively incapable, but deeply troubled by her [abusive] home situation. Her "I don't know" was her way of keeping herself protected; she probably could keep herself from revealing her life only by not revealing anything. With limited knowledge of learners' ways of using language outside of school and of the concerns that may constrain them in school, teachers' evaluations of their students' language abilities are likely to be limited, as the researchers' evaluations were.

Much early research on language took place around isolated tasks in the setting of the school, like responding to a series of pointed questions. The research ignored larger acts of communication like social and small-group conversations where speakers spoke with confidence. Some speakers were judged to use restrictive codes — that is, limited and abbreviated language — but later research showed that these speakers operated skillfully in their own home environments. In a context where they could count on shared values or knowledge, they communicated with ease and sophistication. They didn't need to elaborate everything in words in order to communicate, because so many of the codes of conversation were common and hence assumed. Say two best friends are talking in the booth next to you at the diner. One says, "What's the matter? He say anything?" And the other answers: "Oh you know. Same as it ever was." "Tarmac again?" "Another metaphor!" They say the last phrase together and they both laugh. Now is that conversation in a restricted or an elaborated code? It doesn't make much sense to you eavesdropping in the booth or to us as readers, but someone who knew the two friends and context of their words — why "tarmac" was a metaphor, who "he" was—would understand that the two are not linguistically impoverished, but rich in their ability to transmit precise codes naturally and with complete understanding.

Of course, we do this kind of verbal corner-cutting all the time when we speak to those we know well, and children have spent most of their time speaking to people they know well. One child can send another into gales of laughter by whispering "raisins," if both share an understanding of the context that has made this word into a joke. But children will also produce complex verbal exchanges as well. Within the particular genres of speech that are highly valued in their communities or peer groups—whether they are jokes, riddles, stories, insults—the language of children whose speech was judged restricted, often proved to be, instead, syntactically and verbally rich. When researchers began to leave the laboratory and step into some of the "disadvantaged" environments they had been speculating about—like an urban ghetto in New York or a rural town in the North Carolina Piedmont—they found that the terms *restricted* and *elaborated* didn't do justice to the varying dimensions of language as it was actually used in a community.

In *Language in the Inner City* (1972), William Labov, a sociolinguist, studied the language of urban black youth in a New York ghetto. He faced the problem of eliciting linguistic information, particularly from preteenagers, who were reluctant to speak much in front of someone who represented outside, and presumably hostile, authority. Labov enlisted the aid of a black researcher, raised in the neighborhood, but even he couldn't get much talk at first, until he arranged informal sessions with small groups of boys and brought along potato chips to make a party. Once the boys perceived the occasion as social rather than formal, they talked nonstop with great richness and variety of expression. The data collected provided the basis for Labov's influential essay "The Logic of Nonstandard English" (1972), which showed that BEV (Black English Vernacular) offers a full linguistic system, one that "differs from other dialects in regular and rule-governed ways," so that it has equivalent ways of expressing the same logical content. (It turns out that the missing verb "to be" that Farrell thought must eliminate abstract thinking is simply a perfectly systematic and rule-governed feature of Black English Vernacular: wherever Standard English allows contraction, BEV allows deletion, so that "he bad" represents exactly the same thinking as its equivalent "he's bad"—as anyone who listened to these words would know.)

One sort of linguistic data Labov collected was narrative accounts of significant, "in danger of death" experiences. Black urban teenagers were adept storytellers, and when their narratives were analyzed linguistically, they proved to be syntactically complex, typically showing more complexity than the narratives of adult middle-class white speakers. Further, Labov's work showed the extent to which the peer group provided an alternative source of recognition and evaluation to that of the school. In fact, those two systems proved to be mutually exclusive, so that any teenager who didn't want to be viewed as a "lame" would intentionally use only the discourse style of the peer group, even though all the teenagers had a range of styles they could shift through. Obviously, their use of what mainstream speakers called restricted codes was intentional, and arose from their rejection of the dominant culture. In these studies, Labov put to rest forever the idea that a nonstandard code meant a restricted linguistic or conceptual ability among its speakers.

In *Ways with Words*, Shirley Brice Heath focuses on two rural communities, the black community of Trackton and the white community of Roadville. As in Labov's study, it's clear that each of these communities (the names are fictitious) has distinct patterns of language use that reinforce community norms and values. In Roadville, stories are valued for their morals, and for their usefulness in affirming accepted standards of behavior, and children learn, when asked, to give factual accounts of their experiences, to state explicitly the lesson to be learned from them. In Trackton, verbal cleverness and creativity are highly prized skills, are in fact the only way that children receive significant adult attention, and so within the genres valued in that community— the pun, the ritual insult, the exaggerated "true" story—linguistic skills are highly developed. Like Labov, Heath discovered that communities that earlier research would have predicted to be "restricted," limited in language and hence in ideas, were in fact linguistically powerful as well as diverse.

Geneva Smitherman's study of Black English affirms this fact. Looking at its structure, the ways it's used, and the world view it represents, Smitherman shows how intimately black language is bound up with black consciousness, how important language has been to maintaining a positive sense of self and community throughout a history of degradation and discrimination in this country, and why its speakers continue to maintain their linguistic identity. In her book *Talkin' and Testifyin'*, Smitherman practices her own preaching by making her own language multiethnic, slipping easily into and out of Black English as she writes:

> As James Baldwin has said, America is a country where everybody has status, and in a place where everybody has status it is possible that nobody has status. Thus Americans in general, lacking a fixed place in the society, don't know where they be in terms of social class and personal identity. But, as Baldwin concludes, with nigguhs around, at least they always knows where the bottom bees. (200)

Not only are minority linguistic practices marks of cleverness and creativity in the context in which they originate, but, as Smitherman notes, they often enter the language of the American cultural mainstream and enrich it.

Language in school contexts

So what's the problem if all kids come to school with such extensive linguistic ability, if they're grammatical, understand syntax, use rhythms and intonations, if they're not deprived at all but simply divergent? The problem is, as we've suggested, that what they come with is not understood and not valued by the system that educates them. Because it's not understood and not valued, it's not used or encouraged in the classroom, and an effective connection is never made to the language styles and uses of the school culture. The rich linguistic resources of Labov's teenagers were valued on the street, where tellers competed to prove their bravery and demonstrate their wit, but while "Your mother so skinny she could do the hula hoop in a Applejack" shows creativity and makes a clever simile, it would never find a place in the restrictive environment of the school. The styles and genres of the children Heath studied in Roadville and Trackton were also at odds with those of the schools—the verbal cleverness and attention getting of Trackton children violated school norms for not speaking unless called on, while the reluctance of Roadville children to move beyond the words of a text was seen as a sign that they couldn't think for themselves. Both sets of language styles and behaviors were different from those of the black and white middle class of "Maintown," whose language practices were the accepted ones in the classroom.

Like all children, middle-class children learn the language practices that end up being privileged in the schools long before they learn to read and write, bringing with them to school what they've learned at home. For all these children, the language practices that surround literacy are learned unconsciously and early, not through overt, direct instruction. The Scollons had their two-year-old daughter with them when they were living with the Athabaskans. As they observed her language development, they found that when she told a story, she used patterns of syntax and intonation and controlled the flow of information as if she were reading aloud. Athabaskan children "told" stories, in a more typically oral style, and they associated "reading style" only with school. The older Athabaskan children who heard Rachel couldn't believe that she hadn't already been to school because she spoke school language. Rachel probably wouldn't be seen as an effective storyteller if she were to return to the Athabaskan culture, but she is likely to have been identified immediately as a good reader (whether or not she could decode words) when she entered a typical U.S. school.

Because all uses of language are cultural, representing and reinforcing the culture's patterns of meaning, the dominant patterns of school language are as much a part of school and classroom culture as home patterns are of the culture of communities. Below are some of the features of school language that work together within a larger set of beliefs and values.

1. School language is based on a particular dialect.

As we've seen, all naturally occurring languages and dialects are equally systematic and rule-governed, and they carry the same potential for the expression of meaning, with none inherently better than another. But historically some dialects became dominant because they were spoken by those who held wealth and power — as the London dialect, for example, became the language of commerce and the court. Where the speakers of one regional dialect gain wealth and power and privilege, their dialect soon becomes the "privileged" one — the one that others seeking wealth and power will come to use. As texts began to be printed in the fifteenth century, there was a gradual movement toward standardization, and the standard was set by those who controlled the printing presses. With print, the privileged dialect became more widespread, hence even more privileged. The dialects of those without access to print production remained outside of the dominant public discourse, and their stories outside of the dominant history and culture. In England, these outsiders were those from the outer edges of the kingdom — the Welsh and the Scots, whose land had been conquered but who proudly maintained their national languages — and the ordinary people in ordinary towns who were not part of London government or commerce — and, of course, women. In the United States, the outsiders also included blacks and some ethnic minorities, as well as lower-class whites.

The linguistic variation we have been describing is regional (and, in the United States, we are relatively tolerant of regional variation — of distinct pronunciation and vocabulary and forms — at least in speaking). But linguistic variation is also related to social class; in both Britain and the United States, we perceive class differences most clearly on the basis of the way people speak. And, although, linguistically, social variation is not different from regional, we tend to view it with much more prejudice. A Southern congressman who says "Ah'm goin t' tell y'all somethin" may be treated with amusement, but probably not with feelings of outright superiority, by his Northern colleagues, and he'll be invited to their parties. But the Southern farmer who says "T'aint likely them senators'll tell you nothin" is likely to be seen as inferior by the young lawyer who buys his produce at the farm stand, and even if they meet on the street, both dressed in blue jeans, and neither knowing the other's job, the linguistic clues will mark them as belonging to different social worlds.

All of this is intensified in the schools, which carry out and certify the sorting of people into levels in our society. Geneva Smitherman argues that the emphasis on school grammar, on what linguist Donald Lloyd has labeled a "national mania for correctness," stems from a long tradition of elitism in American life and language matters (185). Schools extend the power of the dominant dialect, ensure the success of most of those who speak it, and make those who don't speak it feel stupid and responsible for their own failure. One result is that school discourse becomes language that most people don't speak. The stereotypical reaction to meeting a school teacher "on the outside" is to cover one's mouth or say, "I better watch my language."

In the classroom, dialect variations are treated as mistakes, as errors, and those who use these variations as mistaken or stupid or perversely stubborn. Students who are most insecure, who have no strong sense of support from a community or a peer group, the "lames" in Labov's research, will either begin to shift to using the forms of the dominant dialect or, as more often happens, fall silent. Students with the strongest social web (and this often includes many of the brightest students) will reject the school's language and the school's rejection of them, and remain vigorous users of their own forms, as the most linguistically skilled of the teenagers Labov studied, or the black students Anthony observed at an inner-city Boston high school have chosen to do. In their choice of language, these students choose a competing value system as well—one that is increasingly at odds with that of the dominant society. As Labov explains:

> The healthy, well-adjusted youth of normal or superior intelligence is a well-integrated member of the neighborhood peer group. For the black youth who saw the situation clearest, it was evident that accepting school values was equivalent to giving up self-respect. When Vaughn says that the Jets hipped him to "the whitey's bullshit," it was clear to him that the rewards of the school culture are illusions as far as blacks concerned. (1982, 155)

Once teachers understand that no dialect of the language (not even Standard English) is inherently superior to any other, that children could extend their ways of thinking and express their ideas and learn to read and write just as effectively in any dialect, they won't be like perverse parents who would respond to the child's request, "Me want milk," with "Wrong. You get no milk until you learn the proper form for a subject pronoun." If teachers don't want their students to limit their speaking and writing for fear of making errors, they must not respond to every offbeat utterance, in speech or in writing, with a demand for a different form rather than with a meaningful response to and praise for the communicative act. When a student writes creatively, "There was trails of fire lit along the path from her eyes to her hand," a teacher is wrong to say, "You aren't ready to do creative writing. You need to learn the basics, like subject-verb agreement, first." At the same time, though, teachers can recognize that the dominant dialect brings academic acceptance and at least some degree of privilege, and they can create meaningful contexts for the learning of standard forms (as in teaching students to edit out common nonstandard forms and giving them responsibilities for school publication of their writing). We'll say more about this in Chapter 5.

2. *School language expresses particular ways of representing thought.*

The "restricted" language that was seen as showing restricted thought is simply a different style of representing thought. Schools demand that responses be extended and verbally explicit. Bereiter and Engelmann insisted that "In the tree" was an illogical, because incomplete, answer to the question "Where is the squirrel?" and that children must be trained in the schoolroom to respond only with the full statement "The squirrel is in the tree" (Labov, 205). And many well-intentioned teachers, hoping to help their students achieve success, followed programs of drilling them to respond to series of questions only with "complete" statements. Of course, the meaning of the answer is just as clear in either case, and there can be no misunderstanding of the meaning of the child's response. The choice of one form over another is simply a matter of style — in this case a rather artificial style versus a natural one. When we're with people who share our meanings and knowledge, we can use shared knowledge and put less into words. If a parent and child have been discussing a squirrel running around the yard, appropriate exchanges may be even more limited — since both parties know what's being discussed, one might say, "Where is it?" or, for confirmation, "Where?"

The less knowledge we share, however, the more we have to specify in order to be understood. As we move out of the home, we naturally use language more explicitly because less can be assumed. When children write to strangers or to some absent authority (like a school principal), they must, of course, fill in more information than when they write to Grandma in New Orleans. But children who have little experience with strangers or formal contexts are likely not to recognize the need for a shift in language style until they've encountered strangers and formal situations. If they're not encouraged to make connections to the more informal and shared communication of home, they'll feel increasingly uncomfortable writing in school settings. Furthermore, in the classroom, where much knowledge is shared, it's only a cultural convention that demands the complete sentence response to a question from the teacher, that requires a pretense that the teacher doesn't know what novel is being discussed in a paper the teacher has assigned, that eliminates the use of first person in "formal" papers. The switch required from intimate to formal or from oral style to written style is even harder for students in this situation, because it's so false.

3. All school language subscribes to particular conventions of literacy.

Because the development of literacy is a primary focus of schooling, the conventions commonly associated with literacy take on particular force in the classroom. Spoken language in schools is judged by standards of style (and also correctness) that are carried over from written language.

Writing is often intended to be read by distant audiences, and it tends therefore toward some features that make little sense in speech. It must be verbally explicit, because it can't assume much shared knowledge on the part of readers, and can't point to things in the writer's immediate context that reader cannot see. It tends therefore to be elaborated, to draw on a larger common culture passed to people in different settings through books, and to refer to earlier words in the text or in earlier texts, rather than pointing to things in the environment. The speaker who says, "What Jim said about that thing yesterday made me feel so — grrrh!" substituting a groan for an adjective, is likely to be perfectly well understood by an intimate circle of listeners. The writer who writes to someone who was not there must recognize that neither "that thing" nor "grrrh" will give enough information to a reader who doesn't share knowledge of the event. She must include information in her text about who Jim is, what he said, a description or more accurate word for "that thing," and a word to express the meaning of "grrrh."

Through the schools, the dominant middle class has incorporated in its speech many of the features common to writing, producing "literate-style" oral discourse. Oral-style discourse (even in written exchanges among close friends) does not generally include these features. One characteristic of the literate style is stating explicitly what things mean. Labov's studies of urban teenage narratives, for example, found that middle-class speakers were likely to stop the story and say, explicitly, what they thought of events — "That was the worst thing that ever happened to me" — while black teenagers were likely to show this meaning through actions in the story — "I never shook so hard in my life." In truly effective storytelling, written or oral, the teller brings the listener or reader into the world of the story by acting as if everyone shares the same knowledge and perspective and assuming that the meaning of the story will be understood from the way events are told. Literate-style school assignments, on the other hand, demand explicit statements of background and of meaning even in narratives, though such statements often work against the conventions of good storytelling.

And, despite what Bruner and others have argued about the value of narrative and the use of narrative as a means of knowing, narrative itself is not much valued in schools; among literate-style uses of language, expository, analytical genres of writing are the preferred modes of discourse.

4. *Schools expect particular patterns of communication, of language behavior, and they demand physical behaviors that fit with those patterns.*

A class can be seen as a speech event, a large unit of discourse — of verbal communication, during which people try to accomplish things with words. The typical class hour, as a genre of speech activity, has its own structure and roles and rules (both spoken and unspoken). The participants, teacher and students, bring to this event some shared knowledge and expectations about what will happen and how, although these expectations may be challenged.

Participation in the classroom speech event is based on defined roles, both formal (teacher, student, recorder for peer group) and informal (class clown, eager beaver). Teachers and students play out these roles in predictable ways. Most often the teacher's own talk is intended to control interaction and behavior rather than to communicate directly about a subject. He may inform, explain, define, question, correct, but he's likely to spend more time getting and keeping attention, prompting responses, requesting, or ordering. And the teacher's purposes may be accomplished in different ways. He may control the amount of speech by ordering students to be quiet, by assigning them individual written work, or by joking with a loquacious student about what happens to a motor mouth.

Studies of classroom discourse show that the most common pattern at all grade levels is a three-part sequence in which the teacher initiates talk by a question or invitation, the student responds, and the teacher evaluates the response. We saw examples of this pattern in the accounts of classroom observations that introduced this book. In the class discussion of *The Canterbury Tales*, the teacher asks a specific student an informational question ("Eleanor," she says, "can you tell me what the Franklin loves to drink?"), and the student answers. If the answer is correct ("Ale"), the teacher affirms it and goes on to another question and another student. If the answer is wrong, or if the teacher sees it as wrong, she'll most often repeat the exchange with the next student. Occasionally, she'll add a second round, asking, "What makes you think that?" Very rarely will a student respond with a questioning of the teacher's answer ("But didn't the book also say that he liked *wine-*sopped bread for breakfast?"). Even in a more substantive discussion — one that focuses, for example, on what the details Chaucer gives about the Franklin might suggest about his character, or on how students felt about the character being described and whether they might find comparable types in today's society — the pattern of teacher question, student response, teacher confirmation continues, and there is rarely an exchange on a school topic that moves laterally, from student to student.

Dickens again provides an example of classroom discourse which, though exaggerated, remains familiar to us. Mr. Gradgrind, checking up on things in his school, steps into the classroom and begins to question the students ("Murdering the Innocents" is Dickens' title for this chapter). He points a finger at "girl number twenty," demanding to know her name. When she replies, "Sissy Jupe, sir," he informs her that "Sissy is not a name. Call yourself Cecilia." He next asks, "What is your father?" And when she replies, "He belongs to the horse-riding, if you please, sir," he responds, "We don't want to know anything about that here." Finally, he tells her to "Give me your definition of a horse." When she doesn't answer, having been cowed into silence by his rejection of her earlier responses, he concludes:

> Girl number twenty unable to define a horse. Girl number twenty possessed of no facts in reference to one of the commonest of animals! Some boy's definition of a horse. Bitzer, yours.

And Bitzer responds:

> Quadruped. Gramnivorous. Forty teeth, namely twenty-four grinders, four eyeteeth, and twelve incisive. Sheds coat in the spring; in marshy countries sheds hoofs, too. Hoofs hard, but requiring to be shod with iron. Age known by marks in mouth.

Mr. Gradgrind concludes:

> Now, girl number twenty, you know what a horse is. (13–14)

Mr. Gradgrind's lesson fits into the familiar teacher question/student response/teacher evaluation pattern. But it also shows the demand for a school-style language that is not only explicit but dependent wholly on definition and taxonomies, without reference to any personal, real-world knowledge. Sissy Jupe's personal experience of horses through her father's work, like her personal identity in her name, has no place in this classroom. A name must have its school form, but here she is really only "girl number twenty," and nothing that she brings with her from outside of the classroom really counts.

In *Classroom Discourse*, Courtney Cazden confirms the continuing dominance of the initiation/response/evaluation pattern, and makes the important observation that "any one event structure is suitable for only some educational purposes" (50). In other words, in some instances it's appropriate to assemble factual information with students, and the initiation/response/evaluation structure may be an effective way of involving students in doing that quickly, but where the same discourse structure is being used for virtually all lessons, it's likely to indicate that all knowing is being reduced to the recitation of facts—as it is in the Gradgrind school.

A teacher can vary this pattern by reflecting on a student's response, by inviting the student to elaborate, by extending the period of silence before responding—so that other students can evaluate the response for themselves—and these changes support better learning within the dominant model. A teacher can also ask questions to which he doesn't know the answers, and actively reflect, with the students, about possibilities, moving toward a more active negotiation of meaning of the sort that Vygotsky would recommend. Significantly changing the dominant model of classroom discourse requires redefining the nature of knowledge, of the teacher's authority for that knowledge, of the teacher's and learners' roles in the classroom. We'll talk specifically about how such changes might come about in Unit 3.

Students often remember their own experiences in the classroom in terms of powerlessness, and Janet's memory in the previous chapter of the "authoritative" teacher provides a strong example—the teacher moved beyond orders to physical acts to compel her students to respond correctly. We hope that this example is extreme. In fact, much teacher discourse is marked by a rather indirect, polite style. The teacher is likely to ask, as in the Chaucer-class example above, "*Can you tell me* what the Franklin likes to drink?" rather than use the direct question "What does the Franklin like to drink?" or the direct command "Tell me what the Franklin likes to drink!" Of course, this politeness represents another social convention of the classroom culture, and it doesn't suggest that the student has any real choice. But it does show just one of the many ways in which school talk is different from home talk, even where both settings are ones in which the adults exercise authority. Parents, of all social classes, more often tell children directly to do as they say—"Put the book away!" rather than "Can we start supper now?" Children from some cultural contexts have no other exposure to the "polite" style of the school, and since they often don't even realize that the indirect statement has the same force as an order, they may appear to be intentionally disobeying *and* speaking out of turn if they respond to the teacher's apparent question with an answer, "Yes, teacher, we can begin the test now," while their books remain open on their desks. Heath's teachers found that their students seemed more cooperative in response to directives. And if you look back to the journal excerpts that introduce this book, you'll see that Donna, the teacher of the class with the apparent troublemaker, successfully uses directives ("Clear off your desks for the test! Put your things on the floor!") as well as the occasional polite or indirect request ("There are too many conversations going on at once") with her energetic, culturally mixed group of students.

Many of the patterns of school talk, and of the school behaviors that talk is embedded in, are significantly different from the patterns of talk and of life in homes of learners who aren't from mainstream, middle-class cultural backgrounds. And these differences extend to larger patterns of language use and to a variety of related behaviors. The Maintown children Heath studied, from both black and white middle-class families, are expected to be respectful of adults and to listen when spoken to. But they're also expected to be conversationalists who can carry on their side of an exchange. They're expected to be orderly, but they're also expected to be responsible and to act independently. They're expected to accept the knowledge of the teacher, but also to get information for themselves, from other knowledgeable people or from books. They're expected to work within established structures, but also to adapt those structures to particular circumstances. And they bring these expectations and practice in appropriate behaviors from home to school, just as Roadville children bring an expectation that they should be silent before authority and the authoritative knowledge of teachers or preachers, and that structures should be accepted and rules obeyed without question. And as Trackton children bring the expectation that they should be clever and assertive with adults, and that they should work out solutions to their own problems.

So Roadville children who are taught from babyhood that they're supposed to speak to an adult only when spoken to and that telling a story is the same as telling a lie end up being passive in a school setting that calls for handraising and student questions and the creation of tales as part of the curriculum. Similarly, Trackton children who are taught at home to compete for attention by interacting freely with adults informally and whenever an occasion presents itself end up being seen as disruptive troublemakers in the classroom, where there are different rules for order and taking turns. These uses of language are embedded in the ways children use time and space: Roadville children are used to doing specific tasks at specific times and places, and won't initiate any change — they just wait for the teacher's instructions. Trackton children are used to carrying out activities for as long as they're interested in them and in locations they choose, and they have trouble accommodating themselves to the school setting with assigned seating and strict time periods for art, reading, physical education.

Practices around literacy in these communities differ from practices in the school too: Roadville adults recite the words of the Bible, and children memorize prayers, but written texts are rarely used to get new information, and they're hardly ever discussed. Trackton adults make reading a group activity, where the words in a letter or in a news article are likely to be shared and negotiated or debated with others in the community. Where writing is demanded, as in filling out forms, it's likely to be done collaboratively as well. Silent reading and individual seat work in school are alien experiences for children raised to hear literacy embedded in collaborative oral practices, particularly when collaboration (as in sharing answers) is discouraged or punished in school. Children from both Roadville and Trackton end up being seen as academically deficient, not because they can't think but because their home practices around language and literacy are so different from the school's.

5. School language asserts a larger set of values.

In *Ways with Words*, Heath describes "the way to be" from the perspective of the middle-class residents of "Maintown":

> The townspeople, black and white, are *mainstreamers*, people who see themselves as being in "the main stream of things."... For them, school is an institution which helps instill values such as respectability, responsibility, and an acceptance of hard work. Early achievement within an institution that rewards adherence to norms of conduct reflecting these values is necessary for success in the workplace, whether as a businessperson, lawyer, politician, doctor, or teacher. Beyond these easily expressed ideals of mainstream behavior in school and workplaces, townspeople exhibit but can rarely articulate other mainstream norms of conduct. They respond to linearity as a criterion of organization: to be neat and orderly is to be in line.... Secondary sources, not the face-to-face network, are authoritative for mainstreamers.... An individual's assertion of formal credentials—either university degrees or public awards and distinction—makes him an authority. (236–237)

As we have seen, these patterns and ideals become those of the schools as well, where Maintown parents are often teachers.

The values promulgated with formal schooling often show up clearly in testing. Labov gives examples from intelligence tests to show that they can't test intelligence apart from values or cultural context. For example, a Stanford-Binet test for seven-year-olds asks, "What's the thing for you to do when you are on your way to school and see that you are in danger of being late?" The answer guide accepts only those responses that suggest hurrying. If the child says, "Go on to school and tell my teacher why I'm late," he fails the test. Labov finds that "No matter what the child does, in fact, he must know what he is expected to say, if he is to pass the test, and say it." And he sees this pattern repeated:

> Throughout all testing procedures, we encounter questions posed to test the child's allegiance to the disciplinary principles of the school system rather than his perception or grasp of meanings. We can only conclude that such questions are good predictors of a child's school performance and find their way into the test situations because without

such moral alignment a child is bound to have trouble getting through school. (1982, 156)

Groups with sufficient resources that have felt themselves to be out of alignment with dominant school values have often responded by establishing their own schools. The Amish, whose literacy and schooling practices Andrea Fishman studied, are one such group. Fishman found that Amish schools provided an education that successfully prepared students for Amish life. But what she saw there led her to reflect on her own practice as an English teacher in a public high school:

> I discovered that I had been misled initially by the Old Order clothes and curricula; my new focus revealed that classroom management and pedagogy so decked out were really little different from those in modern dress at my school. Neither the subjects in the curriculum, the contents of the basal readers, nor the topics of the reports were the core of education at Meadow Brook [the Amish school]; those were the trappings, the vehicles for transmission of what really mattered — the schooling Meadow Brook children received. And it was only the trappings of Meadow Brook that were significantly different from those of my own school; I found the schooling strikingly the same.
>
> As I came to realize that this very different culture with very different ideas about education (and life in general) schooled its children in ways similar to my own, I came to realize that my research had raised some important questions for me to answer, not just as a researcher but as a teacher. How could such different societies be equally well served by such similar schooling? How could we use the same means to achieve such supposedly different ends? How could I do what [the Meadow Brook teacher] did and consider my job well done? (171)

Fishman goes on to reflect on the "teacher-dominated, arbitrarily organized educations" both schools offered, and on the traditional "initiation-response-evaluation based lessons" at both schools. She sees why this sort of schooling is congruent with Amish life, where "a single authoritative voice dominates Old Order life outside school as well as in. . . . In all realms of Amish life, such impersonal authority decides what is right and what is wrong, what is possible and what is not." And Amish educational practices prepare students to take clearly defined places in an unchanging social and moral order. Then she asks herself about her own students:

> But is Old Order life the kind for which my students prepare in school? Will they enter a world governed by a single unquestioned authority with a single moral and ethical code for measuring all behavior? Will they enter a world with places already prepared for them? Will they be told how to take those places, what to do and how to do it? (172)

Of course her answer is "No." The students most of us teach are far more diverse than the Amish and confront a much more complex world. Fishman returns to her classroom and tries to have it respond to the diverse and complex cultural world her students will have to live in. In doing so, she changes her classroom culture, transforming her own classroom and its activities. She stops teaching her students the Meadow Brook lessons "to sit still, be quiet, wait for and follow directions." She changes the initiation/response/evaluation pattern of her classroom discourse. She stops being the one who does all of the talking, and begins to let her students' real language, real voices into her classroom. And in the process she begins to build a bridge between home and school. She also works on another bridge, one connecting school with a larger life in the world, with the larger goals of education. These are issues which we'll discuss in the next chapter, and we'll come back to Fishman's reflections there. But for the rest of this chapter we'd like to consider some other attempts to build this first bridge.

Bridging home and school

One clear understanding emerges from all that we have said here: because language itself is acquired only through its use for communication in meaningful contexts, and because rich and meaningful and familiar as well as new language plays such a crucial part in learning, all language — not only traditional "school language" — must find a place in the classroom. For this to happen, there must be student talk, not the Meadow Brook silence that Fishman describes.

One of the primary ways that home language traditionally has been brought into school has been through formal sharing time or "show and tell" in the elementary classroom. But teachers' expectations for classroom discourse determine whether or not this time will be enriching for students. Sharing-time research by Courtney Cazden and Sarah Michaels shows that teachers whose expectations are determined by literate white middle-class norms in some senses can't even hear the discourse of their students and are unlikely to know how to use or value what they hear. Michaels follows the sharing-time narratives of one young black child who, like others from strongly oral cultures, tends to pull together a lot of incidents that are linked associatively by emotion or theme rather than focusing on one topic and developing it. The child often gathers together a series of incidents about her family life that she perceives as related. But her teacher is focused on school style, and repeatedly admonishes the child for not sticking to one topic, finally silencing her for wandering off track (though the teacher might respond quite differently if she were reading a poem whose structure was guided by precisely the same sort of thematic or emotional association).

The teacher, then, must be concerned both with how to invite her students' language into the classroom in productive ways, and how to respond positively and constructively to that language so that her students can extend what they say and what they know. Tracey is a teacher in a large bilingual/English classroom in an inner-city middle school, struggling with the problem of how to value and build on her students' language:

> I find that certain students of mine *do not* speak in class unless called on—in effect are silenced, even if outside of school they are quite verbal. What I want to know is how do you bridge that gap between home and school language? There's no denying that "school" language is the language of the middle-class mainstream, and if they are going to function in that society (assuming we're not going to try to change all of society from our classroom!) they need to be able to use that language. The example of the child that recounts his experiences and relates many by theme instead of sticking to one topic struck me. I am one of those teachers who would try to encourage them to stick to one topic and develop it. But I think that tendency to jump around between topics is typical of many children. The fact is that it's hard to follow (at least for me—but maybe that's my middle-class background?). I think a child can be encouraged to try to develop one topic in such a way that it doesn't *invalidate* his experiences. . . . Is it wrong to try and do that as a teacher?

Tracey is aware of her expectations about the nature and structure of discourse in the classroom, and she worries about how to help her students learn school ways without silencing them. But it's such silence and silencing that Tracey sees as she observes another English class beginning a unit on poetry. The work of the class looks interesting, focusing on a "found" poem about the suicide of a girl, a poem that Tracey finds "shocking and moving—an excellent way to start a unit." What the teacher has to say, Tracey feels, is organized and appropriate for the students' level. But Tracey is bothered by the silence; the class seems rigid and controlled. "You got the feeling that the law had been laid down long ago and no one tried to test it."

> She did most of the talking and there wasn't much participation, although often times when students did speak, they didn't raise their hand (which might have been expected). About three students made most of the comments; the rest sat there quietly. She didn't try too hard to engage the other students and encourage them to take a risk and participate. She had told me ahead of time that the class was quite dull and that most of them just sat there while a few participated. I kept thinking that that would drive me *crazy*—(as she said it did) and that I would do almost anything to get them more involved. Perhaps

she already has tried everything and is completely frustrated, but it seems that there has to be a way to make them come alive more.

Tracey thinks she finds the reason for their silence, but she wonders again about what might be a better practice:

> I was also surprised at how she "cut" some of them down. When asking for comparisons, some of them were being very vague, or giving impertinent information. A few times she said "no, that's boring stuff" or "too vague!" I tend to be so hesitant to criticize them. Just about anything they say I respond with "Okay . . . what else?" Even if they're way off target, I don't want to discourage them from participating. I wonder, though, if at times it would be better to not be so uncritical, so that they realize when they are being vague, or unclear or are just "throwing out" anything without thinking first. It seems that this is appropriate for a class of more "high achievers," but when dealing with kids that lack confidence in school and need encouragement, it might not be as appropriate. Perhaps, here again, there's a happy medium to be found.

When Tracey observes an ESL class, she finds a different, more relaxed structure, with a teacher who uses colloquial expressions and personal examples to describe words. Tracey admits, "he goes into more detail about himself than I would want to, but he does seem to develop an open, easy relationship with some students." But despite the fact that this class has a more open atmosphere, and while the teacher's responses to student contributions are less overtly negative, there's still not much more room for student talk in this class than in the poetry class.

> One thing that *really* struck me is that the students mostly listen, or if they talk, they talk to each other in their own language. S loves to talk, talks very fast, and barely lets them get a word in edgewise.
> I felt that his tone and choice of words was a little odd—he would say "I try to be nice to you children. . . . Some of you have been good. Others have been silly. Silly isn't good. I like fun but silly is bad." And so on. It seemed a little condescending—as if he was talking to first graders.
> The students had very little opportunity to speak English or show what they knew, or write in meaningful sentences. Most time was spent listening to the teacher. I know that S has done some excellent projects—having the students write their life stories for example, but I feel that in this class he overwhelmed the students with talk. The class becomes a monologue and many of the students are not paying attention. I feel that this was an interesting class for me because I can have the same tendency. I feel that I have to "impart" knowledge to them. This, however, can dampen interest very quickly.

Tracey tries with her own class to avoid the incongruity of a silent language classroom, to build her lessons around the words and knowledge that her students bring with them to her classroom:

I also "observed" my own social studies class with this [student language vs. silence] in mind. We were doing a lesson on "pie charts." I first asked if they knew what "pie" meant in English. Many students volunteered simultaneously "apple pie," "cherry pie," "it's like a cake," or "it has fruit." This kind of yelling out of information always makes me feel *happy* on one hand because it shows enthusiasm, yet a little concerned that it doesn't get out of control. I find that it is a very delicate balance. I will often let them go on for a short time in such an instance, then say, "Sh. That's enough—raise your hand next if you want to say something now." I really hate to stifle their thoughts or creativity but sometimes it just doesn't work; nobody can hear anything, and oftentimes the loud ones completely take over.

The next task was more difficult (making their own pie chart) and I went back to the board. I think we kind of worked it out together; I asked them how they would approach it, got some suggestions. I led them through it asking myself questions out loud and demonstrating. I then had them start and circulated.

Tracey begins the process of helping her students bring their language into the classroom. She elicits their words and their observations, avoiding the teacher talk and student silence of the other classes she observed. But she guides their talk, helping them to be quiet sometimes and listen to each other, thinking through a task with them, moving around to work with individuals as well as with the whole group. In doing so, she helps them connect their ways of talking and working into school ways, while showing them how their knowledge can be translated into school terms.

In order to help students make such connections, the teacher must be able to understand what the students bring. Though he wants to build on their existing knowledge, Pat Conroy can't at first make sense of what he hears from his Yamacraw Island students. He has to be inventive, to find a way to understand them as they talk about what they know. The way he finds is to get everybody involved in translating for him and to him. One of his students, Mary, serves as interpreter:

I designated her as grand interpreter with illimitable powers of life and death over all. When Prophet said something known only to God, Mary would tell me what he said. Sometimes the whole class would help Mary out, and seventeen voices would rise slowly in an unintelligible gibberish, grow louder as each voice tried to be heard, and finally reach a deafening crescendo à la Babel. (35)

Soon all of Conroy's students are involved in this act of translation and become committed to putting what they know into language that he will understand. And as they work to help their teacher understand, they'll work toward speaking to a larger world, a world that will demand elaboration and explicitness.

Many traditional teachers would be shocked if they were to enter

Conroy's classroom, fearing that letting students use their language in the classroom would prevent them from learning new school forms. But unless teachers begin with the language their students know, students will have nothing to connect their new learning to. Geneva Smitherman asserts this position.

> Teachers often ask, "are you saying we should teach the kids black dialect?" To answer a question with a question, why teach them something they already know? Rather, the real concern, and question, should be: how can I use what the kids *already* know to move them to what they *need* to know? This question presumes that you genuinely accept as viable the language and culture the child has acquired by the time he or she comes to school. This being the case, it follows that you allow the child to use that language to express himself or herself, not only to interact with their peers in the classroom, but with you, the teacher, as well. (219)

The teachers Heath worked with were part of the larger community their students lived in, and they knew well the dialect their students spoke. Their problem was not how the words the students spoke might be translated into a language they could understand, but how the knowledge the students had through their small communities and the ways that knowledge was expressed could be translated into school knowledge and school ways. Community knowledge about planting, for example, could be translated into science class knowledge about botany. Heath taught teachers and students alike to use ethnographic techniques, and then the students were told to imagine they were to set up an agricultural resource center in the area, with the task of learning as much as possible about the ways of growing food that were currently being used. They conducted interviews, took photographs, collected documents and artifacts, and then "translated" this into a science book. Heath tells us:

> Learners in this science classroom had become ethnographers of a sort; in so doing, they had improved their knowledge of science. In addition, they had learned to talk about ways of obtaining and verifying information; terms such as *sources*, *check out* (in the sense of *verify*), *summarize*, and *translate* had become part of their vocabulary. They had come to recognize, use, and produce knowledge about the skills of inquiring, compiling, sorting, and refining information. They had not only made use of "inquiry" and "discovery method" skills discussed in science and social studies methods texts; they had acquired the language to talk about these skills." (320)

Heath emphasizes that the translation process here was "bidirectional". As students gathered community planting knowledge and school science knowledge, they used each one to learn more about the other. In the process, they validated both domains of knowledge and integrated them into a coherent system of understanding. Students emerged from their study with a greater understanding of and respect for what was known outside of school, as well as for what was known within.

Heath's ethnographic methods can replace traditional research papers at any level of study. Ellie and two other UMass colleagues, Suzy Groden and Vivian Zamel, collaborated with Heath to set up a project in which basic writers and ESL students in freshman writing classes would do ethnographic research into a variety of home and school language practices. As the students gathered data about many of the features of home and school language use that we have discussed in this chapter, they discovered for themselves the differences and connections between the two styles, making much of their unconscious knowledge about language and writing conscious in the process. We will say more about this sort of activity in Chapter 5.

Schools have generally offered few opportunities for students to make this sort of connection between the worlds of home and school. And most efforts, like "sharing time," don't extend beyond the early years. In high schools, there's little attempt even to pretend that the home language is important in the context of literacy, and while personal experiences or news from the outside world are sometimes taken into the classroom, there are few attempts to make systematic connections between the two worlds. The increasing alienation of older students who see themselves more and more separated from the language they hear in school and the one they speak themselves, from the things they learn in school and what goes on in the rest of their lives, must surely contribute significantly to the attrition problem that plagues the public schools.

The scene described by Anthony at the beginning of this chapter, in which teacher language and knowledge and student language and knowledge run off on separate courses, replicates itself time and time again in our classrooms. As teachers, we are too often caught up in displaying our own knowledge and cleverness to really hear our students. In the classroom David A observed: "The teacher ... did most of the talking, by far, in fact interrupting students often, ironically, after he had called them directly to respond ... and after class he smirked and implied 'well these are the dumb kids, but we do what we can, pushing them along.'" Yet, when David meets with the teacher outside of class, they become engaged in a quite different style of discourse, and he decides "that comfortable banter, listening, speaking, questioning, commenting on the part of both parties is a great atmosphere for learning. When I become a teacher, I hope to establish that 'sit down and relax' atmosphere." When he does have the opportunity to teach, David puts this understanding into practice:

> This was a good day. I felt good speaking with the students, and I got them all to smile, and to listen, and to participate, all of them! When I started, I immediately ran into that brick wall between teacher and

students. But I relaxed, was myself, and talked to the students. I felt they had something to say, and minute by minute they got involved. We talked about *The Color Purple*, and by asking them questions they came around 180 degrees. It was great. It was the *standard class*, my favorites, and they were all looking at me, really eager. . . . They were amazed when they finally understood that I wasn't going to talk very much, that I intended on listening. I was learning. They aren't used to this.

When teachers reject the notion that their students are linguistically and therefore intellectually inferior and work instead with the resources that learners bring with them, they not only discover their students' competence but also find a basis for becoming engaged once again themselves in a new community of learners.

Teachers as inquirers

CHAPTER 4

Cultural Literacy and Multicultural Education

From our discussion in the previous chapter, you can see that the cultures of home and school often compete rather than unite in the individual's learning process. One reason for this competition may be that the environments of home and school are more than just separate, with one informal, intimate, oral, and the other formal, distant, literate: they are opposed in a more fundamental way. The home stresses its own small culture, which sets it off from others. You're a Crawford, your ancestors were Huguenots, you live in the house where your grandfather died, your family pronounces *mayonnaise* like *my-nayse*. All these things help make you unique. Your family stories stress the qualities that make the family different from others and the ways in which your behavior together is different from your behavior with others outside your family or your community group. Your social or ethnic or peer group stresses the qualities its members have in common, but also those that set it apart and give it a distinct identity. But the school brings together individuals from many different family and community groups, and so it emphasizes similarity instead of difference, looking for commonality as a method of teaching all comers. If the school has only students from similar backgrounds, its curriculum may still extend outward, to find commonalities with other groups. We are all learners, the school affirms, we are all readers, we are all Americans, we all share certain values and attitudes. In some ways, the school must call into question — or at least downplay — the values of the home in order to assure a common understanding of an environment beyond the home — of the larger society or of humanity in general.

John Goodlad, education critic and teacher, sees this tension between the home culture of difference and the school culture of similarity as a meeting of opposing forces, with the home a "centrifugal force" pulling away from school uniformity and the school a "centripedal force" that pulls toward it. The opposition needn't be harmful; in fact, it can be productive, helping students to become aware of themselves both as unique and as part of some larger shared community. The ideal to be worked toward in education, according to Goodlad, is the creation of "a kind of balanced tension between the centrifugal tendencies of homes (differences in ethnicity, origin, religion, class) and the centripedal tendencies of schools (moving toward homogeneity)" (1983, 304).

This tension of similarity and difference works in the high school classroom. Where many cultural groups are represented in one class, the teacher may draw from their individual perspectives to create a common understanding that can encompass them all. Where the student body is itself homogeneous, the teacher finds herself with a more difficult task — trying, through the literature read and the topics discussed, to create a framework of knowledge that will extend the learner's understanding beyond those of the community and into the larger culture. Mark, a prepractice student, observes this tension:

> This high school makes me feel at home. It is very much like the high school I attended in Yonkers, New York, in the 1960s. In fact, walking into this school is a bit like walking into the past for me. It took me about two class visits to figure out why. Yonkers is close to New York City, as close as this community is to Boston. And yet the provincial attitude you sense in the students at this high school reminded me of my own adolescent self and the friends I had in Yonkers. . . .
>
> By coincidence, I have had my hair cut at a local salon where the lady taking care of tonsorial needs is the mother of a student at the high school. She confirms what I surmised: Yes, the kids stick together, they don't like outsiders. Her daughter goes out with the son of her husband's best friend — who went to high school with her husband 20 years ago. This makes everyone secure in their cocoon, but leads to a narrow vision of the world and its people. Some of the teachers saw this need and got together so that the course Facing History and Ourselves would be offered.

Facing History and Ourselves is a high school curriculum that uses the Holocaust to foster students' understanding of history and cultural difference. It combines the study of history and literature with a focus on students' thinking about themselves and others, and it offers a valuable perspective to students whose communities offer them only limited experience with people not like themselves.

Increasingly, as teachers have begun to recognize that children's learning is powerfully affected by what they bring with them from home, the tension Goodlad describes has become palpable in the classroom. As students' language is brought into the classroom, inevitable conflicts arise between the perspectives of different students or between those of students and teacher. In the situation described above, it's the prepractice teacher who is most markedly the outsider (despite the similarities he has found between this high school and his own), and it's the students' terms that label him as outsider.

> The class was discussing A Member of the Wedding and the teacher was trying to get the students to focus on the narrow lives of the characters. Some of the students referred to the characters in the story as "geeks"

or "Barneys," the latest slang expression for someone who is a bore. When asked what a "Barney" was, they said that "that was someone who wore a bicycle helmet while going past them at the bus stop. We laugh at those guys."

Well, I wear a bike helmet whenever I ride in the city and as it turns out, I ride to school that way. The students in the class didn't know me but some had seen my helmet on the floor by my desk. The student who mentioned "geeks" in the context of "guys with bike helmets" blushed at her faux pas, and we all had a good laugh at my helmet's expense. But it served to highlight what seems to be going on in this school. If you are different in any way the chances are you will be laughed at or ostracized.

The cooperating teachers in this school have tried to expand the perspectives of their students by having them study the vastly different experience of a group of people not represented in their community, and by having them read about characters in a very different setting whose lives are in fact much like their own in being limited and narrowly defined. Difference and similarity, sameness and diversity, trying to encompass these and use the tension productively — to move beyond the category of "other," of *geek* or *Barney*, and to find the elements to connect these students with others who are unlike and yet like themselves — is a constant concern of education in a multicultural world. (And, of course, hearing the students' terms *geek* and *Barney* gives the teacher a real place to begin.)

Whether the classroom community contains its own diversity or is homogeneous and "provincial," the teacher must locate something that her students can share with others, something that can help them connect the small cultural units of their families and homes, and the language and knowledge that they bring from those units, with a larger culture. In addition to a desire to value students' own cultural settings and what they bring from them, there's an even stronger desire — born of frustration as well as traditional educational goals — to bring students into a larger common culture. In fact, the classroom we argue against here, one that asks students to quietly memorize some body of knowledge and then give it back as a list of terms, a group of dates, a canon of works, is often directed by a teacher who is rather desperately trying to give students something to share in a society that seems more and more diverse.

One of the teachers whose classes Mark observed gives voice to these concerns. She talks with Mark about how "students need to learn that they should treat each other equitably" and "everyone should have a fair chance to succeed." Mark goes on:

> This is how she treats them, fairly — equitably. She wants to teach her students to be responsible to themselves and to their nation in the voting place. "It doesn't matter how they vote," she told me, "so long

as they at least know they should vote. They are our future and I
suppose that's why I care about them so strongly."

So, what are the goals of this English classroom in relation to the
larger society? Some are explicit in the teacher's words: for students to
learn to treat others fairly. Some are implicit, or, as Mark puts it, "seen
in the classroom and not gleaned from conversing with her about
teaching and teaching philosophy per se." One of these is to get all
students, including "remedial" students, "to tap their intellectual resources," to realize they are "worthy of learning something more than
what other might think them capable of." Another is "to show students
that they need to have an awareness of other people who are their
fellow Americans."

The current discussion about the crisis in American education may
seem far from the daily life of this classroom. Yet the larger debate, like
Mark's teachers' concerns, hinges on questions of educational goals.
National educational goals are usually phrased in terms of providing
students with the basic skills and knowledge to fit into an "American
Society" seen as unchanging, or, in a recent variation, to fit into a
society with new technological demands and changing economic conditions. How do the terms of the debate fit with the goals of this
English classroom? And what does it mean to be literate, capable, and
aware within a larger culture?

The education crisis

In 1983, then–Secretary of Education Terrel Bell published a report on
the nation's schools that escalated what had become a growing concern
about the quality of public education in the United States. Titled "A
Nation at Risk," the report painted a depressing and frightening portrait
of America's schools, one that clearly suggested that unless immediate
action were taken to "stem the rising tide" of mediocrity, the country's
economy and hence its place as a world power would be in jeopardy.

The crisis in education highlighted in this report had been developing
for years. Newspaper and magazine articles and television documentaries
pointed to its signs, particularly to a growing anxiety about the "basic
literacy" of America's students, their ability to calculate, to read, to
write, and to reason. The anxiety has been fed by statistics like the high
attrition rates in large cities (more than forty-nine percent of school
children who begin ninth grade in the Boston schools, for example,
will drop out before graduation) and by the numbers of complaints
from employers about high school graduates who are unable to master
the simplest thinking tasks or write the simplest documents, who are
"functionally illiterate." And the anxiety becomes a kind of panic over

the complexity of the social and ethical problems brought into the school for attention, problems once only the province of the home or church. "Why aren't schools administering?" some critics ask. "Why aren't teachers teaching?" say others. "Why aren't parents parenting?" And most crucial of all, "Why aren't students learning?"

This crisis in the schools has been exposed by critics from both the political left and right, by both government and the general public, by teachers and students themselves. Among all these groups there is a kind of unexpressed anger and disappointment about the educational system's failure to meet the goal Americans have traditionally set for their public schools—that they be avenues of opportunity, bridging the gap between those who are wealthy enough to afford education and those who are not. The role of educational institutions in providing opportunities for "have-nots" to become "haves" has been celebrated in American legend from Abe Lincoln learning to read by firelight in his Kentucky log cabin to *Welcome Back Kotter* and *The White Shadow*, recent television shows whose premise is the power of education to change young lives. Underneath these legends lies a conception of school as a more or less neutral place, designed to transmit a pretty much accepted body of knowledge to young people who will, after they finish school, better themselves and, not coincidentally, strengthen the economy of their country.

In 1986, a Carnegie Commission task force produced a report on education that attempted to respond to the stinging indictments made by Bell and others. *A Nation Prepared* begins with a warning that clearly ties national growth to individual educational opportunity:

> America's ability to compete in world markets is eroding. The productivity growth of our competitors outdistances our own. The capacity of our economy to provide a high standard of living for all our people is increasingly in doubt. As jobs requiring little skill are automated or go offshore, and demand increases for the highly skilled, the pool of educated and skilled people grows smaller and the backwater of the unemployable rises. Large numbers of American children are in limbo—ignorant of the past and unprepared for the future. Many are dropping out—not just out of school but out of productive society. (2)

The Carnegie report suggests that the only response to this crisis is to reclaim the traditional educational ideal, the philosophy of individual opportunity tied to national growth that has been so much a part of our national belief about the function of education: "[Americans] rightly demand an improved supply of young people with the knowledge, the spirit, the stamina, and the skills to make the nation once again fully competitive—in industry, in commerce, in social justice and progress, and, not least, in the ideas that safeguard a free society." The report stresses that the American way of life is in danger if schools don't respond to their new challenges:

If our standard of living is to be maintained, if the growth of a permanent underclass is to be averted, if democracy is to function effectively into the next century, our schools must graduate the vast majority of their students with achievement levels long thought possible for only the privileged few. The American mass education system, designed in the early part of the century for a mass-production economy, will not succeed unless it not only raises but redefines the essential standards of excellence and strives to make quality and equality of opportunity compatible with each other." (3)

At the beginning of the twentieth century, the underlying principles for the American goals of education implicit in the Carnegie Commission's report were already in place even though education was designed more deliberately for "the privileged few." In the American democratic state, everyone was expected to have a fair chance, and that constitutional ideal underlay the establishment of free, tax-supported education from elementary through high school. By 1900, education was free (to various levels), compulsory (up to different ages depending on the state), universal, and designed from kindergarten through college. In principle, there was to be equal educational opportunity for all. In fact, only a small portion of the student population completed the entire sequence, but most completed the elementary or junior high school years. Interestingly enough, in those days, three out of four students who took their high school diplomas continued on to college.

The twentieth century has seen an enormous growth of high school populations, and that growth has fueled debates about the best methods for achieving the aims embodied in the rhetoric of bettering oneself and one's society — about how to reach the goals education in America has set for itself. In spite of schools' attempts to recognize and accommodate diversity and in spite of their shared goal of opportunity for all, calls for educational reform have been increasing since the late 1960s. Henry Giroux summarizes this crisis mentality permeating the discussions of critics of American education from both right and left in his introduction to Paulo Freire's *The Politics of Education*:

> For conservatives the language of crisis and critique becomes clear in their assertion that schools have failed to take seriously their alleged commitment to the demands of capitalist rationality and the imperatives of the market economy. The crisis pointed to in this case resides in the lagging state of the American economy and the diminishing role of the United States in shaping world affairs. Many on the radical left, by contrast, write off schools as simply a reflex of the labor market. As reproductive sites that smoothly provide the knowledge, skills, and social relations necessary for the functioning of the capitalist economy and dominant society, public education no longer provides the tools for critical thinking and transformative action. (xi)

Giroux articulates clearly two quite different perspectives on the goals of American education, on what it means to better oneself and one's society. Are schools to provide the skills needed, as the Carnegie report asserts, to maintain the American economy and the American way of life, or are they to support the development of critical thinking and of action that would improve and transform America's social institutions?

Mark's cooperating teachers might say "both." In their classrooms, students work on the "basic skills" of literacy, and they begin, through their reading of literature, the perspective taking that may lead to critical thought, if not to action. But they're working within an institutional context that, itself, isn't neutral.

The inquiry into the nature of our social institutions that began in the 1960s around issues of civil rights and the Vietnam war came, in time, to focus on education, and radical critics began to challenge the traditional notion of education as neutral and objective imparter of knowledge. These critics, Henry Giroux, Richard Ohmann, and others, argued that schools reinforced and accorded privilege to particular codes — certain language forms, types of reasoning, social behaviors, and cultural experiences — in the way they designed curriculum and classroom models.

As Heath's study of the children of Trackton showed, a child whose home communication style included verbal aggressiveness or a lot of movement while talking could be quickly labeled a troublemaker for not staying seated in a classroom that promoted the "dominant code" of passive sitting and waiting to be called on to talk.

Just as the schools, as institutions are not neutral, neither is English, as a field. Its dominant models and methods arise in a larger social and political context, and in a larger culture. In *English in America*, Richard Ohmann argues that English, as a discipline, is tied to the social and political forces that surround the study and teaching of it. And he explores the ways in which the teaching of literature and composition practiced in our schools and colleges is shaped consciously or unconsciously by cultural considerations. He insists that "institutions don't exist in vacuums or in the pure atmosphere of their ideals. They are part of the social order and survive by helping to maintain it" (22).

As part of the social order, the educational institution in general, and the English department in particular, is not neutral in its goals or methods. Ohmann asserts, for example, that, in particular, "the goals of Freshman English were framed in response to the needs of the industrial state and its governing class" (110). Composition teaching conceives writing in institutional terms, and makes dominant social codes into universal truths.

> If the literary style is the "offspring of learning and politeness" and to be regarded as having dignity when it can be seen as more or less sharply opposed to "ordinary, vulgar speech," it is hard not to conclude that the purpose of composition as it came to be conceived in the latter days of rhetoric was the acquisition of certain linguistic forms of relatively narrow currency, which today would be said to represent

good or appropriate English, but which in more candid times could be described simply and without apology, as signs of social rank. (110)

Certainly we have seen that a curriculum that emphasizes correctness of standard forms as intrinsically superior serves mainly to make students who don't speak with those forms feel stupid and responsible for their own school failure and thus for their eventual place in the social order. When teachers take the emphasis off of error and focus instead on building on students' existing competence as a base for new learning, they begin to alter this order.

Ohmann argues that even in approaches to literature, English departments are not neutral, and as an example of this largely unconscious advocacy of institutional values, he cites the New Criticism, the primary critical approach to literature for much of this century (and still the dominant, though unnamed, approach in most literature classrooms). The New Criticism's approach is governed by its belief in the primacy of the text and the irrelevance of the text's author and the text's reader. The text exists in a timeless vacuum, and its true meaning is in its words, to be found by a reader who examines it closely. If the text is removed from the social world of its writer and its reader, then teachers of those texts can escape any consideration of social or political problems.

> A critic and teacher whose work is fun and respectable, but who sees little evidence that he is helping to ameliorate social ills, or indeed serving any but those destined to assume their own positions in the ruling class—a teacher in this dubious spot will welcome a system of ideas and values that tells him that politics and ideology are at an end, that a pluralistic society is best for all, that individual freedom is the proper social goal for rich and poor alike, and that the perfection of self can best be attained through humanistic intellectual endeavor. And this is what the New Criticism and its rival theories had to offer. (86)

In fact, texts and ways of teaching them both shape and are shaped by the real world. And a critical approach to literature that focuses exclusively on finding the "correct" meaning in the text leaves out both the real world texts represent and the real lives of the students who read them. This approach, where the teacher is the one most likely to know the "correct" meaning, reinforces authority-based, fact-centered schooling. It is, of course, important for students to read, accurately, the details that Chaucer uses to portray the Franklin, but what readers make of those details and elements is at least partly determined by the history and culture in which readers read. Modern readers can't help bringing the perspective of a society newly conscious of the dangers of alcoholism to their perception of the Franklin's character, no matter how aware they are that this perspective would have been irrelevant in Chaucer's time. Recognizing that their social lens might differ from a fourteenth-century reader's can lead students to a more complex understanding of texts and their interpretation.

Criticisms like Ohmann's from the left of the political spectrum have helped us begin to see schools as cultures, bound by behaviors and rules that are not at all objective or neutral. They can help the teachers Mark is learning from see important areas of their work from a new perspective and ask questions about their teaching that they might not have articulated before. And the terms *critical thinking* and *transformative action* may cause them to extend their educational goals. But these critics generally analyze the problems of education only in rather global terms that don't speak to immediate classroom concerns.

Recent criticisms of education from observers in the mainstream or on the political right have been critical, not of the ways education works to perpetuate present social constructs and categories, but of the ways it fails in relation to the present order. This concern also leads to a condemnation of the passive, topic-centered instruction current in school practice and a call for emphasis on "critical thinking." Governmental task forces, independent organizations, teachers' groups are all calling for reform, agreeing that public education has become an inadequate avenue of opportunity for the people it serves. The reports typically begin by citing statistics that prove students' declining abilities in reasoning, in writing, in mathematics. The statistics are symptoms of a disease that the reports define and then diagnose, a disease of mediocrity that threatens to create a generation of ill-prepared and hopeless young citizens.

Some criticisms focus on the content of what's taught and what's learned. You've no doubt read disturbing accounts of the numbers of American high school students who can't identify Massachusetts on a map, or spell the President's last name, or, as Chester Finn and Diane Ravitch note in *What Do Our 17 Year Olds Know?*, don't understand why "World War II was so named, since [they'd] never heard of World War I" (viii). Other criticisms focus on skills. A survey of twenty years of reading, math, and science tests released by the Educational Testing Service in February 1989, for example, shows that students fail in "higher order skills," the complex tasks that go beyond simple mechanics in problem solving across the disciplines.

These criticisms just name the problem. The Carnegie Commission goes further and prescribes remedies: changing school structures and provoking consciousness of those structures. Its strategies for change include "active learning" and "redesigned teacher training programs," initiatives within school systems to support excellence in teaching, better testing, and redesigned curricula. It focuses on changes in pedagogy as a possible solution to the problem of inadequate preparation among the nation's school-age population.

In spite of real political as well as philosophical differences among these groups, the concept of critical thinking permeates the discussion, pointing to the need for a pedagogy that would support such thinking. The Educational Testing Service, hardly a radical group, calls for new methods — "discussion teams, cooperative work groups, individual learning logs, computer networking" — instead of reliance on textbooks and teacher-prepared exercises, noting that students must become "doers and thinkers." And those words, used by Giroux and others, are echoed again and again in the references by presidential commissions, teacher organizations, and state-supported task forces to "critical thinking" and "active learning."

The terms provide firm ground for Mark's cooperating teachers. They support directions they're already taking in their classrooms, and they encourage them to extend their efforts. But these terms still leave questions about how to foster active learning and critical thinking, about how to move beyond a set of new methods to create a coherent pedagogy, and how, if teachers accept the critique of Giroux and Ohmann, the learning of their classrooms can lead, in the end, to transformative action. The real issue then, seems to be not *whether* teachers should support active or passive learning, critical or naive thinking, transformative or replicative action, but *how* they should go about making education more relevant, meaningful, and culturally sound. And that discussion pivots on issues of how people learn and share what they learn in a cultural and social setting, issues that are at the heart of what responsibilities an educational system and a teacher might assume. They bring us back to a focus on how people learn that has been central to discussions of education in this century.

The way to learn

In much of the early part of the century, learning by classical methods, memorization and recall, was the rule: students mastered a body of information or group of texts and produced them when called upon to respond. Fewer students attended secondary schools, and those who did were a homogeneous group and brought with them the same values, attitudes, information, and experiences. The methods seemed workable. But as students from other cultures began to enter public school, students whose parents were immigrants or who lived in remote regions of the country newly serviced by better transportation and bigger schools, the old methods of learning began to seem faulty. In the 1920s, the philosopher John Dewey challenged the method of memorization and the concept of knowledge that underlay it, a concept of knowledge as a changeless body of facts. Dewey argued that in order to be effective, education must provide the learner with much more than predigested facts or bodies of knowledge. It must instead allow the learner to become a part of the activity of learning, making knowledge as well as receiving it. Dewey believed that learners could learn anything if their minds were actively engaged in the enterprise of learning. Therefore, he argued, teachers should create active, experience-oriented learning situations.

Alfred North Whitehead, another leading educator, philosopher, and follower of Dewey, continued to refine Dewey's plan for creating better schools by insisting on the importance of individual discovery and of the imagination in the learning enterprise: "Knowledge does not keep any better than fish. You may be dealing with knowledge of the old species, with some old truth; but somehow or other it must come to the students, as it were, just drawn out of the sea and with the freshness of its immediate importance" (97). Like Dewey, Whitehead encouraged educational systems to be responsive to the needs and interests of individual learners. Seen in the context of the changing groups of students who were entering schools in the first half of this century, Dewey's and Whitehead's ideas were profoundly democratic — they asserted the individual's responsibility and power by insisting that the learner's needs should shape school structures.

Responses from the schools—working in the tension

On the surface, modern schools seem to be following the path blazed by Dewey, Whitehead, and other educational theorists by trying to accommodate diversity and allowing for individual activity. After studying Amish schooling, Fishman reexamines the statement of goals which governs her own modern high school, as established by the Pennsylvania Department of Education. She finds that these goals focus on things like "helping all students develop positive self-concepts, maintain emotional well-being, discover their creativity and 'prepare for a world of rapid change and unforeseeable demands,'" as well as on "helping every child to acquire, to the fullest possible extent, mastery of the basic skills in use of words and numbers," and "helping every child to understand and appreciate as much as possible of human achievement in the natural sciences, the social sciences, and the humanities and the arts" (173). The goals seem to her to be "theoretically appropriate to the society in which we live and the principles we espouse." But, as a teacher, does Fishman's own pedagogy meet these goals? Before spending time with the Amish, she didn't ask that question. Like most teachers, parents, and students, she held these goals as ideals but believed that "real schools are not about self images, creativity, and the unknown; they are about English, math, social studies, and science."

For the most part, school curriculum is divided into common subjects, and school structure is based on year-long units of study in these subjects, on what is called the Carnegie unit. A high school curriculum is added up in terms of such units and generally includes four years of English, two of natural sciences, etc. The structure is designed to ensure that students are exposed to a number of disciplines, and it allows some flexibility for the development of individual skills in areas like home economics or art. Since the middle of the century, schools have also offered courses for handicapped learners, for gifted students, for students interested in vocational programs and in college preparation. They often give "life" courses such as personal health, and personal enrichment classes like drama and typing. At the same time, they're assuming new social roles, informing and counseling students on religious, ethical, moral questions, questions that in earlier days were answered by parents or religious authorities. Schools appear to be doing more than they did at the turn of the century to accommodate students' varied interests and abilities, if not their backgrounds, and to give them the opportunity to succeed.

One way that schools seemingly have tried to accommodate the varied abilities of students has been by homogeneous grouping — tracking students in various disciplines into particular levels based on predictions of their abilities and then teaching all students in a track in similar ways using similar texts. Predictions of performance are drawn from standardized tests of intelligence or achievement, previous grades, and teacher assessments of general classroom performance. The rationale for tracking is simple: students move more effectively from one skill to another or one level of development to another when they are surrounded by those who are in their own level, and teachers teach more effectively when they can teach at the same rate to a group of students who will comprehend at the same rate. Students don't have to feel bored by repetitive or too simple work or frustrated by difficult or too complicated work. The ideal is noble: diversity gets recognized and valued as students are placed where they can best perform. And even the practicalities make sense: instruction does not have to be individualized, but can be planned for groups of students who will all be working through the same material at the same pace, thus allowing many students to be served by fewer teachers.

But the actuality is not so ideal: though tracking seems to satisfy the educational goal of equal opportunity and access for diverse populations it also becomes a way to keep from recognizing diversity or accommodating difference. And it limits access more often than it allows it. Students who are tracked at a particular level tend to stay there for the duration of their time in public school, partially because expectations determine placement from year to year and partially because a student who is tracked lives up to the potential assigned to her. As

Hepsie's ten-year-old daughter observed recently, recommending a plan of action to her older brother for improving his performance in school, "Once they think you're smart and put you in a smart class, you really don't have to do that much. If you don't do your homework, they'll say, 'Did you forget, honey?'"

The self-fulfilling prophecy works both ways obviously, and even a fifth grader can recognize it. When learning is seen as the staged acquisition of particular types of information, verified by various standardized tests, the rate at which one passes through such stages becomes an important determinant of scholastic success and classroom placement. But, as Labov has shown us, such tests measure experience with schooling and the adoption of school values rather than ability, and they are grossly inadequate measures of the ability of students from non-mainstream cultures or non-English-speaking backgrounds. One of our student teachers saw the negative effects of tracking in the classroom he worked in and commented on it in his journal:

> The school policy is to group students according to intellectual ability as gleaned from academic performance, and Mr. Y buys right into this. He teaches his "upper level" classes different than he teaches his "standard level" students. The students pick up on this message, just as they would pick up on being treated as if they were a genius. Mr. Y actually asked the students to explain the levels, and the answer was that the upper level were smarter. The standard level students bought this.... By putting students into castes we invite prejudice and elitism. Everyone is unique, elite in some way. Let students communicate their genius to us and to each other. (David A).

As David argues, such a system has significant disadvantages. For students, there's a stigma attached to being assigned a label, at both ends of the spectrum. The students "buy into" the descriptors of the levels they're assigned to and then "fall into" those behaviors. For teachers, the set of assumptions and activities that accompany each track predetermines teaching methods and classroom content. Teachers teach the "smart kids" differently. It can, of course, be argued that there can be no real homogeneous grouping no matter how sensitive the test to group students. And, as David indicates, teachers invite prejudice when they tell students they're college bound or almost smart enough to be in the advanced track or, as another of our students had been labeled, "terminal."

Mike Rose, an English teacher and composition researcher, has described in his book *Lives on the Boundary* the effect of such tracking on the lives of his students. And he begins by recounting its effect on his own life. A misrecorded exam score placed him in a high school vocational track. His immigrant parents did not understand the educational system, and the mistake was found, only by chance, two years later. By that point he had accepted his place in the culture of the school, and the picture of himself as a learner that his placement suggested. He tells how he and his friends protected themselves from the "suffocating madness" of the empty work "by taking on with a vengeance the identity implied in the vocational track," and rejecting "everything you fear is beyond you." Rose writes of those years:

> The tragedy is that you have to twist the knife in your own gray matter to make this defense work. You have to shut down, have to reject intellectual stimuli or diffuse them with sarcasm, have to cultivate stupidity, have to convert boredom from a malady into a way of confronting the world. Keep your vocabulary simple, act stoned when you're not or act more stoned than you are, flaunt ignorance, materialize your dreams. It is a powerful and effective defense — it neutralizes the insult and the frustration of being a vocational kid and, when perfected, it drives teachers up the wall. (29)

A teacher recognized Rose's potential, the school discovered its mistake, and he was shifted back to the college-prep program, to try to make up for the reading and writing and thinking he had missed. Later, after years of working with students in college remedial programs, Rose the teacher begins to ask questions that had not occurred to him earlier about those who were placed in such courses, about whether there were differences in such placements by race or income. And he reflects on the meaning of a term he had thought to be neutral.

> The designation *remedial* has powerful implications in education — to be remedial is to be substandard, inadequate, and because of the origins of the term, the inadequacy is metaphorically connected to disease and mental defectiveness. The etymology of the word *remedial* places its origins in law and medicine, and in the late nineteenth century the term generally fell into the medical domain. It was then applied to education, to children who were thought to have neurological problems. But *remedial* quickly generalized beyond the description of such students to those with broader, though special, educational problems and then to those learners who were from backgrounds that did not provide optimal environmental and educational opportunities. (209)

As Rose discovers, "remedial" labels are more often applied to students from nonmiddle-class homes and nonmainstream backgrounds, as are labels indicating more severe problems. John Ogbu, in an essay on literacy and schooling among African-Americans, cites statistics for the labeling of black children as educationally handicapped. In a representative year, in the twenty California school districts that enrolled eighty percent of black children, "black children comprised about 27.5 percent of the school population but 62 percent of those labeled 'educable mentally retarded'" (143)

The senior and graduate students in Ellie's course on theories of literacy have confirmed this tracking pattern in their ethnographic observations of Boston-area classrooms. In school after school, at all grade levels, they've found the same patterns repeated, with low-level reading groups and resource rooms and classrooms in remedial tracks more likely to be filled with large numbers of minority students. Only in preschool and adult-literacy classrooms were all learners generally grouped together without damaging labels. Of course, such a placement pattern has much more to do with the conflicts we've already seen between home and school language practices and other behaviors than it does with students' actual ability.

In addition to the widespread system of tracking, most schools have developed standard curricula that follow from a group of standard texts selected by school boards and administrators. This approach to the content of a student's learning easily meshes with the system of tracking, for while tracking is supposed to accommodate diversity, a standard curriculum within groups allows for a commonality of experience and might be argued to provide equal educational opportunity among the various school populations. A prepractice student talks about one of the texts in the standard ninth-grade curriculum of the English class he is working with:

> As we were reading, at least one reason for these students' general lack of interest became clear to me: the material being read was inappropriate for these students, with only one exception that I could see. The story, a short novel apparently written for school children, about a cowboy named Red and an "Indian" named Tom, and their adventures on the rodeo circuit, was simply boring. The girls in my group, who were the better readers, and who were conscientiously answering the questions on the reading guide, could not possibly be expected to care about Red and Tom and their bucking broncos. The reading ability of one of the girls, in particular, was so far in advance of the level of the material, that it's a wonder to me that she could manage to keep enough interest even to sound out the words, let alone pay attention to what the words were saying. The boys were somewhat more interested in the story (and one was more or less fascinated by it), but in general they were having a hard time understanding why they should care about horses and tumbleweed. Two of the boys had reading skills that were so rudimentary that they did not know what they had just read, and were unable to answer the reading guide questions even when I stopped their reading exactly at the point where the answer could be found in the text.
>
> Apparently, the reading of this particular novel is required for all ninth-grade basic students at the high school. It's hard for me to understand why that would be required, but it's not hard to understand why students would be generally bored if this is the sort of reading material that they expect to work with. (David S)

David recognizes a basic flaw in the standard text/standard curriculum/standard skill approach to learning followed by most school systems. Individual learners get lost when their interests and needs don't get taken into account. And individual teachers get lost as well, for a uniformly designed curriculum eliminates the particularly designed classroom and encourages the teacher to accept rather than create method.

It seems, then, that tracking is a flawed concept that doesn't accommodate the goals of diversity and opportunity it was designed to achieve, and that the standard curriculum does little to respond to individual learners in a particular classroom context as well. So what is the answer to the problem of providing challenge and motivation for a diverse body of learners? Dewey has answered that learners have to be connected with what they learn, and actively involved in that learning. But while preparing teachers may have read about Dewey in their education courses, they're more likely to enter schools that define learning in a way far from Dewey's notions, schools that demand continual measurement of skills and emphasize forms and facts rather than knowing and understanding. As Fishman discovers, the nature of our schooling leaves us "more likely to achieve Old Order (Amish) goals than our own" (173).

Teacher/researchers like Fishman want their schools to support the development of individual learners and their creativity, and they may turn to other classrooms, in other contexts, to help them perceive their own in new ways. Other teachers want to help their students "tap their intellectual resources" and they may turn, as Mark's cooperating teachers have, to in-service workshops like those offered by the Boston Writing Project to learn more process-oriented methods for helping students become writers as well as readers. Student teachers like David want to "let the students communicate their genius," and they may take a risk and try to alter the dominant patterns of the classroom they have stepped into. But all of these teachers are also responsible to a system that grades and ranks those who will eventually be judged in the larger social system. Teachers may have prepared to nurture genius, but instead find a class that is already labeled "Level 4," where the students see themselves as "Level 4," and have long ago opted out of seeing the significant parts of their lives as having anything to do with school. They'll accept the terms by which they're labeled but reject the arena in which they matter. The conflict teachers feel between what they believe about learners and what the system teaches them about learners is severe and often debilitating. When they see students who have rejected the educational arena, they know the system of schooling is failing but are at a loss to find solutions to make the system work.

Responding to the problem — cultural literacy as old knowledge

E. D. Hirsch's best-selling book *Cultural Literacy: What Every American Needs to Know* is one response to the problem of how to make education work more effectively to produce literate people. Hirsch begins his book by searching for the reasons for the educational crisis and the declining skills of students. He places blame on the structures of schools, those very structures that offered an apparent response to Dewey's concern about the individual learner. Hirsch locates the source of the problem first in curriculum, arguing that a combination of curricular factors — an emphasis on variety of courses and on skills over content — are the real culprits in the deficiencies of American schoolchildren. "That children from poor and illiterate homes tend to remain poor and illiterate is an unacceptable failure of our schools, one which has occurred not because our teachers are inept but chiefly because they are compelled to teach a fragmented curriculum based on faulty educational theories," he says (xiii). Hirsch sees American education as a "shopping mall" where students blindly select what they will study and as a result never learn the fundamental terms that constitute literacy. And he would argue that Dewey's pedagogical ideas have failed, even though, as we've pointed out, they've never truly been tested in public schools. In rejecting Dewey's pedagogical concepts, Hirsch also rejects the philosophical concept of knowledge as dynamic and changeable; he would return education to a nineteenth-century version of a standard curriculum and to a nineteenth-century emphasis on memorization of facts through which that curriculum was taught. And he argues that with a return to that body of knowledge and those ways of acquiring it, students will gain "cultural literacy," or a standard body of information, the lack of which is causing their current failure.

Hirsch's own response to stemming the "tide of mediocrity" the Bell report warned about is a return to an earlier day of a monocultural literacy. In a revealing small narrative, Hirsch recounts a story of his father, who used Shakespearean allusions to end many of his business letters. He would say, for example, as he concluded a letter about the urgency of making a business deal, "There is a tide..." without completing the quotation or even the phrase.

> To say there is a tide is better than saying "Buy now and you'll cover expenses for the whole year, but if you fail to act right away, you may regret it the rest of your life." That would be twenty-seven words instead of four, and while the bare message of the longer statement would be conveyed, the persuasive force wouldn't.... The moral of this tale is not that reading Shakespeare will help one rise in the business world. My point is a broader one. The fact that middle level

executives no longer share literate background knowledge is a chief
cause of their inability to communicate effectively. (9–10)

Hirsch harkens back to a time he envisions when a writer could
make allusions and assume that any reader would understand the reference, where a teacher would not have to teach terms but could assume
that her students knew them. This nostalgia for the past and for a father
who ended his letters with Shakespeare is Hirsch's dream of cultural
literacy. But Hirsch ignores several things in this story that are crucial
to our understanding of how knowledge gets made and shared in
communities. First of all, communities of professional people, students,
community groups, gangs, surfers do share allusions and jargon in
precisely the same ways they did in the day of Hirsch's father's letter.
They do count on a body of information and use it in conversation with
one another. A few years ago, children said goodbye to one another
with the phrase "May the force be with you," an allusion to the wildly
popular Star Wars movies. The phrase became less and less popular
among children the more adults co-opted it for themselves, and soon it
became a strained cliché to be used only sarcastically. The phrase
"There is a tide" is similarly strained and clichéd in some situations, and
one reason for its lack of use may not be so much that it's no longer
understood but that in overuse it lost the persuasive power Hirsch
assigns to it. Furthermore, and this is even more crucial, it's only true
in the narrowest sense that our past was a shared cultural experience.
Maybe Hirsch's father's business associates all knew the Shakespeare
allusion, but it's a safe bet that many of his customers didn't. In this
country, we never have been monocultural; it only seemed that way
because fewer of us—women, ethnic and racial minorities, poor people
of all backgrounds—had the opportunity to be a part of the cultural
conversation.

Responding to the problem—literacy as reseeing old knowledge

The problem with Hirsch's position is not that Shakespeare cannot
speak to students in different times and places. In *I Know Why the Caged
Bird Sings*, Maya Angelou tells us how Shakespeare spoke to her:

> During these years in Stamps, I met and fell in love with William
> Shakespeare. He was my first white love. Although I enjoyed and
> respected Kipling, Poe, Butler, Thackeray and Henley, I saved my
> young and loyal passion for Paul Laurence Dunbar, Langston Hughes,
> James Weldon Johnson and W. E. B. Du Bois' "Litany at Atlanta."
> But it was Shakespeare who said, "When in disgrace with fortune and
> men's eyes." It was a state with which I myself felt most familiar. (11)

Angelou, as a young black child in a rural area of Arkansas, finds in Shakespeare's words a reflection of something that she knows and understands from her own experience. The words of the text speak to her knowledge, and that knowledge provides a bridge to the unfamiliar world of Shakespeare. While Angelou has found this connection on her own, it's most often the teacher's role to help the students find meaningful routes into such texts. Memorizing "There is a tide" as a famous quotation from Shakespeare — as Hirsch would have our students do — won't help them to own that knowledge, or even to remember the phrase past the next exam.

Teachers need to understand that, as Vygotsky has argued, knowledge gets made and shared in social contexts. With this understanding, they can help their students begin to build bodies of shared knowledge. Pat Conroy helps his Yamacraw Island students build the shared knowledge of the larger culture by making "old knowledge" relevant to the learner. Conroy's students were about as separated from mainstream America and as "culturally illiterate" a group as you could find in the United States. Most read only a little and wrote less, and they couldn't begin to read the textbooks that were assigned to them by a school board whose concerns were with uniformity and by a principal who, though black, saw her students as alien and her assignment as so far from the norm that she considered herself to be "overseas."

Conroy begins his work with his illiterate island students with many of the same feelings expressed by E. D. Hirsch and Diane Ravitch and Chester Finn, frustration at what his students don't know — about even the simplest cultural things. And Conroy's frustration is even greater and more understandable, for while Hirsch is disturbed because students no longer recognize Shakespearean allusions and Finn and Ravitch worry about students who don't know who fought in World War I, Conroy faces students who don't know what country they live in, what ocean borders their island, how old they are.

> "What country do we live in, gang? Everybody tell me at once," I exhorted.
>
> No one said a word. Several of them looked at one another and shrugged their shoulders.
>
> "Gang," I continued, "what is the name of this grand old, red, white and blue country of ours? The place where we live. The land of the free and the home of the brave."
>
> Still there was silence.
>
> I was struggling for the right words to simplify the question even further. "Have you ever heard of the United States of America?"
>
> "Oh, yeh," Mary, one of the eighth grade girls, said, "I heared it. I heared it in I pledge a legent to the flag of United States of America."
>
> "Good. Then you knew what country you live in."
>
> "No, just know pledge a legent."

Conroy is dismayed by his students' lack of knowledge, but deeply
angry at the educational system that has left them so culturally illiterate:

> I got madder and madder at the people responsible for the condition
> of these kids. Seven of my students could not recite the alphabet.
> Three children could not spell their names. Eighteen children thought
> Savannah, Georgia was the largest city in the world. Eighteen children
> had never seen a hill. One child was positive that John Kennedy was
> the first President of the United States. Seventeen children agreed with
> that child.... (32, 33)

It's easy to get disheartened by students' lack of knowledge about
concepts that those of us immersed in a culture take for granted. Unlike
Conroy, some teachers see students as responsible for that lack and
laugh about those deficiencies. Richard Lederer, an English teacher at a
private school in New Hampshire, has made a career out of exposing
the cultural illiteracy of high school students across the country. Their
notions of history:

> Julius Caesar extinguished himself on the battlefields of Gaul. The Ides
> of March murdered him because they thought he was going to be
> made kind. Dying he gasped out the words, "Tee, hee, Brutus."

Their absurd spelling:

> Then Elizabeth's navy went out and defeated the Spanish Armadillo.

And their lack of logic and critical thinking:

> The sun never set on the British Empire because the British Empire is
> in the East and the sun sets in the West.

Lederer's compilations of student bloopers are funny and make for
good reading. But if you look back at these missteps, you can see two
things that are disturbing: one, the teacher's attitude that makes these
mistakes the essence of the communication (does the student really
think a giant creature was swimming menacingly through the English
Channel?) and two, the poignant attempt of students to make sense out
of information that obviously made little sense to them. In other words, if
facts are taught apart from context, most won't get learned and those
that do will—almost perversely—get placed by the learner into some
context, however tortured.

Hirsch's conception of teaching leads him to produce a list that he
assures the reader is not "prescriptive," but "descriptive," designed to
expose the information "actually possessed by literate Americans" (xiv).
The literacy list that completes Hirsch's book is an example of such
decontextualized learning and, if taught, would result in lots of new
material for Lederer. For example, under "I" Hirsch lists:

Iacocca
Iago

Iambic pentameter
I am the state
I beam
I been working on the railroad

The list itself suggests a way of knowing that has been privileged in the dominant Western culture that is its source—a knowing of information, of facts. His students would learn "old knowledge" in old ways.

Conroy offers a new way of countering the problem of students' cultural illiteracy—by contextualizing the old knowledge for them, connecting it to the pieces of knowledge they already possess. Conroy reaches his students in this way, helping them learn by making them teachers whose real lives become part of school life. As Conroy teaches his students music, for example, he responds to their curiosity about a record he had in the schoolroom, and lets information and terms and concepts and students' knowledge fall together naturally. One fact becomes part of another fact, and they all become part of something even larger, as students and teacher collectively make new knowledge.

> "Anybody ever heard of the Reader's Digest? This little magazine put out this little record you see here in my hands. This record is a treasure, an absolute delight. A collection of greatness. Now the first great tune I am going to play for you was written by a long-haired cat named Beethoven. Who was that?"
>
> "Bay cloven."
>
> "Close enough. Now old Bay Cloven loved music, and he could write some pretty mean songs. He was the James Brown of Germany. What continent is Germany in (pointing to the map)?"
>
> "Europe"
>
> "Good. Now one of Beethoven's most famous songs was written about death. Death knocking at the door. Does death come to everybody's door sometime?"
>
> "Yeah, death come knocking at Dooney's door last year," Big C said. (46)

Conroy makes use of what his students know, makes that knowledge a story, adds details that are tangential to the main point of his lesson but relevant and potentially memorable, and makes the knowledge connect to what students know themselves about their own lives.

Making literacy multicultural

One way to nurture true cultural literacy is to provide classroom alternatives to a monocultural view of literacy, to make literacy and learning multidimensional, reflective of a number of cultures and responsive to a number of ways of coming to know. In Conroy's classroom, learning takes place through a dialogue in which both students' and teacher's knowledge is valued:

> "Mr. Conroy, ever see how snake eat egg?" Lincoln asked.
> "No, Lincoln, but I'm afraid to ask."
> "He swallow the egg whole. Then he climb up tree, jump off branch, land on ground, and pop egg in belly."
> "That's how I eat eggs, too, Lincoln."
> I returned to the serpent mythology on numerous occasions during the year, exhorting the students to look truth in the eye and to understand that the things we learn in our youth are not always literally correct. With brilliant logic they argued that what I had learned in the city about snakes was not any better than what they learned while living on the island. They had lived with snakes all their lives; I had merely read about them. (50)

Conroy makes literacy multicultural by accepting the knowledge students bring from their own cultural context as part of the knowledge that gets made in the classroom. Yet he doesn't leave them there. Conroy's students lack knowledge of even much of their own history or cultural traditions. Most of them have never heard the words *integration* and *segregation*, for example, and know only that Martin Luther King was a hero, while knowing nothing about why he was heroic. They certainly would never have read any literary work by black writers. But this "new" knowledge too is important.

In her essay "The Poets in the Kitchen," writer Paule Marshall tells of the important moment of discovering the work of black writers. She was an avid reader in school and out of it, had read "everything from Jane Austen to Zane Grey." But she had never read anything by minority writers. "Something I couldn't quite define was missing," she says. One day in a public library she came across Paul Laurence Dunbar:

> I turned to a poem at random. "Little brown baby wif spaklin/eyes/ come to yo' pappy an' set on his knee." Although I had a little difficulty at first with the words in dialect, the poem spoke to me as nothing I had read before of the closeness, the special relationship I had had with my father. . . . I read another poem "Ef you don' get up, you scamp/dey be trouble in dis camp." I laughed. It reminded me of the way my mother sometimes yelled at my sister and me to get out of bed in the mornings. (139)

Marshall heard voices that reminded her of her own experiences, her own life. Those voices validated hers, and they taught her that her own voice might be heard too. She comments on the need for literature other than the standard classic curriculum for ethnic minorities in school:

> No grade school literature teacher of mine had ever mentioned Dunbar or James Weldon Johnson or Langston Hughes. I didn't know that Zora Neale Hurston existed. . . . What I needed, what all the kids—

West Indian and native black American alike — with whom I grew up needed was an equivalent of the Jewish schul, someplace where we could go after school — the schools that were shortchanging us — and read works by those like ourselves and learn about our history. (140)

One way of valuing diversity is to recognize that it exists in the society at large. Even more important is to see that the literature of diverse cultures contributes to our own, whatever it is. "Ethnic writing exists as replenishment," one nonminority teacher, Blanche Gelfant, writes:

It offers alternate modes of expression, alternate myths, metaphors, language, forms. It introduces to our imagination the sensibility of those others who perceive the world in their own way, each different from each, but all quickening to mind and spirit.... The best of American ethnic writing serves the purpose Emerson demanded of great books. It "inspires." It alters our minds. (770)

There's been much talk in recent years of expanding the body of literature considered worthy of study — the canon of great works that forms our cultural heritage. The literature that has traditionally been considered great is a valuable part of that heritage, but it comes from only one of the traditions that inform the world's, and our society's, cultures. When Anthony observed the urban high school class that he described at the beginning of Chapter 3, he found that the text, *Currents of Fiction*, included nothing very current and nothing that represented anything other than Western European culture. But the culture of the students in the class was broader and more diverse, and its potential richness lay untapped.

Another teacher, Eileen Oliver, goes beyond recommending the teaching of ethnic fiction to encouraging an "afrocentric" approach to all literature. In an article in *English Journal* she argues that it's important to give students both new ways of knowing non—Western European cultures, and a fresh way to look at both ethnic literature and more traditional "classic" literature. Students read works by minority writers and begin to learn about the rhetoric and aesthetic of minority texts that have as their origin African rather than European cultural attitudes. "A developing awareness of the black aesthetic requires a sensitivity to the cultural character of the rhetoric, the haunting communication styles of 'epic memory,' the racial ethos of the oral traditions which have survived through oppression" (51). Much of black literature is built on the techniques of the black oral tradition, techniques like the "call and response" or talk-back relationship between speaker and audience. Some of these techniques offer teachers a new way to illustrate the reader/text relationship, and the understandings gained through studying them can support the reading of "classic" literature as well. "If we can extend our knowledge of the universe by adopting a world view," Oliver argues "we will be better able to value art forms of all cultures by understanding what makes them precious." (49–52)

Cultural literacy as sharing knowledge

One of our students, Tricia, had taught in Belize, where, like Conroy, she had intuitively developed the perspective we've been building in this chapter, drawing on her students' language and knowledge and culture and making her classroom multicultural. She reflected on this experience in her journal:

> Having taught in a multicultural setting where the legal language was English but the utilized language was Spanish and/or Creole, I realize the acute need for alternative methods of "reaching" students who don't speak English fluently and who certainly haven't mastered grammar skills. Thrust into this foreign culture, I relied heavily upon my own impromptu ethnographies to merely get by each day. Often, reading Caribbean literature, I had to ask students the meanings of words and customs. Hesitant to relinquish my "control" and, I thought, respect, I finally had no choice and was surprised by the result: a dialogue where students weren't afraid to be "wrong."

Because Tricia had stepped into such a different educational context, she could see how schooling is affected by larger social and political concerns. (And she addresses her reader's cultural illiteracy, with the knowledge about Belize that she shares in her journal.)

> Belize is a small Caribbean country that until very recently was British Honduras. Because of its British background and because it hopes to shed its Third World isolation, the newly independent country's leaders chose English as the "legal" language of the land. While Spanish and a Caribbean Creole are spoken in *all* informal situations, schools, banks and places of business are "hallowed halls" wherein only English, *proper* English, must be spoken. The well-educated Belizean educators have little tolerance for their "obstinate" students who refuse to learn to speak, read, and write proper standard English. For a country striving to create and maintain a national identity (they've been independent for only six years), this dichotomy seemed oddly misguided to me.

Although Tricia's students were very bright, many of them were failing. English was demanded, but it was not treated as a second language, and Tricia spent her time in Belize "trying to convince the country's Education minister to try at least one pilot ESL program." In her own teaching, Tricia tried to overcome the dichotomy that she had observed, having students use the Creole language that they know best to make contact with a larger cultural world.

I had them translate *Romeo and Juliet* into Creole skits. For some poems I had them cut out pictures that supported the imagery in the poem — particularly helpful when they studied Robert Frost's "Stopping by Woods on a Snowy Evening" as many — well, none — of them had ever seen snow. We wrote letters to Presidents Reagan and Gorbachev, Prime Ministers Thatcher and Esquival (of Belize) in Creole, expressing our concern with varied world and national issues. All drew *some* official response prompting these kids to take pride in Creole as a valid "language."

We do need to know how to make knowledge and knowing meaningful to the students we teach, so that the knowing they acquire affects their lives as adults. We need to find ways to make literacy a product *and* a process of the cultures we inhabit, learn from, and, as groups and individuals, affect.

The multicultural teacher

Paulo Freire makes the context of learners' lives, and their competence within a cultural setting, the premise for all his work on literacy. The ability of learners, not their incompetence, becomes the basis of his entire program for achieving literacy among the Brazilian peasants he works with. He tells us that the educator's role is to enter into dialogue with the illiterate, to offer instruments that connect with the learner's reality. "Teaching," he argues, "cannot be done from top down but only from inside out, by the illiterate himself, with the collaboration of the educator." (1973, 34)

Freire's work is important to our view of cultural literacy and multicultural education in a number of ways. Like Dewey and Whitehead, Freire argues that pedagogy should come not from abstract theories but from concrete practices of people's lives. But he offers us a way to move beyond the work of Piaget and Dewey and Whitehead, who promoted a concept of knowledge that gives the learner control, but who didn't consider enough the importance of social and cultural groups from which individual learners draw their strategies and develop their concepts. In fact, Freire provides a kind of educational complement to Vygotsky's studies of human cognition, for, like Vygotsky, he insists on the dialectic between individual and society that develops thought and language, and he explains strategies for making this dialectic a part of the educational process.

We've spent time talking about the traditional goal of education to provide a populace with access to economic opportunity through the improvement of skills. Freire points to another, though not necessarily contradictory, purpose. His work with Brazilian peasants has led him to define a view of education that actively confronts the tension between schools as proponents of a dominant cultural perspective and schools as agents for change. For Freire, the educational experience becomes "an invitation to make visible the languages, dreams, values and encounters that constitute the lives of those whose histories are often actively silenced" (65). Critics of education in the United States have presented two opposing goals for education. One is to provide students with the skills they need in order to function within our society. The other is to help them see that society critically. Freire tries to resolve this tension and to imagine alternatives that can lead to changes in education and in society. In his writings, Freire sets forth and defines a number of concepts that he sees as central to what he calls an "education for critical consciousness." In doing so, he integrates and extends concepts that have been introduced earlier in this chapter, concepts that others have defined in more limited and isolated ways.

1. Freire invents the term *conscientization* to express what he believes schools and teachers need to be about. In defining this new term, he moves beyond the narrower sense of "critical thinking" and "active learning" as we saw them used in reports on U.S. education. Conscientization means *active consciousness in the minds of learners*: learners need to recognize both the personal and social dimensions of the subjects they learn. Tricia, as a beginning teacher, is this sort of learner, she draws consciously on her own past learning, her recent teaching experiences, and her understanding of particular social contexts to understand the concept of multicultural literacy. Freire believes that conscientization will result in "action for liberation," as mental and social freedom allows learners to conceive of changes that can occur in society. When Tricia worked to convince the Minister of Education in Belize to initiate an ESL program in the high schools, she helped to create such change, and she reports that "all school districts in the Northern Districts now teach with ESL methods." As a teacher, Tricia has a crucial role in encouraging this process in the minds of her students as well. To carry out this role, Freire believes, the teacher must know herself and her position with regard to the culture as well as fuse with the cultures around her. "The fundamental role of those committed to cultural action for conscientization," Freire says, "is not properly speaking to fabricate the liberating idea but to invite the people to grasp with their minds the truth of their reality" (1985, 85). When Tricia's students write, using their Creole language to express their concerns about world and national issues to world leaders, they're recognizing and asserting the validity of their language and their lives, and they're changing the consciousness of the people they write to.

2. Freire emphasizes *the power of language to shape consciousness*. He

asserts that teachers must begin with words that name the important elements of their students' lives. (In his case, these students are the poor and illiterate peasants in rural Brazil.) The students can then be given ways to rename and ultimately to reshape that reality, but always in ways that grow out of their own experiences. For Freire, the names of the tools the peasant uses become ways to talk about the peasant's relationship with the land and the owners of the land. For the students in the high school class that Mark described in the beginning of this chapter, the students' naming of guys with bicycle helmets as "geeks" becomes a way to talk about the social categorization that defines the lives of students. The literacy that grows out of the renaming and reshaping of reality will become a *critical literacy*.

3. For Freire, literacy itself can grow out of illiterate people's common experience in reading the world. All learners read signs, and literacy is a way to read the signs of signs. If a peasant sees leaves turned up, he knows that a storm is coming. He is reading a sign for the event. A symbol on the page moves him into one more level of abstraction from the event itself, but the process of reading that symbol is like a process he already knows and uses. This is important. For Freire, *learning is using and developing strategies already embedded unconsciously in all the activities of the learner.* The Trackton children that Heath studied used a familiar strategy to understand the meaning of their school texts. They talked about them in the ways that their parents talked about the newspaper on the front porch. When their teachers did not allow such talk in the classroom, the children often had problems as readers. But Heath's teachers learned to let their students use and build on these unconscious strategies that supported their developing literacy.

4. Because learning begins with what the learner already knows and uses, *the role of the teacher is to make these strategies conscious and systematic.* For Freire, learners are full of concepts and of strategies for knowing them. What they need to do is to become conscious of their ways of knowing and conscious of how to transfer their understanding of their world to an understanding of the word of the written text. Freire recommends that the teacher use texts that students themselves write, "the popular library" of works that students develop out of the circumstances of their own lives. In this way, educators learn to talk with learners, not simply *to* them or *about* them. As the students of Roadville and Trackton go out into the community, to collect the community knowledge of crops and ways of planting, they create texts out of the lives of the community, and then learn to systematically build on that knowledge in the formal terms of school. Freire issues to teachers a strong argument and a warning: to the extent that education provokes and nurtures

learners' consciousness, it is a liberating enterprise. To the extent that it limits consciousness, it is dominating. The teacher herself helps liberate or dominate by the choices she makes in guiding learners toward or away from gaining consciousness.

5. Freire sees *teaching and learning as a continuum for both student and teacher*, where teachers learn and learners teach and where the acts themselves happen simultaneously and naturally: "Only authoritarian educators deny the solidarity between the act of educating and the act of being educated by those becoming educated; only authoritarians separate the act of teaching from that of learning in such a way that he who believes himself to know actually teaches, and he who is believed to know nothing learns" (1988, 41). Conroy's realization that his students teach him — "I wondered if they felt sorry for me because I knew nothing about scrinching" — leads him to see himself as a learner and changes the dynamics of his classroom.

6. Teachers, like students, join in the creation of new knowledge as they participate in the process of discovery and authenticate the knowledge their students create. What comes from such a classroom is *authentic knowledge*, knowledge forged from the joint quests of teacher and students. Real learning, then, means personal, liberating knowledge. For Freire and many of the other critics of the educational scene we've mentioned in this chapter, the kind of learning that often goes on in schools is not made personal or liberating. It is education for pacification or domestication, not for critical consciousness. And it creates students who sit silently, passively, not students who speak and act.

We can see the beginnings of the sort of education Freire calls for in some of the classrooms we've visited in this unit. Our own inquiry has shown us how students like Allison can draw on their own lives and experiences, link those experiences with the literature they read, like *The Diary of Anne Frank*, and use one to help them understand the other. It's shown us how prepractice teachers, like Janet, can draw on their own experiences of schooling to help them see the classrooms before them and explore what learning might be. It's shown us how student teachers, like David, can learn to listen to students' voices and help them find a way out of their silence. It's shown us how a beginning teacher, like Tracey, looks critically at her own class and at other classes as she tried to find ways of connecting home and school language in her classroom. And it's shown us how experienced teachers, like those Mark observed, develop new areas of curriculum to expand students' cultural perspectives or try out new process–oriented methods that will involve students more actively in their own learning. Each of these students and teachers has identified a step along a path toward creating and participating in the sort of learning that can lead to "critical consciousness," to a "critical literacy."

Multicultural education should help students and teachers be critical about their own positions in educational and political systems, teach them to become conscious of how and what they learn, show them that they are not deficient but come with skills and strategies that can and must be valued by the educational setting. In the next units of this book, we'll consider more specifically how critical literacy can be fostered in the English classroom. But like critical literacy, a critical pedagogy contains more questions than answers, more learning than teaching. And so our discussion will continue to offer directions and possibilities, not answers and prescriptions, for an education that grows out of the consciousness of learners. And we'll ask you to continue to be critical participants in and observers of classrooms, to be critical respondents to your own experiences, to be critical readers of this book, and to give voice to your questions and wonderings. You should also be prepared to question yourself, your skills, your motives, and your strategies, to develop your own critical, unquiet pedagogy.

End-of-unit maxims — strategies for changing the course of the stream

Geneva Smitherman writes: "Certainly it is easier to work on fitting people into the mainstream than to try to change the course of the stream" (241). But, like Freire, she would argue that the stream must also be changed. These strategies come from all the chapters in this unit. They are suggestions for helping students feel a part of the mainstream of school culture and, at the same time, for changing the course of the stream of that culture.

1. Build on what learners know. Use students' own references and habits, let them tell their own stories. For children who are bilingual or from nonmainstream cultural backgrounds, the ability to relate new school knowledge to family ways of knowing is crucial so that learners don't end up having to suppress and deny their own backgrounds, like Richard Rodriguez, in order to be a part of the school culture. But the emphasis on connecting home to school should be made even in classrooms where all children are from a mainstream background. Since children come to school already competent as language users, schools need to provide ways to extend their competence rather than replace it.
2. Allow other ways of knowing into the classroom. Consider the implications of gender, class, race, and ethnicity in making assignments, in creating classroom dynamics of groups. And consider the effect of stereotypes in deciding about abilities and potential.

3. **Make room for lots of talk in the classroom.** Knowledge gets shared primarily in oral ways; that means that talk and listening promote literate behaviors. Everything we've discussed indicates that there needs to be a lot of language in the classroom, student talk as well as teacher talk, and student-to-student talk as well as student-to-teacher talk. The writing of the academic essay, something that is now considered a marker of literate behavior in students, was until the twentieth century seen as a more or less debased form of oral speech used primarily as a mnemonic device for oral presentation. Oral delivery was a literate form, often the highest form, as the valedictorian's address to the graduating class still suggests. And oral language should become a "privileged" part of the curriculum once again. Of course, there needs to be written talk as well in the classroom and lots of it. But, just as oral talk should vary from formal to informal and from audience to audience, written talk should take many forms, personal as well as analytical, informal as well as formal, narrative as well as expository, speculative as well as definitive.

4. **Include in your own classroom's literary canon works by nonnative English speakers, by women, by minorities — in order to show the multiple perspectives writers and thinkers take on experience.** Have students bring in literature they have loved, or ask them about cultural groups they'd like to know about, to read something about, and figure out together how to identify an interesting story or poem or essay that would reflect the culture of that group. Teachers sometimes are stymied by their own perceived inability to teach about other cultures they are not familiar with. But literature creates its own world of shared knowledge and invites any reader to enter it, and readers can learn to pick up cues within the text's world that allow them to draw inferences about the cultural perspective the text operates within. The world the text creates then can be re-created by the reader, including the teacher. And in the multicultural classroom the teacher shouldn't think of herself as the only informant in the group; she can draw on the knowledge of others in the classroom community who know more than she about other ethnic groups or races. Learning from them, she shows herself to be a learning member of the group, and she shows them that they have something to teach as well as something to learn.

UNIT 2

Literacy and the Learner

*I*n Unit 1 we talked about the English classroom and its learners in the larger context of what we know about learning, about language, about culture, about society. And we looked as well at the context in which the study of English takes place — looking, as ethnographers do, at patterns of meaning within English classrooms.

In this unit we'll focus more specifically on the relationship between the individual learner and the traditional subject areas of the English curriculum — grammar, reading, writing, literature. These divisions are themselves a construct that has arisen out of the political and intellectual history of the field, and like all of our models of the world, the framework can be restructured and reconceived. So we let these subjects spill out of their rigid divisions. And, although Chapter 6, for example, will look more specifically at what we know about writing, and Chapter 7 about reading, a common focus will run through all four chapters, a focus on the learner who is using language for knowing and meaning making.

We're bringing the premises of Unit 1 to Unit 2: that growth in literacy and in new uses of language, including writing, takes place in and is fostered by a social/cultural context; that the learning of new forms and uses of language, including both reading and writing, requires active use of that language for negotiating shared meanings about real purposes; that the making and reading of literature is continuous with our other daily uses of language, and that all of this involves the imaginative, creative faculty of mind.

We can turn again to the ethnographies written by prepractice students to see how individuals use language to place themselves in relationship to particular contexts. In the selection from Anthony's ethnography of an urban high school that began Chapter 3, the writer tried to create distance and objectivity, and used language that obscured his role as viewer and interpreter as much as possible. There were no first-person pronouns; for example, things became actors — "a milieu provokes inattentiveness" — and where a human perspective was represented, it appeared in a general, impersonal form, as in "one feels slightly uncomfortable." We can surmise that Anthony was resisting being implicated in classroom practices he saw as alienating.

In another ethnography, we find the student wholly involved with her own, subjective view of the classroom she observed. Pam writes first of her own background — of the school she attended in a nearby town and of her expectations as she enters this one. As she moves into the classroom, she tells us not only what she notices but what she thinks about the things she sees.

> It appears to me, as I've observed interactions in the halls before and after classes as well as those in class, that the students at this school do not need an awful lot of discipline. What I mean is I haven't observed any hall monitors; kids walk around without passes; I don't think I've seen one kid walk in late for class; nobody loiters around at their lockers yapping (like I used to); it all seems too perfect ... too controlled, or something. Maybe they're just a lucky school. As I'm walking through a quiet corridor, I peek into other rooms to see kids working, raising their hands with questions, talking with the teacher, etc. which is all *good*, but my God, I've never heard a single teacher yell, raise his/her voice in authority, or anything. Now I know I didn't go to a high school of juvenile delinquents, but we all weren't angels either. Do you know how Mr. Y quiets down his class? He simply raises his hand in the air without speaking. And they all stop. (Heil, Hitler or what?)

The "I" places Pam nicely within her account; we hear her voice, and we hear her thoughts, especially in parenthetical comments like "(Heil, Hitler or what?)," and ironic commentary like "Maybe they're just a lucky school." But the subjective focus has allowed this student, also, to keep her distance, and it has kept her from going beyond her own perspective to discover the perspectives of the students and the teacher.

Each of the stances of these ethnographers — objective or subjective — is a perfectly good starting place for learning. Each assumes a way of looking at the world, and in each case that way of looking is represented by the writer's language. But the contrast in the stances of these learners suggests some questions we want to raise about language and literacy and their relationship to the learner.

Our students found out when they observed a classroom that ethnography involves more than the recording of impressions. And, like ethnography, literacy involves more than just learning to decode words or to write them. It brings with it particular habits of mind and ways of looking at our experience — our characteristic stances. We've seen that language allows us, as human beings, to capture aspects of that experience, to see them for ourselves and to communicate them to others. Literacy facilitates this process. Recording what we see and name and capture, reseeing it, comparing what we have recorded to what other people in other places or at other times have recorded about similar events — all of this helps us to take a broader perspective, to see that our view of an experience and the name we give to it at one moment is not the only view or the only name. What Allison, in Chapter 2, named as "frightening" when she saw it from her perspective as a child (when she could think only of what her mother's illness meant for her) she could rename as not-so-frightening when she saw it again as a teenager (when she became as concerned for her mother as for herself); and she could compare the two perspectives and name the change in them as well: "maturity." In the process she traded her childlike subjectivity ("What does it mean to or for me?") for a more characteristically adult stance, not of detached objectivity but of connected caring and understanding.

Likewise, what our students saw as "objective reporting" or "personal impressions" changed as they studied the patterns of language revealed in their own ethnographies and those of their classmates. Seeing another's terms led them to question and define their own, as Tricia uses her response to another ethnography to examine her own concepts of informal and formal class structures.

> How instructive to read an ethnography of the same classes that I observe! Laura achieved an objectivity which eluded me. Her descriptions were pointed yet detailed and she encompassed the comfortable sense of loosely constructed routine which was so important to this class's successful functioning. Yet her description of the class makes it seem far more rigid than my own which causes me to ask: am I inclined to like and feel comfortable in an informal atmosphere, and did I impose that vision on this class to somehow psychologically affirm my own thoughts: "See, it *can* be done. This class thrives in an informal mode." (Tricia)

In the first unit of this book, we turned at intervals to the experiences of a writer and teacher, Pat Conroy, to reflect on the larger issues of learning and language and context. In this unit we will turn to a novel that continues to be read in most high school classrooms, J. D. Salinger's *The Catcher in the Rye*. The main character of this novel,

Holden Caulfield, is an adolescent who is trapped in the subjectivity so characteristic of adolescents (and which Salinger has named and captured so well with his novel that the name Holden Caulfield has become, in effect, a name for an extreme of adolescent angst). All events have meaning only as they affect him, and most of the time he shows little critical perspective on his experience. Everything that happens, happens *to him*, and happens mostly to annoy him, whether it is the way an elderly teacher looks or the way a former roommate cleaned up. He can't see that others might perceive these events differently. And in his intense subjectivity, he is almost unable to function except in reaction to these things that others do.

But Holden is learning about the world, and his sensitivity extends to his analysis of the motives of others. He realizes that his elderly teacher feels bad about failing him and gives him "the old bull" about how he would have done the same thing in the teacher's place. As he leaves, he changes his language and renames his failure in terms that the teacher can accept. "'Look, sir. Don't worry about me. I'm just going through a phase right now.'" As Holden's responses change, or when he wants others to think they have changed, he changes his language. While he primarily sees what things mean *to him*, he's very involved in thinking about what they mean and in finding words to represent that meaning. Holden's language represents his responses to the world around him, just as the prepractice students' responses to the classrooms they observed were represented in the words they chose.

The important question about language and about literacy is how it allows us to place ourselves in relation to the world — how it supports our process of "making sense" or making meaning. But while language is the primary subject of study in the English classroom, that "subject," and the way it is taught, usually has little connection to the ways we use language to make sense of the world. The study of language, of reading, of writing is too often seen not as a way of perceiving the world or representing ourselves to others, but as a series of technical terms or steps, to be memorized or followed. Yet the learner in the classroom makes sense both of the classroom and of the larger world through language. That learning is a continuous process, one that pulls thinking and naming together with speaking, listening, writing, and reading.

Because our focus in this unit will be on how the study of language and literacy intersects with the individual learner, we'll move from looking at the classroom and school culture as a whole to looking closely at individual learners in the classroom. Teachers continually focus on the individual as they evaluate a student's performance in the classroom: the student's writing, reading aloud, behavior in small-group work, attitude toward writing on the board, friendships with others in the class. These studies are informal, sometimes almost unconscious, as the teacher attempts to match his teaching to a student's learning. But to examine theoretically how a learner works in the English classroom, it's helpful to engage in a more formal look at the individual. The "Strategies" chapter contains suggestions for undertaking a case study of a learner. But the systematic observation of a learner can begin with notes in a journal about a student's interactions with peers, with the teacher or observer, and with her own reading and writing.

The larger life of the classroom and school and the community she's surrounded by shapes the learning of the individual student. And the ways of seeing learning and language that we've discussed in Unit 1 shape our teaching of the subjects of the English classroom — reading, writing, language, and literature. We can begin now to look at learners, and at what they learn, from a new perspective. This unit will explore how the classroom can make conscious and systematic what learners do unconsciously as they become literate — how classrooms can foster the literacy of the individual.

CHAPTER 5

Language and Literacy

The Catcher in the Rye's Holden Caulfield isn't a model student. He's just been kicked out of his fourth private school, where he has failed every subject except English, passing that only because he managed to write pretty good compositions. His roommate Stradlater asks, as a final favor, that he write one for *him*, a descriptive essay.

> "Just don't do it *too* good, is all," he said. "That sonuvabitch Hartzell thinks you're a hot-shot in English, and he knows you're my roommate. So I mean don't stick all the commas and stuff in the right place." (38)

Holden knows that being good at writing compositions is *not* about sticking commas in the right place. But Stradlater has a point. Instruction in English has traditionally focused a good deal of attention on commas — on punctuation and spelling and grammar. Students who have trouble with the surface level of their writing, whose spelling is so-so and whose subjects and verbs don't always agree, watch other people get A's on essays while they get C's and D's, and they soon make the equation: good grammar equals good writing. "If I could just learn the rules and all the exceptions," they say, "I'd be getting A's too." These are the students who want their freshman composition classes to give them a strong dose of grammar. They hope that what didn't take before will take this time, like a vaccination, and that they'll finally be good at writing compositions.

Holden thinks that Stradlater does write "lousy" compositions, that even if he learned everything about where to put commas, he wouldn't solve the problems in his writing. But even students who are good writers believe they're bad because of their errors. "I can't write at all!" one of our students complained. "I know I always have a million run-ons, and I can't spell worth anything either." Even this good writer worried that her mistakes made her a poor writer because she didn't "know any grammar."

When they're not writing but speaking, people still sometimes feel inadequate about their control over grammar. We ourselves have laughed ruefully at the reactions we get when we mention our line of work to a new acquaintance. "You're an *English* teacher?! I'd better watch my language!" As often as not, soon afterwards there comes a lull in the conversation or a discreet ending to it. When confronted by the person they regard as the primary judge of grammatical competence—the English teacher—many people feel suddenly uncomfortable about the language they use. They stop talking before their "mistakes" are found out.

What makes writers, both good and bad, feel that the quality of their writing is determined by whether they have their commas in the right place or have run-on sentences? What makes competent language users believe they are incompetent? To answer these questions, we need to look at the relationship between writing and speaking and the knowledge of school rules of grammar. In this chapter, we'll examine the false assumptions about the relationship between learning grammar and using language, and then we'll consider the ways in which language and grammar can be studied meaningfully and productively in the English classroom.

Grammar = error = good or bad writing

> Funny you should mention grammar problems. My struggles with the set rules of our language have quite long roots. I'm a poor speller. I always remember seeing lots of comments in big red lettering with the word "agreement" marked all over high school compositions, too. Punctuation gives me headaches in the hyphen, colon, or semi-colon and who or whom realm. The strangest part about all of this is that I can ramble off rules with the greatest of ease, pertaining to these aspects of our written language. All throughout grade school and high school I was able to achieve A's in grammar and composition classes because the textbook exercises never gave me any problem. (Clare)

Reflecting on her competence in grammar for an assignment in our prepractice class, Clare comments on the relationship between rules and writing. She knows the rules, but strangely enough they never seem to apply to what she writes. Though she doesn't see herself as a poor writer because she has agreement problems, she knows from experience that to some people, particularly teachers, grammatical problems signal writing incompetence. She also knows from experience that the memorizing of rules of grammatical conduct has meant nothing to her development or skill as a writer.

Clare's confession is revealing but not really surprising. As we saw in Chapter 3, research tells us that people don't learn by memorizing a set of rules or concepts and then applying them to some particular situation. They learn in the context of the situation itself. The rule comes intuitively, naturally, as it proves useful over and over again. The linguistic rule may even be embedded in the deepest cognitive structures of the mind, awaiting the occasion to be activated. Whether it's embedded by nature or implanted by use, a child learns grammar as he learns all language, in order to react to his environment and to act on what surrounds him. The child shifts from "Joey wants" to "Me want" to "I want" over a period of a year in a development of grammatical competence that is regular, predictable, and unaffected by his anxious parents' instruction to "say 'I.'" Yet, despite the fact that common experience confirms what linguists have found—that people know grammar intuitively and that explicit instruction in rules of grammar makes little difference to their knowing—classrooms continue to equate good writing with correct writing and to teach grammar as the way to make that writing correct. *Grammar* becomes the classroom's catch-all label for formal correctness and, for some, for literacy itself.

Typically, grammar is taught as though it were something quite separate from the real language it describes, as though the word *noun* meant something apart from *Joey* as a person who operates in the world, and as though *verb* named something different from Joey's real activity or desire. Students memorize definitions—"A noun is a name for a person, place, or thing"; they don't look at how a noun works in a sentence, or how it refers meaningfully to the world: "Who is this baby Joey and what does he want?" In school, students learn rules of grammar, by repetition or memorization. To test the effectiveness of their memory and of the drills the teacher employs to aid memory, students are often given a list of sentences to mark: "Is this the party to who/whom I am speaking?" Students can complete exercises like these perfectly, but Clare's experience suggests what happens—and doesn't happen—when the grammar drill stops and essay writing begins. There's rarely a transfer. Students learn the rule, learn how to apply it, but for the moment only. When they write, they still write "That is the person who I was speaking to" even when the essay gets returned to them with the word circled prominently.

The linking of error and grammar and the belief that error correcting is the primary purpose of language study are often responsible for students' poor attitudes about themselves as writers. In the prepractice class when we asked students to identify a personal grammatical flaw, each person not only could describe the error but knew its textbook term. Students knew the abbreviations found in grammar textbooks— *r/o, frag, sp, c/s, agr,* or *pro ref*—and acknowledged that their teachers had pointed out these errors again and again on papers throughout their schooling. (Usually in red ink. Of fifteen students writing this exercise, eight of them mentioned red ink as they talked about their grammatical problems.) As our students proved, however, the marks don't tell them much about what the linguistic problem is or how to solve it. "My teachers always told me I had a serious problem with run-on sentences. I still have it," wrote Jeanmarie.

As a prepractice student, Deb commented in her journal on her supervising teacher's ideas about grammar instruction:

> We also talked about the way Mr. Rettman teaches grammar. He, like the philosophy of our class, feels that grammar is important but can be taught through the students' own compositions. He is much more interested in the students' thought processes in composing than he is in mechanics. He said he has been criticized by his colleagues who teach the traditional methods but that really doesn't bother him. To back up our theory he showed me a new software program for the Macintosh computer called MacProof. This software corrects spelling, checks for problems of usage such as racist or sexist words, words that are often confused (it's/its—my worst one!) and imprecise and wordy writing. It even searches for problems in style. This just proves that today, mechanics are just that, mechanical. The actual content is what teaching should be focusing on.

Deb's discussion with her teacher and her belief in herself as a competent writer leads her to recognize that her grammatical errors don't represent her writing ability and that grammar won't be the most important element in her teaching of English. But grammar looms large in the classroom, and students, who feel less than competent in this area themselves, worry a lot about how to teach it.

> I'm writing up a grammar lesson. I don't know any grammar. I need a review if only to be able to say to students "you don't need to know grammar." I was disconcerted at all the misspelled words written on the blackboard during our videotaped presentations. I winced. I am not very keen on the notion that spelling and grammar are acquired through boring repetitive exercises. But as a teacher, mentor, authority figure, I figure it is important to spell correctly, use the semicolon correctly—not fragment my sentences (my terrible habit, I've discovered). (Sara)

If you look back at the prepractice students' comments on their own writing mistakes throughout this section, you'll see that when they talk about error students use words like *terrible, worst, awful*. People—not just our students, but the stranger who "watches his language" when he confronts an English teacher, and sometimes even the teacher himself—see error as a kind of evil, almost a moral lack or at least a shameful lapse in behavior. (There's a history for this view of error as sin. The Scottish moral philosophers in the eighteenth century regarded error as willful disobedience, and these men strongly influenced the teaching of rhetoric and writing during the nineteenth century and even in our own time.) The teaching of grammar, then, becomes the "necessary evil" to purge the greater evil of error.

Matt encountered just such a classroom in his student teaching. It was a classroom filled with what their history teacher described to him as "*basic* kids.... Most of them are as smart as you or I. Their ex-

perience is different, though. And all of this — history, English, math — is totally irrelevant to their lives." Matt describes his cooperating teacher's goals for these students in terms of her desire to remedy the evil of error in their writing:

> A believes that it is her duty, her *mission*, to impart to these kids all those basic skills they have not acquired but ought to have acquired by this time. She is drawing the line. The buck stops here. They *will* learn it and they will learn it by *drill*, by repetition, by testing. She seems to think that they have not gotten this already — that the teachers of these kids have not done their jobs or had some silly educational misconceptions. It is A's job to repair the damage.

Matt questions whether the teacher's mission can be accomplished, or accomplished in this way: "The more I see, the less I am convinced." One reason that Matt questions the zeal of the teacher in drilling students on grammar is that he himself feels the effects of grammar instruction in his own writing.

> My worst grammatical problem is spelling. But worse, is a usage problem. Or maybe it's a grammatical problem too. I think I repeat the same forms again and again, that I lack versatility of expression. Then too, it often seems stiff to me, or mannered. I sampled the writing of five students in the two classes I am observing and found a similar problem. The students are either remedial 11th graders or regular 12th graders. I was surprised to find that there wasn't a clear distinction in the writing of one class compared to the other. A student in the 11th grade class wrote a couple of paragraphs describing a run in he had with a doberman pincer. The writing was good, virtually without error. But it was limited to simple sentences and simple compound sentences: "But I know that the summer is over. I am going to school and I have a part time job." This kid's writing was remarkable because it was so well policed; he knew he wasn't qualified or authorized to get fancy in any way. A 12th grader wrote about the death of her grandfather. It too was very good in the same way. This student, however, tried once to break out of the simple sentence confinement but didn't succeed. "After that it was downhill after operation after operation he decided to go home and wait to die with his family." She really does come close to saying something like "after two more operations, he decided to go home and die," but can't quite get it out. Another student in the 11th grade had this kind of problem throughout his writing. I wanted to go over the whole thing with her and rewrite it in its simplest form. (Matt)

It's interesting how Matt connects his writing to that of the students whose work he reads. He begins with a complaint about his own "grammatical" problems — spelling and "dull" usage — "repeating the same forms" over and over again. When he encounters a student who suffers from a similar usage problem, Matt acutely surmises that it's the student's fear of being wrong, of having the red pen leave its mark, that keeps his sentences simple and his ideas at a surface level. Nevertheless, when Matt reads the work of another student, one who does go beyond the simple form (and not coincidentally at a moment of emotional response), Matt's teacherly desire is to "get it right," to simplify her writing or clean it up — in fact, to repeat the same correct but dull forms he has complained about in his own writing. Matt's introductory subordinate clause leads into a compact and "correct" sentence. But the student's "run-on" conveys the feeling of her grandfather's progressive slide toward death (and could be easily corrected without losing the emotion.) Is his version really better for the telling of this story?

The next semester, as a student teacher, Matt learns more about the "grammar issue" as he remembers that the students in his prepractice class had at least been able to fill a page. The students in his new school don't get more than three or four sentences onto the paper when he asks them to write. They've been drilled and tested for grammatical correctness twice a week during the semester, however. Matt begins to perceive a connection: drills have given these students little practice as writers, and their fear of being punished by the red pen for committing the evil of error keeps them from writing at all.

If one goal of grammar instruction is to reduce grammatical errors in writing, teachers need to begin by ascertaining what will *not* work toward that goal.

1. Memorization is useless, except with some mnemonic devices that are most effective for spelling. (Remember "there is a rat in 'separate' "?) But memorizing rules for comma placement, the list of possible sentence patterns, the number of coordinate conjunctions, the definition of a gerund will not produce changes in students' writing.
2. Applying rules of grammar to sentence exercises or even clever worksheet exercises is not much better. Students will not make the connection to their own writing with the fill-in-the-blanks approach to grammar instruction.
3. Correcting all grammatical errors in a piece of writing by identifying them or exhorting the student to "fix" them doesn't improve the writing, especially if the student is unfamiliar with the grammatical term or construction. "Too many comma splices. This is a serious writing problem" is the sort of note seen on students' papers. But the note is almost never followed by any discussion of what a comma splice might be or even where one lurks in the paper being evaluated.

To understand more clearly why this sort of activity and instruction has no effect on error, we must step back to consider what grammar is and how it relates to writing. The grammar issue is one that goes beyond arguments about whether or not students should be quizzed on their understanding of restrictive and nonrestrictive modifiers. It hits close to the heart of discussions and arguments about literacy itself, about how literacy is established, nurtured, and certified.

What grammar is

In "Grammar, Grammars and the Teaching of Grammar," Patrick Hartwell begins by citing an exhaustive research study done in 1963 by Richard Braddock, Richard Lloyd-Jones, and Lowell Schoer, who concluded "in strong and unqualified terms" that "the teaching of formal grammar has a negligible or, because it usually displaces some instruction and practice in composition, even a harmful effect on improvement in writing" (37–38). Despite this evidence and much that has followed it in the last twenty-five years, the arguments about teaching grammar still fester even when they don't rage. Hartwell summarizes the positions of the grammarians and antigrammarians in terms of what each believes about writing:

> Those of us who dismiss the teaching of formal grammar have a model of composition instruction that makes the grammar issue "uninteresting" in a scientific sense. Our model predicts a rich and complex interaction of learner and environment in mastering literacy, an interaction that has little to do with sequences of skills instruction as such. Those who defend the teaching of grammar tend to have a model of composition instruction that is rigidly skills-centered and rigidly sequential: the formal teaching of grammar, as the first step in that sequence, is the cornerstone.... The controversy over the value of grammar instruction is inseparable from two other issues: the issues of sequence in the teaching of composition and of the role of the composition teacher. (108)

We'll be talking about both the teaching of writing and the role of the teacher in later chapters. What we want to emphasize here is that schools focus on grammar instruction and teachers worry about grammar as error because of commonly held beliefs about how grammar is connected to writing and literacy. Yet there isn't just one definition of grammar and our catchall term really stands for a number of different aspects of language and its use. Hartwell defines five separate meanings for the term *grammar* as it's employed by theorists and teachers:

> Grammar #1 is the "grammar in our heads," the rules we all know intuitively about our language in order to be able to speak it. We talked about this sort of grammatical knowledge in Chapter 3.
>
> Grammar #2 stands for conscious knowing and theorizing about language of the sort that engages the attention of linguists who

study the rules that underlie our production of language. "The rules of Grammar #2," Hartwell argues, "are simply unconnected to productive control over Grammar #1" (115). In other words, conscious attention to rules has nothing to do with the grammar we know unconsciously as users of language, and it is using language, not knowing its rules, that helps us to get new forms into Grammar #1.

Grammar #4, or school grammar, codifies certain rules that students must study and then try to apply to their written work. This is opposed in Hartwell's description to

Grammar #5, or stylistic grammar. This describes the linguistic knowledge of prose style, and it combines rhetorical skill in communication with the active manipulation of forms. This grammar is developed by manipulating language in meaningful contexts and with conscious attention to form.

And Grammar #3? Hartwell names it but leaves it out of his larger discussion, assuming that enough attention has been given to usage, or what he calls "linguistic etiquette." But it's #3 that gives students the most trouble in writing and perhaps in speaking as well. People's notions of right and wrong in language and how that determines performance as well as status come from mistakenly seeing Grammar #3, how we use language, as Grammar #1, our intuitive knowledge about the structures of the language we speak. So we'll talk later in this chapter about how to focus attention productively on the use of language in particular contexts.

Hartwell argues that teachers must stop the "worship" of grammar study and learn to trust more in Grammar #1—the unconscious and organic use of grammatical forms by all language users:

> We need to attempt some massive dislocation of our traditional thinking, to shuck off our hyperliterate perception of the value of formal rules, and to regain the confidence in the tacit power of unconscious knowledge that our theory of language gives us. (121)

Although Hartwell mounts an impressive argument, reflecting a half-century of evidence, against traditional practice in teaching grammar, arguments like his have had little effect on how language is studied in the English classroom.

Grammar and school culture

Despite the evidence of theorists and teachers, and the even more imposing evidence of personal experience and memory, there remains a real disjunction between what schools teach about language and how language really works. If teachers and students know intuitively that teaching grammar as error correction doesn't work to eliminate error, they also know intuitively the powerful traditions of school culture. Traditions are difficult to counter, difficult even to question when a person is a participant in the tradition, as teachers are. And the teaching of grammar in the English class is one of the most time-honored if not the most fondly recollected of traditions. Think, for example, about the way you were taught nouns and verbs. Ask a friend from another community how she or he was taught. Ask your parents. Ask us. We bet the teaching of the noun and verb — "Where's the action?" "Who's doing it?" "Underline the noun once and the verb twice!" — didn't vary much for any of these groups.

Part of the way teachers learn to teach is by remembering and applying to their own situations the ways they themselves were taught, and this is especially true of grammar instruction. Because so many teachers feel uncomfortable with teaching grammar, they fall back on what they read in textbooks and curriculum guides and what they remember. They repeat the lists and rules and drills that they learned and that they see still used in books for their own students. This assimilation of grammar teaching is unconscious rather than critical, making it hard for teachers to see its political and social dimensions. With their attention to errors and exercises, teachers inadvertently end up suggesting that literacy is equivalent to names and labels. With their emphasis on particular forms of language, teachers certify a certain standard and a certain compliance to it, especially in writing, but in speaking as well. The standard is based on the conventions of particular groups of speakers — those with dominant positions in the society. There are debates about whether or not the standardizing of language should be a goal for the classroom at all, given that groups without the "privileged" grammatical code might become even further disenfranchised in classrooms that acknowledge only one code. But in this chapter, we'll assume what so far remains the case, that schools will continue to stress the importance of communication in Standard English, and we'll focus on how to meet that goal more effectively.

The traditions of English instruction are apparent in almost any classroom. A prepractice teacher described in his journal a typical grammar lesson that he observed.

> The rest of the class period was devoted to a grammar lesson. John is going through a grammar outline, having the kids copy it into their notebooks. Here is today's portion of the outline:
> 7. Verb complements
>   a. Complements complete the meaning of a sentence
>   1.) Direct Object
>   (transitive: has a D.O.)
>   (intransitive: has no D.O.)
>   2.) Indirect Object

The whole rest of the period was devoted to D.O.'s and transitive words. There were some exercises consisting of the same verb used transitively and intransitively, which seemed to help get the point across, but the whole concept seemed really not worth the effort: since D.O. and transitive verbs are defined circularly (each in terms of the other) there didn't really seem anyplace for the class to *go*. They were stuck in that circle. Enough repetitions finally got most of them to be able to get to right answers, but it seems very doubtful to me that this lesson will have any lasting benefit. (David S)

David's observations confirm that, in the classroom, knowing grammar consists largely of being able to label and identify parts of speech and that it remains focused on the components of a sentence. In a final reflection on his semester's journal entries, David comes back to this issue.

> Having learned five languages (including English), I know that explicit teaching of grammar doesn't help anyone to communicate — I've been in plenty of foreign language classes in which students can ace tests but can't keep up a conversation in the target language for more than two sentences, and if this is true in a second language, it must be even more true in our native language — and the articles we've read (especially Hartwell) provide convincing proof of this, but still John tries to teach grammar explicitly because he feels it's expected of him. John, of course, also knows all the theory, but he does teach grammar in the end because the school wants and expects him to.

David sees how language gets learned in its communicative context. As for learning *about* language, David goes on to connect this with a larger question:

> How do we get kids interested in what's going on in the classroom? How can we get them to care? It's no wonder that kids who are memorizing word lists and copying down a grammar outline into their notebooks feel that school is silly. What they're doing *is* silly. We need to make the reading and writing that goes on in class a meaningful act of communication somehow. Probably at least part of the "somehow" is to have good writer's workshops, where kids read each others' writing and respond as humans, not as grammar textbooks. John tried some workshops, but they didn't work well at all, I think because his instructions ("Pretend you're the teacher!") did not give students the idea that they should respond as real readers. They thought they were being asked "Where would you put a red circle if you were correcting this?" So we need to make workshops a place where kids get their ideas across, and not a place to display samples of writing so we can "practice grammar." Grammar has to be subordinate to the act of writing/communicating, not the other way around. Maybe that would be a step toward making the whole school experience more meaningful to the students.

The rote learning of grammar and the connecting of grammar and error carry over into all other activities of this classroom, keeping even writing workshops from working effectively. David finds that this fundamentally good classroom teacher feels constrained to teach grammar although he "knows the theory." And he decides: "I guess I'll just have to wait and see how much choice a teacher really has in avoiding these tasks that are close to worthless." But there are other choices for John and for David, other ways to meet the constraints of curricular requirements for teaching grammar, and still make grammar study meaningful.

Teaching grammar by studying language

As you've seen already, most Grammar #1 knowledge (referred to by linguists as competence) is acquired unconsciously without direct instruction. This is true for children learning a first language and for adults learning a second language or a second dialect (including Standard Written English). While older children and adults have cognitive resources not available to young children and can learn and apply rules governing various aspects of life and language, these learned rules become internalized and automatic only with constant use in situations where they are meaningful. David notes that students who "ace tests" in foreign language classes can't necessarily use their language to communicate; on the other hand, travelers in other countries learn how quickly communication occurs when it's necessary to get along. The need for forms is, itself, determined by context. Past-tense forms aren't needed for buying fruit; they're needed when you start having longer conversations with people and telling them about the strange looks you got yesterday when you tried to buy kumquats. As forms become important for real communication, speakers notice them, apply them, and, through practice, begin to use them more and more correctly.

As they're exposed to a wider community of speakers, people begin to recognize the places where their language differs from the forms used by others in that community. They acquire new forms from the language they read and hear, and they can learn to monitor their speech and writing for forms that are not used in this wider community of speakers and writers, for "nonstandard" forms. They can also learn rules of prescriptive grammar and apply rules to the editing of their speech and writing. But unless those rules are internalized through intensive and real communicative use in meaningful situations—in real acts of speaking and writing and reading rather than workbook exercise—they'll never become part of the natural language of speakers. Putting Grammar #2—what a linguist knows about how a language works—into Grammar #1 requires intensive use much more than it requires explicit instruction. Instruction allows learners to see and apply patterns, but it shouldn't get in the way, as it so often does, of thinking and communicating.

 Teachers help learners build their unconscious, internalized knowledge of grammar by giving them lots of opportunities for meaningful speaking and writing and reading. And if teachers refuse to focus on error, they encourage students to take the risk of saying more as they speak and write. But errors occur, and teachers need to know how to deal with them in some potentially useful rather than destructive way. So what does a teacher do about those missing *ed* endings?

The first thing to recognize is that errors are errors only with reference to a set of standard forms. In other words, errors are grammatical; they fit the student's developing linguistic system. That means there's a *reason* for error to occur. In many ways, language learning is like other learning. People learn a new language or dialect and (unconsciously) generate hypotheses about what that new language is like, about what its rules are, based on the data of what they hear and read. Speakers test these hypotheses, try out new constructions, and gradually the constructions they create approximate more and more closely the correct (which generally means the most used) forms of the new language. But during this process, speakers and writers are bound to make some errors. In fact, they couldn't learn anything new about the language unless they *did* make some errors. The errors are likely to be in some way logical or consistent because the learner is searching for patterns, like Ellie's student who, having learned that a noun could be formed by adding *tion* to a verb, then added it to every verb he encountered and produced words like *conflictions.* Similarly, children and second-language learners overgeneralize the *ed* form in English, and once they start using it, they use it for all past tenses, even those of irregular verbs: "I goed," "he singed." In these cases, error is an important sign of active learning, for the error shows how speakers are making predictions and trying out solutions, taking risks with the language they're using.

Teachers want to be careful to encourage experimenting with language in this way, and their attention to error should always be in the context of that encouragement. There are some useful ways that teachers can deal with error:

• Ignore the errors. Most learners reproduce the forms they read and hear constantly and will acquire new forms when they are surrounded by them. They'll start to make new errors, but old ones will drop away. (But we recognize that it is hard for English teachers to ignore the pressures that make this whole issue the focus of English instruction. And some learners, particularly those acquiring a second language, will want to know which constructions they've mastered and which they haven't.)

- Watch for evidence that the student knows the principle behind a particular construction. What learners know is likely to be more than what they produce accurately in any particular instance, and there's no point teaching about a construction that a student already understands.
- Give explicit grammatical information when a student asks or when there is a pattern that a student seems to be working on (like overgeneralizing *ed* or creating forms like *conflictions*).
- Let students work together as editors to prepare student writing for some sort of publication. They'll explain a lot to each other in terms that are easier to understand, and editing will be separated from and not confused with writing.
- Stop teaching error—stop making it seem too important by over-emphasizing it in teaching, and, when reading students' writing, mark only the kinds of error a student seems ready to learn about.
- Recognize that few of the errors students make are actually errors in grammar and that few errors will be confronted in any way at all by students' knowledge of parts of speech. Most of what is considered error in student writing has to do not with grammar as such but with the conventions of written text (punctuation, spelling, apostrophes, contractions—*its/it's*) or with conventions of usage—Hartwell's Grammar #3. As Hartwell argues, studies of reading and writing suggest that "surface features of spoken dialect are simply irrelevant to mastering print literacy."

To sum up, teaching school grammar teaches learners very little about language and doesn't prevent error. It actually detracts from students' development in writing because of the time it takes away from writing and because of the false message it gives learners about what's important in writing. But the study of language can serve a useful purpose in the English classroom.

A rationale for the study of language in the English classroom

Learners acquire most important linguistic knowledge unconsciously in an environment that provides rich data. Because this is true, teachers can best facilitate the acquisition of new forms and uses by creating a language-rich classroom where students engage in real acts of communication. We'd like to emphasize again that it's through engaging in interesting and demanding reading and writing and speaking activities that students focus on language in its contexts and reinforce and extend their linguistic knowledge. But the reinforcement must be genuine, in conversations where the focus is on the meaning of what's said and on its effectiveness as a real act of communication.

Conscious knowledge can supplement and reinforce unconscious knowledge, and some conscious knowledge about language and how it works can, itself, focus students' attention on aspects of their own language use. It can also help learners to become aware of choices they have as speakers and as writers, and how the choices that writers have made shape the literature they read. It can help students see the relationship among language and meaning and communication that is at the heart of English study. Developing "the metalinguistic awareness" — awareness of what language is, of how it works, of terms that can be used to describe it — is, then, a worthwhile goal for the English classroom. And, like all other learning that we'll describe in this book, learning about language occurs most effectively when students are engaged in real acts of discovery.

A first step toward beginning a conscious and systematic study of language is to understand more about the sorts of unconscious knowledge people have. Speakers know about the grammatical system of the language they use. Native English speakers would never make a mistake like putting the adjective after the noun — *the mill red* — even though this is its position in some other languages — *le moulin rouge*. They know, as well, the unspoken rules for how to use language to communicate with other people in particular social contexts, and their linguistic etiquette is just fine for contexts they spend a lot of time in. Much of this unconscious knowledge can be turned into conscious knowledge through study. Metalinguistic awareness is enhanced by reading and by writing and, in turn, by talking about the language choices of readers and writers. When students hear and discuss a variety of styles and linguistic codes (including "nonstandard" ones), they become more aware of language as language. This, in turn, increases their own ability to master different codes — different languages and dialects and the etiquette of use that goes with them. Language then becomes central to the curriculum at all levels and the teaching of writing becomes a primary tool for, not simply a proof of, literacy. Several kinds of unconscious knowledge about language can be made conscious and built on in the English classroom.

Language as structure

Lewis Carroll's poem "Jabberwocky" — "'Twas brillig and the slithy toves/Did gyre and gimble in the wabe . . ." — is the classic text that teachers use to illustrate to their students that they do already know how the grammar of English works. Even though its words are nonsense, students can "make sense" of them because they bring their unconscious knowledge of grammar to their reading of the poem. The two lines quoted above can show students that they know the characteristics of different parts of speech — that *slithy* is likely to be an adjective because it ends in *y*, that the word following the familiar auxiliary *did* is likely to be a verb, that a word that comes after *the* and before the verb is likely to be a noun, and that the noun *toves* is plural because it ends in *s*. Students know a great deal about word order — that verbs generally follow nouns ("toves/Did gyre and gimble"), that adjectives come between articles and nouns ("the slithy toves"), and that prepositions are followed by a noun phrase ("in the wabe"). Students can actually generate many principles of English grammar by working in groups on this poem, naming a great deal of what they know. What they don't know how to name, the teacher can offer terminology for.

And what the teacher doesn't know can be looked up. One of the scariest things about getting away from the grammar book is the fear voiced by nearly all of our student teachers. "I feel so *uncomfortable* teaching grammar! I don't know grammar! I am so afraid that a student is going to ask me a specific grammar question I won't be able to answer." But linguists figure out grammatical rules by asking native speakers if a particular construction makes sense. If it does, it must be grammatical. Then they look for patterns to these constructions, describing what they see. Teachers and students can proceed the way linguists do. If students know the basic parts of speech terms that they learned in fourth grade — nouns, verbs, etc. — they can describe everything else they see. They can talk about verbs ending in *ing* and what they do in the sentence rather than worry about naming participles and gerunds. And teachers need to feel that it's all right not to know all the terms of school grammar. The terms don't always describe the way the language works, and almost nobody remembers them all without the book. Teachers can show students how to refer to the grammar book and find the terms they're seeking to describe what they see.

Of course, there are many other activities that can give students a chance to use and talk about their preexisting knowledge of grammatical structure. One prepractice student wrote a short story, leaving blank spaces for students, and then had students fill in the words. The students guessed what would fit best but then purposely put in the least likely noun or verb, creating very funny variations. (Mad Libs works in the same way.)

Ultimately, this knowledge of structure can be applied to students' own texts and to literary ones. It can be used, not to look for error, but to see what the effect is of stringing together a series of verbs — "he was running, jumping, singing, dancing." Or varying expected word order: "Running, jumping, singing, dancing, the boy ran toward Stone Mountain." These become considerations of style, or the uses of language in particular social contexts.

Language in social uses and contexts

Speakers know the stylistic rules of the language of their homes and communities intuitively, from growing up with them. But school isn't home, even where it extends home values. In even the most parochial school, schooling itself emphasizes more formal ways of knowing and a different style of language use than is generally true of the home—it almost always demands a shift from private to public discourse, from informal to formal style. And where school draws students of different cultures, the shift may be more radical—from very different home styles, such as those Heath found in Roadville and Trackton, to the Maintown style, or even from one language to another, as in the case of Richard Rodriguez.

Most children begin early to perceive differences in style and to use them appropriately. They know that they should use more polite forms at Grandmother's, for example—that while they may get away with saying to Mom at home, "I *don't want* any!" they must say, "No thanks, Grandma, I'm too full to eat brussel sprouts," or in some other way offer an excuse or an apology, if they are in fact brave enough to complain to Grandmother at all. Children perceive much about school style too—remember the Athabaskan children who thought that the Scollons' daughter, Rachel, had been to school, even though she was only two, because she spoke what they thought of as school language?

In fact, differences in styles of using language aren't very different from differences in styles of walking or dressing or driving, and everyone picks these up by being exposed to them and by having members of the community point them out and comment on them: a *geek* or *Barney* is someone with a particular style—someone who wears a bicycle helmet. A previously reasonable teenager who hears from his peers "Look at that geek wearing a bicycle helmet" will refuse from that moment on to wear one, no matter what he's learned from his parents about the risk of injury.

All speakers use their intuitive knowledge of linguistic style to copy the styles of friends or teachers or public personalities. In *Ways with Words* Heath quotes a Trackton resident talking to a group of women who are sitting around on the front porch one afternoon. As Dovie Lou begins to talk about a "know-it-all" neighbor, she shows how the neighbor acts by shifting her style of language to that of a television reporter:

> It was a rainy night, you know ain't no use gettin' fussied up to go out on a night like dat. Tessie 'n I go play bingo. But dat ol' woman, she ak like she some Channel Two reporter or sump'n:

*P. B. Evans was seen today on the corner of Center and Main Street....
The weather tomorrow promises to be cloudy for some.* (168–169)

Dovie Lou would be as conspicuous if she used the formal style of the television reporter for her informal, front-porch gossip as if she used front-porch style to report the news on television. But she knows the features of formal television-news style and can use them to entertain her front-porch audience. In the same way, students know, intuitively, much of what is expected in school style. They are quite capable of mimicking the teacher or the principal or the football coach, capturing both personal idiosyncrasies and a more general teacher style. And they can use their knowledge to write scripts with parts for different members of the school community who speak in different styles. When they talk about what kinds of changes they had to make—changes that represent how Tim, the football captain, Mr. Hanley, the coach, and Ms. Brown, the principal, might describe the winning play in the last game to some buddies, to the team, and to parents at an awards ceremony—they will formalize much of this intuitive knowledge.

Such formalizing activities can help make the features of school, or public, or formal discourse style explicit. A next step is to give names to the intuitive knowledge learners uncover. Students who undertake real investigations—analyses of the differences in style in the editorial section of different newspapers, or of differences in their own spoken and written versions of a story they often tell or hear told, or of differences in typical speech patterns of family members of different generations—will discover that they need terms to describe what they're finding. As they perceive patterns and discuss what they see, the teacher can extend their knowledge, as the parent extends the child's, providing appropriate terms as students grope for them, calling their attention to other features related to the ones they've started to describe.

A class that works with the football-play exercise will soon name particular features—vocabulary words, standard grammar, tone, politeness forms—that are key aspects of discourse style. This initial naming can be followed up by further research—research in which students observe and record (in a notebook or on tape) others' language use in different contexts—at home, at school, at the workplace, with friends or strangers. Focusing on a particular speech act—an apology, a greeting, an inquiry—and collecting data on many instances of that act can be a good way for students to begin to formulate questions and hypotheses about styles of language use, and to see that everyone shifts styles to be effective in getting things done in different contexts. The teenager makes a request differently if talking to one parent rather than another ("Dad, you know how you said I could use your car sometimes? Do you think I could use it tonight?" versus "Mom, I'm taking the car now, O.K.?"). The parent will use a request form rather than a command form to get something done by an adult rather than a child ("Would you mind doing the dishes?" versus "Do those dishes *now!*"). And people make these shifts in predictable ways according to the age of the speaker, the relationship of speaker and listener, their relative positions of authority, and so forth.

Students who begin to observe such speech acts discover a great deal about the particular act they're observing, about general features of language use, and about how initial observations can lead to more questions and hypotheses and can shape further inquiry. As freshmen in classes taught by Ellie and colleague Suzy Groden report, they find commonalities: "It doesn't matter whether you're white or black, old or young, everyone gets insulted by someone one time or another." They note particular details: "I observed when an individual approaches another individual or a group, the interrupter has a humbleness about him, and uses words that he hopes don't offend the other person." They begin to notice other aspects of behavior that accompany the speech act: "I've been watching people being insulted by others. I've watched the expressions on their faces, and their movements to this kind of rudeness." They find larger patterns and generate hypotheses. And they consider ways to extend their research. "I'd like to be able to observe more interactions involving discipline. To see if I could locate specific language use that was similar in all parents and children."

When these students move from the observation of a specific speech act to more general, ethnographic observations of the way language is used in a particular context, they begin to discover larger social patterns as well. One freshman discovered this pattern as he recorded language he heard:

> I've noticed that men and women communicate in different ways toward themselves or each other. Women when they talk among themselves seem to have an untranslatable language. I hear my sister talk to her girl friend and they seem to talk around things. When men are talking to women or vice versa it's usually formal talk. When I'm talking with the guys we usually use a lot of slang." (Albert)

And he began to see more about himself as a language user: "For a week's time I recorded the different situations that I found myself in when communicating. I've noticed that I speak in a different manner to my managers at work than I do the employees."

In this process, students begin to perceive more about the study of language. "I learned how others use language to put people down and make them feel low and dumb as if they did something wrong.... Language plays an important role and is powerful." They begin to see language as interesting and worth learning about in the world, not as dull, repetitive, and confined to a grammar text.

Language in speech and writing

Studies of language as it's used in different social contexts can be extended to focus on the shifts in style demanded by the most common school context—writing. As we said in Chapter 3, those who shape schools or are shaped by them usually end up extending features of written language to the way they speak. Students who observe differences between home language and school language (discovering for themselves much of what we discussed in that chapter) soon become aware of these features. Formally comparing spoken and written language can help students to see such differences more systematically, make their understanding of them conscious, and, in the process, develop language for talking about language.

If you tape-record a story as a student tells it to a group of new acquaintances on the first day of class, you'll find a number of differences from the way that student writes the same story for a class collection. Some of these arise from differences between the act of writing and the act of speaking—differences in the demands on the teller's attention for example. Others come from conventions of style—since letters to friends have been replaced by telephone conversations, most writing these days demands the more formal style that's used with strangers.

When students transcribe the tape recordings of their own or another student's story, they must make decisions that immediately heighten their awareness of some conventions of written text. Sentences and paragraphs, for example, are markings that writers use to provide the coherence and phrasing that intonation and pauses would provide in speaking. And punctuation is something that needs to be worked out in writing; the particular marks needed are not so clear from the spoken words. But many students are horrified at first to discover that they don't speak in complete sentences with no errors: "It was difficult to decide where one sentence ended and the next one began." "While telling a story a lot of the sentences are improper and if you were to write them down they would be incorrect." "The grammar in my tape was not too good, and it probably wasn't good in anybody's."

But the differences between spoken and written texts can't be dismissed as "good" and "bad" grammar, as you can see in the following texts of one story told by Dana, a student in Ellie's freshman class. The first (spoken) version was recorded and then transcribed.

> The thing is you gotta know my father ... he's the ultimate ... ah ... perfectionist ... he ... the person that like ... ah ... I heard you talking before that has a schedule of events of everything and wears like a tie to bed ... he and ... a ... on the other hand my brother ... if I may ... ah ... be so coarse ... as to say ... is the ultimate

hard ass . . . and the thing is that I . . . I think is hilarious . . . no one
else does . . . what my father did was he bought a brand new truck
. . . one of those short Isuzu . . . ah . . . pick-ups and . . . ah . . . it was
nice . . . it was shiny . . . and the thing is you got . . . you have to earn
. . . you have to earn the respect from my father. . . . I shouldn't say
points or anything . . . but to be able to use it . . . and he was . . . and
he used the truck . . . and he took it up a . . . ah . . . up a . . . one of
those parking garages . . . yes . . . and how it went was . . . it goes up
a ramp and curves around . . . like where it's gonna . . . and you park
it and . . . ah . . . a funny thing was he didn't put the emergency
brake on and it was in neutral and . . . ironic . . . it's funny because the
truck rolled down the hill missing like . . . Jaguars . . . Mercedes . . .
you know . . . it's coming down and it's missing everything . . . and it
slams into like . . . a gate thing . . . ah . . . concrete fixture somewhat
like . . . you know . . . that over there . . . to only come home . . . yah
. . . to come home and I . . . and I did . . . I wasn't there so I wasn't
able to see my father's face but to see . . . you know . . . the look in
his eyes as my brother was . . . ah . . . you know . . . who was . . . it
would've been hilarious . . . nn ah . . . to this day my brother con-
tends that it's not that bad . . . I look at the truck and like there's no
rear quarter and it's . . . it's totally . . . ah . . . disheveled and I . . . I
think . . . I . . . it's kinda weird of me to think that's a good thing that
happened to him . . . but . . . ah . . . I think its kinda funny.

As they analyzed his transcribed narrative, Dana and his classmates
discovered a great deal about style and audience that would ordinarily
be taught to students as rules. They found that speakers use a style
appropriate to their audience, and that with peers this style is usually
informal. ("It's kinda weird of me to think that that's a good thing that
happened to him, but I think it's kinda funny.") They decided that
speakers can rely on nonverbal, "paralinguistic" ways of communicating
their thoughts, such as pointing to objects around them. ("It slams into
. . . a concrete fixture somewhat like, you know, that over there.")
They saw that speakers can check audience comprehension as they go
along ("You know?"). They also noticed that Dana had to think out
what his story meant as he was telling it, and that he paused, or filled in
with *ah* a lot so that he could think of what he would say next. And
they noticed that he used a lot of *and*'s to connect his ideas as he moved
from one to the next. In listening again to the tape, they realized that
they had asked Dana questions when he finished his story, that as a
speaker he did not have to worry too much about whether he had given
his listeners enough details because they could ask for more where they
needed them.

Dana's written version of this story was entitled "Perfectly
Imperfect."

My father is a very meticulous person: always pointing out details,
doing things by the book and, if it is possible, showing no imper-

fections. My brother, although nothing of the sort, likes to think he is just like him.

It all happened a year ago when my father bought a brand new small-bed pick-up truck, and my brother finally got a chance to drive it. Apparently what had happened when my brother Don took the truck out was that he did not pull the emergency brake on all the way when he parked it. It would not have been so bad if the truck was not parked at the top of a curvy hill in a parking garage. Needless to say, the truck rolled down the hill only to smash into a cement wall structure at the bottom of the garage.

I guess the only luck to come out of this adventure was the fact that the truck did not hit any parked cars on the way down the hill. It would have been a personal thrill for me to see the look on my father's face as my brother brought the truck in the driveway. My brother finally realized he did a stupid thing and that he was not that perfect anymore.

Dana's classmates found his written style to be more formal and appropriate for a wider audience. This time Dana had put everything he wanted his readers to know into words. ("He didn't just say 'like that over there.' He said it was 'a cement wall structure at the bottom of the garage.'") And he was very specific in his choice of words ("a very meticulous person"). They noticed that his sentences were more complex, that writing had allowed him "time to rewrite and to replace 'and' with 'although,'" and that his writing had been "examined when completed for things like proper grammar." These students also recognized other opportunities available to the writer and not to the speaker. Dana had begun with an introduction to his story that prepared his readers for what would follow, then he told the story, and finally he summed up its meaning. His classmates concluded that "written language allows the writer sufficient time to think and organize his/her thoughts." They saw that writers were more more likely, in their stories, to "say exactly what it means. Dana said his brother finally realized he did a stupid thing and that he was not all that perfect any more."

These students moved on to compare the texts of all of their spoken and written stories, to decide on differences they thought were particularly significant, and to write group research reports in which they reported on these differences, drawing from all their data. In the process, they came to discover for themselves a great deal that's usually taught from a textbook about writing. They made explicit things they already knew about speaking. And they learned to make connections that students don't usually make between the two. They saw in their own speaking and writing much of what language study in the English class should teach them. They gained, in the words of one group, "some practical understandings of the differences between written and oral language." And these *practical* understandings are ones they feel they can draw upon and use, as opposed to textbook knowledge.

In the process of doing this work, these students used language to describe what they were finding out about language — a metalanguage. They applied terms they had heard before like *run-on*, they made up terms for features they had not heard described, terms like *fillers* and *acknowledging statements*. And where they found their own terminology cumbersome — as when they had to keep naming facial expressions and gestures and tone of voice — they asked if there was a term to cover this, and then used that term — *paralinguistic elements*. But work like this goes beyond naming. In discussing what they were finding with other students and with the teacher, these learners had a chance to negotiate shared meanings and to extend what they already knew in the ways that Vygotsky has told us learning takes place. And in writing about what they had learned and in sharing that writing with others, they again used language to focus and to push their thinking.

Students don't need pages of workbook exercises on sentence boundaries to do this sort of study. They can see where sentences end in written texts or "run on" in spoken texts and can generate principles of punctuation. They do not have to memorize lists of conjunctive adverbs and rules for when to use them; they can see that a writer can replace *and* with *however* and that such changes can be used to "make clear connections." And they can write their own text (or, as these students did, letters to incoming freshmen) discussing things they find important to remember about formal written language. But they also learn that there are times when it's better to use an informal, familiar style and that their ways of speaking with friends and peers aren't inferior to school discourse but are appropriate to the context. They confirm their competence as language users and enter confidently into learning new, school styles.

Language in the study of literature

Much of what students begin to discover about language from studies like these can carry over to their study of literature. They can look at how different characters speak and how that language helps to "characterize" them. In *Hard Times*, for example, the dialect of each character is closely connected to both social position and moral position. And as characters change, so does their language. The harsh and pompous discourse Mr. Gradgrind uses to assault the students about facts at his school changes as he begins to learn the lessons of Sissy Jupe and to see that facts cannot be separated from human contexts. Gradgrind, who had reprimanded "girl number twenty" for being possessed of no "facts" about a horse, and who praised the student Bitzer for offering the terms "quadruped gramnivorous," is disturbed to find the adult Bitzer to be quite heartless. In the end, Gradgrind seeks feeling from Bitzer, and he speaks of memory and pain, not of facts: "Bitzer, I have but one chance left to soften you. You were many years at my school. If, in remembrance of the pains bestowed upon you there, you can persuade yourself in any degree to disregard your present interest and release my son, I entreat and pray you to give him the benefit of that remembrance" (282).

The main character in Toni Morrison's *Sula* changes styles also, shifting back and forth between a new, formal school style ("The rest of my stuff will be on later") and her old black community style ("Don't you say hello to nobody when you ain't seen them for ten years") when she comes home from college. She brings with her "lovely college words like *aesthetic* or *rapport*," words that sound "comfortable and firm" to her old friend Nell, who cannot really understand Sula's new behavior. And in *I Know Why the Caged Bird Sings*, young Maya Angelou gets in trouble with Momma because she uses a common colloquial phrase "by the way" without recognizing that it comes from a context outside of her home, and that in Momma's world, the phrase is blasphemous when used in other than a religious context, to refer to "the way of Our Lord." Students who have analyzed their own uses of different styles can perceive a great deal in the language of these characters.

What students learn from representations of language in literature can carry over to their understanding of their own use of language as well. One of our student teachers discovered this in her own teaching:

> 2/24—I got some really good ideas from meeting with the other student teachers yesterday. In part of my homework assignment for tonight I took out three lines from *A Raisin in the Sun*; the lines involve nonstandard grammar. I asked the students to tell me what they notice about the language in the three quotes. How does that language differ from the language that they usually read? What is a *dialect*?

> 3/18—I was particularly amused by a [peer editing] incident involving two female students who are friends. Marvia was reading her story making "corrections" or changing to standard grammar as she read. Lina, who was reading the story over Marvia's shoulder, suddenly snatched the paper away from Marvia, exclaiming, "Girl, you aren't reading what's on that page. You write in some kind of dialect!" It was a pleasant exchange and Marvia did not seem to take offense. I was pleased because all the work I had done regarding *dialect* during *A Raisin in the Sun* had paid off. Students were obviously able to use the word, able to recognize a dialect, and attached no stigma to it. A dialect is not an inferior form of a language; a dialect is simply a variety of a standard language. My students are well aware of this distinction. (Margaret)

Margaret creates ways for students to learn about language through all of their work. Understanding about dialects helps them to read this piece of literature, and seeing dialects presented in literature confirms their own experience with language and gives language variation a place as an accepted topic in the classroom.

Students can identify other features of their spoken language that carry over into the literature they read. They are likely to find more repetition in spoken language, for example — a striking feature in a formal speech such as Martin Luther King's "I Have a Dream" speech, or in early literature like *Beowulf*, and in literary "tales."

Language as style in writing

One of our prepractice students who had written about her concerns with grammar began talking about her response by saying, "I remember my teacher telling us one day that she was teaching fragments because all of us had them. And I kept thinking — if you teach it, don't you expect us to learn it?" After we finished laughing, we realized that teaching error instead of teaching grammar was the problem we wanted to address. So, in a short assignment, students made use of their confessions about error by creating small lessons on that problem that they might use with a class. As they generated these lessons, they quickly discovered that a shift away from talking about error becomes a shift toward thinking about style and about choices that a writer makes. Matt, who had felt his own sentences, and those of the students he observed, to be "simple" and "limited" and lacking "versatility of expression," wrote:

> I would like to gather up more student examples of the kind of problem I've described above. I would like to have whole essays consisting of simple sentences, essays consisting of mostly simple sentences and some attempts at diversity, and essays that are made up mostly of failed attempts at diversity. I would talk about how to combine sentences, how to make diverse sentences error free, how to simplify when necessary.

Priscilla's lesson would bring together her own writing and a discussion of the run-on sentence:

> We need to identify "real life" not textbook error. I'll hand out a draft of my own in-process work and several students' work and then groups will identify and make possible corrections, sharing their suggestions with the class and hopefully taking those suggestions back to their own writing.

Another student, Mat P, would focus his grammar lesson on the colon:

> I will pass out xeroxed copies of my sentences where I illustrate the uses of the colon. I might write "We could only agree on one conclusion: the Celtics need Larry Bird." After discussing all the examples, I'll pass around copies of newspaper articles where colons are used and have students read aloud to hear the effect the colon has on the rhythm of the sentence and becoming aware of how the punctuation affects the meaning of the sentence. Later students will sit in groups and construct

sentences using colons. As homework, students will write a short essay, relate it to whatever piece of literature we are studying at the time, and incorporate three colons into their writing.

Reading aloud "to hear the effect the colon has on the rhythm of the sentence," thinking about how the punctuation affects meaning, looking at writing-in-process and making suggestions about it, writing with the options of simplicity or diversity—these are all matters of style in writing. The lessons these students would teach address things that they perceive as "grammatical problems," but, as we've seen, one person's error is another person's (or community's) style. And looking at and talking about those styles, rather than about errors, will allow students to try out what they learn about language in their own writing.

Choices about style in writing are related to concerns about purpose and audience—concerns we'll discuss more in the next chapter. But often these choices overlap with concerns about correct usage. For example, throughout this book we've made choices about the formality of our style. Because we've conceived of the book as a conversation about teaching that grows out of our conversations with many teachers and with students preparing to teach, we've chosen to keep some features of our conversational style—to use contractions like *we've*, for example—or to allow prepositions to stand at the end of sentences or clauses—"the purpose the students were writing for" instead of "the purpose for which students were writing." We've been conscious of using both the feminine pronoun and the masculine, to suggest that boys and girls, men and women are the teachers and learners we imagine. We make similar choices in our classrooms: Ellie consciously chose, and now unconsciously uses, forms like "It's me," to avoid the image of the hypercorrect English teacher. Hepsie steadfastly maintains the Southern dialect feature of dropping the end of *ing*—so that *going* becomes *goin*—asserting the place of this regional variation in the discourse of the wider community. Our choices are related to larger values about language and the messages our language conveys, as well as the immediate purpose or context for our words.

Language as a means of getting things done in the world

People use language, "speech acts" instead of physical acts, to let people know how to get places, to show that they are sorry for other actions, to get other people to do things for them—to assert themselves and act on the world in a variety of ways. To get things done successfully with language, however, everyone must use conventions that other people accept. Getting other people to accept your linguistic forms is in itself an assertion of power. And the conventions for what forms to use are determined in part by communities.

In his book *Word Play*, Peter Farb describes language as a game — a game in which players unconsciously know the rules as well as the strategies of the people they usually play with. He tells of an interaction between a black psychiatrist visiting the South and a Southern policeman.

> "What's your name, boy?" the policeman asked.
> "Doctor Poussaint. I'm a physician."
> "What's your first name, boy?"
> ... As my heart palpitated, I muttered in profound humiliation: "Alvin." (3)

Farb uses this example to illustrate what happens when two people from different communities, who play by different rules, meet. In the larger American speech community, it's not acceptable to address people by race, or to insist on familiarity (or subordination) by calling a stranger by his first name. The policeman does both (*boy* being used as a racist designation for a black man in the South). Dr. Poussaint, a professor at Harvard, plays by the rule of using professional identity to introduce yourself. But the conflicting rules for this word game are really a part of a larger system of power relationships. And in this case, it's the white policeman who holds the power, who refuses to play by Poussaint's rules, and who insists on the speech forms that will force Poussaint to display his inferior status in this Southern white community.

In the classroom, a teacher may assert authority directly, "Put your books away for the test!" or indirectly, "You are about to have an opportunity to demonstrate what you know." No one's language is neutral. The forms people choose, at any instance, place them in relation to others and assert their meanings and intentions.

Students can begin to observe the ways in which people use language to get things done, and the ways in which they use it to demonstrate power or authority or acquiescence in the world around them. They can discover, in literature, the ways in which language affects other people — the way in which a greeting in one of Doris Lessing's *African Stories* can change the relationship between a young white girl and a tribal chief, or the way in which the mother in Tillie Olsen's "I Stand Here Ironing" has had to give into the nameless, faceless authorities she refers to only as "they." They can read, in Maya Angelou's *I Know Why the Caged Bird Sings*, the scene where Maya's grandmother goes into the office of the white dentist who has refused to treat her granddaughter: waiting outside, Maya imagines her grandmother powerfully confronting the dentist, verbally whiplashing him, using her words to drive him out of town. Those students then can write about situations in which they have felt powerless or powerful — perhaps writing first in their journals, then informally to a friend, and finally formally to a person who has some authority in the situation, noting their own shifts in language and style. Students can also begin to study the language of bureaucracy, of politics, of the government doublespeak that creates expressions like *collateral damage* to mean civilian casualties in a war.

While linguists have begun to look at the power of language and how language is used to accomplish particular ends, that subject has traditionally been the focus of rhetoricians. Over the centuries in education as well as criticism, one of the primary ways to explore language as language has been to analyze discourse in terms of its rhetoric. As you probably know, the art (though certainly not the practice) of rhetoric began in ancient Greece. In Greece's democratic state, the legal system was based on advocacy, and therefore the ability to speak and to persuade were highly prized skills. Skilled at speaking to particular audiences for particular purposes in particular contexts, the rhetorician recognized the importance of responding to diversity and to different ways of knowing. Rhetoric can, in fact, be defined as a concern with context — with the elements that surround the text of a piece of discourse. These elements together constitute what Aristotle called "the art of the available means of persuasion."

Jesse Jackson showed that he knew much about those available means in his speech before the Democratic National Convention that preceded the 1988 presidential election. Here's a section of that speech, in which he compares himself — the contender for the nomination — to the party's nominee, Michael Dukakis:

> There's a great gap between Brookline, Mass. and Haney St., the Fieldcrest Village housing projects in Greenville, South Carolina. He studied law; I studied theology. There are differences of religion, region, and race; differences in experiences and perspectives. But the genius of America is that out of the many, we become one.
>
> Providence has enabled our paths to intersect. His foreparents came to America on immigrant ships; my foreparents came to America on slave ships. But whatever the original ships, we're in the same boat tonight.
>
> Our ships could pass in the night if we have a false sense of independence, or they could collide and crash. We would lose our passengers. But we can seek a higher reality and a greater good apart. We can drift on the broken pieces of Reaganomics, satisfy our baser instincts, and exploit the fears of our people. At our highest, we can call upon noble instincts and navigate this vessel to safety. The greater good is the common good.

Jackson establishes his own character in this excerpt, a man who has lost the candidacy but will work for the election. Drawing parallels between himself and the candidate allows Jackson to make larger conclusions about the nature of America, where the immigrant and slave ships meet, where "out of the many, we become one." He uses Brookline and Fieldcrest to stand for the larger differences of privilege, class, and race. And he uses allusive language to make his point. The metaphor of the ship evokes Jackson's major themes in the speech, steering a new and courageous course toward unity, making the greater good the "common good." Jackson plays with the metaphor in several senses, calling on his listeners' sense of humor with the wry phrase "we're in the same boat tonight" and on their recognition of allusions with "our ships could pass in the night." Jackson's use of language in this passage works to bring his message home to the party that needs his support.

What we've done here is to conduct a brief rhetorical analysis of this bit of Jackson's speech by looking at his language — the syntax and the meaning — in terms of his purpose, his appeal to an audience, his character as a speaker. Studying the language in this way exposes the writer's agenda, illuminates the effect and the elements of this discourse. We'll say more about rhetoric later. What we want to do here is show how rhetorical analysis — that is, looking at the elements of discourse within their contexts — can help learners achieve metalinguistic awareness, see language as language, and become able to manipulate language for their own purposes.

Here's a text written by a student who'd been given the first part of a fairy tale, one that appears in John Fowles' novel *The Magus*, and whose assignment was to complete it. First, Fowles' tale:

> Once upon a time there was a young prince, who believed in all things but three. He did not believe in princesses, he did not believe in islands, he did not believe in God. His father, the King, told him that such things did not exist. As there were no princesses or islands in his father's domains, and no sign of God, the young prince believed his father.
>
> But then one day the prince ran away from the palace. He came to the next land. There to his astonishment from every coast he saw islands, and on these islands, strange and troubling creatures whom he dared not name. As he was searching for a boat, a man in full evening dress approached him along the shore.
>
> "Are those real islands?" asked the young man.
>
> "Of course they are real islands," said the man.
>
> "And those strange and troubling creatures?"
>
> "They are genuine and authentic princesses."
>
> "Then God also must exist!" cried the prince.
>
> "I am God," replied the man, with a bow.
>
> The young prince returned home as quickly as he could. "I have seen islands, I have seen princesses, I have seen God," said the prince reproachfully.
>
> The king was unmoved. "Tell me how God was dressed."
>
> "God was in full evening dress."
>
> "Were the sleeves of his coat rolled back?"

The prince remembered that they had been.
"That is the uniform of a magician. You have been deceived."

Students didn't discuss the story much, though they were curious about how it ended. They wrote using as many or as few details as they wished, but they had to complete the story. One student ended the tale this way:

"tell me how the islands look," said father.
The son said they had big + giant trees,
Very large mountains, and the Islands had people on it in little villages.
The father said, "How interesting are you sure it was real;" the son replied, "yes, I was there in real life."
The father said, son you said you seen princesses too.
Yes I did father, they are very pretty with their long dresses on and shinning rings, and bright eyes. Father you said all of those things were not true. No, the father said, "I did not say that I said I didn't want those things in my domains.
So in 20 years the King made his domains out of an Island, he found out the God was ever where and finally he found some princesses and they all lived happily ever after.
The End

When our prepractice students read this fairy-tale ending, some saw only its weaknesses — its "deficiencies in mechanics and literary development," its "errors involving capitalization," its "improperly aligned dialogue." Now, it's true that the writer has some real problems with error. For these readers, the errors seem to compromise the piece so completely that they can't look at anything else. But for a teacher to respond to this piece of writing in the way these students have done would do the writer no good. The writer would feel chastised, punished for his mistakes maybe, but his next attempt at writing might be the same — or even worse — as a result of the corrective comments. The comments wouldn't have improved the writing or even the writer's attention to error.

How can other readers, teachers and students, look at such a piece of writing to enhance both the writer's understanding of language and style and their own? The answer is to examine it in the same way as the Jesse Jackson piece above, to look at what the writer does or is trying to do, and at how he does it. In other words, readers can consider the essay rhetorically. The reader can ask about the voice of the writer, the audience for the text, the subject the text addresses. She can ask herself about the context in which the writing was produced, what its purpose is for both reader and writer. Most of all the reader asks what this writer knows and how he uses that knowledge. That question is important in reading any text, but it's vital in reading the text of an unsophisticated writer like this one.

These are some of the things the writer of this text knows:

- The writer understands intuitively the form of the fairy tale and uses that knowledge to produce his text.
- The writer is not familiar with the conventions of punctuating dialogue, but knows that there are such conventions and attempts to use them.
- The writer moves between general and specific ideas, from description to narration, from dialogue to authorial summary.
- The writer understands and uses vocabulary from the first part of the fairy tale.
- The writer understands and builds on a theme.

Reading the essay in this way can allow other students to formalize the knowledge that they drew on as they responded to the same assignment. It can also help the teacher discover constructive ways to converse with students about their writing, as another prepractice teacher does:

> In responding to the student who completed the fairy-tale narrative, I would assume the role of engaged reader who wanted to find out what would happen next in the conflict between the king-father and the prince-son. What happened to make the king want to fashion his kingdom out of an island twenty years later? Some events seem to be missing. How did the king find out that God was everywhere? And what happened to his son? Is he part of the cast of characters who live happily ever after? I would note these questions as an interested reader, not teacher as examiner, on the student's response as an impetus for the student to elaborate. (Sela)

Looking at the rhetoric of this piece of writing allows Sela to emphasize the language it uses. It allows an appraisal from more than one angle and it encourages her to see the text as literature, as a piece of discourse with a writer, a subject, and an audience. Sela is reading as a reader, discovering places where she'd like more, noting places that confused her. Her suggestions are good ones.

Sela might also want to respond to the grammatical and surface features that disturbed the other readers. This student may not have figured out how to use some conventions of written texts — like dialogue punctuation — systematically, but as a teacher, Sela could point out how to use the orthographic cues in Fowles' text as a model for the student to follow. Most of the other errors that appear here have to do with conventions of writing, as well: capitalization, sentence punctuation, spelling. Yet these conventions are used correctly in some places, and in preparing an edited text, the writer could be encouraged to apply his knowledge of their use more consistently.

A great deal of linguistic knowledge is represented in this student's text too. In fact, only one nonstandard grammatical form appears here, where the king says, "you said you seen princesses." This past tense form is probably common in informal exchanges in the writer's own speech community, but it would probably violate the student's expectations of "the king's English." A reader might react with surprise to this nonkingly style without discouraging the writer. The one error in noun–pronoun agreement — "the islands had people on it" — remains an area where the writer's grammatical knowledge might conflict with the standard; and the teacher who found other examples in the student's writing might gather them to use as a basis for discussion and explanation.

By affirming grammatical knowledge and focusing on rhetorical style, the teacher can help this writer become conscious of the language he knows and uses competently. Such positive attention to language becomes an important means of supporting a student's further development as a writer who, unlike Stradlater, can see that writing involves more than just being able to "stick all the commas and stuff in the right place."

CHAPTER 6

Writing as Composing

Writing extends the ways in which we use language to name and understand the world, to get things done in it, to communicate with others. It gives what we say and think a permanent form, allowing us both to return to what we have said or thought before (and to develop historical perspective) and to rethink or reform it. Because writing allows time for forming and reforming, the forms that writing takes become a focus of our attention in a way that's generally not true of speaking. The nicely shaped essay, the carefully crafted poem or short story becomes as important and as interesting as the message or meaning conveyed. It is natural, then, that readers and writers will be concerned with form. But form does not come "formed" — it evolves in ways that are appropriate to the particular context and purpose of a piece of writing, and it evolves during the writer's process of figuring out, within that context and purpose, what she wants to say and how. As Ann Berthoff says, "Forming is the mind in action. It is what we do when we learn; when we discover or recognize; when we interpret; when we come to know. Forming is how we make meaning" (1981, 5). Focusing only on what has been formed or how it must be formed, as teachers often do in classrooms, leaves out much of what writing is about, and keeps writers from understanding what it really means to write. It keeps both teachers and students thinking of writing only in terms of its most traditional form in the English classroom — the finished essay.

In the classroom, a concern with form too often becomes a focus on format. The teacher enters his English classroom with a writing assignment in hand. What's the first question his students will ask? If it's a typical classroom, that question is likely to be "How long do you want this paper?" The question isn't a bad one, but it does indicate something troublesome about the way students view the writing they accomplish in school. They focus on what's outside the writing assignment itself — its length, its format — rather than on what the task requires of them as thinkers. In part, that focus derives from a very real sense that the physical things about writing are the things most susceptible to control. "I may not know what to write about," students say, "but I can write the specified number of pages and have a title and underline the thesis sentence." But the question about length or title page also comes from students' belief that writing is a task quite separate from themselves, with right and wrong answers determined by the authority of the teacher. Writing in school is most often seen by students not as an active means of discovering what they think and know, but as a routine and essentially passive kind of decoding, figuring out what someone — the teacher or the text — wants them to do.

At first, it may seem paradoxical to think of writing as a passive act. After all, the writer controls the pen or keyboard, puts words on the page that come from his brain, decides when to make new paragraphs, where to put punctuation. But when you think of the writing assignments you've written in your own school lives, you'll probably remember only a few where you felt in control of what you had to say. More often than not, you were looking to please rather than to talk, and your motivation was likely to be the prospect of a good grade rather than the opportunity to explore and present ideas. This outside aim directed the words, paragraphs, even the commas you placed on your page. "I was always trying to write the way I knew the teacher thought I sounded," one student wrote in her journal, characterizing her own high school writing experience. Other prepractice students make similar comments about their school writing: "The most damaging aspect of school writing was the necessity of pleasing the teacher"; "Instead of concentrating on the writing, I was concentrating on the teacher"; "School writing has always seemed to be structured by the teacher, rather than by the student." As a result, when students do begin to seek more from their writing, they find their efforts to direct their own writing continue to be hindered by a preoccupation with what the teacher or the professor will value: "For the most part, my experiences with school compositions have been frustrated by my inability to go beyond attempts at perfect writing."

The responses of these students reflect the traditional focus of composition teaching on form and structure — on analyzing the formats of effective compositions and teaching students to replicate them. When a teacher, Janet Emig, began in the late 1960s to look at what writers actually did when they wrote as well as at the papers they produced, she found that the process of planning, writing, stopping, rereading, revising was similar for all of her twelfth-grade students. Yet for each individual student there were profound differences in the written products, depending on whether the student was engaged in school writing or in "other," more personally motivated writing. The "other" writing Emig found to be more fluent, with more complex syntax, a surer sense of voice, clearer intent. Based on her research, Emig argued that there were two dominant modes of composing for student writers: school-based or *extensive* writing, and self-based or *reflexive* writing. Extensive writing, assigned by teachers and controlled by extrinsic factors of length, correctness, evaluation, led to writing that was generally shorter, less complex, less interesting, and less fluent, while reflexive writing, motivated by the writer's need or desire, produced longer, more complex discourse. Emig encouraged schools and teachers to find ways to allow reflexive writing into classroom instruction, and in the past decade theorists have begun to examine how reflexive writing—in journals, freewriting exercises, diaries—might be made part of a school setting.

When they write without the pressure of formal demands, writers often begin to feel like writers, to know the pleasure of writing. The prepractice students who commented on the constraints of school writing also wrote in their journals about using writing to fuel their own learning, and about what they might apply from their experience as writers to their own teaching.

> My enjoyment grows when I relax with the subject and "freewrite" and refuse to worry about perfection in the first draft. I suspect that high school students may benefit from an allotment of freewriting time in any or all English classes—by taking the sting out of "correctness" when they receive their assignments back. (Anthony)

> An English class taken early in my high school career introduced me to, and kept me in the habit of, keeping a journal. I have since filled three bound books with what Joan Didion calls "pieces of the mind's strings too short to use." So ingrained is this desire to "get things on paper" that I've often found my thought pattern is more ordered when I write and so I rarely tackle a paper, digest an idea, or incorporate an image without first writing about it. (Tricia)

Letting "pieces of the mind's strings" form the basis for school writing makes that writing easier and more effective, in the end, for student writers.

When Holden Caulfield agrees to write the "description essay" as a favor to his roommate, Stradlater, he turns the school writing task into personal reflection, makes an *extensive* task *reflexive*. Even though he's working under constraints set by both the assignment and his roommate, for Holden this is not really a school task. What begins as a favor becomes an opportunity to write about something meaningful to him—an opportunity to describe the baseball mitt of his brother, who has recently died, and to think about him. He begins describing the mitt, on which his brother had written poems in green ink. Holden remembers Allie—how everyone thought he was intelligent, and nice, and how he used to laugh at the dinner table, and how he [Holden] broke all the windows in the garage when Allie died.

> Anyway, that's what I wrote Stradlater's composition about. Old Allie's baseball mitt. I happened to have it with me, in my suitcase, so I got it out and copied down the poems that were written on it. All I had to do was change Allie's name so that nobody would know it was my brother and not Stradlater's. I wasn't too crazy about doing it, but I couldn't think of anything else descriptive. Besides, I sort of liked writing about it. (51)

Stradlater returns and reads the composition. He is annoyed because what Holden has written doesn't conform to what Stradlater sees as the assigned task. A school essay has to be "right."

> "For Chrissake, Holden. This is about a goddam *base*ball glove."
> "So what?" I said. Cold as hell.
> "Wuddaya mean *so what*? I told ya it had to be about a goddam *room* or a house or something."
> "You said it had to be descriptive. What the hell's the difference if it's about a baseball glove?"
> "God damn it." He was sore as hell. He was really furious. "You always do everything backasswards." He looked at me. "No wonder you're flunking the hell out of here." he said. "You don't do *one damn thing* the way you're supposed to. I mean it. Not one damn thing."
> / (53)

Holden doesn't do things the way he's supposed to do them, and he's flunking out despite the fact that he can write good compositions. He's involved in the much larger task of making some sort of meaning out of the events of his life — out of the death of his brother and the ways that he has felt and acted since then. His school writing could help in that process, but most school tasks don't allow room for any connection with the real world — including the real emotional world. Most tasks are like the essay question on Holden's history exam, which he failed — the one that asked him to give back a lot of information about the Egyptians. His one paragraph response to that question is, as he says, "crap": "The Egyptians are extremely interesting to us today for various reasons. Modern science would still like to know what the secret ingredients were that the Egyptians used when they wrapped up dead people so that their faces would not rot for innumerable centuries. This riddle is still quite a challenge to modern science in the twentieth century" (16). Even in this "crap" there's a connection to what preoccupies Holden, a connection a teacher could have helped him to explore — to discover what other people, like the Egyptians, thought about death and afterlife and how that belief system and its practices gave shape to the lives of the living. But where writing is used only for giving back what the teacher is looking for on an examination, there's no opportunity for the student to use school writing to discover genuine areas of interest or concern.

Writing in school

Writing has most commonly been used in school in just the way Holden Caulfield's history teacher used it — as a way of testing to make sure that students have done their reading or listened to the teacher's lectures. From the earliest school years, reading has traditionally dominated the school curriculum. Little writing has been included, and what has been has taken the form of workbook exercises related to the reading task or the occasional book report that proves a student has read a library book. Where writing has finally been taught, in the upper grades, it's been taught in much the same way as reading — as a step-by-step decoding of words and letters rather than as a larger, constructive, meaning-making activity. And writing instruction has emphasized the teaching of traditional grammar and has focused on small units as building blocks for real writing. (This focus continues in college "remedial" writing courses, which typically begin with the sentence and end with the paragraph.)

Yet children who grow up in a print culture are natural writers. They see writing as a meaningful activity from the time they are very young, and most will spontaneously "write" stories and "read" stories in the way they spontaneously draw pictures, long before they actually learn to read or write. The two-year-old daughter of the Scollons, who accompanied them in their fieldwork with the Athabaskans, "wrote" stories in scribbles and "read" them with book-reading intonation, convincing the Athabaskan children that she attended school. Her interest in writing was unusual in an Athabaskan community, but common where children see reading and writing as ordinary adult activities like going shopping or driving a car — activities to be "played" and emulated.

Recently, "whole language" programs in some elementary schools have begun to build on this natural interest in reading and writing, and to connect reading and writing as the similar, constructive, meaning-making activities that they are. In whole-language classrooms, children begin to write as they begin to read, and they draw on their existing knowledge about books and about the world. Typically, children might tell their own stories to a teacher or older schoolmate, who writes them down so that they can read them out to the class. Quickly these children begin to write, on their own, words from the story that are important to them, keeping their own dictionaries, practicing the words by using them again in new stories, where they write the words they now know while the teacher fills in the rest. The teacher offers support and direction for students' activity while leaving them in control. Where learners are interested in and have authority over the texts they produce, they become highly motivated to write and to read. Such integrated reading and writing produces real writers as well as better readers. (Researchers like Donald Graves in *Writing: Teachers and Children at Work* have provided wonderful accounts of the work of these writing-focused classrooms for young learners.)

Tracey, the bilingual classroom teacher from Chapter 3, reflects on how much students like to write when they feel in control:

> Children love to write, yet many of them, by the time they get to the seventh grade, have developed a fear of writing. I have seen students feel completely at a loss as to what to write in certain instances, yet in other instances feel enthused. Perhaps it is this idea of *control*. When they feel they have ideas and can "let it flow," they feel in control. As a descriptive writing assignment one time, I showed them a picture of a wild car, a classic one, all painted with abstract pictures of people and flames. They *loved* it and had no trouble writing about it as if it were their car. They told me all about it, where it came from, what they liked to do with it, and so on. Other times I've seen kids "stuck" while writing, and I've given them a little idea I think that particular individual would like, and it often seems to give them the start they need.

In high school, more writing is typically demanded of students, at least in English classes. But the forms it takes allow less opportunity for student writers to be in control of what they produce. Much of the writing is in the form of notetaking or of short answers or short essays on tests, but there is also, at least for students in the upper tracks, some essay writing. Yet most of this writing is used primarily to evaluate what students have read and learned. And the student is writing to an examiner no matter what the "assigned" audience might be. This pattern was confirmed by a 1980 study by Arthur Applebee, sponsored by the National Council of Teachers of English, on writing in the secondary school.

Applebee surveyed nearly eight hundred teachers of major high school subjects from schools across the United States about the amount of writing, the kinds of writing, and the purposes for writing in their classrooms. (These teachers had been identified by their principals as "good" teachers, and probably had their students do somewhat more writing than other teachers did.) He also collected samples of student writing from these classes, and information from the students about their perceptions of the sorts of writing they did. Applebee found that although forty-four percent of class time involved writing of some sort, most of it took the form of notetaking or providing short, informational responses, like one-sentence answers to study questions, and overall, only three percent of class time (and three percent of homework time) involved writing a paragraph or more. (Even under the category of "essay writing," he sometimes found the real activity to be mechanical — "the 'essay' test that asked the students to write 'The Star Spangled Banner,' and social studies 'writing' assignments that involved copying out whole sections of the text") (32). Most of this writing (eighty-five percent of samples submitted by teachers) was to convey information about the subject, rather than to explore personal connections and ideas.

Of informational writing, most took the form of reporting or summarizing, with some analyzing — categorizing and making logical connections. Only three percent of writing samples went beyond these forms to "theorizing" — making hypotheses and drawing deductions from them in a systematic way. And eighty-eight percent of the writing in the samples was addressed to the teacher, in the role of examiner, as the primary audience.

Where the focus is on instruction in writing itself, rather than on examination and evaluation of other learning, more essay writing may be asked for, but its emphasis continues to be primarily on forms and organizational structures. (This too is confirmed by Applebee's study: when students reported receiving any instructions from teachers before beginning a writing task, these were most likely to focus on form; eighty-seven percent of students in English reported receiving instructions on form, while only thirteen percent cited discussion of the topic, as part of the introduction offered by the teacher to a writing assignment.) Typically, writing instruction focuses on the five-paragraph essay with an introduction, three main paragraphs, and conclusion, and/or on surface structures of spelling and punctuation and "grammar." Longer writing assignments, or "term papers," stress forms to be used in each stage, from writing a topic sentence to adding a bibliography. Such "essay writing" is rigidly separated from creative writing or personal writing. In either case, writing is seldom self-motivated and is seldom seen as a tool of inquiry or learning. And while teachers may begin to observe student writing processes or patterns in their writing behaviors, writing is almost never the subject of student inquiry, even in the composition classroom.

Responses from our students confirm this general pattern.

I remember a huge research paper in high school about an animal. I chose the rhino. The paper was to be a whole semester's effort. We were given time to collect material and information. We were then forced to take notes on index cards, one thought or action per card. The cards were turned in for inspection and graded. Next came an outline passed in and graded. Then rough draft, editing, rewriting, and, ultimately, final draft. The idea was simple. We were supposed to arrange the cards into a type of outline on the floor. We would rearrange as we saw fit.... After critical examinations we passed our final drafts in. The results reflected the process, bland and impersonal. The papers were information-packed but painful to read.

The same year I had a creative writing class. Our teacher made us write what seemed to be hundreds of short papers where we worked at avoiding facts. Most of the papers were observations of objects or events. The reading emphasized not your actual observations but the manner in which you conveyed these observations to others. One paper I remember was an instructional paper. It didn't matter what we instructed or how accurately we instructed it. All that mattered was that we conveyed to the class the steps necessary to do something. The papers lacked a purpose.

Somewhere between the two forms of writing lay the best method. A method where you could make an entertaining, flowing paper that said something significant. Unfortunately, no one ever connected these ideas for me. Research papers were not taken seriously if they had little jokes or flowery descriptions in them. Creative writings seemed to be frowned upon if they stated anything concrete. Just as trained, the students would write what was expected, not necessarily good writing, but what we were taught to write. (Peter)

What makes good writing?

While most English instruction (and the textbooks it's based on) suggests that writing is good if it follows the prescribed form, writers all know, intuitively, that the forms they choose when they are engaged in real acts of communication are related to the people they are talking or writing to and their reasons for talking or writing. Dad might expect an information-packed monologue from each of his children about their school days, but the same day will be described in different words, perhaps in brief vignettes, in a conversation that is providing entertainment for friends. The scientist will report her findings differently in a scholarly journal than in a letter to a colleague. It's only in school, where most students are not writing for real, communicative purposes, that the question of form gets separated from its natural relationship to audience and purpose and no longer evolves out of a real context.

Historically, rhetoricians have paid attention to the quality of texts, not only to the forms they took, but to how well suited these forms were to accomplishing the speaker's or writer's intentions. The forms named by rhetoricians in the past continue to dominate our thinking about texts, and are worth reviewing. But a catalog of forms cannot re-create the act of forming — the relationship a writer or speaker establishes between ideas and form for a particular purpose at a particular moment — and the making of choices that are at the center of any theory of rhetoric.

Form is the appeal (classical rhetoric)

Aristotle, the most influential of the classical rhetoricians, developed a series of classifications and divisions of speech that have been used and modified and challenged for centuries. In *The Rhetoric*, he focused on the relationships among the speaker (writer), the audience (reader), and the subject. Speakers and writers manipulate these relationships toward the desired end of persuasion, and the best rhetoricians are those who can gauge form, style, and approach according to their appropriateness in particular contexts. Aristotle divided the speech into five component parts, each one based on a relationship achieved among speaker, audience, and subject. (This three-way relation is often referred to as the "rhetorical triangle.") The parts were:

> invention (how a speaker went about gathering data);
> arrangement (how a speaker put data in an appropriate form);
> style (how a speaker controlled data through eloquence);
> memory (how a speaker used past knowledge for a present occasion);
> delivery (how a speaker paid attention to listeners).

Aristotle's categories became tools for teachers to guide their students' production of oral and written texts for hundreds of years. With the exception of memory and delivery (the two that appear most closely linked to the oral mode), they're used still in textbooks and classrooms. Aristotle produced lists of topics to aid invention, examples of form to aid arrangement, suggestions of word choices to aid style. He developed these taxonomies as possible strategies for speakers to use in forming texts: they showed speakers ways they could proceed as they began to think and speak. He offered twenty-eight *topoi* — summaries of the lines of argument that discourse might follow. Speakers should consider, for example, the opposite of the thing in question. "Observe whether that opposite has the opposite quality. If it has not, you refute the original proposition; if it has, you establish it" (Bk. 2, 23). This sort of practical advice extended to a consideration of the audience as well: in speaking to elderly men one must consider their personal characteristics: "they have lived many years; they have often been taken in, and often made mistakes; and life on the whole is a bad business. They are cowardly, and are always anticipating danger . . . people always think well of speeches adapted to, and reflecting, their own character: and we can now see how to compose our speeches so as to adapt both them and ourselves to our audiences" (Bk. 2, 15). Although Aristotle's taxonomies may seem limiting, or even laughable, they described not so much rules for composition as possibilities for composing. The classifications of arguments, audiences, speakers gave the composer strategies for conceiving the texts he produced.

Form is all (eighteenth- and nineteenth-century rhetoric)

The eighteenth century was interested in knowledge and its classification (this was the period in which the encyclopedia was invented), and so rhetoricians placed emphasis on Aristotle's second aspect of a text — its disposition, arrangement of ideas — rather than on invention, and they developed a classification system that allowed all discourse to be categorized based on how ideas were arranged. Called the "modes of discourse," these classifications allowed teachers to concentrate on the structures and forms that comprised the category and helped students mimic those forms in writing of their own. Eighteenth-century rhetoric focused on the modes of description, narration, exposition, and argumentation. In the nineteenth century other discourse modes were added — comparison-contrast, definition, process — as subheadings for exposition. Percy Boynton organized the chapters of his 1915 textbook *Principles of Composition* according to the modes of exposition, argumentation, description, and narration. If you look at modern textbooks (like the 1989 *Patterns for College Writing* published by St. Martin's Press), you'll see that the modes continue to be an organizing and defining principle for writing. In many texts, the classification is hierarchical, with narration taught first and argumentation last (presumably because it requires the greatest sophistication from writers).

Of course, one thing wrong with such taxonomy is that none of these modes exists in anything like pure form. Narration always contains description, and often subtle argument; argument always contains exposition, and often narration. Yet generations of students have learned these forms as wholly distinct and produced them as separate forms in their writing for school. (And that may be one reason school writing is seen as something so divorced from real life or real-life writing. The modes of discourse, so popular in teaching still, just don't exist in the real world.) Another problem with teaching the taxonomy of modes is that they are too often taught without reference to the ways in which the reasoning represented in these forms helps us to make sense of the real world. Students write papers in a variety of courses that ask them to describe a chemical reaction, to define the term "chauvinism," to compare and contrast the positions of the United States and USSR on strategic arms limitation, papers in which description or definition are part of what is needed to achieve an understanding of the subject. But they also sit in composition courses where they are asked to write a "definition" paper, a "comparison and contrast" paper, with no concern at all about what will be defined or compared. The format becomes all-important.

Form is function (the new rhetoric)

In the late twentieth century, emphasis has increasingly been placed on the function (or the purpose) of discourse rather than its forms or its techniques. A writer's reasons for using certain rhetorical techniques and particular forms becomes the guiding principle in making decisions about what constitutes effective writing. This stress on purpose can be seen as a stress on rhetorical context (a writer has to know his audience to understand the forms he should use to persuade, entertain, or inform them). Some modern theorists like James Kinneavy and Kenneth Burke have focused on the aims of texts as they were represented in the texts themselves rather than in the author's intentions. Kinneavy has reformulated the nineteenth-century modes by focusing on the aim (or "guiding purpose") of texts — on whether they are literary, persuasive, referential, or expressive — instead of on their characteristic forms.

James Britton uses the linguistic categories of expressive, poetic, and transactional discourse to represent the kinds of writing that writers do. Like Kinneavy's, his categories divide written language according to its aims or the functions it serves, but he takes into account the writer's intentions as well as the qualities of the text produced. *Expressive* writing, like Emig's reflexive writing, is based in the self-expression of the writer, and its function is to reveal and affirm and discover the writer's identity and relationship to the world. Britton describes it as "writing that assumes an interest in the writer as well as in what he has to say about the world." For Britton, expressive writing is at the heart of all writing. It's "psychologically prior" to the other two functions of writing he names. *Transactional* writing is writing that functions to get things done, to act on the world by carrying out transactions with others. And *poetic* writing is that which focuses on "*making* something with language, rather than *doing* something with it" (1982, 53).

These recent approaches to rhetoric shift emphasis from the features of the text that's produced to the writer and the communicative act. Britton's work has been particularly important in helping to establish a writing curriculum throughout British schools that begins with young children using language to make meaning of their worlds and develops their ability to use writing for these three functions in more and more complex and sophisticated ways. We'll say more about his work shortly.

What makes a "good writer"?

Just as there's been a change, recently, in the rhetorical theory that defines good writing, there's been a change in the theory of instruction that answers the question of how to teach people to be good writers. Newer answers appear alongside traditional ones in the classroom.

1. The writer is born, not made.

This maxim carries the aura of the Romantic poets who valued above all the poetic genius, the writer who awaited inspiration. Like the poet in Coleridge's poem "The Aeolian Harp," the writer must await inspiration by being ready and able to recapture and reproduce it. The harp itself is a passive instrument, placed in a window to catch stray breezes and make music. The poet has to remain still and listen well. In this Romantic view, the good writer is someone to whom Nature has given special talent. All a teacher can do in a classroom is to find the good writers and encourage them as much as possible, while helping the others to be competent. "Chances are the next Hemingway is not sitting in your classroom" is a maxim offered to new teachers in a recent issue of the *English Journal*. And many students, as well as teachers, accept this maxim. How many times do students say, "It's just harder for me to write because I'm not naturally talented"?

2. Imitation is the sincerest form of flattery.

For centuries, the prescribed method for writing improvement was to help students learn from models of good writing. Students would read examples of persuasive oratory, eloquent description, clear analysis, would study the forms represented in the readings, and then would imitate these forms in their own writing. Here's a sample assignment from Boynton's 1915 *Principles of Composition* mentioned above:

> After reading the exercises, examine the following list of subjects and indicate with reference to each one whether it is the sort which lends itself to enumerating by classes, to chronological treatment, or to interpretative treatment. [The topics include: The Chinese Drama, The Five Great Species of Literature, Rival Merits of Portland and Seattle, The Value of Moving Picture Shows.] (220)

Students are expected to recognize and imitate the methods for development of topics after having read those methods. Their ability to do that kind of imitation is independent of their knowledge of or interest in the subject. (Only a very few students would actually be able to discuss the rival merits of Portland and Seattle.) Despite the fact that such tasks begin far from what students know and can build on, this classical method of recognition of form and imitation of it remains a popular strategy in most college composition texts (and thus high school texts), and many collections of readings — "readers" — used in college composition courses still follow these principles. (It is, for example, the principle that has guided the selection of readings to represent each mode of exposition, from narrative to argumentation, for *Patterns for College Writing*.)

3. Process makes perfect.

This maxim represents the most recent movement in writing instruction. It follows from Emig's initial observations of her students' writing processes, and from the many other studies that followed hers. The different behaviors that Emig found the writer to move through in producing a piece of writing, and the terms she used to define them, are representative of what other researchers found. She described these activities:

- Invention (sometimes called prewriting) — all the activities a writer engages in to get ready to write a draft. These may include reading, taking notes, talking, outlining, making lists, freewriting.
- Drafting or writing — all the activities a writer uses to get from beginning to end of a piece of writing. These include starting and stopping and thinking and moving away from the text as well as actually composing chunks of it.
- Revision — all the activities that change a draft of writing. These include rereading, moving bits of text around, scratching out, adding. Revision may result from the writer's reading to herself or to others, or from leaving the text alone for a time.
- Editing — all the activities that put the text into appropriate form. These include making changes in syntax, mechanics (spelling, punctuation), format (footnotes, bibliography, headings).

These activities look as if they represent a linear process in which the writer moves step by step from a prewriting stage to a drafting stage to a revising stage to an editing stage. And unfortunately that is too often how the writing process is taught. But, in fact, the writer moves back and forth among at least the first three of these activities — stopping drafting to think of new ideas or going back to change what was written earlier. And within the process there seems to be some sort of global planning or monitoring of how the piece is progressing as a whole as well as local shaping of the immediate section. The writer also has to move back and forth between her own developing ideas and her sense of how these ideas might come across to an audience. (Sondra Perl refers to these two movements as *retrospective structuring* — writers' shuttling back and forth from their sense of what they wanted to say, to the words on the page, and back to address what is available to them inwardly — and *projective structuring* — writers' shaping of the material so that their meaning carries over to the intended reader.)

A writer on the writing process

While all writers have a "writing process," and writers' processes include similar features, there's also a great deal of variation in the attention different writers give to different parts of the process, as well in the ways in which one writer will proceed in different tasks. Here's part of a response from a student on her writing process for school assignments:

> Whenever I write a paper, the process is basically the same. I spend the greatest proportion of time thinking about the assignment, what is this paper going to say, what questions will it answer, what questions will it raise, when the paper is due is relative to how much time I toss ideas

around before actually getting the yellow pad and pencil. I then attempt my first rough draft, complete with crossouts, misspellings, and arrows. Using a legal pad simplifies the numbering of pages, and I just keep writing until I think it's all out there. Of course, in between recording my thoughts, I have to move around and rethink my writing. From my initial draft, I pull out what seems to be the best of what I want to say. I rewrite this on white paper, in ink, dictionary in hand. The next step is to type the first finished copy and then edit. The paper is never really finished; I just have to turn it in because there is no more time. (Valerie)

Valerie is conscious of the strategies that move her writing along. Most writers don't consciously reflect on their writing processes, but, like Valerie, they find, when asked, that they have a defined set of strategies that got them from one stage of their writing to the next. These strategies — which together become the composing process — vary of course from one writer to another. Valerie moves through the same basic stages that Emig found for her student writers as she proceeds from a beginning to an end, yet many of the specifics within each of these stages are idiosyncratic.

Valerie's invention techniques included "tossing ideas around" in her head, thinking of questions that her paper might try to answer and try to raise. And for many writers, the initial stage of the composing process involves this kind of thinking: coming up with ideas and rejecting them, asking questions — all internally and often almost unconsciously as soon as an assignment is given. For other writers, starting their writing immediately is necessary to get them started thinking. Some talk with friends or other class members, sharing questions and ideas. Some writers make long lists. Some try not to think about the assignment at all. Formal invention techniques that teachers can employ to stimulate this early part of the composing process are often referred to as *heuristics*. These may include brainstorming and listing ideas with a class or small group, writing freely about all the ideas that initially occur to the writer, rereading entries in a double-entry/dialectical notebook. Ann Berthoff talks of "assisted invitations" to composing, and suggests three activities in particular: listing and classifying, naming and defining (finding general terms that can cover a variety of things named), and asking "HDWDWW?" (How Does Who Do What and Why?) (1982, 50–79).

The next step — drafting or writing — is sometimes the only one that writers consciously think about because it's the most conscious step. The words get physically written on the page. Some writers complete this stage quickly; like Valerie, they "just keep writing" until a draft is finished. Some writers write in fits and starts, leaving the unfinished draft for hours or days before they write the final sentence. As they write this first draft, they cross out, start over, replace words often, being careful about their words, being careful to be as correct as possible the first time out. Peter Elbow calls this kind of writer *critical*. Other writers seldom stop to look back at their words as they write them. They produce work quickly and without much hesitation and often end up with more than they need. These are *creative* writers in Elbow's terms. Of course, these distinctions aren't mutually exclusive. Elbow talks about these two contrasting styles as the stereotypes on two ends of a continuum, admitting that they're mixed in the actual practice of writers. Valerie, in fact, uses both styles as she works on her draft. And many writers continually reread their work as they proceed through a draft, not to make corrections but to keep rethinking where they've been and where they're going. Nevertheless, these distinctions between creative and critical are useful in thinking about the next stage, revision.

Writers' revision strategies vary like the other elements of the process. Revision might take place on a very large scale, where entire pieces of the draft are removed, or groups of paragraphs are added, or sections are reversed. Or it might occur on a much smaller scale, with changes limited to sentence and word changes. Writers revise to make the draft make more sense or sound better to themselves, and they revise to fulfill the requirements of an audience they know or have imagined. Donald Murray (1980) calls these two types of revision *internal* and *external*. Any writer engages in both types of revision as she looks back at her draft. In internal revision, Murray finds, writers read what they have written to discover what they have thought and said. They move in and out, from a whole piece to a sentence, out to a paragraph and back in again to a sentence. But they think primarily in terms of how the flow of ideas on the page works for them. In external revision, writers think about how they communicate, and they work to create coherence and order so that a reader can follow the thought. They make sure of transitions between paragraphs, logical connections between ideas; they step outside their texts to take on the role of reader. Valerie talks about two times when she revises. The first involves rethinking her writing in between recording her thoughts, and that revision is probably primarily internal, focused on her developing ideas. The second comes after she has completed a draft, when she pulls out "what seems to be the best of what I want to say." Although she doesn't say so, it's likely that she's stepping back at this point, to look at her text as a reader and to take on a reader's perspective.

As we indicated earlier, these three stages of composing — inventing, drafting, and revising — intertwine and shape one another. The writing process is recursive, and the writer keeps circling back to see where she's been in light of what she's writing now. So the writer who is revising may decide to reinvent by changing a thesis or adding a story. But the last stage of the process, editing, is different from these others.

It doesn't generally interact with these other stages. In fact, if it does, it often blocks writers' fluency. Editing or proofreading is the most mechanical, and therefore least important, stage in the process. But it's often given the most attention by textbooks, by teachers, and by students themselves. Students edit by looking for errors they know they commit, by asking others for help, by finding answers in handbooks. Or they try to avoid error altogether by limiting their words. Fluent writers save editing until last, until they have finished revising and are satisfied with their text. Then they proofread what they have written, read it aloud, have others read or listen, check punctuation or usage in a handbook, check spelling in a dictionary (or with a computer spellchecker). They don't let editing interfere with their writing.

Writing process pedagogies focus on facilitating the writer's development of fluent composing processes and on helping writers change aspects of their process that hinder their writing. The teacher's role is to help students become aware of what they do when they write and to help them expand their repertoire of effective strategies for composing. Instruction centers on finding the writer's unique ability to come to terms with language in her own way. Process instruction in writing also follows from developmental theory in learning. Like all learners, writers take on new tasks and solve new problems as they mature and develop more and more complex strategies for interpreting.

The process model of writing has begun to find its way into the classroom in part because it attempts to recognize diversity, that one writer may approach tasks differently from another. (Although where textbooks have followed the process approach, they tend to suggest uniformity in the linear movement of writers through distinct stages.) Peter Elbow, Donald Murray, Ken Macrorie are all exponents of a process approach that recognizes the writer's individuality and power in shaping language.

Writing as a way of knowing

The double vision of what makes good writing and what makes a good writer has come into single focus in the work of composition theorists in recent years. The perspectives of modern functional rhetoric and of composing process theory meld as the composing process is seen as a process of forming and shaping texts to particular aims and that forming is seen as connected to ways of knowing. Britton's work has been particularly important in making these connections.

Britton began his study of writing by looking at the ways in which children used language, in a variety of forms, to make sense of the world. In an early essay on children's reading and writing of poetry, he says:

> The process of creating our world is continuous in our waking hours and we interpret experience without being aware that we are doing so: we act, that is, upon assumptions without ever being aware that we have made them. But the process is intensified whenever we stand back and work over past experiences, whether in conversation, in writing, in acting, or in painting, or in any other way. In doing these things we discover meaning. (1982, 14)

Writing extends the process of thinking and making sense of the world and of communicating that sense to others. In writing, students express ideas that are important to them, tell stories they want to tell, speculate, solve problems, and discover questions. Writing can do things that oral language can't do, and that's one reason to emphasize it in the classroom.

Through writing, writers transcend the immediacy and everydayness of experience, see that experience from new perspectives, and discover general patterns. Writing about home, the writer finds that he can talk about the general characteristics of home as well as his real one on Greenleaf Avenue. He can write about past events and resee them in terms of what he now knows. Allison, the student writer in Chapter 2, came in this way to reconceive her responses to her mother's illness in terms of her own growing maturity. Writing allows an escape from the imprisonment of the here and now or, as Piaget called it, "the irreducible present," a reseeing and recategorization of experience. In other words, writing can make it easier for people to think abstractly and to reflect even on their own thinking, abilities that are critical to study in most disciplines. And where writers are engaged in real acts of communication about what they're discovering, the need to communicate can push their ideas toward elaboration, modification, clarity.

Outside the classroom, writing is used in the real world in a number of ways. It's used to overcome the limitations of the spoken word—to record and store information on forms, in lists, in notes, extending the limits of memory. People use writing to communicate when the person they want to talk to isn't present—as in the note to a teacher explaining a child's absence or the now-rare letter to a friend, extending speaking across time and across space. Many of the uses of writing are continuous with the uses of speaking, and one mode can support the other.

Writing can be used both to act and to comment on actions. Britton talks about the distinction between language used to get things done (which he calls *participant* language) and language used to evaluate or comment on the actions or experience of the speaker and listener (which he calls *spectator* language). The spectator is not really inactive, as the word might suggest, but is reflective—looking back at a past experience or looking at another's experience, recounting it or reliving it or hearing another recount it. Spectator language allows speakers to think about the acts and events they have been involved in—to evaluate those acts and events and figure out what they mean from various perspectives. When Allison recounts the story of "when my mother got sick," she is not only conveying information to inform a reader about an event, but she is reflecting on the meaning of the event to her, as "one of the first and most frightening things I remember as a child." And the language of reflection runs throughout her narrative, as Allison thinks about the events and thinks about her thinking about the events: "I just thought"; "What did I know"; "I was very confused."

People undertake this sort of reflection alone some of the time. But much of the communication between people also involves this sort of language. As Labov has shown, conversations are full of narrative accounts of events in which the teller tries to re-create the event and negotiate a shared sense of what the meaning or significance of the event might be. If Allison had been describing her childhood responses to her mother's illness in a conversation with a friend, that friend would probably have said, "That must have been frightening," and showed that she shared Allison's understanding. Britton suggests that gossip, too, is an oral form of spectator language; such language strengthens a connection between speaker and listener and reinforces a story and attitudes to a story already known. Heath's accounts, in *Ways with Words*, of conversations on the front porches of Trackton or in the kitchens of Roadville show how such gossip and storytelling reinforces the norms and values of a community while creating a social connection among its members and building a shared pleasure in the shape or cleverness of the telling.

Literature — in essays as well as short stories and novels — is a written form of spectator language. Britton uses the concept of spectator language to break down what he sees as a false separation of literature from the texts produced by ordinary speakers and writers. "Whenever we play the role of spectator of human affairs, I suggest we are in the position of literature." Like gossip or conversational narrative, literature comments on human affairs, but in a formal, rather than informal, way. Whether it's Salinger, choosing to begin Holden Caulfield's story with "If you really want to hear about it," or Allison choosing to begin with "One of the first and most frightening things I remember," the writer who is making choices about form — about whether this will be a first- or a third-person narrative, about whether it will begin in the middle of events or with an overview — is involved in an essentially literary endeavor.

In using the terms *spectator* and *participant*, Britton focuses on the role of the speaker or writer in the communicative act. He connects these roles to the functions of language by showing how the participant uses *transactional discourse* to get things done in the world, and the spectator uses *poetic discourse* to provide formal expression of the meaning of events and to provide pleasure in the telling. But both the transactional and poetic functions of language, Britton believes, begin with the speaker's attempt to express and characterize ideas in tentative, associative, emotional and often esoteric ways, in *expressive discourse.* Only later does expressive language branch out to meet the needs of an audience in communication. (Though Vygotsky would say that the language we use, even for this expressive function, is shaped in communication with others in a social/cultural context.) Britton sees this primary function of language as "the matrix out of which all other functions of language grow." It is language close to the self, unstructured, and is the mode in which we frame the tentative first drafts of new ideas. Such language is fostered in journals, in personal and unevaluated bits of writing, in freewriting of all kinds.

Because he sees expressive discourse as the beginning point for all language, Britton believes that teachers need to see expressive writing as important in its own right and to make it a starting point for writing that will eventually communicate. Expressive discourse may represent the first thinking in a text that will be shaped into the transactional discourse used to inform, report, or persuade, or, like poetic discourse, it may involve retelling and reflecting on acts rather than acting. For students as writers, it can be enabling to see their expressive tellings as continuous with the literature they read—to see that they too work with forms, move back and forth among journal entries and conversations and stories and poetry—and teachers can learn to nurture their students' experiments with form.

In the 1970s Britton and his colleagues undertook a study of writing in British schools (one that Applebee used as a model in studying writing in American schools). He found that there was little expressive writing in most classrooms, and that lack was limiting the effectiveness of instruction in transactional and poetic writing. Britton studied, on a large scale, an issue closely related to the one that had troubled Emig in her study of her students' composing processes. When Emig looked at how students wrote, she found that students' school writing was far away from the kind of fluent, experimental, and associative writing they accomplished in their own reflexive responses.

Case studies of high school students written by prepractice students reveal this difference between extensive and reflexive writing. In one, Jennifer observes a twelfth grader writing poetry for herself and for school. Sara, the student Jennifer observes, is concerned with traditional forms in her school assignment, commenting that it's really hard "to think up words that rhyme." In contrast, in the reflexive poetry writing she does at home and reads to her family, she allows herself to have more choices and to experiment with form: "She appears to relax the insistence on rhyming each line, and the rhythm varies throughout the poem," Jennifer notes; "she experiments with the Dickinsonian dash throughout, but does not worry as much about punctuation at the end of every line." Sara writes the reflexive poem in the first person, because she "sees the reflexive poem as a more accurate representation of her style, and voices that confidence through the use of 'I.' " Of course, such experimentation could take place in school contexts, allowing the development of new modes of expression and of a closer fit between the writer and the writing produced. But because schools give little place to expressive, fluid, or still partly unshaped writing, they effectively remove this sort of learning from the classroom. If expressive language precedes all other functions of language, if writers need time and space to find out what it is they want to say, what they desire to speculate about, then to exclude it in English courses is to exclude a primary — and for Britton crucial — element in the process of shaping experience into language.

By concentrating only on writing as performance, teachers close off a potentially powerful strategy for students to make sense of what they're learning. The writers these classrooms produce may become competent in reproducing the forms someone requires of them, but they'll often have difficulty taking authority for their own words or for connecting their learning to their own experience. They won't be, in our sense of the term, good writers or produce, in our sense of it, good writing — they're more likely to reproduce Holden Caulfield's response to his history essay than to invent his meditation on his brother's baseball mitt.

Why students can't write

Although many teachers would assent to what Britton says about writing as a way of knowing and interpreting, and about the importance of expressive writing to this process, in teaching writing as in teaching about language, most of what goes on in a classroom is determined by long-standing traditions of school culture. And students receive an underlying message about what's valued from the larger set of classroom practices, despite the emphasis of instruction in any one area. Although the teacher may want students to respond in genuine ways to one another's writing, continual emphasis on grammar instruction may convince them that correctness is really the important value, so that they comment only about a "misplaced comma."

Two areas of emphasis in school-based writing work against fluent processes of composing and against thinking in writing. One is the concern with error and the emphasis on correctness at the surface-level of what is written. The other is the emphasis on "correct" structure — on format rather than forming.

Surface errors and deep blocks

For students from both "standard" and "nonstandard" backgrounds, an excessive concern with form and correctness blocks the development of skill in writing. For many beginning writers, that concern focuses on errors and other surface features. The student who stops in the middle of a sentence to look up the spelling of a word in the dictionary disrupts the process of composing and often loses the sense of the larger developing idea. Many of these writers hesitate to write very much at all out of a fear of making mistakes that for them decide whether they are good or bad writers. They decide to keep their sentences and their ideas simple and thus avoid being wrong. (And this response has been reinforced by their having been told they're wrong so often and for so many years.) The problem is magnified for the basic writer or the second-language learner, because these groups have typically been evaluated as writers wholly on their mistakes in grammar and syntax; as Janet Emig says, on the "accidents, rather than the essence" of their discourse. But all student writers have this fear of being wrong, so they often produce less writing and writing of less complexity. Our pre-practice students discover this as they interview students for their case studies. The responses Pam received were typical:

> I asked: "What about writing? Do you like writing?"
> Darell said: "Not really. If I write too much I have to stop because I get tired. When I get tired, I make mistakes."
> I asked: "When you write something, what atmosphere works best for you? Where do you go? What do you need?"
> Darrell said: "To the living room, or my room. I'd rather be at home because I can have more time to get it right, make sure there's no mistakes n'stuff."
> I asked: "How do you make sure it's 'right'?"
> Darrell said: "I go back sometimes and rewrite what I wrote, change the words around til it sounds right."
> I asked: "What exactly do you *do* when you write? Do you try to write in any specific *way*?"
> Darrell said: "I just try to think about what I'm *supposed* to write, and then I write what comes into my head."
> Finally I asked: "If you had the choice to answer a question by writing out an answer or by speaking/saying what you thought, which way would you choose?"
> And Darrell said: "I'd rather write it down than say it out loud because I'd have a better chance to get it right."

Pam comments on these responses:

> A couple of things struck me as I interviewed Darrell. One of the most prominent was his extreme concern for doing things the "right" way, and, in my opinion, earning the respect of his teacher. Darrell,

like most students, knows that the bottom line in getting good grades is getting, or coming up with, the right answer or response. What I find disturbing about this, with specific reference to his writing process, is that making his work "right" overrides any concern for thought development or thought stimulation. When Darrell writes, he first enters into the process by trying to think about "what I'm *supposed* to write," rather than thinking perhaps about what he has *read*, what *he* thinks about the reading, and *then* formulating a response. What I noticed here, upon going over my notes on the interview, was his use of the word "supposed"; he undoubtedly must feel that the teacher is going to grade him on how close he comes to writing out some preconceived "right" answer in the "right" way.

Darrell's concern with writing in the way that he is "supposed to" echoes our prepractice students' memories of their own school writing. Such a preoccupation with getting things right to please the teacher can create deep writing blocks for students. Mike Rose studied college writers who were *high blockers* or *low blockers*. He found that high blockers had often internalized a set of rigid rules about writing (generally from their previous writing instruction) that interfered with their attempts to follow out their ideas in composing. In interviewing students, he found that they expressed a number of these rules directly: "Writing has to be logical"; "You're not supposed to have passive verbs"; Words shouldn't be "too simple," or "too colloquial"; "Writing is not good if it contains too many prepositional phrases" (1984, 49). When asked what these rules meant, students sometimes didn't really know. But students who depended on such rules were found to edit prematurely:

> [They were] composing with the aid of a number of rules—some absolutely expressed, some not fully understood—which are appropriate to determine the final texture of prose but are very inappropriate when one is working out ideas in rough draft or simply glossing an assignment sheet. The result, as was seen, is not only limited production but an actual stymieing and even forgetting of one's thoughts. (50)

That such interference with composing is common, even for writers who ultimately produce good writing, can be seen in the reactions of the many prepractice students who, when they read about Rose's high blockers, responded "That sounds just like me."

Format versus form

"Rightness" can be seen not only in terms of surface errors or features of style like the number of prepositional phrases. It's as frequently set in rules of format—rules that, when applied rigidly and prematurely, have an equally limiting effective on a student's composing and ultimately on the quality of his writing. Wrongheaded approaches to writing tell students to:

1. Get a topic.
2. Make an outline based on the prescribed mode of discourse (comparison–contrast; process–analysis; argument).
3. Follow the essay form. A paper should include a thesis sentence that contains three points, and five paragraphs with one paragraph to introduce, one for each of the points in the thesis, and one paragraph to conclude. (You may recognize this form as the "3.5 essay" or the "three-fold thesis essay.")
4. Include a topic sentence for each paragraph.
5. Use the inverted pyramid to move from the largest point to the smaller details.
6. In your introduction, tell your readers what you're going to tell them. In the body, tell them. In the conclusion, tell them what you've told them.

When we look at the opening paragraph of a neatly typed, final copy of a "Definition Paper" (that was its title), written by a writer in freshman composition, we can see the teacher's or textbook's rules for proceeding step by step through a defined format behind what the student has written in the opening paragraphs.

> In this paper I will define the word "dynasty" in a sports sense.
> The reason these teams stand out above the rest is for three or four reasons. Their ownerships are the most stable organization in their sports. Another reason was the great coaches and also the great athletes these teams had and the leadership these athletes provided their teams.

The student has chosen (or been assigned) a word to define and has actually managed to find a way to connect it to the one topic that interests him — sports. He's following the prescribed mode of discourse (definition). He's begun by telling what he's going to do ("define the word 'dynasty' in a sports sense"). He has included a thesis statement with at least three points ("the reason . . . is for three or four reasons"). As you might predict, he has three middle paragraphs (though they, in fact, talk about three different dynasties rather than the organization, the coaches, and the athletes). And he concludes by telling what he has told ("In conclusion the reason these teams stand out from all the others are three reasons"). Along the way there are hints of his genuine interest in the subject of sports, if not in defining "dynasty." He has detailed information about the teams he describes — the owners and coaches and the players they hired. But his interest is so constrained by the format that he can only fit it in the slots — he can't really create any new understandings.

The teacher's responses to this paper consist mostly of marginal comments. After the first sentence she writes, "Add a little here explaining what you mean more fully." After the second: "The reason is for reasons." After the third: "This needs more detail." And after the fourth: "Tighten." She also adds an admonishment to "keep verb tenses consistent." We'll talk about responding to student writing in Chapter 10, but for now we'd like to make three observations. Most of these comments do not really engage with the meaning of this writer's text but are the sorts of typical comments that studies like one we'll talk about by Nancy Sommers have shown to appear on paper after paper, as if placed there by a rubber stamp. They mix concern about expanding the text in the way a writer would on an early draft with editing concerns about consistent tenses. And they give the student little guidance about what to do next as he leaves this final paper and goes on to work on the next assignment—a comparison and contrast essay.

In all instances, focusing on format first defines and limits the questions we ask. *Definition* becomes an isolated task rather than a part of how we build larger understandings. The five-paragraph essay forces the writer to see only three main points. The comparison and contrast essay, in which three comparable points are discussed for each of the things being compared, results in essays like this student's next one, in which he compared Boston and Los Angeles "in weather, historical and in a sports sense," concluding: "So this is my compare and contrast paper of two cities, Boston and Los Angeles." (We have included the full text of this essay in the "Strategies" chapter at the end of the book.) While comparing things is a fundamental aspect of coming to know something new by relating it to what is already known (Hepsie's niece saw the elephant she called "big dog" as both like and unlike the dogs she knew), the process itself is messier than form-oriented pedagogies would suggest. There are, in fact, many features of life in Boston and Los Angeles that might be salient to an individual, and the process of listing and categorizing and sifting through those features might end with the identification of three key areas of comparison, but the process itself would support the generation of new understandings, rather than the "I said I would do this and I did it" conclusion.

Nurturing good writers and good writing

Learning about writing is like all other learning: it involves active discovery, doing, risk taking. Good writers are made by writing—by following out their ideas, trying out connections and relationships between them, experimenting with ways of expressing them. And good writing is made by writers who do these things—who work with their writing and do not close off the process prematurely. Teachers can help students become good writers who make good writing in a number of ways.

1. Teachers can help learners tolerate the uncertainty and confusion of writing-in-progress, hold off premature formatting and editing, and let their writing find its form.

Ann Berthoff has repeatedly emphasized the relationship between thinking and forming (her first book was titled *Forming/Thinking/ Writing*). For Berthoff, the process of composing is a process of generating ideas, or chaos, of naming those ideas and opposing them to others. Composing, then, is a process of seeing and reseeing relationships and developing more and more strategies for interpreting.

> I believe we can best teach the composing process by conceiving of it as a continuum of making meaning, by seeing writing as analogous to all those processes by which we make sense of the world.... Thinking, perceiving, writing are all acts of composing: any composition course should ensure that students learn the truth of this principle, that making meanings is the work of the active mind and is thus within their natural capacity. (1981, 69)

To let this process of making meanings happen, writers have to learn to tolerate chaos and ambiguity.

> Meanings don't come out of the air; we make them out of a chaos of images, half-truths, remembrances, syntactic fragments, from the mysterious and unformed.... When we teach prewriting as a phase of the composing process, what we are teaching is not how to get a thesis statement but the generation and uses of chaos; when we teach revision as a phase of the composing process, we are teaching just that—reseeing the ways out of chaos.
>
> Now chaos is scary: the meanings that can emerge from it, which can be discerned taking shape within it, can be discovered only if students who are learning to write can learn to tolerate ambiguity. (1981, 70)

Writers need to learn to tolerate ambiguity to keep the mind active and ideas developing. It is writers' fear of chaos that causes premature closure, that leaves ideas explored in surface or incomplete ways, and that often causes writer's block as well. Coming to premature closure, fitting writing into final forms while the ideas behind it are only partially formed, most often creates writing that looks adequate but lacks depth of thought or a feeling of completion. It elicits responses like those the teacher gave to the definition paper: "Explain what you mean more fully"; "This needs more detail." As writers learn to tolerate chaos, they let themselves engage in a process of forming, in which the thoughts and their evolving forms grow together. The forms they try help them to think — drawing out ideas as well as giving shape to them. Berthoff tells us that "it is the power of language as a form that creates order from chaos" (1981, 79).

Britton refers to this process as shaping — shaping that begins to take place from the moment an idea is uttered (aloud or on paper), but with shapes that are not fixed and final as long as the thinking continues. We both find and shape our ideas as we write, and the shaping helps the finding.

> I want to associate spontaneous shaping, whether in speech or writing, with the moment by moment interpretative process by which we make sense of what is happening around us; to see each as an instance of the pattern-forming propensity of man's mental processes. When we come to write, what is delivered to the pen is in part already shaped, stamped with the image of our own ways of perceiving. But the intention to *share*, inherent in spontaneous utterance, sets up a demand for further shaping. (1982, 141)

In this "shaping at the point of utterance," finding a shape as we begin to utter our thoughts in speaking or on paper, the shape we find as we begin to share our thoughts helps us make sense of what we have been thinking, so that the thinking and the shaping (like Berthoff's composing and forming) work together. "The act of writing becomes itself a contemplative act revealing further coherence and fresh pattern." (1987, 143)

Peter Elbow talks about the writing process in similar ways, as "allowing yourself to proceed without a full plan ... trying to let the words, thoughts, feelings, perceptions try to find some of their own order, logic, coherence ... trying to get your material to do some of the steering instead of doing it all yourself" and waiting for a "center of gravity" to emerge. Elbow calls the larger process of letting writing shape thinking a process of "growing" through writing. He also talks about "the smaller process: bubbling, percolating, fermenting" of ideas, and he calls this "cooking." Several kinds of interaction cause the cooking of meaning to go on either in the head or on the paper — interaction between words and ideas, between metaphors, and particularly between people.

Elbow has drawn on his own experience as a writer and his own blocks — with writing his dissertation, with writing articles — in generating his ideas about writing and how to teach it. Writers are often blocked by imposing the rigid critical standards appropriate to finished writing on their very first efforts; they want to produce a final text immediately. When Elbow described the process of "cooking" as one that, for many people, takes place on paper rather than in the head, his metaphor gave others a way to think of their own writing processes and to accept their own half-cooked first drafts. And it was in struggling with his own composing problems, as well as those of his students, that Elbow discovered "freewriting" — writing as quickly as you can for a period of time with the only constraint being that you have to keep the pen moving on the paper, even if you keep writing "I don't know what to write" — and then rereading this writing to find a "center of gravity" — a point of focus or interest that you can go on from. Writers who began a task with freewriting freed themselves from thinking that this writing had to be structured and polished, freed themselves to develop their ideas. Elbow eventually came to describe two modes of writing: writing in words (freewriting), and writing in ideas (pullling back and looking for overall perspective and structure). He tells us: "It's not that one is better than the other; not even that each has a different function. It's the interaction between the two that yields both clarity and richness — cooking. Start with whichever you prefer. But make sure you use both and move back and forth between them" (1986, 43). Elbow too is trying to capture the active relationship between generating ideas and finding an overall plan or structure. And like Berthoff and Britton, he emphasizes that it's the dialectical movement in writing — back and forth between thinking and forming — that yields "clarity and richness."

Using writing to generate ideas and to organize and shape them has some similarities to doing the sort of ethnographic inquiry and writing that we discussed in Chapter 1. Most research begins with a series of questions that come out of a model or theory of what will be found — a working hypothesis or a plan. Within the logical framework of the model, the research might test or explore a series of possibilities. But too rigid a model sets limits on the nature of the exploration. Anthropologists studying other cultures discovered that preconceived models could not be applied to those cultures, that predetermined questions reflected what was important to our culture but not necessarily to the culture being studied. They found that gathering rich data and not eliminating any possibilities was the only starting point for gradually coming to know, from inside a culture, what was in fact significant there — what kinds of questions to ask, what sorts of thinking were "smart" or "dumb" in that culture's terms. At the end of *Amish Literacy*, Andrea Fishman describes how inductive and open-ended her ethnographic work on Amish literacy turned out to be, and how her findings — the significant patterns that emerged from this study — remained hidden and implicit until her third draft. So for the ethnographer, too, writing is a discovery process.

> While I knew I couldn't predict what I had to say before I did my research, what I discovered did not jump out at me and scream "Here

I am!" as I must admit I expected it to. I had to write it down, at
length, and then read what I'd written, before I actually realized what I
had to say about what I knew. (210)

Like the ethnographer, the writer engaged in writing as an act of
inquiry and discovery needs flexible models and loose plans that can be
revised, depending on what is discovered. Teaching students to use
freewriting, assigning journals in which they can begin their thinking
about any subject with expressive writing, assigning sequences of small
tasks that encourage them to keep writing about something until their
writing begins to find its own shape can help them find both what they
have to say and how to say it. But like the ethnographer, the writer
must also give final form to her discoveries. Classroom work on sorting, on categorizing, on grouping and regrouping specific ideas and
details, labeling these, creating mid-process outlines that give a preliminary structure to a writer's early chaos — all of these activities can
help the writer shape a final, coherent form. We'll say some more about
them in Unit 3.

2. Teachers can help learners see and understand their own processes of writing, discover, as Elbow did, what helps them to get unstuck, and find ideas.

When students who have become comfortable with their own writing
begin to observe their writing processes, they discover that these processes are not neat and linear at all. They find that their writing, like
their reading, is "initially fragmented," that they "try things out, test
ideas, take risks," that they move in different directions at once — back
to earlier ideas, forward to the direction they may be going in, down to
small, specific details, and up to connect to a larger theme. The picture
these students present is like what Janet Emig found when she began to
study the composing process of her twelfth-grade students and like the
chaos-generating process Berthoff describes.

Beginning writers, too, can begin to observe and reflect on their
own processes. Ellie's basic writing students answer a set of questions —
a self-evaluation of writing progress — part of the way into the semester. The questions make the goals of the course explicit, and they
give students a chance to think about what they have accomplished and
what they are working on. While students do many kinds of writing
over the semester, a major purpose of the course is to help students
succeed in college writing tasks. The questions help students think
about the process they go through in writing such essays, and the
essays they produce.

1. Describe the process you go through when writing an essay. Do
   you jot ideas down freely at first and then come back to choose

particular points to expand on? Do you write more than one draft? Do you stop frequently to read back over what you have written to see if you have said things as clearly and as fully as possible? Do you change things around within a draft, moving a sentence or paragraph from one place to another? Do you change words, eliminate words or sentences that don't fit, add words when they are needed to make things clearer?

2. Consider the relationship between your writing and your thinking. Are you writing longer papers? Do you try to think about what things mean and explain them? Do you push yourself to think about what things mean and explain them? Do you push yourself to think more about the subject, even after you have written your first ideas? Do you actually learn something as you write?

3. Consider the structure of finished essays. Do your finished essays focus on one main topic? Do they move logically from one point to another? Do you include both specific details and a larger generalization or characterization that those details support or that can be drawn from those details? Do you decide, in the end, on the most effective order in which to discuss particular details?

4. Consider the perspective of a reader. Do you let the reader know right away what you're writing about? Do you include enough information so that any moderately informed reader who picked up your paper could make sense of it? Do you use paragraphs to lead your reader through the groups of your ideas? Do you leave the reader with a final point, drawn from the rest of your discussion, which shares whatever insight or meaning you have discovered in writing the essay?

5. See yourself as an editor. Do you proofread your paper before handing it in? Do you keep a list of words you frequently misspell and try to catch them? Do you use a dictionary when you have one available? Do you try to catch other errors that I have pointed out and explained? Do you reread papers that have been returned to you and look at explanations? Do you ask a question when you received a comment or explanation that you don't understand?

They are also asked questions about their own learning: "What have you learned about writing or about yourself as a writer that you didn't know or see as clearly when the semester started?" "Where you learned something new, what helped you to learn it?" "What would you like to do or have more of?" "What do you want most to work on next in your writing?" Students can describe much of their own processes; they compare notes and learn one another's strategies; and the questions reinforce the idea that their processes and their development, and not just their finished products, are an important focus of the curriculum.

Just as students have a great deal of knowledge about language that has never been made explicit, they know a lot about writing and about themselves as writers. Eliciting this information helps the teacher find out where students are following rigid rules and misguided advice, and where they follow practices that should prove effective. And encouraging students to make their own knowledge explicit helps to make that knowledge available to them, to use consciously. One student's response, "I knew in the beginning that I wrote poorly, but now I'm not as intimidated as much, so I find it easier to write," suggests that helping students to see and reframe their knowledge about themselves as writers can be an important aspect of our teaching of writing.

Beyond process pedagogies

In spite of the effectiveness of process approaches to the teaching of writing, many students continue their established pattern of failure even when they're in process-oriented classrooms. Process approaches work well where the community and school mesh and where expectations of teachers, parents, and students coincide. When learners already have the discourse strategies and styles of language use of mainstream literate discourse, process approaches have helped them develop and extend their abilities to use those strategies and to discover new ones. But the process approach often fails to take into account learners whose discourse strategies and expectations may diverge from those of the mainstream.

In an article titled "Skills and Other Dilemmas of a Progressive Black Educator," Liza Delpit recounts her experiences as a young black teacher trained in writing process approaches. She began teaching in an urban school setting where parents' expectations for school writing were that children would learn an academic dialect through methods that seemed contradictory to the process approach. While process approaches generally value the individual writer's style over prescribed form or finished product, black parents wanted their children to learn how to produce those products and those forms, feeling that they need to develop skills, not fluency. Delpit speculates:

> Maybe these writing process teachers are so adamant about developing fluency because they have not really had the opportunity to realize the fluency the kids already possess. They hear only silence, they see only immobile pencils. And maybe the black teachers are so adamant against what they understand to be the writing process approach because they hear their students' voices and see their fluency clearly. They are anxious to move to the next step, the step vital to success in America — the appropriation of the oral and written forms demanded by the mainstream. And they want it to happen quickly. They see no time to waste developing the "fluency" they believe their children already possess. (383)

And she goes on:

> I run a great risk in writing this—the risk that my purpose will be
> misunderstood, the risk that those who subject black and other min-
> ority children to day after day of isolated, meaningless, drilled "sub-
> skills" will think themselves vindicated. That is not the point. Were
> this another paper I would explain what I mean by "skills"—useful
> and usable knowledge which contributes to a student's ability to
> communicate effectively in standard, generally acceptable literary forms.
> And I would explain that I believe skills are best taught through
> meaningful communication, best learned in meaningful contexts. I
> would further explain that skills are a necessary but insufficient aspect
> of black and minority students' education. Students need technical
> skills to open doors, but they need to be able to think critically and
> creatively to participate in meaningful and potentially liberating work
> inside those doors.... if minority people are to effect the change
> which will allow them to truly progress we must insist on "skills"
> *within the context* of critical and creative thinking." (384)

How can teachers answer Delpit's concerns? How can the writing
classroom work to develop the skills demanded by a minority community within a context of meaningful communication and critical and
creative thinking?

Process approaches can support the acquisition of new dialects, but
they do so indirectly. While they build on an existing *repertoire* or
background knowledge of a writer, they often stop short of considering
how to translate that repertoire directly into new forms. Too often,
students whose social class and cultural background vary from the
idealized practices of the dominant school culture leave their schools
without "skills" *and* with little sense of themselves as learners, with
poor writing abilities, and with little enjoyment in reading.

Mina Shaughnessy was one of the first to document the cases of
some of those learners on the margins of the dominant culture. Her
unprepared, nontraditional freshman composition students were unable
to produce the kind of written discourse she had expected them to
write. They were learners whose composing processes did not produce
coherent texts. And they were painfully aware of it. One student wrote:
"I don't believe society has prepared me for the work I want to do that.
is in education speaking, that my main point in being here, If this isn't
an essay. of a thousand word's that because I don't have much to say.
for it has been four year since I last wrote one" (1977, 19). Shaughnessy
let us know that something beyond process—the individual in negotiation with her text in a series of stages—was necessary to talk fully
about what happens when writers write. Shaughnessy's students followed processes all right; processes that their particular backgrounds
and cultures and school experiences had helped them develop. But
those processes didn't fit the mainstream of school experiences, and

they consequently had almost no strategies for accomplishing writing in school, the extensive writing that Emig defined. In addition, these writers had no experience with using writing as spectator language or doing reflexive writing, and so were locked out of the powerful tool of writing as a way of helping them begin to think of what they wanted to communicate.

Shaughnessy's solution was to work with students' errors, to find in them evidence of systematic thinking that underlay those errors — thinking about what writing was, about what writers do with language, about what Standard Written English is like — and to respond to the developing system of each individual learner (as well as to the typical patterns of basic writers). Her work is still enormously useful in dealing with these patterns, and we recommend it to teachers of basic writers. But Shaughnessy's work still focused on the patterns of errors students made when they began to use a new form of discourse. It didn't make explicit connections between the larger realm of linguistic knowledge students brought to the classroom and the new knowledge they were expected to develop. Recently, there has been a shift in the focus of work in composition, as theorists have begun to recognize the importance of community and of the linguistic resources that students bring from that community and play off against as they move into new uses of language — particularly writing. The work of Shirley Brice Heath is, to a great degree, responsible for that new direction in research.

Heath's study of home and school language patterns suggested directions for writing pedagogy that would answer the concerns of Delpit. Helping students in the writing classroom become researchers of their own home and school language practices would allow them to be engaged in the sort of *transactional* writing generally demanded by school — writing that was not generally either reflexive or poetic but that had the aim of getting something done in the world (report writing, for example), and to use that writing to do real things, to report on things that had value and meaning to the students, and to gain thereby the sort of motivation and interest that Emig found only in her students' reflexive writing. Students who asked real questions, undertook real research in their communities, and then translated what they learned into school terms might still keep journals and reflect on what they were discovering, but they would also describe those discoveries in the discourse of the school. They would work in groups and respond to what others had drafted, and be readers to one another's texts, but they would also — together — shape final texts in school formats. They would validate the knowledge represented in their homes and communities and approach their schooling from a position of knowers who were learning something new, rather than from a position of not knowing. And in the process (and this would involve a process), they would make their knowledge of home and school styles and what was needed in shifting from one to the other conscious and explicit.

The sort of work Heath recounts and advocates meets Delpit's criteria. It builds useful and usable knowledge that contributes to students' abilities to communicate effectively in standard, generally acceptable forms. It is meaningful work that takes place in a meaningful context. It supports the development of critical thinking. And within that context, it helps students to explicitly recognize and practice and develop the new uses of language — the "skills" that they will need to have in order to succeed in mainstream society. As these students do all sorts of writing, from observational note taking to analysis, from reflection to interpretation, they engage in the process of writing and discuss their processes: "What did you do next?" "Why did you do that?" They find meanings. And they discover a relationship between context and form that will help them plan and shape and meet the needs of real audiences, of real readers, as they discover their meanings.

Tracey, who found that her students loved to write, though they had developed a fear of writing in school by the time they reached her class, shares many of these concerns. She worries in general about the fact that

> I want everything to be fun and exciting and stimulating for them, but I also feel that there are times when they must just learn how to sit down and concentrate and study, that some things require discipline and concentration. That there are certain skills to learn — setting to a task, studying for a test, doing an assignment, handing it in, organizing oneself.

And these concerns carry over to her teaching of writing. She describes one sequence of activities around a traditional task, the writing of a book report.

> I decided to plan the approach carefully, and not just tell them generally how to approach it and let them "go to it." I have given them a writing assignment before and have been overwhelmed with what I got. They've made an effort, in general, but they need so much work! The idea of rewriting it *kills* them, and if they do, they basically just copy it over. I met with each student individually — it took forever and I wasn't happy with the results.
>
> So ... this time I broke them into pairs. They had to tell their partner what the book was about. If the listener didn't understand, they could ask questions. This was very successful. I then had them think about how it went. Did they leave out important details? Did the listener understand? Did this help them clarify the story?
>
> I then explained that when we are talking, we can say "Oh yeah, I forgot to tell you that he found the key to the treasure when he was little ..." or "I forgot to say that he had a sister who ...," but then when we write we've got to plan it out first or we'll confuse the reader.

Tracey then takes her students through a process of drafting a report on a novel they had read as a class—jotting down notes, writing some sentences using the notes as a guide, modeling for them how she would think her way through such a task. The next day she models again with "Little Red Riding Hood," has students work individually on notes about their own books, and tries "to get around to as many as possible," asking questions about their books and answering questions about their writing. But five students remain stuck.

> We went to the back table and had a very good work session. I just got them started telling me what the book was about and I took notes for them. When they understood how I was doing this, they could continue. I think they finally got the idea. I will continue this process and see how it goes . . . that's where I am now.

There's no one simple strategy, no sequence of steps or set of practices that will help all learners in all circumstances to develop as writers. Teachers who know some of the theory we have discussed in this chapter, who are sensitive to their students and the contexts of their students' lives, will still have to discover their own ways to work, day to day, with the writers in their classes. Tracey is doing an excellent job of trying out, reflecting on, and revising classroom practices. As a teacher, she is much like the fluent writer who keeps a larger plan or goal in mind, but tries things out to see whether they move her along toward it, taking into account the new things she discovers and learns along the way. For classroom teachers, as well as for student writers, being overly concerned with "getting it right" can block the development of effective processes.

At the end of the semester, when Tracey reviews and reflects on her teaching of writing over the semester, she sees how much she has come to know, or know that she knows.

> I see that one of the major themes I wrote about was *how to teach writing*. This problem has been with me for 1 1/2 years and I feel like this course gave me the chance to sort out some different approaches and ideas and I feel that I have a stronger theoretical background behind me. I like the idea of prewriting and journal writing and have initiated these in my class. I feel the journals have been quite successful so far. I also had my students write up the results of an interview they did and was so pleased with the results. I felt that all the laborious work and small group meetings I did for their book reports was worthwhile! They realize now that writing is a *process* and did 1st, 2nd, and even 3rd drafts on their own. They read each others' papers and helped each other with them. They were able to organize their ideas into coherent paragraphs and present the information to the class. They had actually learned how to write a paper! I felt proud and satisfied.

CHAPTER 7

Reading and Meaning

In the last chapter we described writing as an active, constructive process—a process that writers use not just to present "right" answers in "correct" formats but also to extend ways of using language to make sense of the world. When people read, they are actively involved in creating meaning, in the same way they create meaning from all of life's experiences. So reading, like writing, should be seen as an inventive, constructive activity. In reading and writing texts, students gain control over their own processes of learning. But reading and writing are more than just similar acts. They are *symbiotic*, to borrow a term from biology; that is, they mutually reinforce, enhance, and shape each other. Reading helps writers discover structures and forms and voices just as writing helps readers uncover meanings and strategies. And reading, like writing, depends on what readers bring to it, as well as what they find through it.

> If you really want to hear about it, the first thing you'll probably want to know is where I was born, and what my lousy childhood was like, and how my parents were occupied and all before they had me, and all that David Copperfield kind of crap, but I don't feel like going into it if you want to know the truth. In the first place, that stuff bores me, and in the second place, my parents would have about two hemorrhages apiece if I told anything pretty personal about them. They're quite touchy about anything like that, especially my father. They're nice and all—I'm not saying that—but they're also touchy as hell. Besides, I'm not going to tell you my whole goddam autobiography or anything. I'll just tell you about this madman stuff that happened to me around last Christmas just before I got pretty run-down and had to come out here and take it easy. (Salinger, 3)

Reading the opening paragraph of *The Catcher in the Rye*, we can see some of the things readers draw on in creating meaning from this text. They come to this book with several kinds of existing knowledge in their heads that will help them make meaning of the text they read. First, readers bring to the reading, as they do to every activity, the accumulated knowledge and experiences of their lives. Readers know, for example, about childhood and about parents—perhaps about touchy fathers. No reader's experience will have been exactly the same as Holden Caulfield's, and individual experiences may even interfere for a time with an understanding of Holden's story, but the experiences themselves provide an opening through which readers will look at Holden's experience. Readers know, as well, about language and about texts. This story is told in the first person, and in an immediate present, not in the distant past ("Once upon a time") or about a removed third person ("He had a terrible childhood"). As modern readers, familiar with openings that place them *in medias res* and with stream-of-consciousness narration, readers are tolerant of entering a scene they know little about and of entering the mind of a character who has not been formally introduced. In fact, familiarity with these conventions could keep readers from realizing immediately that the speaker is actually talking to someone, not just thinking to himself. But the language of the text becomes familiar. "If you really want to hear about it" is colloquial, slightly aggressive, and addresses another person. And the language tells even more: the choice of words (*lousy, crap, stuff, touchy, goddamm*) is informal, slangy, and would be used only with peers or intimates, or by a speaker who was not particularly concerned with fitting into a formal context — like a teenager.

As readers read Salinger's opening, they draw also on a larger cultural framework, like the reference to David Copperfield. Readers can make sense of this novel without knowing who David Copperfield is, but the association with another book places the speaker's childhood somewhere in relationship to other novels of childhood, and it reveals something about Holden's general education or background. And if readers know *David Copperfield*, they may even hear in Holden's voice the echo of David's opening words: "Whether I shall turn out to be the hero of my own life, or whether that station will be held by anybody else, these pages must show."

Finally, readers draw on a developing knowledge of the particular text. The first clause, "If you really want to hear about it," tells almost nothing of the world of this text. But by the time they read "I'll just tell you about this madman stuff that happened to me last Christmas," readers have learned quite a bit about this rather angry and hostile young person who has had a lousy childhood and who doesn't feel like going into it, though he seems to be expected to. So when they read "I got pretty run-down and had to come out here and take it easy," they think that he (and somehow this sounds like a "he") has perhaps had some sort of mental breakdown ("madman stuff") and is talking to an adult in authority (probably a psychiatrist) and they are ready to predict that the speaker will in fact explain what has happened that has gotten him there. And the voice has engaged readers enough that they probably have decided they do really want to hear about it.

Examining even this passage of one novel makes it clear that much of what's demanded of readers is similar to what's demanded of writers. Not only must readers be active and working hard at constructing meanings, but they must also make choices, guess about possibilities, ask and answer questions as they proceed. In fact, this opening paragraph from the *The Catcher in the Rye* insists that readers question, since it hasn't explained much. It hasn't begun with the standard narrative introduction ("Holden was a deeply troubled sixteen-year-old who, after suffering a nervous breakdown, found himself in a sanitarium, telling his story to a psychiatrist"). Perhaps most important, readers must keep options open and not shape the developing story into a final form too quickly, avoiding the premature closure that Ann Berthoff warns against in writing. If readers decide, for example, that the young speaker is going to tell about what readers might consider real "madman stuff" — violence or murder or self-mutilation — they will be very puzzled waiting for Holden's account of school and girl troubles and general confusion to turn into the story they've predicted. So in reading, just as in writing, readers use all sorts of knpwlege to help shape a general plan or schema for what this particular text is going to be. But they keep that plan flexible, just as they do when they write, altering it as new understandings emerge.

As readers read a book, then, they are also "reading" the book, interpreting the words on the page and creating meaning from them. What readers come to know as they read, the meaning they make, is a product of past experience (including cultural and social backgrounds) and present experience (reading). In other words, meaning comes from the language in the reader's head as well as the language in the text.

> Reading does not consist merely of decoding the written word or language; rather, it is preceded by and intertwined with knowledge of the world. Language and reality are dynamically interconnected. (Freire 1988, 29)

In *Literacy: Reading the Word and the World* Paulo Freire describes his own beginnings as a reader, and the ways in which he learned to "read the world" before he learned to "read the word". He sees the two — the world and the word — as continuous; just like reading words, reading the world requires understanding the symbolic nature of objects as signs to be interpreted. As an example of the continuity of reading the word and the world through signs, Freire recounts his own experience as a young boy who first learned to read the changes in a mango's color as a sign of the fruit's ripening or the behavior of animals as signs of their playful or angry moods. He tells us:

> My parents introduced me to reading the word at a certain moment in this rich experience of understanding my immediate world. Deciphering the word flowed naturally from reading my particular world; it was not something superimposed on it. I learned to read and write on the ground of the backyard of my house, in the shade of the mango trees, with words from my world rather than from the wider world of my parents. (32)

Freire was fortunate because his school experiences extended this early introduction to reading, so that texts, like the world, offered signs to be interpreted and understood, rather than "scanned, mechanically and monotonously spelled out." What he learned about the nature of reading and writing through his own experience shaped how he saw his role as a teacher:

> I would find it impossible to be engaged in a work of mechanically memorizing vowel sounds, as in the exercise "ba-be-bi-bo-bu, la-le-li-lo-lu." Nor could I reduce learning to read and write merely to learning words, syllables, or letters, a process of teaching in which the teacher *fills* the supposedly *empty* heads of learners with his or her words. On the contrary, the student is the subject of the process of learning to read and write as an act of knowing and of creating. The fact that he or she needs the teacher's help, as in any pedagogical situation, does not mean that the teacher's help nullifies the student's creativity and responsibility for constructing his or her own written language and for reading this language. (34–35)

All teachers are shaped by their early experiences as readers and as writers. But unfortunately school experiences have too often been divorced from the contexts of real life and a continuous reading of the world. Like many writers with both useful techniques and rigid rules, teachers carry a mixture of false notions of what reading is and what texts are, along with a few effective strategies that help them understand the texts they read.

What we do when we read

Here's a student's account of her reading:

> I noticed while reading a book by Faulkner that I was constantly trying to put his thoughts into a complete idea. I would constantly go from one page to another in hope of gaining his point. When that did not work, I found myself flipping back pages to see if I had missed something. I then began to try and associate the characters of the book with other books that I have read.... If the name Snope was mentioned I would try to recall what part he played in another book and by doing so, hoping to get to the inner meaning of the text I was reading.
>   At one point I tried to picture myself as a character of the book. One of the characters in the book *The Hamlet* is called Flem. Whenever Faulkner describes him, which is through the eyes of another character, or lets him talk for himself the book becomes fuzzy. I can never really grasp the meaning of what is taking place. So at one point I tried to portray myself as Flem. I began to actually realize the emotions of what the character was going through. I began to despise people and use meanness to get to them....

As I read on I began to notice that Faulkner had a great way of exhausting the semantic possibilities of words. Words that would first appear as innocent, would eventually come to acknowledge a totally different thing. I would constantly have to reread a passage to try and catch the true underlying meaning of sentences in the book. Still at times, I would have to wait for class to find out the real meaning....

What has come to my attention is the fact that while in high school all the books I read appeared to only have had one level of meaning. Now, however, I realize that every book can be interpreted with different meanings. I might find the theme to be one thing, and someone else another. Who is right? Who can say? (Geraldine)

Reading is usually an unconscious process. Readers pick up a book and either get it and get into it or don't get it and set it aside. Only with school reading do they feel compelled to stick to a book even when they're not getting it. Geraldine is struggling with the reading of a difficult novel for a literature course, and, for the first time, trying to notice what she does in the course of that struggle. Her account shows several things about what she does when she reads. She tries to get an overall sense of what the book is about: "I try to put his thoughts into a complete idea." When she's unsuccessful, she tries other strategies. She draws on her knowledge from other reading — here the knowledge of what parts these characters played in other books by Faulkner. She imagines herself as a particular character, drawing on her own experience of what it's like "to despise people and use meanness to get to them" in order to understand his perspective. She associates words with her own preconceived thoughts and emotions. In every case, she brings her experience — of emotions, of words and their meanings, of other texts — to the reading of this one. And she draws on all of that knowledge to help her make sense out of the words on the page.

Geraldine has definite ideas about reading and about texts. Despite the fact that she draws on her own experience, she believes that the "inner meaning" of a book is in the text itself. So she flips back pages to look for it there. She rereads passages "to catch the true underlying meaning of sentences." And when she doesn't catch it, she waits to get to class to find out "the real meaning." Yet she is beginning to find that "every book can be interpreted with different meanings," and this leaves her more confused about the "reading" of a book.

Although Geraldine still tends to see meaning as something fixed on the page, her own process of reading is an active one. Not only does she use her past experiences to shape her reading, but she uses the immediate experience of the text itself, as she flips back to earlier pages and as she redefines words as they recur. Her reading process isn't linear, moving along word by word and controlled by the sequence of words in the text, but recursive, moving back and forth within the text and between the text and her experience of the world. It's not only active but interactive and therefore dynamic.

Still, though Geraldine's questions begin to acknowledge that the reader has a role in the process of creating meaning, she isn't ready to consider that role an active one. (Her use of the passive voice exposes the passive view she takes of her own reading: "Every book can be interpreted with different meanings," rather than "Every reader interprets a book differently.") For Geraldine, the fundamental issue continues to be one of correctness or truth, as she asks "Who is right?"

Geraldine's picture of what meaning is and where it resides, a picture given to her in high school, is much like that of many readers. And her questions express the uncertainty many readers feel if that picture starts to change. Her concerns lead us into the concerns of this chapter: how reading is taught in school contexts, how fluent reading works, how fluent reading is like fluent writing, what teachers can do to create fluent readers, and how they can reconceive the relationship between readers and texts — particularly literary texts.

Reading in school

If, as Freire reminds us, readers read the text as they read the world, and shape its meanings as they shape understanding of life's experience, why does Geraldine have so much difficulty seeing the reading process as an active one and acknowledging her own role as an interpreter? Why is her experience of reading, unlike Freire's, discontinuous with her experience of the world? Most likely it's because she didn't learn to read and write under the mango trees in the backyard of her house, but learned in the sort of classroom Freire would not teach in — the classroom where learning to read and write is reduced to memorizing vowel sounds as in "ba-be-bi-bo-bu."

In fact, the theory that's dominated reading instruction in the United States has focused on just this sort of reduced literacy — on having children learn the alphabet with sound/letter correspondences, teaching children to sound out individual letters, then to blend those sounds to form words, and finally to read out series of words to make sentences. There's much emphasis on moving from alphabetic symbol to the sound that it represents (phonics), on "decoding" from symbols to spoken words, and little emphasis on the meaning of the words and sentences that are decoded. Jeanne Chall, an influential reading educator who represents a moderate version of this traditional reading pedagogy, suggests that individuals move through a series of separate stages toward facility in reading. After a "prereading" period, in which children develop perceptual skills needed for beginning reading and acquire general knowledge about letters, words, and books from the larger literate culture, children enter stage one, an "initial reading or decoding" stage (grades one and two), in which they learn to associate letters with the corresponding parts of spoken words, and then stage two, "confirmation and fluency" (grades two and three), in which children learn "to use their decoding knowledge, the redundancies of the language, and the redundancies of the stories they read" to gain fluency and speed with familiar materials. In Chall's view, it's only in later stages (grade four and up) that readers begin to use reading to discover meaning and come to new understandings (41−44).

The implementation of Chall's stage approach to reading in classroom instruction has led to emphasis on decoding individual words and phrases *before* a student is allowed to understand how those words and phrases work toward larger units of meaning. While Chall sees that some children don't require emphasis on the code in order to learn to read ("Brighter children and those from middle and high socioeconomic backgrounds also gain from such an approach but probably not as much. Intelligence, help at home, and greater facility with language probably allow these children to discover much of the code on their own, even if they follow a meaning program in school"), she would maintain the emphasis on isolated skills for nonmainstream children ("Children of below-average and average intelligence and children of lower socioeconomic background do better with an early code emphasis"). (83−84)

There's little compelling evidence to support Chall's position. The discussion in Unit 1 demonstrates that school often presents unfamiliar expectations and practices to children of nonmainstream families, and early standardized reading materials do little to make meaningful connections to their existing knowledge and experience. Reading is meaningful only when it connects with the learner's existing ways of knowing. When it doesn't, all that the child will acquire is a mechanical skill in translating letters into sounds. Early reading instruction that focuses heavily on decoding and ignores the ways in which children make meaning by drawing on their knowledge of the world only contributes to the frequently noted failure of "children of lower socioeconomic background" when they must begin to read for meaning and to acquire information.

During the "learning to read" period (generally grades one through three), school reading instruction most often consists of two activities: reading orally in groups (usually "tracked" according to "reading ability"), and completing, as deskwork, workbook and worksheet activities that reinforce the attention to discrete skills (matching up the letter *b* with words that begin with that sound, for example). Oral reading demands that the child pay most attention to sounding out each word correctly, rather than to working out the developing meaning of the text. It's perfectly possible to sound out the words without thinking about their meaning at all. (Parents become good at reading aloud to their children while thinking of other things, and can often complete pages of a story without remembering anything of what they've read.) Schools implicitly recognize the fact that focusing on sound alone impedes the development of fluency in reading, and later discourage "lip reading," to get readers to make the transition to reading silently.

Students in Ellie's theories of literacy course traced their early experiences with literacy and with reading. They wrote of their preschool years as involving storytelling and/or storyreading, playing house or school, playing family alphabet or word games (particularly in the car; many students mention road signs as an example of their earliest reading), and learning from watching parents that the reading of books and newspapers and the writing of letters were important activities. But their accounts of literacy past school age tell of two different sorts of activities. Outside school, they continued to participate in games, fantasy play, informal reading and writing (baseball cards, comics, notes, and letters), and, for some, reading library books and writing poems and stories. But in school they described being placed in reading groups — high or low — where they were praised or reprimanded. (Several students recounted embarrassing experiences in these groups. One told of how she thought she could read until she was called on to demonstrate. Then she stumbled over a word, and was told that this was a "baby" word and that she would have to be placed with the nonreaders.) They remembered school reading texts as boring and repetitive, and particularly hated the SRA series with its cards of short readings on different topics followed by comprehension questions, the competition to move through the colored sets of reading cards (often with wall charts marking students' progress), and the requirement that they work through all of the early sets before going on to the longer, more interesting stories. They also remembered spending a lot of time on worksheets, and even on flashcards, which focused on the reading of isolated words. One student found an old report card that showed a low grade in reading, with the teacher's explanation that the child was taking too little time with her worksheets because she was too eager to turn to her library book.

What was striking about this set of responses was the disjunction between students' early experiences around literacy in their homes and families and their experiences in schools. These students, many of whom were or would be teachers, had either succeeded in school tasks or had, after being tracked away from college (one student wrote of having to spend four years of high school learning the correct form of a business letter), come back to school at a later point in their lives. Those who had succeeded had enjoyed being praised. But no one remembered traditional school reading instruction as enjoyable or interesting. No one attributed a later love of reading and learning to their work in reading groups, on worksheets, with SRA or other basal reading texts. And no one talked of doing any writing, except for short worksheet answers, in conjunction with early reading. Their early school reading had focused on isolated decoding skills and fragmented, meaningless tasks, and eventually on getting the "right" answers to questions that followed reading selections. For most students in high school and college classrooms, the pattern of early reading instruction was similar, and it has influenced their practices and attitudes toward reading, particularly school reading.

How fluent reading works

In *Understanding Reading*. Frank Smith looks at the relationship of reading to ways of knowing through language. He demonstrates that because of the limits of short-term memory, it's impossible for readers to move step by step through the sounds or words of a text. Fluent readers predict what is likely to come next in a text, and scan large chunks of text quickly, to either confirm or discount those predictions. In reading, readers are constantly creating a schema for the text and revising that schema as they get new information.

> The twin foundations of reading are to be able to ask specific questions (make predictions) in the first place, and to know how and where to look at print so that there is a chance of getting these questions answered. (176)

In asking questions and seeking answers, readers depend on the existing frames of knowledge we described above: knowledge about texts, and knowledge about the world outside a text. And, although Smith doesn't say so specifically, both of these kinds of knowledge are, in fact, cultural.

Most children in a literate society do have some knowledge about some texts. Growing up in a culture in which print *is* seen as meaningful and is widely used, children develop, long before they actually learn to read print themselves, a sense of what print is and an understanding that reading is somehow linked to matching up clusters of alphabetic symbols with the things they represent. Cereal boxes, street signs, billboards, all suggest that the symbols on them stand for words that have meaning. Growing up in a pervasively literate society, children learn to read not only the signs of color or behavior significant and meaningful in the world of Freire's childhood, but also some of the signs for these signs, the printed words—the mango sign over the display of fruit in the market.

Teachers can help learners extend their own developing literacy not through workbook exercises sterilized of their associations with real life, but from stories that come from learners' growing knowledge of the world. As Unit 1 shows, people learn by linking new knowledge to old, by using what is already known to guess about what isn't yet known. Through time and experience, those predictions get revised and strengthened. As they read, then, learners look for connections with their own experience in order to make sense of the events of the text and they use their own language in order to make sense of language in a text, drawing on intuitive knowledge of familiar syntactic patterns, for example. Consequently, when school reading is completely separate from a reader's experience or language, it fails to support or extend literacy.

Smith argues that there is nothing more important to the development of fluent reading than to be read to. Children who are read to learn intuitively about some of the most important elements in reading, like voice, rhythm, context. They learn to hear the "reader-voice," the sound that directs their own later silent reading. The writer Eudora Welty describes the voice this way:

> Ever since I was first read to, then started reading to myself, there has never been a line read that I didn't hear. As my eyes followed the sentence, a voice was saying it silently to me. It isn't my mother's voice, or the voice of any person I can identify, certainly not my own. It is human, but inward, and it is inwardly that I listen to it. It is to me the voice of the story or the poem itself. The cadence, whatever it is that asks you to believe, the feeling that resides in the printed word, reaches me through the reader-voice. (14)

Readers who hear voices in texts listen for meaning, and they will later read for meaning.

Children who are read to come to another kind of shared knowledge about texts — that texts have particular forms and unfold in particular ways. They learn naturally about genres of literature: that when they hear "once upon a time," a fairy tale is about to begin, that when they hear two lines that end with rhyming words like *snow* and *go*, a regular pattern of rhymes is likely to follow. They connect meanings from the text to their own experiences, but at a comfortable distance, as they listen to the story of a little girl whose curiosity leads her to danger in a forest with talking bears. Heath and others who have studied the family reading practices that best prepare children for extended school literacy describe the ways in which parents discuss a story with the child, anticipating possible outcomes (what the bears might say if Goldilocks doesn't run away), making connections to things the child has seen in the real world (the bears they saw in the zoo last weekend), seeing ways in which the events of the story are comparable to real events ("Remember the time at Uncle Ned's that you wandered off to a neighbor's yard and got scared when the man asked what you were doing in his garden?"). The parent builds connections between the child's knowledge and the world of the text; the parent's questions help the child to extend that knowledge, providing a supportive structure for the child's learning through a process referred to as *scaffolding*. In Heath's *Ways with Words*, Maintown parents who talk about books with their children, like Trackton families who gather together on the front porch to discuss a letter, engage in reading as a constructive, and social, and affirming act.

But in school reading groups, reading aloud and even being read to focuses on the errors — or the "miscues" of reading — rather than on its meanings, and there is therefore a lot of emphasis placed on reading each word correctly. Smith's study of the reading process demonstrates that readers don't read every word when they read to themselves; in fact, they *can't* if they're to read for meaning. The brain acquires information in chunks, rather than in individual letters or words, and fills in larger patterns from small bits. So readers predict, skip whole words and phrases, looking for clues to confirm meaning. This process happens rapidly and unconsciously, but you can see it happen if you watch the eyes of a reader reading. You'll see the eye move back and forth very quickly along the line of type rather than focusing from left to right. The reader is storing information and picking up new information, predicting meaning and circling back to repredict, and all almost without conscious or deliberate effort.

You can see this process in your own reading. If you read the sentence "The captain ordered the mate to drop an ——," you fill in the remaining letters based on the context you've predicted. You no doubt predict the word *anchor*. The language of the sea and the association between drop and anchor tell you that's the right word without your reading it. But suppose the sentence continued and you read on: "— and the furry, long-nosed animal scurried across the deck." Your eye would instantaneously take you back to the *an* —— to see where you'd misled yourself. You would read *anteater* and continue, with some greater interest in the text perhaps than before, for you'd be wondering why an anteater would be aboard the ship. Misreading is often not misreading at all, but mispredicting, and that's a normal part of the fluent reading process.

When we understand the way reading works toward meaning, it's clear why worksheets or flashcards that remove words from context lessen rather than enhance ability to read for meaning. If teachers use flashcards or worksheets that remove words from sentences, so that the child can no longer tell that the letters *goat* name a thing that *kicks* or *runs*, they make the job of reading unnecessarily hard, if not impossible. And if teachers focus attention in reading groups on sounding out letter combinations without helping children draw on their knowledge of syntactic contexts, on their expectations about the relationships of subjects and verbs in English, they divorce reading from other uses of language, and create a situation in which children who're quite adept at using their language to represent their world become "poor readers."

Reading whole texts helps readers see words in their familiar syntactic settings. And talking about texts helps readers connect those words with a familiar world. Learners who discuss real-world goats and their behaviors before they read "The goat kicks and runs" will be able to predict "kicks and runs" from what they know of the nature of goats, as well as from what they know about sentences, or they'll be able to move back and read *goat* once they read about the animal's behavior. Selecting texts that draw on what readers know of the world can help them proceed confidently. So it's important that the world of the text confirm knowledge that the beginning reader brings to it.

But what about the child who's never seen a goat? What about texts that call on readers to understand something beyond their experience of the world? The child who knows nothing about the workings of a farm, who has never seen seeds planted or sheep shorn, will bring little or no experience to the reading of *My Animal Friends at Maple Hill Farm*, just as the teenager who knows little about Puritans will have trouble finding a way into *The Scarlet Letter,* and the adult who knows little about physics will have trouble finding a way into Stephen Hawking's book on cosmology, *A Brief History of Time.* Like Pat Conroy's island students, who couldn't identify their island, their state, or the ocean that surrounded them, and who found only alien words in a geography book, readers who have no *repertoire* or knowledge of subject outside the text have difficulty making meaning. While it's important for beginning readers to have some texts that refer to the world they already know how to read, as it was important for Conroy's students to read about the snakes whose habits were already part of their knowledge (if not Conroy's), it's also important to extend the experience of learners and to create new common knowledge in the classroom. A class of city children reading *Maple Hill Farm* can talk about animals they do know, squirrels and dogs and pigeons and cats, as a way of creating connections to a text about farm animals they have not seen.

Establishing such knowledge depends a great deal on talk (and talk encourages active learning). The combination of oral reading groups and seat work does not provide nearly enough productive talk for beginning readers. Traditionally, children haven't spent much time in their reading groups discussing what they're about to read or have just read, and they generally haven't had the chance to work together even on decoding or on worksheet activities. This is true despite the fact that in many communities adult reading practices are communal and constructive. The reading that people do in the real world is almost always related to contexts, things they know or have expectations about. Reading in the real world is almost always done for confirming and extending, or reseeing and questioning, what's already known and the principles of "real life" reading can and should be applied to even early reading pedagogy. Simply talking about stories before they're read and during the process of reading can accomplish a great deal.

The behaviors Smith describes for fluent readers are like those of fluent writers. Both are actively involved in the construction of meaning. Both keep an overall plan in mind as they go along, but a flexible rather than a rigid one, so that it can change as new meanings unfold. And for readers as well as writers, being able to take risks is important to developing fluency and to moving to deeper levels of interpretation. But in most schools, where reading is separated from writing, students have little opportunity to see that the two processes are similar and related, and that the active construction of understandings is central to both. In school, writing usually follows reading because it is used as a proof that reading has taken place. Reading precedes writing because it is used to give content to the writing.

The "write to read" or "whole language" pedagogies in the early grades mentioned in the last chapter present reading and writing and speaking and listening as related activities in an integrated curriculum, rather than as fragmented bits of skills. Beginning readers are engaged with their own stories, and they quickly learn not only to read out the words that appear in them but to write those words as well, gradually expanding their "dictionaries" of significant words, which they use again for new stories. The difference in approach makes a real difference in children's attitudes about reading. Gloria Norton, a teacher in a whole-language program at a bilingual school that Shirley Heath worked with, asked children from different elementary schools what reading is. Children who were learning to read in traditional school ways thought reading was "answering questions," "working in workbooks," "sounding out words," "figuring out what the teacher wants." But children from her school, who had been writing and reading their own stories, thought of reading as "living in a world that the author creates."

Other teachers of reading have likewise found the value of making the words for reading come from the context of learners' own lives and stories. Sylvia Ashton-Warner, working with poor Maori children in New Zealand, asked her pupils to tell her the words that were important to them — the words they wanted to own — and she would write each of these words out on a card for the child to carry around and use. The significant words for these children were often those that exposed the violence of their home lives — *knife, rage, fight* — and were linked to subjects that were immediately important to their reading of the world, words and subjects not to be found in the nationally prescribed textbooks. Like Ashton-Warner, Freire found it essential to use *generative* words for the texts of his literacy programs, words from the "word universe" of the learners, "expressing their actual language, their anxieties, fears, demands, and dreams," and often inserted pictures representing real situations in the learners' lives (1988, 35). With these texts, learners engage in a critical reading of their own situation of the world that supports their developing reading of text.

Reading in high school

Unfortunately, by the time many students reach high school or college classrooms, they have been affected by years of instruction that treats reading and writing as separate skills, with both separated from the activity of learning and experiencing. Many of these students will have been labeled *problem* or, more euphemistically, *developmental* readers. And they see themselves this way. "I don't like to read," one student said. "I always was in the low group." The emphasis on correct performance in these reading groups has made such readers fearful of taking risks, making predictions, putting their own associations into texts they read; they have too often had painful experience with being judged wrong. They may still sound out words, not knowing how to read for meaning. They hesitate to ask questions, for questions seem to offer proof of their failure to understand. And they see little reward in keeping at this painful activity. The basal readers used in early grades, with their limited, grade-leveled vocabulary and their bland stories, have made reading seem uninteresting. Because progress with basal readers is measured by movement through the series, there has been little encouragement for students to extend their reading outward in other directions. And the workbooks and exercise sheets that accompany basal readers have taught teachers to surround reading with discrete, decontextualized exercises rather than the sort of discussion and writing that would provide reading with real context. By the time students enter high school, too many of them have decided that reading is confining, not broadening, and that it should be confined to school.

For all readers, basic and advanced level, fluent and halting, first grader or college freshman, however, the tenets of the reading process remain the same. We want to summarize them once again here.

1. *Reading depends upon whole contexts.*

Vocabulary lessons are the high school equivalent of flashcards. To remove a word like *lithe* (a word that appears on the lists of a standard high school vocabulary test) from both its syntactic context (from the larger sentence in which it would act as an adjective, describing and modifying a thing, a noun), and from its semantic context (the meaning that it might take on in a real situation, as a quality that could inhere in real people or objects), leaves little chance for a reader to predict its meaning or connect it to what the reader already knows, and forces "learning" through rote memorization.

Ellie's family gives context to this kind of rote learning by making vocabulary tests a dinner-table game. Each week they take the list of unrelated vocabulary words her son Kenny has to learn, and they all try to place the words they know in contexts that are clever and amusing. Ellie's favorite newly contextualized word is *lithe*, and Kenny still remembers the meaning a year and a half after they came up with *Saturday Night Lithe*.

A similar classroom exercise can give students the opportunity to recontextualize words by playing with them and thus creating ways of retaining their meanings. A better way to help students learn new words, however, is to find real contexts in what students are reading and writing and discussing in class. Students will learn the meaning if they have a reason to, and a good reason is that the word expresses a quality they want to describe.

Too much time in high schools is spent on vocabulary instruction from separate vocabulary texts. We learn new words best as part of larger meaning-making activity, to name and label what we perceive in the world, and to make finer discriminations among things or to present different aspects of them in different situations. Because of limitations on the memory, no one can remember very many words learned outside a meaningful context or schema. Dictionaries are useful in confirming the meaning of a word that readers have heard or read in a particular context. But since they give decontextualized meanings, they don't help readers actually use the words they contain.

It's easy to see the effect of such decontextualized vocabulary instruction in the sentences that students produce. "My skirt was corrugated from being in the suitcase," Ellie's daughter, Karen, wrote after looking up *corrugate* in the dictionary for a recent homework exercise. In a 1987 article, "How Children Learn Words," Miller and Gildea look at vocabulary teaching in schools. They point out that the average seventeen-year-old has learned vocabulary at a rate of five thousand words per year for over sixteen years, while in school vocabulary instruction they learn no more than a hundred to two hundred words, and most of these do not become part of their useful vocabulary. Miller and Gildea give many examples of sentences like Karen's. In each case, the students have applied the dictionary meaning in a way that would seem correct. For example: looking up *correlate* — "to be related, one to the other" — produces "Me and my parents correlate, because without them I wouldn't be here." Looking up *meticulous* — "very careful" — produces "I was meticulous about falling off the cliff." Looking up *stimulate* — "to stir up" — produces "Mrs. Morrow stimulated the soup." And the examples go on in this way, providing more and more material for Lederer's *Anguished English*.

When readers don't understand the meaning of a word or phrase, they try to make sense of it in terms of the things they do know. Like

Holden, who makes meaning from a phrase he's misheard: "If a body catch a body comin' through the rye." Holden makes this line of a song mean something to him, and the meaning he makes of the line comes to represent the meaning that he's trying to make about his life. He would be the catcher who would try to keep kids like himself from going over the cliff. Holden has created the sort of context that readers need in order to make sense of words and phrases.

2. Reading depends upon knowledge of the world.

Hirsch has rightly emphasized the importance of shared knowledge to successful reading, and the need for readers to acquire a great deal of new knowledge in order to become skilled. But for students who don't bring that knowledge base, Hirsch would create a common fund of cultural knowledge in the classroom by having students memorize the content of lists of culturally important facts. When students in groups discuss Hirsch's list of culturally important terms, sharing their associations and working together to construct common understandings, they ask questions, make associations, scaffold, use their own frames of knowledge and meaning, and stimulate others to do the same. They also use linguistic knowledge, and they draw on personally based experiential associations. In working together to pool shared knowledge, they create a new context of meaning for these words, creating a framework in which they fit. Hirsch's term *Poohbah*, for example, falls outside the cultural frame of reference of many students in our university classes. But remembering some associations with Saturday morning cartoons, they decide that the term refers to someone of importance, or self-importance. They may never get to the "correct" association of the term with Gilbert and Sullivan's *The Mikado*, but they do come to a common understanding of its culturally shared associations. The very things these students do to create meaning from the list are the things all readers do as they read. And teachers can use such group processes to create shared knowledge.

By high school, much of the knowledge of the larger culture and the world comes through books, and a knowledge of other texts becomes an important part of what it means to be literate — to be able to understand the references and allusions that work to define a world of shared meaning based in books other people would have read. The first paragraph of *The Catcher in the Rye*, with its reference to David Copperfield, shows the importance of this kind of knowledge. Because Holden is a reader who makes sense of his life in part through the things he reads, readers are drawn increasingly into a web of references to other literature that create a framework of meaning for Holden and for readers: *Out of Africa*, *The Return of the Native*, as well as *David Copperfield*.

Holden has internalized the judgment of others and his string of school failures to conclude that he is "quite illiterate." He sees no contradiction between that judgment and the fact that he reads a lot (and is a good writer). Holden sees himself as illiterate because he doesn't put things in school terms, either in his writing (he'd rather describe his brother's baseball mitt than the room that his roommate's teacher suggested) or in thinking about his reading. He reads out of personal interest and need, and he doesn't describe what he reads in terms of literary criticism, but in terms that show how a book answers those needs—what knocks him out is wishing that the author was "a terrific friend of yours." The fiction that deals with fundamental human concerns like that of Dinesen of Hardy draws this response; he'd like to call up "this Isak Dinesen" and talk to her whenever he felt like it.

For students to develop, through reading, a broad cultural perspective, they must read broadly. Memorizing lists won't do. And this reading must connect in some way with their world and the things they already know, while expanding beyond that world (and beyond the traditional canon) to provide new perspectives. But too often the readers who turn to books to learn about the world have had to discover on their own—and in contradiction to what the school teaches—what books offer. They find their own meaningful context in spite of, not because of, classroom reading instruction.

Malcolm X was such a reader. In his autobiography, he talks about his early love of school, particularly of English, which abruptly ended the day his well-intentioned English teacher suggested it was unrealistic for a black man to aspire to become a lawyer, that he should consider carpentry for his career. At this point the young Malcolm X closed off school. Like so many students, he begins just to go through the motions. "I came to class, and I answered when called upon. It became a physical strain simply to sit in Mr. Ostrowski's class" (37). And his formal education ends shortly after, with eighth grade. But years later, in prison, when challenged by a visitor who argues that he knows nothing of his own black heritage—"You don't even know who you are ... you don't even know your true family name, you wouldn't recognize your true language if you heard it"—he begins to read again in a new context, searching through history and philosophy for that knowledge. As he reads, he writes long letters to Elijah Muhammad that connect his learning to his life as a Black Muslim. He talks with other prisoners, joins a debate team, begins writing himself out of a desire to explain what he's learned. In prison, he expands his world to become the "self-educated" and articulate spokesman for a large group of followers. Though, of course, it's really his exchanges with others that have provided the context for this education.

Teachers often try to encourage their students to engage in such "self-education" by offering outside reading lists that will expand their cultural knowledge and will encourage them to read for pleasure instead of necessity. But students read these books in isolation, with no discussion. Without encouragement to make personal connections to the

classics that appear on these lists, individual readers become easily discouraged by the difficulties and turn away from them. There's no
reason high school students should be required to spend the summer
before their junior year reading *Wuthering Heights* and then hate forever
the thought of reading anything by the Brontës or even from nineteenth-
century British literature. It would be better to use out-of-school reading
to extend interests created and developed in class—to read a second
Dickens novel, or to turn to an American critic of his society like Mark
Twain—to use ideas discovered in the classroom to support additional
reading. In their honest desire to give students enough background
reading to support their learning, teachers need to be careful about
assigning long lists that serve mainly to frustrate rather than support:

> I believe much of teachers' insistence that students read innumerable
> books in one semester derives from a misunderstanding we sometimes
> have about reading. In my wanderings throughout the world there
> were not a few times when young students spoke to me about their
> struggles with extensive bibliographies, more to be devoured than
> truly read or studied. (Freire 1988, 33)

Such reading is not generative or empowering.

3. Reading is supported by talk about texts.

Despite (or perhaps because of) our early experience in reading groups,
reading is most often seen as a solitary activity. Certainly long works of
fiction, which ask readers to enter and live in the world being created
for us, require close attention. And yet, to the extent that readers really
do enter the world of the text, they reenter the world with new
perspectives and new ways of seeing things that can best be used in real
life if connections are talked about. This process of connection works
both ways: making the connections with the real world of experience
explicit helps readers enter the world of the text, and helps them bring
the world of the text back into real experience. Talk connects the books
written and read with the words said and heard and makes both text and
readers become part of one extended conversation about human life and
experience. Needing this kind of talk, Holden visits a former teacher
whom he'd liked. He talks about a class that he failed, in Oral Expression,
and how the students had to "stick to the point" when what interested
him was the digressions, how the teacher, Mr. Vinson, kept telling him
"to unify and simplify all the time," and how "you can't hardly ever
simplify and unify something just because somebody *wants* you to."
The teacher responds with advice and encouragement:

> Many, many men have been just as troubled morally and spiritually as
> you are right now. Happily, some of them kept records of their
> troubles. You'll learn from them—if you want to. Just as someday, if

> you have something to offer, someone will learn from you. It is a
> beautiful reciprocal arrangement. (246)

Holden's teacher has the general idea, but he doesn't have it quite right. Entering into a larger conversation with others who have thought and worried and written about common human concerns *is* important and valuable. But the reciprocal arrangement doesn't have to mean that one studies and reads and learns from others, and then, having acquired all the knowledge, turns to pass it on. The conversation, the one that Holden is seeking, needs to go on *along with* the studying and the reading; it's an important part of the learning. And it can take place inside the classroom with peers and with teachers.

In working with teenagers and adults who haven't yet learned to read successfully or critically, teachers can begin to undo some of the damage that's been caused by a limited model of reading instruction. They can try to discover generative themes and texts in literature that will speak to learner's hearts and souls. Teachers prepare readers for reading these texts by making connections with readers' lives explicit and showing how experience might be *re*presented in the text, by making informal, unconscious knowledge formally stated and conscious. They can encourage learners to be predictors and questioners, asking them what is likely to happen next and encouraging them to use the unfolding text as a context for what is still to come. They can read *to* students, so that students can hear the expanding power of the words, and read *with* them, exploring possibilities as a Maintown parent might do in reading to a child. (In fact, one-to-one "lap-reading" has been a particularly successful route to remediation for delayed readers.) Teachers can initiate group reading and talking about texts, so that students can bring real-world strategies into the classroom and begin to establish, through sharing, the shared knowledge they need. They can encourage readers to ask questions as they read, and help them know how to find answers both within and outside the text (in library reference materials, for example), and encourage them to revise their understandings as they read. And, finally, teachers can encourage readers to write.

4. Reading is supported by writing.

Writing is important to reading for all learners, not just for children, because it establishes and records active engagement with the text in a continuing act of interpretation, an interpretation that derives from both the text and the world. A limited view of reading, which many students hold, is that the meaning is wholly in the text, buried there like a golden treasure, and the accomplished reader (usually only the teacher) is the one who knows how to find it. Such a view emerges from classrooms where the teacher's questions concentrate only on facts, where there is only one right answer to any question, where texts contain answers the teacher knows and the students must find: "What was stolen from Silas Marner before he found the child?" "What was the name of Pip's stepfather?" "What does Hester Prynne's scarlet A symbolize?" And it emerges from writing used only for the teacher's evaluative purposes, so that the student can show possession of these "right" answers. Reading instruction that asks students to read isolated paragraphs and look for the "main idea" reinforces the notion of one "right" answer.

When readers write as they read, they record their speculations, their predictions, and their associations with a text, and the writing becomes a way to help them interpret actively the text they're reading. Journals, in-process notes, responses to sections of texts, bits of created dialogue, all are ways of encouraging meaning making by making writing a tool for interpretation.

Readers and texts

This chapter began with a paragraph from *The Catcher in the Rye* and talked of the ways reading the text both drew from and built knowledge, combining readers' experiences with life, reading, and culture and an evolving knowledge that came from reading the text itself. Once they have learned to read, readers tend not to pay much attention to this complex process of making sense of and interpreting texts. Unlike readers, literary critics have made the interpretation of texts their primary concern and have traditionally focused on texts themselves, not what readers bring to them. They've seen knowledge as fixed in the text, not evolved by a reader in the process of reading.

The idea that knowledge is in the text, existing apart from what readers bring to and make of it, is a dominant theory of literacy, of the differences between spoken and written language. But in few sentences, either in texts or in life, is the meaning wholly in the words themselves. Whether the teacher says or writes, "You did a great job on this essay," the meaning must still be interpreted by the student based on both the immediate context (the other words that were written, or the teacher's expression or tone — whether sincere or sarcastic) and the larger context (the past practice of the teacher and the past experience of the student).

Although primary attention has usually been given to the text itself, and to the elements within the text that support interpretation (like the New Criticism in most of the twentieth century), literary criticism has occasionally shifted its emphasis over the years, pausing every so often to focus attention away from the text and the knowledge within it. In the nineteenth century in the Romantic period, criticism looked toward the writer, and now, in the late twentieth century, it often looks toward the reader. The Romantic movement glorified the soul of the poet, whose inspirations were "divine" and who simply translated the world for readers to appreciate. Romantic critics believed the best way to locate meaning for the text was therefore by understanding the poet's mind at work, understanding his life and the sources of the writer's inspiration as the real way to understand the text. If you were a Romantic critic, knowing as much as possible about J. D. Salinger's life would be the key to a good reading of *The Catcher in the Rye*. And, of course, a Romantic critic would have a tough time with Salinger, since he's spent his life trying to prevent anybody from knowing anything about that life.

The arguments that grew up around an approach to interpretation that focused primarily on the author resulted, in the twentieth century, in a "New Criticism." "We don't have access to the poet's mind," the New Critics said, "and, what's more, why should we believe what the poet says about his work?" "The word uncag'd, never returns", wrote Horace in the first century B.C., and the New Critics focused their attention on the word as it existed apart from the creator of it, as it lived by itself in a text. New Criticism — a movement designed to shift the attention away from the author and onto the text — has dominated critical responses to literature and the teaching of literature for most of this century. Most current university English professors were trained in this tradition, and most English majors have studied in it. For New Critics, any literary text can and should be read apart from the context of time and author, meanings can be found by accomplished readers, and the same meanings are found through all accomplished reading. If readers differ in their interpretations of a text's meaning, one reader has the right interpretation or later will get the right one. The right reading comes about through the techniques of *close reading*, with intense attention to language, to metaphor, to thematic structure, to genre. The New Critic who reads *The Catcher in the Rye* might begin as we did earlier in this chapter, looking at the words of the text, seeing what the language is like, how themes get brought up and reinforced, how character is developed, how narrative conventions like first-person narration are used.

More recently, in the last twenty years, literary critics have argued against New Criticism by insisting that the reader makes the crucial difference in interpretation; that texts don't mean very much apart from the reading of them. The tree that falls in the forest makes no sound, they might say, unless there's someone there to hear. While New Criticism asserts that because different readers interpret in different ways, critics must stick to the text, reader-response criticism asserts that it's precisely because they interpret in different ways that critics have to look at readers' interpretations. For this reason — the emphasis

on the hearer or reader and the consequent variability of interpretation—
reader-response critics are sometimes called *subjectivist* critics; because of
their emphasis on the object of the text. New Critics are characterized
with the opposite term, *objectivist*. The better term for the reader-
response critics is probably *reader-oriented*, for while these critics vary in
the degree to which they assign responsibility to the reader in making
meaning, all insist on taking the reader into account in the interpretive
process. Reader-response critics would look at various readers' reactions
to the opening of *The Catcher in the Rye* to find out what meanings they
made from the text, and to see, perhaps, how important knowing
about David Copperfield might be to their early enjoyment of the
novel, how much readers identify with Holden's teenage struggles,
where and how they make predictions about what will happen next.

One strand of reader-oriented criticism attempts to combine subjective and objective perspectives on reading. *Transactional* critics try to
account for the ways in which the world the reader brings to the text
and the words the reader finds there work together in creating an
interpretation. The work of one such critic, Louise Rosenblatt, has been
particularly influential with teachers because it provides an approach to
literature that takes into account the needs and perspectives of learners
without denying the importance of the text in shaping the reader's
understanding. Her approach looks at the text and its author *and* the
reader. In Rosenblatt's description, both reader and text merge in the
act of interpretation, into what she calls the "event" of creating the
"poem." Because she is so useful to teachers and so clearly connected to
the arguments we've been making here, we want to summarize some of
the most important tenets of her theory of reading literature. The
connections to Frank Smith's studies of reading are clear:

1. The reader is active, building meaning out of responses to a text.
2. The reader pays attention to text as only one element in producing
   meaning, and draws as well on associations, feelings, images, ideas
   evoked by the text's words.
3. The reader's past experience is important to making sense out of
   verbal signals on the page—"built into the raw material of the
   literary process itself is the particular world of the reader" (11).
4. The reader's response is self-ordering and self-correcting. The confident reader will enter into a reading knowing that he'll recognize
   where elements don't fit, where adjustments have to be made to
   achieve a coherent meaning.

If the reader is active and necessary in interpretation, Rosenblatt argues
that the text plays an important role as well:

1. The text is a stimulus, activating the reader's experience with literature and life.

2. The text is a blueprint for ordering, rejecting, selecting what is evoked from the reader.

In Rosenblatt's model, the reader and the text are put into relationship with each other. So meaning is not the property of the reader or of the text, but emerges from the transaction between the two.

> Part of the magic — and indeed of the essence — of language is the fact that it must be internalized by each individual human being, with all the special overtones that each unique person and unique situation entail. Hence language is at once basically social and intensely individual. (20)

The transaction is not merely then between the reader and text in producing the poem or the event of meaning. It is a transaction between individual and community, between thought and language, and thus reading illustrates, symbolizes, and provides a specialized instance of what humans do all the time as they experience and reflect on experience in their worlds. The very physical signs of the text — its verbal symbols — allow the reader to break through his own individual world and move outside and beyond the personal world. Transactional literary criticism insists that the text be part of the event of meaning, so that the text becomes a way to influence and check a reader's response while the classroom community helps students to corroborate their own subjective interpretations.

Rosenblatt would revise the usual distinction between literary and nonliterary texts, focusing not on differences between kinds of texts but between kinds or purposes of reading. (This is comparable to Britton's revision of the rhetoric of discourse in terms of functions of or purposes for writing.) Rosenblatt distinguishes between two types or uses of reading, which she calls *efferent* and *aesthetic*. Both are defined in terms of the reader's purpose, and she asks, "What does a reader read for?" In efferent reading, the reader reads with an eye toward what she will get out of the reading, what will remain after she completes reading. We read efferently when we study for a test or prepare to recite or look for relevant quotations to use in an essay, or when we're trying out a recipe or replicating an experiment (just as Britton would say that we engage in transactional writing when we write for these purposes). In aesthetic reading, the reader reads to be involved in the moment of reading itself. "In aesthetic reading, the reader's attention is centered directy on what he is living through during his relationship with that particular text." (25)

In most classrooms, these two sorts of reading are separated (as are creative and expository writing) according to the content of each book, and there's the assumption that books in most disciplines will be read efferently. (In high school, even the reading of literature is most often assumed to be for the purpose of extracting information and not for aesthetic response.) But, in Rosenblatt's terms, texts themselves are not inherently either efferent or aesthetic. A book on cell biology may seem efferent by definition to many readers, but a reader with an interest in cells may appreciate the moment of discovering something new about their formation. And a writer like Lewis Thomas will write a biology book that most readers will respond to aesthetically. Hepsie's math teacher in high school used to talk about the beauties of the quadratic equations in the eleventh-grade math book. Her appreciation for the skill of a student who mastered one on the blackboard was an aesthetic reaction to the balance of the formula as she saw the student develop it. In contrast, when Hepsie's English class studied prosody (patterns of rhyme and rhythm in poetry), students looked at Marvell not to experience "To His Coy Mistress" but to figure out the pattern that emerged from the poet's careful manipulation of lines and stanzas. They read the poem for what they could learn about formulas from it. In other words, they read efferently.

For the teacher, two questions arise immediately about reader-oriented approaches in the classroom: how does a teacher effect the sort of transaction between reader and text that would help students enter the works they read through observing their own personal response and making connections with their own experience, building toward a reading not just of that experience but of the literary work? And how does a teacher help her students find the aesthetic reading instead of always and only the efferent one?

A cooperating teacher who was also one of our graduate students explored these issues in her master's essay. As a teacher in a large high school in Boston, she had often found that her "low-level" students were "turned off by" the books they read—even by those that seemed relevant to their lives. Their own experiences did not help them enter the world of the text, but were irrelevant to or interfered with their ability to enter it. While she was thinking about her students' reading, Joyce herself had a similar experience with a text she expected to find relevant, Andrea Lea's novel *Sarah Phillips*. Joyce had expected to find confirmation of her own experiences of family, religion, and race in this novel. Instead she found herself frustrated and angered by the protagonist's actions and responses.

> The fact that Sarah and I share a common race had me especially eager to read the novel. Unfortunately, I hoped for too much satisfaction from the reading because of this issue. Experience taught me to believe that no matter how many varying backgrounds black Americans have, they have a commonality which may be as simple as mutual respect for the same race. Sarah complicated my thinking on this issue when I read of her desire to reject her blood and by implication her race. (13–14)

Just as Elbow used his own experiences with writer's block as a starting point for learning about the composing process and developing effective pedagogy in composition, teachers can use their experiences as readers to help them understand and respond to the reading of their students. In this case, Joyce explored reader-response theory and decided to observe in detail her own responses, as an active reader, to this surprisingly frustrating text. She wrote about her own experiences, and she annotated the text as she read. She kept a double-entry notebook in which she noted parts of the text annotated the text as she read. She kept a double-entry notebook in which she noted parts of the text that evoked her responses and then reflected on those parts and those responses. She reread, letting her prior experience of the text reshape her expectations and using what was in the text, rather than what had been in her experience, to predict what was to come. And when she had come to an understanding of this text and of the process that she as a reader had used to gain this understanding, she applied what she had learned to developing a sequence of writing and reading and double-entry notebook assignments for her students that would allow them to move back and forth between their experiences and a text they were reading.

For her students, Joyce adapted the activities that had supported her own reading. She wanted them to learn to focus their attention on different areas of the text, so she had them use the double-entry format twice, once with students' selection of excerpts and reflections on them, and once with her selection of excerpts for them to reflect on. The second set of selections moved students toward a larger experience of the text—toward considering, in a now familiar format, aspects of the text they'd not found immediate connections with, and toward using this new experience of the text to resee their earlier reading of it. Although Joyce found that her students continued to respond more from their experience of the world than of the text, "they were able, in the end, to connect that experience with the larger themes of the text" (36).

Reading for the pleasure of the text, like bringing the experience of the reader into a consideration of the text's meaning, has important implications for the English classroom. Reading sometimes for pleasure rather than for information can free students to engage with and really think about the things they read, to develop beyond presenting the safe facts of the text (the details of plot, characters' names, etc.) to seeking the significance of those facts. Students can come to interpret the events of a story, the images of a poem. They can make associations with their own lives and see how their own experiences affect their readings of the text. They can read actively and imaginatively. And in doing so, they move from what's known to what's unknown and use the latter to resee the known, to see larger significance in familiar events.

As students bring their different readings into the classroom, they can talk with others, in a community of readers, and see the common meanings that are made as different readers come together, and share their different readings of the text. But this classroom interaction can raise new questions for the teacher who wants to honor each student's response to a text and yet create a functioning interpretive community in the classroom. Marjorie Roemer raised these concerns in a 1987 *College English* article, "Which Reader's Response?" Roemer recognizes the appeal that reader-response theory has for teachers like herself, who "see themselves effecting a more dynamic, more empowering classroom situation with readers who are being invited to make active and personal engagements with the texts they encounter." But she worries that classrooms communicate "a set of dominant values and manners." It's likely that those values will be in conflict with the readings that at least some students will take from the literature they read, and that there will still be a silencing of whatever experiences lie outside of the dominant community.

> The teacher is not merely directing her class through a survey of methodological styles. If she is really eliciting reader response, she is opening a space in her classroom where diverse cultural codes of all kinds will be contested.... Much critical debate proceeds as though the world were divided between old "new critics" and new "poststructuralists" [including reader-response critics], but the divisions in the world are much deeper and more complicated than that. (914–915)

It's a continual challenge to the teacher to recognize the force of her own authority, not to subdue students' divergent responses to the texts they read, but to encourage readers to *name* those responses, as Freire would have them do, and through that naming to resee the world and see ways of acting on it. But making a place for those responses in the classroom and opening up dialogue with students about the texts they read is an important place to begin.

Teaching *The Catcher in the Rye*

A student teacher who observed and then taught classes on *The Catcher in the Rye* reflected on approaches to that reading in her journal. She (and, through dialogue, her cooperating teacher) moved from an approach that focused on "right answers" and an acceptance of students' passive response, to a transactional approach, bringing together the experience of the reader with a close examination of the text and attention to the author, combining writing and reading, encouraging readers to become active learners, and trying to create a community that values the experiences that shape different students' responses. Sela begins by imagining alternative ways of introducing the novel so as to engage the imagination of the students.

> I felt frustration as I watched B put a set of questions on Chapter 1 on the board for kids to answer in class. Then, she added another set of questions on the overhead for kids to do as homework regarding Chapter 2. To me, it was a very mechanical way to begin one of the most controversial contemporary novels, or to begin any piece of literature for that matter. Kids were obviously unengaged. They needed a means of stimulation to get them involved.
>
> If I had been able to kick off *Catcher*, I would have given them some background on Salinger, who certainly is something of a character. It also might have been interesting to distribute excerpts from book reviews that came out when the book was published to show what diverse response it has engendered. In addition, I would have pointed out that *Catcher* has been the most censored book in American educational history, and I then would have asked them to be on the lookout for possible offensive material as they read it. Even considering the peculiarity and obscurity of the title as an introductory activity would have given kids motivation to want to read the novel and find out where the title comes from.

She recognizes the importance of background knowledge and of putting such information in terms that are familiar to students.

> Something that shocked me was when B asked me if I knew the "David Copperfield and all that crap" reference on the first page. Kids thought it was a reference to a contemporary magician!! They don't take into account that the novel was published way back in 1951, before the magician in question was on the scene. When I replied that David Copperfield was the name of a Charles Dickens novel about a boy who had a lousy childhood, [they] said that [they] hadn't heard of it. . . .
>
> She asked me to clarify his *Out of Africa* reference, so I began by asking how many kids had seen the movie version a few years ago? Some had. Then, I explained that this had been adapted from a novel written by a European woman who had married a wealthy man and moved to an African plantation, where she began to write. . . .

As students move from mechanical question answering to reading and discussion, they become involved.

> This morning I felt much better at how the class shaped up. B had them start reading Chapter 3 out loud, pushing to elicit responses to the text. Kids got involved and really seemed to enjoy the narrative. They laughed at the humorous parts without indulging in any silliness. I was impressed at how mature they were about the farting incident.
>
> B asked them why Holden would call himself "illiterate" and yet make all kinds of references to works of literature that he had read. Kids felt that he meant that he had trouble reading what he read. One kid added that maybe Holden was referring to his lousy vocabulary. B

asked them if Holden in fact had a poor vocabulary and what evidence
there is, if any, for difficulty in reading. "Is he being too hard on
himself?" she asked. "Is he putting himself down?"

I finished up the reading of Chapter 3 with the kids. Two Vietnamese
girls volunteered to read, and I helped them out when they stumbled
over words. One of them was having trouble with "sonovabitch," and
I joked that by the end of the book she'd have no trouble saying it.
Kids laughed.

Through discussion, students become aware of their conflicting
readings. Sela uses this opportunity to turn their attention back to the
text.

Several kids again asked how old Holden is, and I explained that he is
16 when the events of the story take place. Someone interjected that he
thought Holden was 17. I responded that when Holden is recounting
the events of the story after they happened, he's 17. Since kids still
seemed confused, I had them turn to page 1 again and look at his
reference to getting run down and having to take it easy at "this
crumby place." I explained that this is Holden's not very direct way of
letting us know he's had a nervous breakdown and that the narrative
represents his looking back at the events leading to his mental collapse.

And Sela draws on students' own experiences to help them understand
the motivation and responses of the novel's characters.

Before considering Stradlater's attitude about girls and Holden's feelings
about Jane, I mentioned that as we continue to read the novel, they
should pay special attention to Holden's encounters with women—to
note which ones are upsetting to him and which ones are satisfying to
him.

In helping the kids perceive Stradlater's lack of respect for women,
I pointed to his remark about a previous date being "a pig" and asked
them what that shows us about Stradlater. It was interesting to me
that Loretta didn't think it showed a lack of regard. She emphasized
that he was calling a "specific girl" a pig rather than saying that all
girls are pigs. Kim added that "maybe the girl really was a pig," so
Stradlater was justified in calling her one. I wasn't sure if the kids
attached the same meaning to "pig" that I do, so I asked them what
the term suggests. Somebody said, "fat," and Randy replied that
Stradlater wouldn't go out with any fat girls, that since he was so
handsome he'd want a gorgeous girl. Then, I asked them what having
to think about Jane's name and then getting it wrong—calling her
"Jean"—shows us about Stradlater. Had he been paying attention
when he met her? What was he interested in? Randy answered "himself."
I asked the girls how they would feel if they were out on a date with a
guy and he called them by someone else's name. Loretta replied, "I'd
tell him to take a hike."

To follow up, I'll have them write on the following topic: "With
whom would you rather go out on a date, Holden or Stradlater?
Why?"

While these discussions went on, students wrote in journals in class and wrote essays at home. In fact, beginning-of-class journal writing was first instituted because the cooperating teacher wanted an activity that would help with discipline, demanding students' immediate attention as they entered the classroom. Sela suggested that they write in journals about their responses to the previous night's reading and she found that this significantly increased their involvement in the discussion. Writing answers to the teacher's text-based comprehension questions was postponed until after class discussions (and was sometimes done in small groups) and by that point students were comfortably involved with the text (sometimes enough so that they questioned the questions). Little by little, these students and their teachers worked at finding ways into this novel, through writing and reading and talking and developing shared knowledge and negotiating common understandings. In the process, students changed their roles in the classroom from passive and silent to active and engaged.

The reticence and disengagement of many high school and beginning college readers arises from the fact that reading seems so external to them, wholly dependent on outside authority. The most successful college "remediation" programs are not those that work on isolated skills in either reading or writing, but those that help students resee their relationship with what they read and write, that help them feel their own interpretive authority as readers. The approaches to reading we've discussed in this chapter empower readers and allow students to have authority over their reading. In particular, they open a way for writing to be used to enhance reading and interpretation, as a way of reading the text. Too often students see both the texts produced by other writers and their own writing as very distant from themselves. They fear to take authority for interpreting others' texts in the same way they fear to take authority for their own. But as students are encouraged to see reading and writing not as separate activities with subsets of discrete skills to be mastered but as interpretive acts, they learn to see their own reading as imaginative and their own writing as literature; they see themselves as engaged imaginatively in using language to make meaning of the world.

CHAPTER 8

Imagination in the English Classroom

One of the reasons the disparate activities of literacy haven't been more fully integrated into the English classroom has been that teachers haven't seen how to connect those activities with any kind of real coherence. How does one teach *Julius Caesar* and sentence combining and the comparison/contrast essay at the same time? How is it possible to teach skills of reading and speaking and listening and writing in an hour-long class? And why try to transcend those individual activities when textbooks, course guides, and evaluation procedures set them so firmly in separate categories?

If they give the imagination a place in the classroom at all, teachers consign it to one of those discrete activities that students pick up and discard when the moment requires. The imagination is in this view a limited act, like paragraphing or summarizing, that helps students write the occasional short story or poem or tall tale. The curriculum in place in English departments across the country supports that view. Vocabulary is separated from reading, punctuation is separated from sentences, sentences from paragraphs, creativity from analysis. Not suprisingly, teachers infer that the real work of the English classroom centers on rules and applications, on individual and discrete units of information, rather than on some larger activity of learning that would arrange individual bits into a pattern. As a consequence, students are taught to regard what they do when they read *Julius Caesar* as something entirely different from what they do when they write about it and both as different from the grammar exercises that accompany the unit of study. And none of those activities is presumed to call upon the imagination. The study of language in class becomes entirely removed from the uses of language in and outside class. And it's that separation of the skills of literacy from their embodiments in literature and in talk that encourages students to divorce what they do in one class from another class and divorce what they do as learners from what they do as people. A student in a history class is angry if a teacher comments on her writing. "This isn't English!" she'll complain. A student assigned a task that takes her out of the classroom to observe or to talk to people reacts with surprise and often suspicion. "Are you sure this is all right?" or even "Are you sure this is school?"

But for the most part, unfortunately, students aren't surprised by their classroom assignments because those assignments seldom take them beyond the boundaries of the skills of the discipline; they complete their tasks as they're required to do and then quickly move on to more significant activities: talking to one another, planning lives and futures, playing sports, finding hobbies. It seems clear that before educators can create an integrated curriculum in English, they must show students how their real lives put them at the center of their classroom lives, how what they do in life contributes to what they do when they read and write. More than that, educators must help students realize (and this means they must realize it themselves) that the process of living is a process of interpretation, which means that students come to the activities of reading and writing with lots of useful strategies.

How do we go about putting together life outside and inside the classroom? An integration of the elements of literacy involves recognition of the act of mind that is required to read, to write, to listen, to speak. That act of mind is the ability to interpret, or, to put it as philosophers from Coleridge to I. A. Richards to Susanne Langer to Ann Berthoff have done, to use the imagination. In this chapter we want to talk about the imagination as the central element in a classroom that creates active learners. To do that, we need to redefine the imagination by explaining its function in learning and then show how it works in classroom strategies. All learning — and all that we've been saying about language, writing, reading — depends on the imagination for the making of new meaning. People learn by building on and extending what they already know. And it's in imagining — forming concepts and testing them — that they leap beyond what is known, creating new connections and new knowledge.

The imagination in school

Schools traditionally have consigned the imagination to the creative writing class or the creative writing assignment because it has been classified as *affective* rather than *cognitive*, dependent on *feeling* rather than *analysis* for its methods and hence not useful for engaging the more frequently assigned, and therefore by implication more highly regarded, activities of analyzing, arguing, reporting, summarizing. Creative writing assignments serve as a break from other more "serious" writing tasks, as teachers assign poem or fiction writing with frequent exhortations to "use your imaginations!" How many times have you heard a teacher tell her students to use their imaginations as they begin to write literary analysis or the research paper?

The truth is that when a teacher tells students to use their imaginations, he states a foregone conclusion: students can't do anything but. Imagination is the force that allows the student to make knowledge out of experience. Coleridge defined the imagination as "the prime agent of all human perception" (452). For Coleridge, and for us, the imagination names the active mind, and the mind's activity is a process of making sense of the world through discovery of connections and formulation of concepts. The imagination therefore forges the essential link between the outer and inner world, between object and perceiver. "An object is not datum, but form constructed by a sensitive, intelligent organ," Susanne Langer says (4). The mind's primary activity—the process of sense making, of formulating and categorizing the "blooming, buzzing confusion" that is the world—is an imaginative one. Another way of saying all this is to say that we can't know anything about objects apart from our perception of them; in knowing, the connection between object and perceiver is intimate and necessary.

But when classroom teachers fix the imagination in the realm of fantasy creations that students accomplish in their off time, they short-circuit the connection between world and mind that is necessary for learning by falsely dividing the knower from the known, or the student from her object of study. In *Reclaiming the Imagination*, Ann Berthoff uses excerpts from the writings of thinkers from many disciplines to explore the role of the imagination in the making of meaning, and she argues that the imagination needs to be *reclaimed* by teachers of writing for just this reason: the imagination is the power that allows knowers to make knowledge. Like I. A. Richards, who coined the term, Berthoff believes that classrooms should become *philosophic laboratories* where teachers and students explore ways of knowing, and she lists the tools they should use: "Among the speculative instruments needed in our laboratories are forming, thinking, knowing, abstracting, meaning-making, acting, creating, learning, interpreting: Imagination names them all" (1984, x). In other words, Berthoff shows that the activities we stress in the classroom are in fact imaginative; the key is to make the shaping and forming that go on in composing, in reading and writing, conscious and active so that the imaginative faculty becomes engaged. Knowing isn't following a procedure but imagining one; knowledge isn't fixed somewhere apart from that imagining but created through it.

The imagination, then, is the mind's ability and need to form by reconstructing and formulating experience in terms of what it knows already and what it needs to know. Given what we're beginning to see now as its importance in learning, engaging the imagination should be a primary—maybe *the* primary—responsibility of teachers. Alfred North Whitehead was quite specific on this point as he discussed the function of the university. We quote his words at length here because they're equally applicable to all classrooms—high school and elementary as well as university:

Thus the proper function of a university is the imaginative acquisition of knowledge. Apart from this importance of the imagination, there is no reason why business men, and other professional men, should not pick up their facts bit by bit as they want them for particular occasions. A university is imaginative or it is nothing—at least nothing useful....

Imagination is a contagious disease. It cannot be measured by the yard, or weighed by the pound, and then delivered to students by members of the faculty. It can only be communicated by a faculty whose members themselves wear their learning with imagination.... The whole art in the organization of a university is the provision of a faculty whose learning is lighted up with imagination....

The combination of imagination and learning normally requires some leisure, freedom from restraint, freedom from harassing worry, some variety of experiences, and the stimulation of other minds diverse in opinion and diverse in equipment. Also there is required the excitement of curiosity, and the self-confidence derived from pride in the achievements of the surrounding society in procuring the advance of knowledge. Imagination cannot be acquired once and for all, and then kept indefinitely in an ice box to be produced periodically in stated quantities. The learned and imaginative life is a way of living, and is not an article of commerce. (133–134)

Whitehead puts together the learned and imaginative life in the classroom, and thus breaks down the dichotomy between personal knowledge and "book learning." And he reclaims the imagination as a powerful force in learning rather than as a useful skill for creating engaging plots.

Yet, despite the important role that philosophers like Whitehead have claimed for the imagination in all human knowing, we've made little place for it in schools. Although we give some attention to the imagination in some parts of the school curriculum—in art, music, drama classes—if imagining isn't valued throughout the curriculum, it's unlikely to be truly fostered by teachers in any of their classes; and where it's suddenly and arbitrarily demanded of students, it can't flourish. A student who was carrying out an ethnographic study of the literate culture of a sixth-grade classroom made the following observations of what could have been an imaginative activity.

My first encounter with this constructive environment occurred during art class. The children, rather than making a drawing as I anticipated, built windsocks. They were given the instructions step by step by the teacher as they were doing the project. The directions were conveyed in a straightforward linear method with short concise statements that were easy to follow. For example "Glue the paper onto the rolls. Cut shapes from the construction paper. Glue shapes onto rolls." Etc. She constantly repeated these phrases so that the children would continue to work together as a class. There were, however, chances for an individual's creativity.

But when the teacher told them to cut out whatever shapes they wanted, some of the children were a little flustered. A majority, actually, needed some encouragement about what forms to cut, while others had difficulty deciding which paper to choose. Eventually the teacher was forced to prompt the children by suggesting particular shapes. When that did not help, Miss L. then encouraged another student to draw a shape, cut it out, then pass it along so the more indecisive students could trace it.

A second incident occurred when a child went ahead of the group to the next step. He applied his streamers to the outside of the roll instead of the inside. When the teacher saw this she brought attention, albeit constructively, to the differences between his windsock and the one displayed. She was not critical of his creativity, she assured him his sock was nice and all right, but she was critical of his not waiting for proper instructions. (Marie)

Marie's observations show how quickly the imagination, even in a "creative" activity, loses its place to the dominant classroom focus on conforming to rules for procedure or format. In this classroom, imagination or "creativity" is just one prescribed step in a series of steps. When students are unable to switch from following the teacher's prescriptions to creating their own composition—to deciding on and arranging their own shapes—the teacher, frustrated by their inability to take her lead, gives them forms to trace. When a child uses his imagination to invent the next step in the process—to see a relationship between what was previously constructed and the final object—he's reprimanded for moving ahead. Although the teacher is, at least overtly, "not critical of his creativity," she also makes it clear that this creativity has led to error. It may, in fact, be important to the functioning of a windsock that the streamers be placed on the outside rather than the inside. But the child doesn't get a chance to discover this, to explore the congruence between form and function, to encounter problems and invent solutions. Rather, he learns that his creation is wrong because it's different. In the same way, students of written composition, if given only rules of prescribed forms ("Be sure you have an introduction, three main paragraphs, and a conclusion!") or prescribed steps in a process ("Has everyone finished brainstorming? Good. Now we'll draft for the rest of the period, and then revise tomorrow"), are unlikely to be able to respond to sudden demands for writing that shows depth of insight and understanding—to be able to compose. They may find it hard to imagine fitting relationships between the forms they'll use and the ways their writing will function.

Most classrooms in high school and college are, in fact, far away from the philosophic laboratories Berthoff envisions. A long series of divisions—administrative, curricular, philosophical—keep the activities of learning separate from one another and prevent students from making themselves part of their work in the classroom through their imaginations. The administrative structure of schools itself becomes a pervasive dividing force in learning. Structures like the system of tracking by ability groupings, condemned in almost all recent studies of American education, remain in place in part because administrators, parents, teachers, and students themselves can't even imagine another structure, another alternative to labeling students in classrooms based on certified and rigidly defined standards of performance. And it's this "paralysis of imagination," as Theodore Sizer describes it, that limits the possibilities of American high schools.

How does the imagination work?

There's been a long discussion in Western philosophy about imagination, what it is and how it works. Plato placed imagination at the lowest rank of mental faculties because he thought imagination merely imitated perception, which in itself was lower than discursive reasoning, scientific knowing, and rational intuition. The opposition between imagination and reason, with reason most often being given privileged status, has been with us ever since. From Descartes to the eighteenth-century Rationalists and up to the Romantics, the two mental faculties were seen as divided, even competing for dominance, within the individual. In part because the imagination was ineffable, without clear rules or absolute systems, reason and the system of logic that supported it was — and is — held in higher esteem. As we've indicated, Coleridge is an exception to this long tradition; he placed the imagination at the center of thought and at the center of the individual's power to interpret, emphasizing the creative imagination that moved the soul of the interpreter. But the glorification of the imagination with the Romantics was short-lived. And the turn toward objectivity, rational experimentation, and the preeminence of the text in this century led philosophers and literary critics to embrace even more strongly the rational and logical at the expense of the imaginative.

Even Piaget treats imagining as an early stage in the child's development of thought, something to be transcended as the child matures. Piaget notes that the imagination, seen especially in games and play, allows the child to represent objects and situations not present in perception, but that it's only a stage in the child's development toward nonimagistic symbolizing. He draws on a model of scientific thinking in his study of children's development, and scientific thinking is usually thought to be in opposition to the imagination, providing objective and accurate information about reality, while the imagination gives subjective and inaccurate accounts.

But others have seen the imagination as central to scientific thinking, as well as to poetry or music. In *The Origins of Knowledge and the Imagination*. Jacob Bronowski, the mathematician and biologist, discusses the place of the imagination in all knowing. He suggests that "every act of imagination is the discovery of likenesses between two things which were thought unlike" (101), citing as an example Newton's use of the metaphor of a ball thrown around the earth to think about the moon's rotation. Bronowski says that such discoveries of new likenesses open up a closed system of relationships, of one-to-one correspondences and systematic decoding, to things that haven't been included in the system so far. And, from the perspective of the existing system, the new discoveries tend to look wrong, even if they're ultimately more right than what has gone before. "All imaginative inventions are, to some extent, errors with respect to the norm" (111).

Likewise, Jerome Bruner finds two connected modes of imagination. He describes the *paradigmatic* imagination as "the ability to see possible formal connections before one is able to prove them in any formal way" (1986, 13). The paradigmatic mode helps learners create formal systems. But the ability to imagine possible worlds as well as to perceive actual ones in turn lets people step outside of the systems they have constructed, outside of the "given" of the logical paradigm, to see things in new ways. And narrative and metaphor aid in that process. "The artist creates possible worlds through the metaphoric transformation of the ordinary and the conventionally 'given,'" Bruner says (49). So, for Bruner as well as Bronowski, whether the existing system is a bureaucratic structure, a format for lessons, a poetic form, or a scientific problem, coming to new understandings involves moving outside of the existing system, reconceiving it and seeing it in new ways. And to make that kind of change, learners must recast what they know in new terms.

Seeing old things in new ways

For Janet, a biology major, participating in a prepractice class for English majors led to her reconceiving the teaching of biology. She records her new thinking in her journal:

Most science projects do not really ask questions. There are no new questions and new answers. They are projects showing us that a student knows enough to look up things in an encyclopedia, copy the information, draw pictures of the subject, etc ... but not much use of reading and writing to truly discover knowledge.

I am thinking that a good exercise for science students would be to write about pictures and diagrams. Write from observation of electron micrographs, follow their thoughts and explorations through writing, learning to explain a process such as the lytic cycle of a virulent virus in writing after only seeing a picture or model of it. I like the idea of turning the visual into literal. I think it fits nicely in learning science.

Descriptive writing applied to what is seen under the microscope or
observed in a field site. Keeping a naturalist's journal. Mrs. W, like
most teachers, is aware of "getting through the material," teaching for
the test, keeping to the structure....

   I'd like biology class to meld with art and writing. I see the
possibilities to have students observe, draw, and write and make
beautiful journals of their learnings. I find it distressing to see how
"low interest" biology class is at this school. It is such an engaging
topic, really, which affects us daily. I've learned that the key to
turning people onto it is to bring it "home" to them. It's got to be
colorful, exciting, visual, and personal too.

In thinking about how to engage her students' imaginations in the
biology classroom—how to help them turn the visual into the literal,
the lab report into the beautiful journal, to see the workings of a virus
as colorful and exciting—Janet is using her own imagination, reconceiving the categories of biology, writing, art, and opening up what
Bronowski describes as a "closed system of relationships." Unlike the
art teacher who could see her student's windsock not as an invention
but only as an error—a violation of a sequence of *proper instructions*—as
a science teacher, Janet will see her students' ways of doing and seeing
things, where they differ from her own, as *imaginative inventions*.

   In talking about knowing before, we've emphasized connecting the
known and the unknown. New information is fit into the framework
of the old so that it can be understood. But the connection between
knower and known also implies that the old is seen in a new way,
reenvisioned in light of the new, just as Janet is reenvisioning the
familiar (and codified) ways of teaching biology through the new terms
provided by an English prepractice course. Both activities are creative
processes. But how do teachers come to see old things in new ways and
new things in old ways in the classroom?

   In writing about the role of the ethnographer in depicting the
culture of schooling, Frederick Erickson talks about "the philosopher's
technique of deliberately making the familiar strange."

   Upon entering a non-Western society the fieldworker doesn't have to
   do this. Everything is unfamiliar and much is strange. But when
   describing institutions of his or her own society, the ethnographer
   must adopt the critical stance of the philosopher, continually questioning
   the grounds of the conventional, examining the obvious that is so
   taken for granted by cultural insiders that it becomes invisible to them.
   Often it is the taken for granted aspects of an institution that in the
   final analysis turn out to be most significant. (62)

"Making the familiar strange" can help any researcher or learner find
new patterns of significance, new meanings in what had previously
been taken for granted.

   Many of the methods for making the strange familiar and the

familiar strange are techniques associated with the writing of poetry. But these terms describe as well methods for allowing the imagination to connect categories of experience and move toward understanding. In fact, some of the most useful poetic techniques—*juxtaposition, metaphor, repetition*—are names for strategies all thinkers use to connect experiences imaginatively.

The forming of categories—placing one experience against another to draw inferences about them—is in poetic terminology the use of *juxtaposition*. A child sees her first clown, a high school student reads his first Shakespeare play, a freshman writer confronts her first research assignment, by juxtaposing some category already in place in the mind with the new uncategorized experience. New categories get formed: clowns are scary and have red noses; Shakespeare is tough; research papers require drafts. And old categories get rethought. Uncle Paul looks like a clown; Tennessee Williams is easy; short essays might benefit from drafts. Juxtaposition takes separate experiences and lines them up, providing a strategy for the learner to use to connect elements that appear disparate. Juxtaposition is so much a part of the way we experience that most times we're not even aware of how continuously we use it. A look at any comedy team shows how even humor depends a lot on a mostly unconscious ability to juxtapose. Lucy and Ethel, Laverne and Shirley, Penn and Teller, and Laurel and Hardy are funnier together than they are alone because their audience is forced to juxtapose them: their disparate physical types and their different personalities. It's not just the differences between the two that provoke the laughter but their odd pairing.

Teachers use juxtaposition a lot in their programs of instruction, typically by putting two examples together and asking students to compare them. In teaching writing, juxtaposition helps students evaluate correctness or appropriateness of expression—the effective opening paragraph versus the deadly dull opening paragraph; the flowing cumulative sentence versus the stilted periodic sentence; the simple versus the complex thesis. In teaching literature, juxtaposition isn't used as frequently because students usually study one work at a time, and the key to juxtaposition is a kind of simultaneity of experience. This simultaneous looking provokes connections, as we've mentioned, and teachers can make it work to help students select alternatives, not simply decide on worth. Two good essays—student or professionally produced—can be discussed together to show the effect of rhetorical choices on meaning. A topic handled scientifically can be put against the same topic explored in poetry or in the personal essay. Thoreau is a good choice for this kind of juxtaposition: he wrote in one way in his journals about his years on Walden Pond and in another, more consciously rhetorical way about the same experience in the actual book. Juxtaposing Sophocles' *Oedipus Rex* and Woody Allen's parody of Greek tragedy, *God*, provokes interesting connections between comedy and tragedy, between the role of characters and audience, and shows that the themes of humans' position in an incomprehensible world are concerns that transcend the barriers of time.

Readers of poetry respond deeply to juxtaposition because the odd pairing is often more visible in the sparse lines of poetry than in a fuller narrative. In Henry Reed's poem "Naming of Parts," the glaring contrast of images — loading a gun and watching a spring day outside the window — makes a powerful statement against war. The soldier/narrator is learning the names and uses of the parts of his gun, his attention wanders to the window, and the instructions from his superior officer mingle with his reverie on nature. Neither the gun nor the spring day alone would evoke the same meaning that the two placed together do:

> And this you can see is the bolt. The purpose of this
> Is to open the breech, as you see. We can slide it
> Rapidly backwards and forwards: we call this
> Easing the spring. And rapidly backwards and forwards
> The early bees are assaulting and fumbling the flowers:
>   They call it easing the Spring.

By using the same terms to describe the workings of the machinery of death and of life, Reed heightens the contrast, and readers learn about the speaker's attitude as well as about their own feelings as they are disquieted by the quiet placement of Spring and war.

Like juxtaposition, *metaphor* allows us to use the categories we've created and go beyond them; perceivers overcome the rigidity of the categories themselves by *doing something* with them. Metaphor is defined in poetry and memorized dutifully by students as "comparing two unlike objects without using like or as." But its original Greek meaning was "to carry beyond," and that original meaning expresses something significant about the power of metaphor to making meaning. Metaphor is comparison, but comparison designed to make the interpreter see something new about at least one of the points of comparison, to lead the interpreter to see through or beyond the things immediately in front of him. William Blake's famous poem "The Sick Rose" offers a nice example of the way in which metaphor leads readers to "carry beyond" an image or object to learn something new:

> O Rose thou art sick.
> The invisible worm
> That flies in the night
> In the howling storm:
>
> Has found out thy bed
> Of crimson joy,

And his dark secret love
Does thy life destroy.

In this poem, two things are compared, but one of the terms being compared is never mentioned, though the suggestive content and the placement of words cue the reader that the rose is being compared to something. It's not difficult to see the rose as a woman (the metaphor was a commonplace one even in the eighteenth century) and the details about love and fear suggest a human relationship. From that awareness, it's just a small step to perceive the heavily sexual message in the poem. Yet metaphor leaves this step to the reader's imagination — the reader must enter the world represented by the rose, and resee life in its terms. Metaphor forces the reader to locate the second term to be compared (the rose as female) and to take a third step by speculating on the implications of the connection (the implications of sexual experience). Metaphor, in fact, insists on more than a connection; it requires an identification. The woman is a rose; the man's love destroys. The reader has to think about the characteristics of roses as well as the associations with night and worms in order to experience the literal and metaphorical meaning of the poem.

Robert Burns' poem "My Luve" asks the reader to proceed rather differently. Burns provides a set of specific comparisons: "My luve is like a red, red rose," "My love is like a melodie," and the reader must systematically line up and compare two categories of experience, bringing them together in much the same way as in juxtaposition. The less explicit comparison of Blake's metaphor creates some ambiguity, leaving more room for the reader's interpretation. But in both cases, connections that are made are ones that pull the reader into the poem through experiences and associations — cultural, historical, and personal.

As a rhetorical technique, metaphor keeps the audience invested in the meaning of the words being spoken by making them actively make the meaning. In his campaign speech mentioned earlier, Jesse Jackson used the metaphor of his grandmother's quilt to represent the pieces of America, in its various constituencies, which must be sewn together to make any real difference. "Working mothers, working in the factory, you are right to complain about inadequate wages. But your patch isn't big enough." Like the quilt, Jackson's listeners have to piece together the patches to see themselves as part of the network of cultural groups that can make a political change. In her short story "Everyday Use," Alice Walker uses the same metaphor — the quilt — to represent the black woman's cultural heritage. The daughter who sees the quilts as priceless artifacts that shouldn't be put to everyday use is the daughter who has distanced herself from her heritage, even as she loudly proclaims it through the styles she adopts. Like Jackson's listeners, Walker's readers are given the patches — the metaphor — and asked to enter the world represented by the quilt and understand the terms of that world.

Some philosophers, logicians, or positivists, like John Locke, urged the elimination of metaphorical expression in discourse because it presented to readers too many possibilities for confusion and ambiguity and because it seemed to reflect feeling rather than the more highly valued abstract thought. But metaphor is deeply and irrevocably embedded in ordinary, as well as in literary, language. And philosophers in the last century have begun to realize that it's so embedded because metaphor supports an imaginative construction of ideas, ideas that mediate between the individual consciousness and what surrounds it. Metaphor is an important tool of the active, forming mind.

Lakoff and Johnson's book *Metaphors We Live By* supports that contention by arguing that metaphors represent a vital organic mental process with great power to aid conceptual thinking.

> Metaphor is for most people a device of the poetic imagination and the rhetorical flourish — a matter of extraordinary rather than ordinary language. Moreover, metaphor is typically viewed as characteristic of language alone, a matter of words rather than thought or action. For this reason, most people think they can get along perfectly well without metaphor. We have found, on the contrary, that metaphor is pervasive in everyday life, not just in language but in thought and action. Our ordinary conceptual system, in terms of which we both think and act, is fundamentally metaphorical in nature. (3)

Lakoff and Johnson agree with other theorists who argue that every system has a "root" metaphor or underlying figure that determines the system. A school, for example, may become metaphorically a correctional facility, a workplace, a garden for nurturing the young (*kindergarten*). Even where the metaphor is implied rather than stated (as it most often is), it will manifest itself in a variety of details — in how people are addressed (*Mr. Wood, Susan, girl number twenty*), in the kinds of activities and behaviors accepted and encouraged, in the structure of the physical environment.

Metaphor is so ubiquitous in the language and in thinking that most people don't recognize it as a strategy that allows them to name and control reality. "Winning an argument" (metaphor: arguing is war), "wasting your time" (metaphor: time is money), "my wheels are turning now" (metaphor: the mind is a machine), all are examples of how much metaphor is part of everyday language and, Lakoff and Johnson argue, of thinking, and they show that metaphor not only names reality but affects and even determines it. When teachers think of school bureaucracy as *red tape*, they may let themselves be more bound by it than a colleague who speaks of bureaucratic *hurdles* to be leapt over. Metaphors also help teachers see their work and their students. Some of these are imaginative and clarifying: one teacher, Bruce Rettman, comments about his students, "I suppose freshmen and sophomores are convinced existence is a multiple choice test; juniors and seniors know they can expect a few essay questions." Some are simply clichéd and reductive: "She's a late bloomer." "He's a round peg in a square hole."

Several philosophers and theorists of writing have used metaphors deliberately to make their discussions imaginative experiences for their readers. Peter Elbow's "cooking" metaphor for the writing process allows readers to imagine the bubbling, growing, and changing that accompany the producing of a piece of writing. Berthoff creates a metaphor of the opposable thumb to describe the relationship between perceiver and object, and Langer makes the metaphor of music the title for her work, her philosophy "in a new key," as well as the image for the symbol-making mind.

When students themselves make metaphors to describe what they do when they write they often find themselves discovering more than they knew consciously about what they do as writers. The metaphor, when it's chosen thoughtfully, seems almost inexhaustible, and students sometimes go on and on, discovering new implications of the metaphors they have made:

> Why do I write or better, what is it like when I write? Writing is like the way you feel when you think you're in real bad trouble and finding out you're not in trouble at all — that it was all a mistake. Writing is a feeling of giving up the controls of your car that's speeding 60mph and finding out that somehow it's ok. Someone or something else is driving. I just keep my foot on the gas. When I'm honest and motivated I don't need to control things — they just happen. When I'm unsure — writing something I don't know about or don't care about — I lose it. CRASH Boom-king-kang-a-lang. (Michael)

Metaphor is so intrinsic to our common understanding of the world that we're generally not even conscious of it. Cartoons like Gary Larson's depend on our being forced to see the literal meaning of common metaphors. The airplane pilot says to his cocaptain, "Let's get this baby off the ground," and we see them seated on the back of a baby, near a control tower, surrounded by flying babycraft. Or the passenger in a cab says to another. "You have to watch this breed, they turn on you," and the cabdriver — a dog — smiles wickedly as he begins to make a sudden turn.

Howard Gardner has found the language of very young children to be filled with metaphors, used especially in play to rename objects (the pencil as rocket ship). But children become increasingly uncomfortable using metaphors during their school years, perhaps because, as Gardner suggests, of the very fact that metaphors transcend category boundaries. Categorization is important to cognitive development and is also given strong priority in schooling, so it's hard to be sure whether the school curriculum alone, stressing logical categories over imaginative leaps outside of categories, is responsible for the decline in metaphorical language among school children. But young students who are encouraged

to write poetry respond with wonderful metaphors, and this suggests
that the metaphorical impulse is still strongly present but remains dor-
mant until a safe situation for its reawakening is found.

Children are also inclined to create metaphorical understandings of
the unfamiliar words they hear from adults. In one excerpt included by
Berthoff in *Reclaiming the Imagination*, the novelist Walker Percy writes
of "metaphor as mistake," of the ways in which seeing something as
something else, even when this results from a misunderstanding or
misnaming, creates a heightened perception and understanding. He tells
of his own experience as a boy, mishearing a guide and thinking that
the Blue Darter Hawk was a Blue Dollar Hawk. To the boy, the
metaphorical *blue dollar* gave the bird's movement significance that was
lost with the straightforwardly descriptive term *darter*, and he was dis-
appointed when the mystery of *blue dollar* was erased by the correct
term. When Holden Caulfield mistakes the words of the song "If a
body meet a body coming through the rye," replacing *meet* with *catch*,
he creates the metaphor of the catcher who will keep children from
falling off the edges of life. In each case, seeing something as something
else, even mistakenly, invests it with new meaning.

Student writers may use metaphor as a conscious strategy for
representing what they know. Here are the opening paragraphs of a
paper written by a student in an ESL freshman composition class.
Notice how the writer of this paper has used a metaphor (or rather two
contrasting metaphors) to frame her understanding.

> "Gold Mountain" what a fancy name is! This is the most popular
> name for the U.S. in Hong Kong. According to the name, I could
> think of that American people were very rich. These was easy money
> in the country. I was told that the U.S. was a good chance for
> education since colleges in my country were scarce and I was hardly
> having any opportunities.
>
> Are American people really rich? Compare with my country's
> people, perhaps they are. Americans have higher living standard.
> People live in big houses in which they share their own rooms. In
> average, every one has a car or more than one. People go to vacation
> every year. They seem to have a lot of money and time. For our
> people, they are rich because American money is worthier. It is 7
> times to the Hong Kong dollars. In America, there is not hard for
> people to get good lives if they work harder.
>
> In my eyes, America is not a gold mountain at all but a working
> machine. Everyday, people work hard for their money. They are so
> busy that they don't have time to communicate with their friends....
> (Winnie)

This student, like the freshman writer of "definition" and "comparison
and contrast" papers in Chapter 6, is drawing on one of the modes of
discourse defined by rhetoric. She, too, is comparing two things—but

not just for the purpose of filling out a prescribed format. She's trying to work out an understanding of the differences between what she imagined the United States would be like before she arrived, and how she has found it to be. But her new understanding is complex. Some of what she thought before turned out to be true, and yet the metaphor that captured her earlier understanding no longer seems appropriate. In representing what she now sees, she rejects the familiar Hong Kong metaphor of the "gold mountain" and replaces it with her own metaphor: "working machine," going on in the rest of her essay to explore its implications. In finding a new, more appropriate metaphor, she's found what she really thinks about her new country and its wealth.

The metaphorical language of literature, while it may initially create some difficulties for student readers who aren't used to it, can also help readers to make connections between things that are familiar to them and the meanings of the new texts they read. Toni Morrison's novel *Sula* is filled with metaphor. Comparisons are rarely made explicitly — readers aren't told that the Sula who returns to town as an adult is seen as dangerous by Jude, the husband of her childhood friend. But they're told that the birthmark over her eye begins to look to Jude like a copperhead. Readers learn to see the townspeople's view of natural events with human significance — when robins die evil is among them. Morrison warns the reader early on that an outsider, a "valley man," who entered the town of Medallion would not find the meaning of life in this town by just looking at the surface. "It would be easy for the valley man to hear the laughter and not notice the adult pain that rested somewhere under the eyelids, somewhere under their head rags and soft felt hats" (4). The valley man must enter into the world, must feel the movement of the spooncarver's fingers or let the voice of the church tenor "dress him in silk," just as the reader must come to an understanding of the novel by paying attention to feelings and associations, rather than simply by looking for a set of exact meanings to correspond to the words on the page. Nevertheless, those associations are triggered by the words on the page, and attention to those words, like the valley man's attention to the tenor's voice, leads to understanding.

For the reader of *Sula*, an understanding of the perspectives of the novel's characters can come, in part, through following out the metaphors that express those perspectives. For example, Jude's idea of marriage, as he weds Sula's best friend Nel, is presented through an extended metaphor. "Whatever his fortune, whatever the cut of his garment, there would always be the hem — the tuck and fold that hid his raveling edges; a someone sweet, industrious and loyal to shore him up" (83). Students who read these words, who write about what they seem to mean, who work out the literal meanings of *cut of his garment*, of *hem*, of *raveling edges*, and who then talk about aspects of marriage that they might represent, making explicit their associations and connections, learn to use metaphor to help them enter the world of the novel. They learn to use and connect two areas of the familiar—here the garment with its cut, its edges, its hem on the one hand, and the characteristics of marriage in general—to come to know the unfamiliar, the particular ideas about marriage held by a character in this novel.

Metaphor moves one step beyond juxtaposition by making the comparison less explicit and forcing the interpreter to imagine both the second and a third element in the construction. The interpreter must find a third thing that puts the two elements being compared into a relationship. In what ways is marriage like a hemmed garment, allowing Morrison to "yoke" them together to represent Jude's view? Metaphor forces readers not only to see two things together, what they share and how they differ, but to create from those two things another term, another image that goes beyond comparison and contrast and toward mediation or synthesis.

Another poetic and fictional technique that is an organic conceptual activity is *repetition*. Repetition is used in poetry for effect—you might remember Edgar Allan Poe's famous raven quoting "nevermore" again and again—to heighten reader awareness. The word or phrase or instance repeated becomes increasingly important in the interpretive scheme of things; readers are paying attention unconsciously because they hear the same thing more than once. Joseph Heller's classic antiwar novel *Catch-22* makes repetition one of its primary rhetorical techniques. At points throughout the long novel, the phrase "Snowden's secret" appears and reappears. The reader begins to recognize its importance and to wait for clues to the secret, coming to understand that the revelation of the secret will be a revelation of thematic intent. And what is the secret? "Man is garbage," the main character Yossarian says when he discovers under Snowden's jacket a terrible and mortal wound. "Readiness is all." This shattering occurrence becomes Yossarian's cry for an end to war—the sudden, shocking realization of his own mortality. Heller doesn't simply repeat the phrase "Snowden's secret" but carefully places it in various contexts: when the bombing mission fails, when Snowden's biography is explained, when Yossarian's consciousness awakens. The reader sees the secret in larger and larger contexts because the secret has been repeated in various forms, and the reader's understanding of its meaning is therefore expanded.

Repetition is an important thematic technique in *Sula* as well. When the young girls, Sula and Nel, are playing with a little boy by the river and he slips from Sula's hands and drowns, we are told that they stand there staring at "the closed place in the water," expecting him to come back up laughing. Through the rest of the novel "the closed place in the water" is evoked each time the meaning of Sula's actions or the question of trust in the relationship of the two women comes into question. This repetition guides the reader in connecting a now familiar event with new contexts and raising a set of questions, if not answers, that are fundamental to the novel. And, through repetition, the event of the drowning becomes, itself, a metaphor, standing for those questions about Sula's responsibility and trustworthiness that need not then be explicitly named at later points.

Student writers learn quickly to use repetition in comparable ways in their own writing. A freshman, writing of her family's experience being lost while her father was piloting a small plane from their home in Antigua to St. Maarten, began by telling her story to the class and using their responses to help her build tension and suspense. Group discussions also led her to see why she had chosen to tell about this event, and how it showed her family responding to difficulty in characteristic ways. By her second written version of the story, she had divided the story into several distinct episodes of trouble, each one marked by repetition of a phrase that had not appeared in the earlier version — "no one panicked." After effectively highlighting the story's meaning with this repetition, she cleverly turns it to ironic effect in her ending, where we finally learn how frightened her father had been under his calm surface:

> The first place we went after leaving the plane was to a gift store in the airport in order to buy a pair of shorts for my father. It seems that for some strange reason, the pants he had on during flight had developed an odd stain right in its seat. But, no one panicked. (Aqeelah)

This student has come to use repetition as a technique for connecting a series of episodes, for highlighting their similarities, and for showing them as representative of a general theme. But her discovery of this technique has itself come about through repetition used as a process. In repeating her telling and writing of this story, in reseeing the story several times from the perspectives of several readers and listeners, she comes to know it in new ways.

This notion of seeing and reseeing has been used by composition theorists to help students think more critically. Berthoff's dialectical notebook asks students to respond and then later respond to their responses, to repeat the experience but to learn from that repetition, rather than filtering down experience into existing categories. One of her most interesting assignments in *Forming/Thinking/Writing* is an exercise in repetition, where students examine the same natural object — a nut, a wildflower — for a week and write about it. The object rarely changes, though sometimes it begins to disintegrate, but the observer always does change, learning to see more by looking more.

Langer notes that repetition is never simply repetition, but always analogue; one experience is lined up against the experience repeated. You've probably read the same novel at different times in your life and had completely different experiences each time. The novel hasn't changed, but you, of course, have. Your experience with reading, in life, in school, has altered your perspective, given you new reference points from which to evaluate your reading. You enter now familiar territory, not the same unfamiliar territory you covered before. And so you move along differently, making new discoveries. If the repetition of a reading takes place in different circumstances — at a different time of your life or even in a different course — the changes in you and in the context of your reading may lead you to new understandings of yourself or of your context as well as of the text.

Repetition is often unfairly linked in classroom practice to its adjectival form, *repetitive*, and that word is usually a pejorative. The only teachers who repeat are those who *have* to in order to teach "those students" who can't remember instructions or who willfully disregard them. But in its imaginative sense, all teaching is repetition, repeated experiences of writing, reading, listening, and talk that generate new and more accomplished writing, reading, listening, and talk. In a class where an entire group of students gives speeches one after the other, the experience for the class is one of repetition. Usually the students who come later deliver more effective speeches. And if the speech making is repeated as an activity several weeks later, the entire group gets better. Why is this? The repetition has allowed them to make connections among the method their fellows used, searching out what succeeded, recognizing and discarding what failed. Teachers should use repetition to frame units of study, allowing students to make links between how what they learned about the uses of setting in *The Tempest* affects what they perceive about setting in Stephen Crane's *The Open Boat*, for example. Repetition in teaching provokes imaginative reconceiving.

We've shown how poetic techniques of repetition, metaphor, and juxtaposition are much more than the choices a creative writer makes according to his subject matter and disposition. They are parts of everyone's mental operations and as such intimately a part of the imagination. In fact, if teachers were to think of poetic techniques in this new, conceptual way, it might make the teaching of poetry to high school students easier. The choices of the poet are the conceptual strategies his readers use to experience the poem.

The last and most obvious technique of poetry is also an organic conceptual activity, and that is *form.* Of course, all writing, and all experience for that matter, is embodied in some form. As Kenneth Burke says, in literature "form is the appeal" (123). Readers read meaning through the forms they perceive and use forms to imaginatively connect them to meanings. As interpreters as well as creators of texts we depend on our consciousness of form. But poetry is recognized as such by its form. Readers see that a piece of writing is poetry by the form it takes on the page and create expectations and interpretations based on their understanding about the form of the poem.

Several years ago, one of Hepsie's fellow graduate students wanted to demonstrate to the class something about the relationship of form to poetic experience, so she conducted an experiment in which she handed out a small poem to the class. It read something like this:

> The winds of the Santa Ana
> blow hot over the parched land
> and move to the cold Pacific
> seeming to die
> but gathering energy
> for a new assault.

The class read the poem, tried to grasp its metaphorical connections, talked about its techniques and its narrator. Then they were told that the "poem" was actually a paragraph taken straight from an eighth-grade geography textbook, and that a stanza had simply been created from its lines. It was a perfect illustration of how expectations for form control the imaginative response. Students who create "found poems" by forming lines and stanzas from the texts of news articles or their own essays gain new understandings of form and meaning that can help their reading of poetry and all literature.

In his book on teaching children to write poetry, *Wishes, Lies, and Dreams*, Kenneth Koch discusses this generative use of form. Students begin by writing a poem together.

> The way I conceived of the poem, it was easy to write, had rules like a game, and included the pleasures without the anxieties of competitiveness. No one had to worry about failing to write a good poem because everyone was only writing one line; and I specifically asked the children not to put their names on their line. Everyone was to write the line on a sheet of paper and turn it in; then I would read them all as a poem. I suggested we make some rules about what should be in every line; this would help give the final poem unity, and it would help the children find something to say. I gave an example, putting a color in every line, then asked them for others. We ended up with the regulations that every line should contain a color, a comic-strip character, and a city or country; also the line should begin with the words "I wish." (10)

Koch collected the lines, shuffled them, and read them aloud as one poem. The students then wrote whole poems in which every line began with "I wish."

> A few days later [the regular fourth-grade teacher] brought me their poems, and I was very happy. The poems were beautiful, imaginative, lyrical, funny, touching. They brought in feelings I hadn't seen in the children's poetry before. They reminded me of my own childhood and of how much I had forgotten about it. They were all innocence,

elation, and intelligence. They were unified poems: it made sense
where they started and where they stopped. And they had a lovely
music—

I wish I had a pony with a tail like hair
I wish I had a boyfriend with blue eyes and black hair
I would be so glad.... (12–13)

As Koch points out, the form gives the poems unity, and it's a form
that's easy and natural to use. Here the form involves repetition of the
line "I wish," and the repetition has the effect that we've been discussing of
placing the wishes in relation to one another, and allowing each to
reflect and shape and be shaped by the ones that have gone before. It
can be varied ("sometimes I wish"), and it allows the writers to draw
on their personal knowledge while helping them to recast that familiar
knowledge in new ways.

Other forms Koch used were the repetition of comparisons with
like: "The sea is like a blue velvet coat."

> I encouraged them to take chances. I said people were aware of many
> resemblances which were beautiful and interesting but which they
> didn't talk about because they seemed too far-fetched and too silly.
> But I asked them specifically to look for strange comparisons—if the
> grass seemed to them like an Easter egg they should say so. I suggested
> they compare something big to something small, something in school
> to something out of school, something unreal to something real,
> something human to something not human. I wanted to rouse them
> out of the timidity I felt they had about being "crazy" or "silly" in
> front of an adult in school. (15)

In addition to providing a generative form, here Koch gets children to
hold two familiar things (the sky and something in the classroom) in a
relationship to each other that changes each (extending juxtaposition
into metaphor).

> Each assignment gave the children something which they enjoyed
> writing about and which enabled them to be free and easy and creative.
> Each also presented them with something new, and thus helped them
> to have, while they were writing, that feeling of discovery which
> makes creating works of art so exhilarating....
>   The repetition form, which I often suggested they use, turned out
> to have many advantages. Repetition is natural to children's speech,
> and it gave them an easy-to-understand way of dividing their poems
> into lines. By using it they were able to give strong and interesting
> forms to their poems without ever sounding strained or sing-song, as
> they probably would have using rhyme. And it left their poetry free
> for [a] kind of easy and spontaneous music. (20)

Koch helps even young children to use the familiar phrases of everyday
language in formal ways, to pull out aspects of their thoughts and
experience and to use repetition, juxtaposition, metaphor to set these

phrases off from ordinary, conversational speech and to mark them as having a heightened significance — as standing for and representing that larger experience in some way. This is the function that the formal use of language — whether in oral genres like prayers or sermons or songs or stories, or in written genres like drama or fiction or the essay — performs. In such use, the attention is on form in its power to reshape experience (rather than on form to meet social expectations for getting things done, as in the business letter). In highlighting and marking words by the forms given them, writers indicate that what they're expressing at this moment, in this form, is both representative and highly significant. Language takes on a dimension beyond the functional or, as Britton would put it, transactional uses, and becomes instead a comment on the functional activity. Language becomes *poetic* to use Britton's term, and language used this way is making literature. Like the children of Koch's poetry class writing about comic-book heroes, writers who use poetic discourse can begin to see seemingly ordinary comments and responses in new, representative, and imaginative ways.

While form is too often taught as a requirement for correctness rather than as a medium for invention, even the structures of the college essay can be generated imaginatively, drawing, as in Koch's work, on students' familiarity with form. In *Beat Not the Poor Desk*, Marie Ponsot and Rosemary Deen show how the whole curriculum of a freshman writing course can grow out of students' knowledge of form. They want students "to discover what they can do with what they know about the larger shapes of effective language," to bring those structures under their conscious control, and to extend their knowledge of those structures to the essay structures of the freshman writing course. And they begin with structures that have dominated human consciousness for a long time, those of oral tradition — the fable, the parable, the myth — structures found "among the earliest products of imagination" (13).

Using familiar forms can help alleviate some of the anxiety of student writers, while providing vehicles for imaginative creations. If students know that a fable is short, that it has animal characters in it, and that it teaches a lesson, they can use that knowledge to generate relationships and oppositions between characters, between a story and its moral in fables they create as well as the ones they interpret. They might resee relationships between people they know or use fables to explore the workings of the classroom or of peer response groups. They might read *Animal Farm* to see how Orwell created a political fable. Students come to classes with knowledge about many other forms, and these can all be useful to provoke imaginative conception in writing and talk.

Of course, teachers teach form in much of the work they accomplish in the English classroom. As we'll discuss in a later chapter on curriculum, textbooks and course guides typically organize their discussions around

considerations of form—the comparison/contrast essay, the sonnet. Form can be taught for its own sake, in which case it's not very imaginative, or it can be taught to help students recognize their power as interpreters in reading and writing, in which case it becomes generative. Sentence patterns, for example, can be taught as limited grammar exercises. In *Forming/Thinking/Writing*, Berthoff offers a repertory of sentence patterns that provide ways of putting meanings together, and talks about the way in which even punctuation can contribute to the making of meaning. (The semicolon, for example, provokes ideas through juxtaposition.) She provides some forms common in academic writing but probably unfamiliar to her students; by making formal features of academic writing explicit for her students, she helps them see how to work within a new culture, how to imagine within a new culture.
Her structures:

1. A structure for listing and renaming.
   _____,_____,_____:_____.
2. A structure to relate condition and result, cause and effect.
   If_____, then_____.
3. A structure for articulating a comparison with a difference.
   Just as_____, so_____; but if you consider_____, then_____.
4. A structure for stating differences with something in common.
   However_____, _____.
5. A structure for restating with a greater degree of specification or generality.
   _____; _____. (81)

If you try to fill in the blanks in these sentences with ideas about the imagination, you'll see how generative they can be: "Repetition, juxtaposition, metaphor: imagination" as Sentence 1, for example.

Teachers can build on forms students already know and suggest that they try out new ones. But part of students' imaginative work in the classroom will be to make connections themselves between the forms they know and what they're learning. One of our student teachers created a lesson in which some students would write to Ann Landers about problems in the school, and others would invent Ann Landers' response. Students' responses to this lesson showed that they know the forms, that they can re-create the voices, that they understand the usual nature of the advice-column response. We think of form as something we have to impose from without. Teachers sometimes think of students as coming with a cloud of ideas that they must shape by providing the forms in which to fit those ideas. But students also come with a knowledge of form, and teachers can help them use those forms to find their own conjunction of shape and idea. And students will encounter new forms as they read and write, and begin to reshape concepts of form according to the forms they already possess. A student who doesn't know argumentation as a form can discover that what she knows about the Ann Landers form gives her a way to make what the teacher says about argumentation her own.

Imagination and interpretation

The techniques of juxtaposition, repetition, metaphor, and working with form are part of the larger activity called *interpretation*. Like the elements it draws on and looks for, interpretation is an activity of the imagination. And it too emerges not just from one area of work within the English classroom but from all of thinking, as a part of how people make sense of the world. The fact is that everyone is always interpreting. Any time we recount an event, we're selecting the aspects or details we think are significant, and those details fit with an evolving sense of larger patterns of meaning. Langer suggests that even in the first moment of perception, humans interpret, seeing or noticing primarily those things that fit in some way with a conception of the world, rather than taking in details that aren't significant to the personal life or immediate culture. Language reflects the relationship between perception and interpretation, as the Eskimos' seventeen words for snow reflect their interpretation of the physical facts of their world. Living and working in a world where survival may depend on snow conditions requires Eskimos to pay attention to subtle differences in snow, to snow "nuances," while inhabitants of more southern city climates content themselves with *snow, ice,* and *slush*. Of course, as city dwellers have taken up skiing, they have generated their new vocabulary for changes in snow conditions.

Narrative—as represented in the stories we tell all the time, in all of our conversations—is the most basic form in which we interpret and, in effect, create the world. In telling stories and recounting events, people select from the flow of life experience a sequence of elements perceived as related and important. Through that selection of events, through the words used to reconstruct them, as well as through explicit statements, people demonstrate what they believe events mean and why they're significant, and that demonstration constitutes their interpretation. When people are motivated to recount an experience, they all become effective narrators—able to shape the telling to fit an interpretation of the events. Labov's work has shown for example, that when urban adolescents choose to tell a story to their peers, they use complex linguistic strategies to convey meaning, strategies like metaphor and repetition. But in school narrative assignments, like "Tell about what you did on your summer vacation," good storytellers may produce only brief, superficial essays. Not understanding the purpose of their telling, they aren't motivated to tell much, especially about what the event might mean. The reader is left wondering "So what?" or "What's the point?"—which is precisely what the writer no doubt wondered as he wrote.

The narrator who can choose when to tell or what to tell will select details that present or lead to an interpretation of events. When Holden Caulfield says, in his opening words to the unnamed psychiatrist who's listening to the story that will follow, "The first thing you'll probably want to know is where I was born, and what my lousy childhood was like," he suggests one possible frame for his story, one that fits with an interpretation he thinks the psychiatrist would like to give it. He could choose to begin with his childhood and tell about its difficult events. But he doesn't want to reduce his recent troubling experiences by letting them be fit into that story, into any authority figure's interpretation, so he quickly rejects the frame, refusing to make this a story of a lousy childhood: "But I don't feel like going into it, if you want to know the truth." And he substitutes his own frame: "I'll just tell you about this madman stuff that happened to me around last Christmas." It's Holden's interpretation of the "madman stuff" that the psychiatrist— and the reader—will be interpreting.

Reading literature demands the ability to imagine the possible. One group of students, entering the University of Massachusetts through a special admissions program for students who didn't have traditional academic backgrounds, were given a reading selection from *The Diary of Anne Frank* and asked to write about what they'd take with them if they had to go into hiding. These students could consider only the objects of their present worlds. They couldn't imaginatively construct the possible world of being in hiding, where credit cards and loud boom boxes would have negative value. Such students really need practice in imagining, not more punctuation exercises or work with study guides, to prepare them for their work at the university.

Literature helps thinkers imagine the possible. It selects particular elements from general human experience, both real and imagined, and describes them in a language that, because it's formal, says "this is important," "this has meaning," "this suggests something about the world and the way it operates or might operate." Holden's story suggests, at one level, a personal meaning, a way in which Holden understands and interprets the world. But as a formally presented work of narrative fiction, it's also something larger, representing aspects of life that will be familiar to some of its readers, and representing something about the human condition in a particular time and place. The concern with form in literature is more important than whether or not a work is judged "fictional"; autobiographies like Anne Frank's *Diary* or Maya Angelou's *I Know Why the Caged Bird Sings* go beyond personal meaning to represent larger understandings about human life and experience, as

Salinger's work does. For the student, like Allison in Chapter 2, the movement back and forth between the formal representations of others' experiences in literature and the formal representations of her own in the essays and stories she is writing provides entry into the world of active and imaginative interpretation.

Interpretation and texts

Interpretation has often been seen in classrooms as a game, a scavenger hunt, where students try to find the phrases and meanings that the teacher will eventually point to as significant. Interpretation treated this way is a decoding, a non-meaning-making activity where students don't create meanings but locate them in texts they read. They locate by using some sort of key given to them by the teacher or the text — questions to guide their reading, significant passages highlighted and explained, special words defined and contextualized. As is true in any scavenger hunt, those who find the most items on the list win, those who locate the symbols, themes, recurrent images with the most assurance and perseverance get rewarded.

Why do we practice literary interpretation anyway? What's the point? What do we discover by engaging in it? Traditionally, literary texts have been seen as difficult to read or understand — by teachers and their students — so teachers have felt duty-bound to interpret or translate those texts, to put "the meaning" into terms students will understand. In her famous essay "Against Interpretation," Susan Sontag says that interpretation as it is traditionally conceived and practiced presupposes a discrepancy between the clear meaning of a text and the demands of readers:

> Interpretation is a radical strategy for conserving an old text, which is thought too precious to repudiate, by revamping it.... Interpretation is not (as most people assume) an absolute value, a gesture of mind situated in some timeless realm of capabilities. Interpretation must itself be evaluated, within a historical view of human consciousness. In some cultural contexts, interpretation is a liberating act. In other cultural contexts, it is reactionary, impertinent, cowardly, stifling. (1966, 6–7)

Too often in the classroom, interpretation is the latter — stifling students' interest and engagement with their reading by emphasizing rules and one-word answers. Sontag is worried about interposing interpretive rules between the reader/viewer and the work of art, so that she can no longer experience the work immediately and directly, but only through the lens of the dominant interpretive strategies of her historical period and cultural context.

> Real art has the capacity to make us nervous. By reducing the work of
> art to its content and then interpreting *that*, one tames the work of art.
> Interpretation makes art manageable, comfortable. (8)

But it does so of course, only for those who have been initiated into the
accepted interpretive methods. For the teacher, interpretation is made
comfortable by the familiar categories of plot, character, point of view,
which mark our present mode of interpretation (just as, for the medieval
scholar, interpretation focused comfortably on the then familiar search
for analogical and allegorical meanings). Interpretation like this can
sometimes reduce the work by forcing it into narrow ideological
channels. Sontag shows how Kafka's work can be read by different
schools of interpreters in several ways: as a social allegory about the
insanity of modern bureaucracy, as a psychoanalytic allegory revealing
Kafka's fear of his father and his castration anxieties, as a religious
allegory representing the "inexorable and mysterious justice of God"
(8). Students who've been schooled in the dominant cultural mode of
interpretation will be comfortable with their era's dominant interpretive
activities. But such categories can also reduce the work to what fits
neatly into them, and the interpretive act can become a kind of routine
decoding rather than a way of creating new understandings.

Such a routine, for example, shapes a prepractice student's teaching
of a model lesson on "The Secret Life of Walter Mitty." He begins with
some good questions about what Walter Mitty was and what he wanted
to be, building on students' own responses to the story, evoking their
memories of the text, pulling those responses into the public arena, to
become part of the class's shared knowledge. But suddenly he turns
from this evolving discussion and puts the familiar terms *plot*, *character*,
setting on the blackboard. At this point the students settle back, seem to
say to themselves, "Oh — he's doing the plot and character routine and I
don't have to think about anything else." A few students plug in the
expected answers, but the work of the class and of Thurber too has
been reduced to just these elements, and the dynamic energy of the
earlier discussion is lost. The terms are useful, but if they're not integrated
into the discussion, they can prevent readers from taking an imaginative
perspective on their reading. It's often more valuable to turn literature
lessons around, so that any formal terms come out at the end, after
students have worked with the text and groped for their own ways of
describing and analyzing it. Having students look for examples in the
text that indicate to them what Walter Mitty was like/wanted to be,
and studying these examples closely, would bring out much of what
goes into this story — including the terms — without reducing it to the
same old game.

Much interpretation involves reading something as something else —
making a word or a text or a work of art a metaphor. Sontag's *Illness as
Metaphor* shows how disease (tuberculosis in the nineteenth century;

cancer in the twentieth) becomes a metaphorical description of cultural traits and societal attitudes. This "seeing something as ——," when it's novel and generates new understandings, is fundamental to the sort of interpretation we'd like to foster, being careful to see the metaphor making as imaginative rather than reductive. Metaphorical connection, made imaginative, allows — even insists on — the direct interpretive response of an individual reader. And that is perhaps its greatest value in the classroom. Nowhere in the interpretative approaches that have dominated the education of most teachers has there been room for direct interpretations of a relatively naive reader, for an acknowledgment of the relevance of that reader's experience and knowledge to the meaning of a text. Teachers themselves, when teaching a new work of literature, will most often turn first to the "accepted" interpretations, whether from their own class notes, or from the books they can grab off the library shelf, rather than trusting and using their own interpretations to encourage students to do the same.

This does not mean that the teacher should ignore all literary criticism. But we suggest that she remember that all critics are readers first. One of the reasons we argue in favor of a transactional or reader-oriented approach to the teaching of literature is that its aim is to make explicit the necessary imaginative link between reader and text. Interpretation happens in the moment where a reader encounters a text, Rosenblatt argues. In that moment is the "event" of the poem, the meaning that is a combination of reader and his world with text and the world it creates for him. This is the imagination in action, the moment of connection of one experience to another. The forms criticism may take, its rhetorical choices, its discussion of sources, the voice of its writer vary according to the imaginative construction the interpreter places on the reading experience. Becoming aware of and comparing critical strategies, including the reader's own, supports both the interpretive act of reading and the interpretive seeing of different ways of reading.

It's clear that the imagination is central to all real learning in the classroom and in the world. The ways in which teachers can imaginatively re-create the classroom as a community where the "learned and imaginative life" can flourish in the ways that Whitehead wished will be the subject of our inquiry in the third and final unit of this book.

Maxims — strategies for enhancing the literacy of learners

1. **Recognize all uses of language as continuous and whole.** The language we use in the classroom is an extension of the language we

use in the cafeteria or at home. The language we write is an extension of the language we speak. Eact time we use language for one purpose we reinforce the skills we will apply to other purposes. So if we want our students to be good readers and writers, we must encourage our students to use language in many ways, both old and new, in the classroom.

2. **Use meaningful work to support the learning of language and literacy in the classroom.** We know that all new uses of language are learned in meaningful contexts, whether in writing, reading, speaking (or listening), and that decontextualized, fragmented exercises and activities teach students how to do well at those activities but not how to become fluent readers and writers or how to use formal linguistic styles in their writing and speaking. Rather, we foster literacy when we engage students in reading, writing, and speaking and in talk about how we read and write and speak.

3. **Treat writing and reading as similar processes — constructive, recursive, and often messy.** In both reading and writing the learner constructs tentative understandings and then goes back to alter these early understandings from a later perspective. Allow room for expressive, exploratory writing and for tentative, exploratory reading, and let communities of readers and writers talk about how these can be shaped into more formal writings or "readings."

4. **Make the imagination central to all classroom learning.** When students begin to make connections between apparently unlike things, when they observe how their minds work in constructing and reconstructing the world, the literature that they read is connected with their own thinking and their own writing. And when students experiment with forms for representing their own understandings, when they see how even their daily conversations depend on shared conventions about form, they begin to see how the forms of literature become meaningful.

UNIT 3

Theory Into Practice

In this unit we'll be talking about how to implement some of the theories and practices described in the first sections of this book. "How do you do it?" is always an important question for teachers, and too much of a teacher's preparation in universities has left out that essential component. English courses have taught subject matter and education courses have taught pedagogical methods, but for most teachers the two have never met in an integrated theoretical and practical approach to classroom instruction. This is one reason some teachers are resentful of theory: it's all very well to spell out what's needed and how theory proves what's needed, but sometimes a very different matter to put any of it to work productively in an actual classroom in a real school.

Yet, as we've seen in earlier chapters, as soon as teachers try to understand the learning of real students — of individual readers and writers — they discover that theory and research help them to make sense of what they see. When they learn from theory and observation that writing with real purposes in mind alters the relationship between the writer and his writing, they begin to look for ways to make school writing more meaningful. When they learn that students come to the classroom as competent language users with an intuitive knowledge of grammar, and that new uses of language are acquired through use rather than through learning rules, they begin to create meaningful ways to talk about new uses of language. When they know that writing and reading are similar and related processes and that how people read affects directly how they write, they begin to encourage students to read as writers and to write as readers.

So far, while we've referred to some of the ways in which we and other teachers have tried to accomplish these things in our classrooms, we've focused primarily on the relationship of new practices to the learning of individuals. But individuals are also learners within larger classroom contexts. And so the question becomes "How can we remake whole classrooms so that they support what we know about how individual readers and writers learn?" To answer that question, we must return to the school and classroom culture that we began to explore in Chapter 1, this time looking not for patterns of meaning represented in the structures as they exist but for strategies to revise those structures so that they express the meanings we want to create. Like writers engaged in a genuine composing process, once teachers have begun to discover new understandings, they must reenvision what's gone before. For teachers, like writers, the composing of the English classroom will be a process, in which they both look ahead to see where they want to go and look back to see where they've been, carrying a flexible plan that will get revised as it gets reseen with real students.

Nevertheless, teachers do need to have a plan, and they can begin to create one by looking at key relationships within the culture of their classrooms. Once they've decided they want to foster active learning and inquiry, extend cultural and multicultural understanding, develop all aspects of literacy through work in meaningful contexts, teachers need to reexamine existing relationships of students and teachers and curriculum, to ask how they can be revised so that teacher and learner work together within a curriculum to nurture literacy.

In this unit we'll return to our observations of classrooms, particularly to the classrooms of two teachers, John Welsh and Bruce Rettman, who're engaged in revising their plan for teaching and learning. If we accompany a prepractice student as she steps into the classroom of one of these teachers, we can see that changes in the relationships of teacher and learners may be marked even by subtle alterations in the physical setup of the classroom.

> The classroom is set up on six rows of about four desks each. The blackboard is in the front of the room, with a podium which Mr. Rettman usually conducts the class from. On the side of the room is Mr. Rettman's desk, and two other tables beside it where Stan, the student teacher, sits, and where I observe from. Behind me, on the radiator, are stacks of newspapers. On my table also is a box where the students hand in their journals and pick them up once they've been

reviewed/graded. The back wall is a bulletin board with a map and other posters of school concern. (Deb)

In many ways, this description seems to present a fairly typical picture of the English class, rows of desks, blackboard at the front, posters on a bulletin board located behind the students. But there are some unusual features, like the location of the teacher's desk, that might change the way student and teacher interact in this environment.

> The kids filter in: Mr. Rettman is floating around the room casually greeting the students. They obviously feel comfortable talking to him about their assignment worries.... He starts out a lecture by briefly going over what was talked about last class. He uses the board, and the students take notes in the right side of their journals. On the left there will be a place for their interpretation of what went on in class....
>
> Mr. Rettman gives a quick writing assignment. He is sitting at his desk and writing too. This assignment also takes place on the right side of the journal. Then he has the students randomly read their responses. He writes key ideas from the responses on the board.
>
> Mr. Rettman sets up conversation so that students want to respond. Hands are up all over the place. He *walks all over* the room during discussion; now he's in the back and kids have to turn around to talk to him. Mr. Rettman reads *his* response. So he gives an opinion. Then he gives a responding assignment for the right side of the journal.
>
> Next he passes out a dittoed article from the *Boston Globe*. He has students move into "response groups" (already assigned groups for journal and other discussions) and asks them to discuss the differences between this article and the story they just read. I sat in on a response group and the kids all responded!

One of the simplest, and often most neglected, strategies for creating an environment in the classroom where teacher and student interact is to change the position from which the teacher speaks. Bruce places his desk away from the front and center position where students would expect to see it. In this way, students change their angle of vision during the course of any class from the front of the room where the blackboard is, to the side of the room where the teacher's desk sits, to the back of the room where he walks. This more fluid situation leads them to disperse their attention around the room and leads to their looking at one another as well as at the teacher. And their looking at one another is a key factor in making a class *interact* rather than simply *react*.

Another way to achieve interaction in a classroom is to recognize, and nurture, the relationship between the school and what students know and do in their lives outside the six or seven hours a day they spend in schoolrooms. The newspapers sitting in Bruce Rettman's classroom and his assignment with the *Boston Globe* signal an involvement with that outside world within his classroom. Deb finds that this involvement carries over into students' conversations:

> This is unbelievable. A student, before class, asked if anyone had heard the news this morning because there was an invasion in the Persian Gulf. It seems so strange for me to hear these *kids* talking seriously about world issues.

As we've discussed in Unit 1, learning means being able to connect the known to the unknown, the personal to the public, and a classroom in which those connections are made explicit is one in which students will see relevance to school activities because they see relevance to the larger activities of living.

We can see then that several elements, interdependent and dynamic, must be altered from traditional stances in order to support a classroom that is shaped by inquiry as well as knowledge—one that's home to a community of learners.

1. Classroom activities—writing, reading, speaking, listening—need to be reenvisioned, both the substance of those activities within a curriculum and the way they get produced in the classroom. Students and teachers need to engage in real inquiry, real dicovery, real negotiation.
2. The relationship of the classroom to the outside world needs to change. Teachers and students bring lots of "outside" knowledge to the classroom, and the classroom needs to be a place where such knowledge is valued, and where it's connected to the learning that goes on within the classroom.
3. Teachers and students need to resee their relationship in the classroom by redefining authority and control for themselves. Students need to take authority for learning in activities designed to ensure responsibility and action in the classroom. Teachers need to resee their authority by recognizing the way it can be shared as well as dispensed. The curriculum needs to foster shared control over tasks, over interpretations, over evaluation.

The "Strategies" chapter suggests some of the activities that can foster such changes, as well as some ideas for the sort of flexible and responsive plan or blueprint that can be used to guide the new work of the classroom.

In the chapters of Unit 3 we'll talk about the ways in which these changes will reshape the roles of learners, the roles of teachers, and the traditional curriculum. Finally we'll imagine a possible world in which an unquiet pedagogy transforms not only the ways in which we teach but what's taught, in a new, unquiet, curriculum.

CHAPTER 9

Creating the Classroom Community: New Roles for Teachers and Learners

One of the most persistent questions that new teachers have about a classroom is how to keep order. "What do I do about discipline problems?" a student teacher will say. In the traditional classroom, the teacher's role is too often that of the disciplinarian, the keeper of order. And that leaves students with two conplementary responses — to submit to or disrupt that order. But in the kind of classroom we're advocating here, the notions of discipline and order, and the roles teachers and students have in maintaining an ordered classroom community, need to be reconceived. Order doesn't mean the arrangement of desks, and discipline doesn't mean a silent classroom. Instead, structure comes through an underlying program of activities that moves students through real and meaningful work and makes everybody in the class feel invested in that work. Discipline comes from engagement and activity, imposed more from within the group and the learner than from the teacher's desk. Responsibility for classroom order is shared.

The new roles of teachers and students in this classroom community will be characterized especially by new patterns of talk and silence. In the traditional classroom, where authority rests with the teacher, the right to speak resides with him as well. There's a particular irony in an English classroom that supposedly focuses on the development of language skills yet limits students' opportunities to use language to express what they're learning. According to Shirley Brice Heath, in the typical high school classroom there's no more than two minutes of talk for any individual student in any given class, and in videotapes of classrooms throughout the country an observer can see clearly that many days go by when there's no classrooms talk at all except for the brief replies students make to direct questions from teachers. This silence is not golden. We know that talk is important to learning. But it's also important to both negotiating and practicing a consensus about how classroom activity will be ordered. In the very act of having a conversation with someone there are rules of order that get followed — rules for taking turns, listening, keeping the voice at an appropriate pitch, staying on or changing the topic. Talk itself allows students to construct a kind of order in the classroom.

But it's the "children should be seen and not heard" notion of discipline that's dominated our schools. Heath's work in Roadville illustrates that children who've internalized the idea of keeping silent in school end up being passive learners wholly dependent on the authority of the teacher and unable to invent their own paths to knowing something. These children will often "misbehave" when the teacher goes out of the room because they've learned too well that it's the teacher's job to keep them quiet and on task; when the teacher leaves, all learning stops and anything goes. Unfortunately, their misbehavior only forces more stringent methods of keeping them quiet. Such a view of talk and silence inevitably creates conflict between the two and a conflict between teacher and students. The teacher has the right to talk and the students have the right to remain silent.

In the new classroom community there are still moments for silence. Students and teacher have time to reflect on something that's been said, to write in journals, to read individually. This sort of silence and stillness in the classroom reflects active involvement, and it's interspersed with periods of talk and outward activity. It's quite different from the silence that's occasioned by a faulty conception of discipline — that children should be seen and not heard.

Real learning takes place in the negotiation between talk and silence among learners themselves, not only between teacher and student. Because people have been so conditioned to the authority of the teacher, it's difficult for students to see themselves in an equal conversational relationship with the teacher. One thing that group talk does is to allow students ways around their meek and quiet submission to the teacher's voice. Before we can create a true interactive classroom, therefore, we have to create alternatives where students can talk and not merely answer.

What we've been suggesting about the dialectic between silence and talk, and stillness and movement, in creating a new kind of classroom order mandates new attitudes toward authority. Literally, an author is the creator: a writer or designer, one who determines the outcome of any enterprise. Students who are authors in the English classroom are more than the writers of their own essays. They're the designers, cocreators of the learning that goes on. And as creators, they've both freedom and responsibility for the product — the classroom structure.

But for students to become authors and creators and speakers in the classroom suggests new roles for them and for their teachers.

Examining teachers' roles

What we've said so far implies that learners should be responsible for what happens in the classroom in ways that traditional methods of instruction and learning haven't allowed for. If students are active rather than passive, they bring their backgrounds acquired in particular communities and families to bear on what they read and write. If students are inquirers rather than responders, they discover methods as well as facts. They learn how knowledge is created because they've used their imaginations to interpret the worlds around them. And learning that knowledge is created in communities, they learn that they help create the small community of the classroom itself.

There are few models for these new roles and this sort of classroom community. Real-life accounts by teachers like Pat Conroy (*The Water Is Wide*), Sylvia Ashton-Warner (*Teacher*), Jonathan Kozol (*Death at an Early Age*), and George Dennison (*The Lives of Children*) provide moving portraits of the learning of engaged students in restructured classrooms. But common cultural experience, reinforced by fictional accounts in movies and books, focuses on the authoritarian teacher and passive or rebellious or worshipful students. And in fiction, as opposed to real-life accounts, authors seem to fall back on the stereotypical student-teacher relationship, where the all-powerful teacher who may or may not be a benevolent despot influences powerfully (for good or ill) the completely powerless students in his charge. You remember from Unit 1 Charles Dickens' teacher Mr. Gradgrind, who weeds out conjecture from facts by grilling his quaking students, and who succeeds only in cowing most of them into silence.

A more positive but no less dominating teacher appears in other fiction, in novels like *The Corn is Green* and *Goodbye Mr. Chips*, in recent movies like *Dead Poet's Society* or even *Stand and Deliver*, based on a real-life story of an inspiring teacher's work with Los Angeles ghetto kids. Muriel Spark's novel *The Prime of Miss Jean Brodie* tells the story of such a teacher, whose relationship with her students and their learning provides an interesting counterpoint to the new roles we'll reflect on in these chapters. Miss Brodie's eccentric and interesting ways, and her suggestion that those who follow her are special, win the loyalty of her students. But like Gradgrind she demands silence: "You were not listening to me. If only you small girls would listen to me, I would make of you the crème de la crème" (22).

Miss Brodie is loved by her students and disdained by the school authorities and the rest of her teaching staff for her unorthodox methods of instruction, which consist primarily of telling stories of her own life and travels, interspersed with facts about geography and art. Her method is to make learning personal by making it live through her own experience, and through her stories Miss Brodie engages the interest of her students while she broadens their experience of the world and the range of their background knowledge. Outside school her stories inspire her students' own self-sponsored compositions — mostly stories about her lover who was killed in the war — and their own research — primarily into matters of sex. But they don't leave room for students' language and discovery.

Miss Brodie often embodies the familiar metaphors used to decribe teachers. As we said in Chapter 8, metaphors do more than describe concepts; they also order observations and determine the way we look at concepts. Metaphors, as linguists Lakoff and Johnson argue, are "not only grounded in our physical and cultural experience; they also influence our experience and our actions" (68). So the metaphors most commonly used to characterize teachers both describe and *influence* the ways in which teachers are seen by students, the community, and themselves.

The teacher as hanging judge

"She's going to kill me for not having done my homework." "He hates it when we forget the title." "She told us this was our last chance to improve." This is pretty familiar student talk. This teacher, like Mr. Gradgrind in Dickens' novel and countless others in film, is the arbiter of taste, of correctness, and of worth. Students work to please this emblem of rightness, knowing that their best efforts will probably be met only with a grim smile of pity. The judge/teacher is basically an enemy, the one who carries the gradebook like a shield and her pen like a sword, and her students are guilty until proved innocent. Innocence is proved only when students somehow divine the answers that she deliberately withholds in a sadistic maneuver that proves to her students how little they know. If most teachers vary completely from this stereotype (and we hope they do!), many people don't know it, and they still retreat into silence upon meeting a teacher or going to visit their children's classroom.

The teacher as god

Sometimes the judge/teacher isn't an enemy but simply someone so remote from the students and so removed from real life that students believe she lives only inside the classroom. Once, when Hepsie was teaching high school, she saw one of her ninth-grade students at a rock concert. "I can't believe a *teacher* would come to this," he said. He even ran to get two of his friends to show them that she was actually sitting in the stands. He was obviously shocked at seeing a teacher in the real world — his world — because her behavior didn't fit his stereotype. The stereotype of the teacher as god is certainly a more positive one than that of the hanging judge, but it's no less damaging to real interaction in the classroom. A god always knows everything perfectly. A god can't be expected to understand imperfection, even when he might not punish for it. A god doesn't know experience because he doesn't live it. Sometimes students who admire their teachers begin to think of them as flawless, and they consciously try to adopt some of their teachers' personality traits or actions. This is especially true in earlier grades or in classes where students are preparing to be teachers and see teaching behaviors they like. While making the teacher a model isn't necessarily a bad thing (both of us have teachers in our pasts who've been — and who continue to be — models for our own teaching), believing the teacher is godlike prevents students from wanting to exchange ideas and assert their own authority in a classroom.

The teacher as guide

In this most positive of all the stereotypes, the teacher is the experienced traveler who's been through the wilderness and returned to lead the new generation out of it. His experience allows him to be wise, and his larger vision lets him facilitate the workings of the classroom. The teacher who nearly dropped out of high school as a teenager and returns to his rundown neighborhood to help teenagers who are like he once was or the teacher who has made life choices she regrets and wants to prevent her students from making the same mistakes both fit the teacher/ guide stereotype, and such images recur in movies and in novels.

Miss Brodie presents herself, at times, as godlike in her powers to mold the lives of·her students: "Give me a girl at an impressionable age, and she is mine for life." Others see her as dictatorlike, and even one of her girls, Sandy, sees for a moment "that the Brodie set was Miss Brodie's fascisti, . . .all knit together for her need" (47). But Miss Brodie herself attributes her method to carefully thought-out educational principles, which are like those of the guide.

> Miss Mackay wishes to question my methods of instruction. It has happened before. It will happen again. Meanwhile, I follow my principles of education and give of my best in my prime. The word "education" comes from the root *e* from *ex*, out, and *duco*, I lead. It means a leading out. To me education is a leading out of what is already there in the pupil's soul. To Miss Mackay it is a putting in of something that is not there, and that is not what I call education, I call it intrusion, from the Latin root prefix *in* meaning in and the stem *trudo*, I thrust. Miss Mackey's method is to thrust a lot of information into the pupil's head; mine is a leading out of knowledge, and that is true education as is proved by the root meaning. (54)

Unfortunately, what Miss Brodie would lead out of her pupil's souls are really the obsessions that are in her own. And later, in adulthood, Sandy is asked, "What would you say was your greatest influence during the 'thirties? I mean during your teens. Did you read Auden and Eliot? . . . Did you take sides in the Spanish Civil War at your school? . . . What was your biggest influence, then? Was it political, personal? Was it Calvinism?" And Sandy responds, "Oh no. But there was a Miss Jean Brodie in her prime." (52)

Real people, however, often do attest to the influence of their teachers as guides for them during their youth. *An Apple for My Teacher* is a wonderful collection of narratives from famous writers who write about the effect teachers they admired had on their careers. All use the "teacher as guide" metaphor to explore their relationships. The metaphor is a good one to suggest much of the action that goes on — and should go on — in the classroom. But it can't embody the teacher's entire activity. If the guide leads, then the others follow. And they don't know where they're going! Taken to its logical extreme, the teacher as guide puts the students in a classroom in exactly the passive, waiting postures that we're trying to escape from. As a stereotype, Miss Brodie isn't much better than Mr. Gradgrind.

What all these metaphors have in common is the underlying recognition of the teacher's power — used for good or evil. The truth is that whatever metaphors we operate with unconsciously or intentionally in our depiction of the teacher, and whatever words we use to articulate our role — facilitator, colearner, evaluator — the teacher's authority in the classroom is inevitable and inescapable. However, as Freire explains, assuming authority doesn't mean being authoritarian:

> Only authoritarian educators deny the solidarity between the act of educating and the act of being educated by those becoming educated; only authoritarians separate the act of teaching from that of learning in such a way that he who believes himself to know actually teaches, and he who is believed to know nothing learns. (1988, 41).

The teacher who sees the oneness between the act of educating and the act of being educated, between teaching and learning, must still acknowledge rather than deny the power of the teacher's role. She must learn how to use her authority to make authorities of her students.

New roles for students — active and collaborative learners

One of the real problems for teachers in escaping limiting postures, once they themselves become aware of them, is that their students often promote the stereotypes actively and don't like to see them altered. Students in a classroom carry traditional ideas about the teacher-student relationship, about the authority in a classroom, about their own roles. If teachers refuse to be simply punishers or dispensers of truth or scout leaders, students may resist. New, less stereotyped teachers' roles mean new roles for them as well, and students operate with stereotypes of themselves too, ones that tell them that being quiet, passive, and accepting are the behaviors they should get rewarded for; being aggressive, challenging, talkative are behaviors to be punished. They might choose the "bad" student role or the "good" one, the "clown" or the "nerd," but they're clear about what determines each of the categories. Many students want to have classroom roles and classroom activities not only spelled out but spelled out in letters that put students on the margins, rather than in the center, of the action. These students are the ones who will in frustration or anxiety say to a teacher, "Just tell me what you want, and I'll do it."

The student as active learner

One idea of teacher/student roles is as ancient as the Greeks. Socrates' student Meno is exasperated by his teacher's refusal to "just tell him" what to do, what the truth was, in his case, regarding the teaching of virtue. Meno is astounded when Socrates, the teacher, admits that he not only doesn't know whether virtue can be taught but doesn't even know what it is. "What!" Meno says. "Is this the report we are to take home about you?" Socrates forces Meno to reframe the question, to speculate about it, to come to his own answers through Socrates' careful strategies of illuminating the problem for him. One of the striking things about this dialogue is the way Socrates confesses, in fact makes a point of asserting, his own ignorance of the final answers to the questions his students ask. "All I can say is that I have often looked to see if there are any [teachers of virtue], and in spite of all my efforts, I cannot find them.... I don't know what virtue is and, not only that, you may say also, that to the best of my belief, I have never yet met anyone who did know" (Hamilton, 354). And Meno is confounded by his teacher/guide/god refusing to tell what Meno is sure he knows.

The stunned admirers in Miss Brodie's class wonder aloud and write about subjects they have discovered an interest in.

> Jenny was a reliable source of information, because a girl employed by her father in her grocery shop had recently been found to be pregnant, and Jenny had picked up some fragments of the ensuing fuss. Having confided her finds to Sandy, they had embarked on a course of research which they called "research," piecing together clues from remembered conversations illicitly overheard, and passages from the big dictionaries. (26)

These girls, who sit silently before their beloved Miss Brodie and her stories in the classroom, are quite different outside. They draw on what they've learned from the world around them, on what they can learn from books, and actively work to gain new understandings.

Coming to know is an active process, in which the learner must be engaged in acts of discovery and inquiry, and, as Vygotsky has shown, this process always takes place within a particular social/cultural context, with language internalized from and shaped by that context. Most real-world learning takes place in interaction with others, but most classrooms isolate learners from that kind of interaction. The group in the classroom mirrors the way most people learn outside the classroom. The individual who negotiates between what he knows already and what other members of a group share with him creates dynamic knowledge, knowledge that gets made as group and individual interact. While teachers can establish activities that actively engage students as individuals in their learning (and many individualized learning programs for computers are designed to do this), we argue that knowledge, because it is fundamentally shared and social, is fully created and negotiated only in collaborative contexts. So, while helping students become active learners and assume authority for their own learning, teachers must also create opportunities for them to share in knowing and coming to know.

The student as collaborative learner

For learners of all ages, interactive, collaborative learning in pairs and groups supports shar*ing* knowledge (as opposed to the memorizing of facts that E. D. Hirsh advocates for creating culturally shar*ed* knowledge). Kenneth Bruffee, who has focused much of his work on the development of collaborative learning in the English classroom, tells us:

> To think well as individuals we must learn to think well collectively — that is, we must learn to converse well. The first steps to learning to think better, therefore, are learning to converse better and learning to establish and maintain the sorts of social context, the sorts of community life, that foster the sorts of conversation members of the community value. (640)

The patterns of interaction and communication that members of a community value are too often alien in classroom contexts, particularly at the high school and college level. But we can support them by using groups in many ways in the classroom — for writing and responding, discussing, questioning, problem solving, researching, reporting. Such groups encourage learners to take active roles and to assume new responsibilities.

Working in groups

> The class broke up into 6 groups. The task was to paraphrase a poem by Anne Bradstreet. Marla and I and John walked around from group to group, offering help. One of the groups was especially frustrating. The "leader" of the group was a girl who is constantly insisting that she doesn't understand what's going on. She took charge of this group, would say what the poem meant, but then wouldn't know what to write down as a paraphrase. All of us had the same experience with this group: we ask what does the poem say, then Sue says it and then says "What do I write?" "You just said it." "No, I don't know what words to put down." "The words you just used." "But what do I write?" And so forth. John didn't have any better luck with her than Marla and I did. The other groups were mostly very good. (David S)

David's observations show that simply forming groups in the classroom will not automatically bring about interactive and collaborative learning. Teachers must think as well about how to form them and to make them work, taking into account group dynamics and the personalities of individuals.

Effective groups are usually relatively small (four or five people), allowing each person a chance to talk and a chance to listen to everyone else in the group so that several perspectives are always influencing the group's work. And they are usually long-term, allowing students to establish relationship with each other that build trust. A student who shares her thought or her writing is taking a risk: What if she sounds stupid? What if she's made mistakes? What if everybody else knows more about the subject than she does? What if they laugh? When groups retain their members, each student learns to take risks because continuing dialogue and trust have time and space to develop.

All groups will need some support from the teacher as they get to know one another and learn new roles. Personality clashes or discipline problems may develop as students work together in groups, and teachers will need to make themselves part of individual groups to help them move in positive directions. While the group David observed welcomed the intervention of the teacher or prepractice assistants, it was only to get an authoritative answer. Actually becoming a member, rather than an authority, in the group for a little while—attending to interactions rather than answers—is necessary for teachers at some points during a semester's work.

Some of the activities of the group should center on developing procedures and reflecting on processes. Consensus building is one of the most important processes to nurture in group work. A group game (like the one included in the "Strategies" chapter at the end of this book, where each member is given a clue to the solution of a mystery and must combine it with everyone else's clue in order to solve the case) provides a nonthreatening starting point for encouraging each member to contribute. Such activities teach inductively a lesson about how a group functions: how ideas get shared, how associations get made, how plans develop, how interpretations develop.

Group tasks should be varied to accommodate the variety of activities in the English classroom itself. It's crucial that groups do real work, moving toward new understandings about significant elements in the class's study. The best insurance against distractions in the group is the clear sense of purpose that brings the group together — in other words, the activities the group will engage in. The assignment of paraphrasing a poem by Anne Bradstreet was a clear task for the group David observed. But this group, at least, seemed to need clearer steps toward that purpose. Questions or sequences of steps distributed by the teacher can help groups remain effective. Students might generate their own steps as well once they have the task clearly in mind. Students might decide on interpretations for a particular story or essay they've read, they might write together, they might read one another's work, they might help revise their peers' writing or revise together some published piece.

A group's members come to define their own roles, and leaders, facilitators, synthesizers will emerge in any situation where individuals interact, but it's important to allow students to try out particular roles (president, recorder, reporter), and to rotate them. The group David observed didn't have defined roles, and perhaps that's why a self-appointed leader dominated both the discussion and the recording of what was said.

The work that groups do — examples from the 3 R's

Reading

Reading groups in the high school and college classroom can do the very things most elementary school reading groups didn't. They can create collaborative and supportive environments for reading and understanding and interpreting texts. But many students need support to enter into such group work after early negative experiences in reading groups. David comments on one reading-group structure he observed, and then reflects on the problems that continue to keep a group from working together effectively.

> After the quiz, John broke the class into three groups to continue reading a novel they started last week. John, Marla, and I each took one group to lead. The kids read aloud, and were answering questions on a study guide. The kids were sort of shy, but they read OK and

seemed eager to at least find the answers to the study guide questions. I'm not sure what I think about using study guides. On one hand, it does seem to focus the students' attention on the reading; but on the other, they might tend to just look for the answers and then be done with it, not going any further than that. But maybe with the guide they get more out of it than not? I don't know — would have to experiment myself and see what difference it makes.

A later entry:

> After vocabulary they broke into the same three reading groups that we had a few weeks ago. This time I got the tough group: three of the five have exceptionally poor attitudes. It was really rough going, hard to keep them under control. I think I noticed a pattern to their behavior, though. It seems that what they do is act exaggeratedly stupid, deliberately making mistakes to be funny. I wonder if this isn't a defense mechanism of some kind: since they are afraid of making mistakes, maybe fearing being humiliated by their errors, they deliberately exaggerate their errors. So that way a mistake is not really a mistake, it's just something they're doing to be funny. It's safer for them not to really try; that way they can't fail. But even if that's true, what can be done about it? It seems like it would take a long time to overcome their fear of failure, if that's what the motivating force is. But I'm sure it could be done somehow, just by remembering that they're people too.

The classroom teacher may have to experiment with different structures for getting reading groups to work together effectively, and will need to observe carefully and be responsive to the workings of individual groups. But, even with these difficulties, reading groups can do a great deal to help make the language of literature come alive for readers in the classroom. In particular, they can help them to establish shared knowledge and shared understandings for interpreting literature, and much of the focused work of literature classes can be carried out actively and effectively in groups.

Dramatic literature offers unique opportunities for groups to work productively, since drama is created as a collaborative effort among actors, writer, director, stage designer, and audience. In fact, one of the real problems in interpreting drama — envisioning its performance — is circumvented by group work where group members can take on those roles. Groups can work to translate stage directions into sketches for sets, or "block" the movements of the actors on stage by interpreting characters' motivations in a scene. They can read scenes aloud, prepare roles, do staged readings of sections of the play for the class. They can rewrite scenes and talk about aspects of the characters' background motivations. In doing this work, the group re-creates the play: the relationship between actor and character, between audience and writer, between production and interpretation that constitutes the rhetoric of the dramatic text.

Like drama, poetry is an oral mode, designed, at least originally, to be performed. Unfortunately, poetry has been made to seem esoteric, hard to grasp, and students often come to a unit of poetry with groans of boredom or anxiety. The group helps resolve both problems. Small groups can begin by reading the poem aloud. Often whole vistas of interpretive possibility open up when a poem is really heard and not merely read silently. Groups can share in reading the poem, providing interpretations, speculating together about meanings. Reading aloud and commenting, students can build on associations that individuals might have to a particular image or story and combine ideas to create a response to the poem. And groups can write poems as well. Kenneth Koch's work with children writing poems, discussed in Chapter 8, shows how effective group work can be in stimulating creativity as well as teaching something about poetry. Students learned how form helps create meaning in poetry, how repetition generates new ideas. But it was their work in groups that let them get around their suspicion of poetry as something they were incapable of understanding or producing.

Students are most familiar with interpreting fiction, but they often feel unsure about interpretations of "difficult" stories and consequently want confirmation that they've found the "right" answer when they speculate about a theme or technique in a story. Groups can help students negotiate these responses and give them a sense of assurance about their own interpretations. They can point out alternatives for interpretation and help individuals see new angles on story elements in a nonjudgmental way. Because so much of the reading of fiction centers on the reader's background knowledge, the group can create a larger, more complex repertoire so that interpretation becomes richer. Groups can write endings of stories, discuss characters, structures, themes. They can move fiction into drama by writing dialogue for narrative. They can connect fiction to nonfiction by locating real events that remind them of fictional ones. Students can collect bits of stories they know, narratives of their families or communities, and bring them to the group to connect with stories they're reading. In these ways, they learn something about the structure of narrative, the use of dialogue, the ways readers interpret character through real-life example. Collecting different family members' versions of the same story, for example, provides a way of learning something about point of view. Re-presenting these stories for a classroom or group audience can raise issues of form and shared knowledge.

Writing

There's been a great deal of study among composition researchers about the role of the group in nurturing the writing process in two of its stages: invention and revision. Brainstorming is often used as a group invention process where ideas on topics proliferate because everybody contributes and makes associations quickly. Once these are listed, groups can create categories and refine them, and the process of getting ideas for writing — often the single most difficult part of writing for many students — is accomplished fairly painlessly.

Composition theorists have concentrated even more discussion on the benefits of group work for writers during the revision stage of the writing process. Writers who have real audiences listening and responding to their writing learn firsthand how writing is a communicative act; they learn to take responsibility for their words, to defend and modify them based on reactions from the real people sitting around them. One of the primary benefits of group work at this stage is that writers learn that some of their ideas, or points, or transitions, are made only implicitly; that is, they're never stated or even alluded to very clearly. When a writer reads his own work to himself, he often continues to make these links as he reads because he knows what he means. When he gets a paper returned with "vague" or "no transition" or "more specific" written in the margin, he may not realize that it's those "missing links" that have caused his reader (the teacher) confusion. But in writing, reading, and speaking to the audience of the group, the writer can see immediately by puzzled faces where implicit connections need to be made explicit. Furthermore, because the group is composed of peers who are not only evaluating but writing themselves, the fear of what Elbow calls "giving one's writing" diminishes and trust has a chance to develop. With it comes a sense of confidence and authority over the words of the developing text.

Students need to learn to be effective responders in this group effort. David observes a class in which students participate in a "writing workshop," responding to other students' writing:

> Then they did a sort of workshop. The teacher had copied two students' papers, and gave everyone a copy. The workshop instructions were something like, "Pretend you're the teacher." Interesting to see how kids took that: all their comments at first were about fixing punctuation and spelling. But for the second paper they started to talk about the ideas, maybe because the second paper was much better both in content and in mechanics.

Students like these may wish to make a lot of corrections, especially in spelling or word choice because they've been taught to feel that these factors mean good or bad writing. Or they may simply praise the writing, especially if they hope someone will judge their own efforts more sympathetically when they themselves have been sympathetic or if they don't know what to respond to in order to be helpful. "It's fine, I guess" was a typical response in a later group that David observed. Teachers can help students become good responders by giving suggestions of elements to look for in writing, by providing activities that encourage responders to write suggestions or ideas, by showing groups how to respond to drafts through their own responses to the drafts of students in the class.

The benefits of the group for the individual's writing process are considerable. But peer-group editing and response aren't the only ways writing needs to be employed. As we suggested earlier, the group should produce writing *as a group*, sometimes responding to questions, sometimes suggesting ideas, sometimes producing an extended piece of discourse. There are different models for collaborative writing: some groups divide the work and then blend it, sometimes one person pulls together the work of several different writers, and sometimes members of the group generate ideas and texts together. Groups probably should explore more than one of these alternatives as they write. David observes one of these models for writing in groups — collaborative thinking with individual writing. (And he points out the need for the teacher's active support and assurance in such work.)

> More group work: each group got a picture from the Revolutionary Period. The assignment was to write a story based on the picture. Each group exchanges ideas, but each student writes his/her own story. Marla and I walked around, offering help.
> This was interesting — a lot of the groups had many very good and imaginative ideas, but didn't want to use them. The kids thought their ideas were dumb, and it took a lot of convincing to get them to actually start writing them down, but except for one group (the one with Sue in it that had the same problem with the Anne Bradstreet poem paraphrase — "what do I write?") they all started to write pretty good stories. As before with this sort of activity, it just took a few good questions and some assurance that they were on the right track to get the groups going. They seem to need that assurance a lot — there is overall a terrific fear that they're not doing something right. Important to let them know that they are doing it right, and definitely not focus on whatever they might be doing that's less than right.

Collaborative writing is the way much writing is done in the real world, where groups of people often contribute in one way or another to a common report. (And the use of computers in the writing classroom, especially when terminals must be shared, sometimes supports more collaborative efforts.) Writing with others also shows students dramatically how many ways there are to say something. When you write by yourself, you're tempted to believe you have to find one right choice, one right word for the idea you have in your head. But when a writer writes with someone else, she becomes conscious of the rich possibilities there are for interpreting in writing in part because she's forced to talk about them. This kind of talk helps the writer clarify her own choices and extend the range of possibilities for her own writing. When two thinkers are working together, each adds to the work in ways that allow for new steps to be made.

Collaborative writing can also help individual writers recognize their own voices. The process of negotiating one's voice with others' to create a new, blended voice lets students begin to hear their own individual voices clearly because they hear them in terms of those other voices.

Finally, even mundane tasks — correcting sentences — when they're done in groups and reflected on together become occasions for generating understanding about how decisions get made as well as about the decisions themselves. Peer editing for a class publication of student work, for example, can help students become aware of the forms and uses — and the rationale — of Standard Written English.

Research

The image of research in the humanities has been precisely that of writing itself: The lonely researcher sits in the library pouring over the work of other and older lonely researchers who've sat in libraries pouring over the work of still other and even older lonely researchers before them, in a kind of infinite bibliographic regression. Our colleagues in the social and the physical sciences have long practiced collaborative research in groups and teams, having understood the value of group effort in research. In some ways what we have to say here about research is much the same thing we've said about writing in general. Researching ideas and material together provides the benefits of real audiences and responders, and even more important, allows for ideas to get further developed in the kind of conceptual scaffolding that happens when thinkers move between external and internal modes of communication.

But, in speaking of research, we need to talk once more about the nature of inquiry. Research begins with questions: about the world, about texts, about oneself in relationship to the world and to texts. The questions thinkers ask build upon knowledge that they already share with others, and the ways they go about answering build on ways that others have sought answers. Consequently, doing research in groups makes this implicitly shared questioning and answering explicit and supports the learning of students who are discovering how to be researchers. In group research, multiple perspectives and the validity of results are tested by lots of different approaches or experiments that provide angles on a problem. Researchers working together are making new knowledge by building on one another's work, asking questions that they had not until now thought to ask. Collaborative research takes the emphasis off of form and format and puts it onto the process of discovery, with more than one perspective informing the project.

Groups and the larger classroom community

We've been discussing the advantages of group work so far in terms of how learners learn and how knowledge gets made. In general, the group is an important element in the interactive class because it functions to put learners in control of their own environment. When the group meets, students in the classroom talk. Their interaction spreads control throughout the room and allows them to feel that they're helping to make the conditions in which they learn. As they talk together and before the class as a group, their performance puts them in control. Their authority as a group makes for interaction with other small groups and promotes real discussion rather than simply response to questions. Oral performance in the group is a kind of publication, a presentation of findings and of interpretations. Group writing that's distributed to the class at large is another kind of performance that lets students assume control over classroom activity. And all knowledge becomes shared knowledge.

Groups are also important because of the ways in which they affect the dynamics of the class as a whole. The class is a larger group (sometimes much too large, with thirty-five or forty students). While small groups allow students to contribute in ways that would be hard with limited time in a very large group, they also can encourage new patterns of large-group communication. Students who report on group findings to the whole class have the backing of four or five other students. They don't have to be lonely risk takers, and the group voice generally helps them find their own. Students who've contributed actively to small-group discussions become much more comfortable contributing actively to a larger one. And a teacher who's circulated and listened to students' ideas and asked the sorts of questions that help small groups extend their thinking will listen more and ask better questions of the class.

But there are other, less tangible, advantages to small-group interaction in the classroom both to the individual and to the community. Like most educators, we believe that one goal of education is to help students develop as ethical and responsible human beings. In order for people to become ethical and responsible, they have to practice negotiating their needs and desires with those of others around them. Sadly, today many of our students come from homes and families that are "dysfunctional," to use the sociologists' term: homes where severe problems — social, economic, psychological — prevent communication and create isolation. As adolescents, all students from whatever kind of home background are struggling with a tension between the two poles of an extreme self-consciousness and an overwhelming need to lose the self in a group of peers. Learning effective patterns of group interaction in the classroom can give students practice in maintaining their selves and their values while working responsibly toward consensus with the group. In the group, listening becomes as important as speaking, and restating others' views becomes as important as defending one's own. The roles of group members become a kind of microcosm of later interaction in jobs and in the home, where people must sometimes lead and sometimes follow, sometimes accommodate and sometimes defend. Trust happens in group work, and that trust can affect the relationship between students and teacher as well.

> The other groups were mostly very good.... The kids seem to be getting more comfortable, and comfortable with us too. They've actually started calling us over to help, which is worlds away from what they did at first, when they'd try to get rid of us when we offered help. So that's good. I guess they are slowly coming to trust us and to believe that we can help them.... And I'm coming to trust them more too, coming to realize that for the most part they do want to do well, and are willing to try. I'm still sort of trying to find the right level of speech for them, still trying to get a sense of what kind of background knowledge they have.... But in general this was a super experience, spending the whole class period going around to the groups and mostly being successfully helpful. (David S)

New roles for all individuals in the classroom community — readers, writers, respondents

As David's observations show, in the new classroom community both the students and the teacher must learn new roles. David is learning to teach within the classroom of an experienced teacher who is himself reexamining his classroom roles in the midst of shifting expectations. As a long-term teacher in a school with a traditional and sharply defined curriculum, John Welsh continues to do many things in traditional ways — teaching grammar from an outline (Chapter 5), giving constant quizzes on vocabulary words (Chapter 6), even though he "knows the theory." But John is a teacher in transition. He's not just digging into old ways, and he's certainly not giving up. Rather, he's trying out new ways in his classroom, doing more group work, holding writing workshops, developing peer responding and editing skills, and giving students opportunities for collaborative writing. Not all of these new ways are immediately successful — students who've just completed grammar exercises are likely to look first for errors as they respond to other students' writing. But as students gradually learn to function in new ways in the classroom, they enter into new relationships with their teachers — at first just by asking for a little of the teacher's help while they work with each other.

John himself is a learner, as well as a teacher. He's returned to graduate school in English to find new ways of thinking about his subject. He enthusiastically takes on prepractice teachers, not just to "train" them in his ways, but to learn what they are learning, and to think collaboratively about what's going on in his classroom:

> One of the most important things I keep in mind is to always feel like a first-year teacher, not to follow the same preplanned program of lessons and methods for each class, but rather to be always alert to trying out new ideas, ways to do things differently . . . in order to get some response from the students. , . . The experienced teacher needs, just as much as the inexperienced, to be willing to try something for the first time. . . .

For John, an important part of the teacher's learning is understanding how to respond to and support learners in his classroom. He goes on: "It all comes down to personality: your personality, their personality, how those two interact, how accepting they are, how accepting you are." David sums up his cooperating teacher's perspective:

> John's philosophy of teaching, then, might be summed up as follows: what happens in school is for the students; the teacher needs to know who those students are, and accept them as they are; and the teacher needs always to do whatever is best for those students, to help them learn in whatever way is best for them.

Such a teacher will respond as an individual to students as individuals, but he'll also help these individuals become a contributing part of the classroom community, and understand the relationship between self and other in learning. Here, then, are some of the reciprocal roles that teachers need to foster for themselves and for their students.

Informed reader and spokesperson

The literary critic Stanley Fish locates the basis for interpretation of literary work in what he calls the *interpretive community*, a group of readers who exist in a kind of circle of interpretation, a circle that might be as large as the group of literate human beings or as small as the classroom. In this community, members bring what they know and believe about a text to a discussion and by negotiation determine for themselves meaning and significance of work. The *informed reader* in this community is a hybrid of ideal and actual; in Fish's words such a reader begins as "a real reader (me) who does everything within his power to make himself informed." As this real reader reads, he tries, simultaneously, to keep his mind open to whatever responses the text might evoke—"making my mind the repository of the (potential) responses a given text might call out" — and to suppress whatever is "personal and idiosyncratic" in those responses. "In short the informed reader is to some extent processed by the method that uses him as a control" (49).

Just as the individual informed reader tries both to be open to possible responses and to eliminate responses that are wholly idiosyncratic, a community of readers will bring out a variety of possible responses from its members while making it clear which responses are not shared by others in the group and are, in fact, idiosyncratic. The classroom can function as this sort of an interpretive community, where the group meets to negotiate meaning and significance in the activities they accomplish. Fish is talking only about a means to arrive at decisions about the interpretation of literary work, but his discussion bears a clear relationship to the activity of individual students in the English classroom. The student needs to find ways to become the informed reader: the person who makes her mind the repository of responses to texts (or to ideas, or to events, or to discussion) and who can suppress or pull out what is important only to her, only personally relevant, and therefore idiosyncratic in her responses. To become informed readers, students should read a lot, and respond, both in speaking and in writing, to what they read. Teachers can promote such reading by providing time for both reading and responding in the class. There should also be time for students to share what they know, to present their ideas to others and to represent the ideas of other readers. To become an *informed spokesperson*, as Fish might put it, students should have lots of opportunity to speak in both informal and formal ways, engaging in the talk that fosters learning.

The teacher should also serve as informed spokesperson, guiding and pushing discussion into areas that he knows are productive because of his greater experience with texts. He also provides writing activities that allow his students to become more and more confident, skillful interpreters, activities that he designs based on his thoughtful exploration of his own interpretive strategies as a reader and writer. Consequently, the teacher as informed reader or spokesperson becomes both guide and provoker; he knows the territory because of greater experience with the text to be read, and he has greater interpretive ability because of that experience. And he uses that experience to create other informed readers in the classroom. "Each of us," Fish says, "if we are sufficiently responsible and self-conscious, can, in the course of employing the method, become the informed reader and therefore be a more reliable reporter of his experience" (49). One of the main tasks of the teacher as informed reader, in fact, is to allow other informed readers to emerge in the classroom.

One of our prepractice students, Sara, observes her cooperating teacher in this role:

The assignment had been to write a first draft on a story by John Gardner — a rewrite, basically, of *Beowulf*. Ms. N instructed everyone — including myself — to move into a response group. The groups were divided by threes and fours. Ms. N had written questions on the board to be included in the essay. One student read her paper and others went over it thoroughly. They read Kelly's paper with the nearly practiced eye of an English teacher. They picked out words Kelly might change, and even restructures a few of her sentences and seemed to be having a heck of a good time doing it, too. At 9:10 Ms. N asked everyone to finish up. She had been visiting each group in that 45 minutes and talking to each one, making suggestions, leading them back to the story, making them think of similarities. Reflecting on this, I can just now see her expertise in teaching. She was able to keep the class in near complete order while each student, each group of students, worked amongst themselves. Though she hardly appeared to be teaching, she really was.

Sara observes several important aspects of the work of the teacher as informed reader here. First, the teacher provides her own model for the group to work with in the form of a list on the board. The list itself, though, has grown out of class discussion where the group has decided on the key issues they thought their essays should explore. The teacher moves among groups with questions in her mind that focus her energy and the energy of the groups she visits. Although she has a clear agenda for the activities of the groups, she builds that agenda by consensus rather than by directive. And she is systematically creating other informed readers in the classroom with her approach. Notice that Sara says that the group members read "with the nearly practiced eye" of the English teacher. They don't correct; they talk about choices and alternatives and they read aloud, all the things that an informed spokesperson might do with a piece of writing she's responding to. This approach provides a way for the classroom to support any number of informed readers.

The teacher as informed reader directs, guides, promotes inquiry by engaging in it herself. Something as simple as sharing a response to a first reading of a story ("When I read the first paragraph of *The Awakening*, all I could think about was where I had taken my kids on vacation last year") can show students how the personal association may become part of the interpretation or may be pushed aside when it's not important enough to the reader's interpretation. As the teacher talks with students in small and large groups, as she shares her responses and reactions, she shows not only that the personal and the extracurricular can find a place in the activity of the class, but she demonstrates a method of inquiry that keeps asking the questions "What difference does it make if I think of it this way and not some other?" "What else do I need to think about or find out about before I can make a decision?"

Writer, journal keeper, author

Bruce Rettman has been consciously transforming his and his students' roles in the classroom. In response to some questions we asked about his teaching several years ago, he spoke as the informed reader—a teacher who is engaged with his subject.

> As a student, my favorite subject was English. I was always tremendously interested in what my teacher was saying about literature. As a result of that, I make an automatic assumption that my students are as interested as I was in literature and in writing. My assumption of interest converts to enthusiasm and intensity in the classroom. My students never leave my class without recognizing that I am involved in what I do, that my passion, my being, is somehow wrapped up in these poems, stories, plays, novels I discuss with them.

But for Bruce, the work of transforming his classroom really began when he began to participate, as a writer, in a community of writers through the Boston Writing Project:

> I had taken nothing that influenced my teaching until the Writing Project Summer Seminar with Joe [Check] and Peter [Golden]. I learned about teaching writing from them, learned to use writing as a way to learning. Naturally, I had devised techniques of my own through the years that were effective, but I had never been able to see those techniques in the context of a broader philosophy, and I had never been equipped with so many ways to lead students to write. This year I'm using double entry journals with my freshman classes. I've also used response groups. I think what I'm doing is transferring the responsibility for good student writing from me to my students. Peer editing seems to be the most healthy method I've ever introduced to my classroom.

In an article written for the *Boston Writing Project Newsletter*, he tells us how participating in the Boston Writing Project brought him new understandings of how to work with writing in the classroom.

> The Institute allowed me to see expressive writing as an end in itself and as a way to other writing. It allowed me to look at methods of helping students as they wrote, as they developed drafts. It has suggested a hundred ways to develop competent peer editors and to form constructive response groups. It has shown me ways of response that are affirmative and constructive, not damning and critical. It has made me aware of the need to provide opportunities for a variety of writing experiences. It has shown me how to create in my classroom the sense of a community of writers by providing ways of publishing. Withal, what I will do will be firmly grounded in a theory that makes sense. (2)

But the Writing Project provided more than new approaches and the theory behind them. It created an opportunity for Bruce to become a learner and a writer again, and to do it in a community of other learners and writers. For teachers, as well as learners, who are involved in renegotiating their classroom roles, the community becomes crucial.

> An important aspect of our institute is the sense of community it expresses. If individuals grow, they have to do it in a community or the growth is an aberration. What was inspirational to me was to listen to knowledgeable, committed colleagues express their thoughts so well. Our discussions allowed me to grow as a teacher. We met long enough to allow whatever scars we bore to be seen. That community was also important to me as a writer. . . . From time to time, I tried to publish poetry with only limited success. I've never published a piece of prose other than letters to the editor. The institute got me to publish some prose pieces, so now I have some I may be able to do something with. (2)

Bruce re-creates this community of readers, writers, learners in his classroom. As a prepractice student observes: "Mr. Rettman reads aloud many portions of the story. He always assigns some sort of writing assignment — today it's to jot down some words/phrases that show imagery and the representation of senses from the passage which he read aloud. And he always writes when the students do" (Deb).

Looking at Bruce's comments and Deb's observations, it's clear how much his attitude toward writing, described in his Boston Writing Project article, is mirrored in his teaching strategy. He insists that writing be central to students' activity in the classroom; they write in order to talk in groups, they write to help them interpret texts, they write to begin thinking out ideas that will become essays. Bruce's own experiences with writing as a tool for discovery in his Writing Project work have clearly influenced the direction he takes with his classes. He writes with the class to become a learner himself and compares his jottings with those of his students so that his voice becomes just one of a chorus of voices that explore an issue or idea. But he writes too because he has made writing in and out of class central to his activity as a teacher. In that teacherly activity, he's deeply invested in being a learner, and Bruce is aware that learners can use writing to learn.

Teachers can write in more than one way as they encourage new roles for themselves and new directions for their classrooms. One of the best is Bruce's method: to write some of the assignments themselves that they assign to students. Writing along with the class, either during class or for homework, the teacher becomes one of the group members working along on a task and so establishes her role as writer and learner. And one of the benefits of writing responses to assignments is, of course, that the teacher discovers the hidden difficulties or ambiguities of a writing task that she might not have envisioned in making up the writing assignment.

The teacher might also keep a journal along with the class. Long before his participation in the Boston Writing Project, Bruce kept a journal and had his students keep journals: "The impetus though, had been my reading of Boswell's *London Journal*, not an informed pedagogy." But students begin to locate their own reasons for writing once they begin to write a lot in a journal. Both students and teacher can use journals to observe and speculate about the things they observe, in the classroom, in their reading, in the world. Whether the format is that of a log of observation notes, a double-entry notebook that combines observations with reflections on those observations, or a dialogue journal in which a teacher or another reader asks questions and responds to entries, the journal helps writers clarify and extend their thinking. Many journals become a combination of several of these "types," sometimes personal and experience-related, sometimes double-entry or critically reflective, sometimes assignment-based. Teachers and students should experiment with strategies that make journal keeping pleasurable and habit-forming, and often the varying of task and response makes the journal both useful and self-illuminating.

Journals used in these ways are not always private, but they are at least owned by the writer. Any reader of another's journal needs to be careful. Because journals are designed to provide room for a freer exploration of ideas without formal constraints, readers should never judge or even comment on forms unless the writer is deliberately testing out a new form that she obviously would appreciate response to (sometimes, for example, students will include the drafts of poems as journal entries and ask for suggestions), and responses should focus on ideas and meanings. If used well, the journal becomes a place all learners go to with pleasure to help them work out problems, speculate about reading, plan writing, and make sense of their hectic lives. We'd like to think that journal writing might become a lifelong habit for some of the writers who begin it.

Like Bruce Rettman, both teachers and students can become authors as well as writers and journal keepers. The Boston Writing Project provided an initial forum for Bruce's writing, in the *Boston Writing Project Newsletter*. Many schools have literary magazines and newspapers that publish students' and teachers' work, and this is certainly a good way for students to see themselves as "real" writers. Work published in the classroom itself carries a similar message. In many elementary school classes where whole language approaches to reading and writing are used, classroom work is published in newsletters or books, and students write, illustrate, do page mock-ups, and then produce final pages, bind them, and make book jackets; and when the process is complete they hold a publishing party for parents and schoolmates at which proud writers circulate and talk about their books. Students can publish their work in similar ways in high school and college classrooms, and formal class collections can make the members of the class feel that their writing has an audience beyond the teacher.

It's also helpful for students to read the informally or formally published writing of other students — to see students' work as literary text. Hanging Loose Press, a small press that publishes the work of a number of poets, has recently produced a wonderful anthology of poetry written by writers of high school age. Edited by poet/teachers Dick Lourie and Mark Pawlak, *Smart Like Me* is now being read in high school classrooms; it gives students an opportunity to think seriously about the work of other writers like themselves, and can help them take their own work seriously. School literary magazines publish the work of young authors. And some avenues for publication support the work of less polished and confident writers. At South Boston High, Katie Singer has directed, for a number of years, a project in which students, many of whom would have been considered basic writers, collect and write stories of families and communities, as well as of their own experiences. Their publication, *MOSAIC*, is now read in many classrooms in the public schools. With its multicultural student staff and multicultural perspective, it's provided an important picture of what all members of a community can contribute to our larger social understanding, and in the years following the busing of Boston school students into segregated neighborhoods, it provided an important model for cooperation as well as a route to pride in authorship.

Teachers should also write outside class for work of their own, for professional meetings, for articles and essays, for any number of public or personal arenas. As Bruce has found, the teacher who writes for himself feels the process he teaches internally; he teaches the process with authority because he is experiencing it. And the teacher who shares such writing with students not only teaches them about the writing process but gains helpful readings in response.

Respondent and correspondent

Where the classroom has become a community for readers and writers, all its members take on new roles as respondents to the writing they read, as correspondents to other writers. The teacher in this community is no longer only an evaluator of student writing, and no longer the only reader of student writing, but an informed reader who models useful responses.

In a well-known study of teachers' responses to their students' writing, Nancy Sommers (1984) found that "teachers' comments can take students' attention away from their own purposes in writing a particular text and focus that attention on the teachers' purpose in commenting" (161), and that "this appropriation of the text by the teacher happens particularly when teachers identify errors in usage, diction, and style in a first draft and ask students to correct these errors when they revise" (162). Sommers found that teachers often given contradictory messages to students, telling them to find meanings and develop ideas at the same time that they must correct errors and create final, edited sentences. And teachers did not suggest that there was any priority to be given to one or another of these concerns. A typical comment was "Check your commas and semicolons and think more about what you're thinking about." And, in fact, most comments had little to do with a specific piece of writing done by an individual student. In Sommers' terms: "Most comments are not text-specific and could be interchanged, rubber-stamped, from text to text" (163). They consist of rules like "Avoid the passive!" rather than of reasons and strategies for doing things differently.

Students who've received such responses from their teachers learn to respond similarly when they move into writing groups. But both students and teachers can begin to respond to writing in new ways.

Responding within the context of the writing task

The first thing to consider in responding effectively isn't really what to write on a paper or even how to read it, but how the writing task was designed in the first place. What's the purpose of this particular piece of writing? Is it to explore initial thoughts and ideas on a subject? Then an appropriate response is to consider those ideas, to add a contribution to this imaginary conversation, to ask real questions or make real associations. Journal entries or short in-class writings are a good way of evoking a writer's initial thinking, and response journals, in which readers respond briefly but genuinely to a writer's daily entry, can provide a mechanism for getting real exchanges going. Is this piece of writing an early draft? Then again, a genuine response to the ideas, with real questions or pointing to places that cause real puzzlement, will guide the writer toward the next draft. For a later draft of formal writing, the reader may want to assume the role of the more distant "audience" a writer addresses, and follow the conventions of written discourse that suppose the reader doesn't share much contextual knowledge with the writer. Finally, there are occasions where it's important to serve as an editor, to help writers work out final details, clarify jumbles, and correct errors, always remembering that editing is really a last stage of the writing process, quite distinct from earlier ones.

Responding as a reader

When responding to the texts of other writers, readers must first read through the piece to find out what the writer is saying, what the general effect might be, avoiding the all-too-real temptation to judge or correct the writing *before* its intentions are even established. Marginal comments, shorthand marks, and questions written while reading are useful, though, in this first reading of a text, for such text markers help readers monitor the progress of their own reading of the text. Marginal comments can show the ways in which the reader is making sense of the written text. Perhaps even more important, such comments — speculative, questioning, suggestive — establish a conversation with the writer.

Only after the whole piece is read should a reader make summary responses, suggestions, corrections. When readers begin to read a piece of literature, they assume a relationship not unlike a contract: the writer in good faith attempts to communicate and the reader in good faith attempts to engage actively in that communication. The contract is strong enough that even when readers begin in utter confusion, as they do when they open Faulkner's *The Sound and the Fury* and hear the disconnected rambling voice of mentally retarded Benjy, they continue, searching for connections, listening for clues, making sense. Once readers begin to do the same thing in their reading of student writing, they discover many of the writer's intentions, purposes, strategies, moves. They discover the essence and not merely the accidents of the writer's discourse.

Readers can also record the general effect of the text on their process as readers, noting that "I was thinking that you really wanted me to pay attention to your motorcycle ride, but then you started to say quite a bit about the fact that your friend bought his helmet on a trip to Florida. Why did you want me to know about this? Does it help to explain something about the accident?" And writing comments in full sentences at the end of the paper or on a separate piece of paper requires that readers become correspondents as well.

Responding as a conversational partner
We have talked about how important it is to think with writers and respond in real ways. But we have few models for conducting effective dialogue in writing; few of us carry out real exchanges of ideas in writing, and most of us write letters only to make a complaint or to formalize an agreement. Letter exchanges — with the teacher, with other students, with outside penpals, with an informed expert — can create the sort of extended dialogue that fuels both thinking and writing. Prepractice students who exchange letters with freshman writers have found that the writing of both participants changes, through a process of negotiation, as each partner responds to the thought and words and meanings of the other. Emily, for example, began to move away from her teacherly, academic style when she discovered that her freshman partner's writing had "a very honest direct quality" in contrast to her "more distanced, detached language." At the same time, Emily found that her partner moved toward Emily's style of analysis and evaluation, using phrases Emily had introduced into their dialogue, and applying them to her own experiences: "In relaying my experiences to her about transferring to UMass, I wrote self-evaluative comments in the midst of my text

and commented about having 'grown up' from being out of school and being 'ready' to learn. At first when I read this I thought Angie must be uncomfortable for some reason and repeating back to me my ideas rather than her own. But at a closer look I saw that she had really applied the phrase about 'growing up' to her own context/experience."

Engaging in this sort of negotiation of meanings through writing-response groups, through correspondence and written as well as spoken conversation, enhances the development of a writer's thought and language, and develops the writer's sense of audience. At the same time, creating a community of respondents in the classroom or correspondents beyond the classroom generates a great deal of writing while shifting the burden from the teacher, who's no longer the sole respondent to all student writing.

Responding as an editor

When students write constantly, and write to learn, then the final papers they produce after a sequence of assignments or journal entries or small writing tasks will be, in fact, final rather than preliminary. There are likely to be few of the kinds of gross confusions in ideas that Nancy Sommers saw teachers marking along with surface errors. Final papers will explore ideas more clearly because they'll have been developed and elaborated over time. At such a point, readers can focus on issues of form and organization and logical relationships — can serve as informed editors.

But where and how does an English teacher attend to errors? Mina Shaughnessy, whose book *Errors and Expectations* we discussed in Chapter 1 as an example of effective teacher inquiry, offers some guidance. Shaughnessy saw her students' errors as examples of their existing models for written language and standard usage. As we said in Chapter 5, each learner of a new language or new uses of language develops an *approximative* system — a systematic set of rules and generalizations about how the language works — and revises this system based on new data. Rich data — lots of reading and writing and speaking and listening — provide the best support for the development of this system toward the final goal of standard written language.

Pointing out errors before a writer is ready to attend to them effects little change. But writers know what they're paying attention to, and they know what their own questions are — so one way of discovering what sort of response to error is likely to be useful is to ask students to underline constructions or punctuation marks or word usages that they have questions about as they write, and to ask questions about those things at the end of a draft. Another way is to be observant. Where a new sort of error appears in a student's writing — where the page is suddenly littered with semicolons, used differently each time, or where relative clauses, in strings of *which*'s, suddenly appear — there's evidence that the student is trying out something new. For beginning writers, the reason for common orthographic features might be puzzling, and as they begin to observe these features, they might overgeneralize their use, producing, as Ellie's daughter Karen did at one point, a series of papers with an apostrophe before every final "s" before asking "What is that high-up comma for again?" At this point, while the writer's attention is on the new feature, explicit teaching about it can help the writer to use it effectively. Syntactic knots, misused words, erratic punctuation are almost always evidence that a writer is moving beyond what's safe and under control and extending his uses of language. Many of the errors that appear during such a period of experimentation will be corrected automatically as the writer moves on, and it's important that he not be discouraged from trying out new ways of using language.

Many of the errors that writers make in a piece of writing have nothing to do with their underlying knowledge, or linguistic competence, but rather result from some aspect of the writing situation. Everybody makes scribal errors when thinking and writing (or typing) quickly, and we don't always catch them, even when we proofread, because we can't help paying attention to meaning more than forms. Developing writers are particularly likely to make errors when they're intently focused on meaning. Reading aloud allows writers and their reader/ listeners to discover the discrepancies between what they say (and intend) and what they've written, and orally read writing is often self-corrected.

For the teacher, the way to deal with error is best reconceived by sharing responsibility for it with the student. Having students ask, at the end of a piece of writing, the questions they had about grammar and mechanics as they wrote or edited is one way to share responsibility. Peer-editing groups is another. (Students who've wrestled with the same problem can often give the clearest explanation of what's wrong and how to change it.) When students are really working to extend their thinking and language, really taking risks in writing, old errors will fall away, but new ones will appear, and the error rate will stay constant or even increase.

But students can learn to be responsible editors of their own and of other students' writing. They can note certain types of errors that they do understand but keep making when they're writing under stress. And they can use an individualized editing checklist to eliminate those errors. This works particularly well for spelling. A student may not remember how to spell a word, but he can remember that he often gets it wrong, and that he should look it up. (And teachers can ask students to share responsibility for blackboard editing as well, sending a message that it's not a terrible thing, even for the teacher, to make errors, but that everyone can work to clean up public texts.)

Evaluating and grading

While much of the responsibility for the work of the English classroom will be shared in the new classroom community, the larger institution that this community resides in will continue to demand the traditional accounting of students' work and progress in the form of grades. Until that larger institution is transformed, the ultimate responsibility for this accounting will rest with the teacher.

We're convinced that one of the reasons teachers have focused so extensively on error in responding to their students' writing is that error provides an "objective" basis for grading: "If you have two sentence fragments or three spelling errors your mark will be reduced by one letter grade." Even teachers who've thought a great deal about how to support the development of their students' writing will sometimes develop elaborate schemes for quantifying issues of form and error so that their teaching will stand up to the scrutiny of other department members who oppose process approaches to the teaching of writing. Some teachers "maintain standards" by dividing content and style, or mechanics, giving two grades. ("You have B ideas but a D+ style.")

Grading is detrimental to learning in most instances. Students who learn to work for grades tend to work only for that reason. (Just as a recent study showed that children who were given rewards for philanthropic acts were less likely to perform them out of human sympathy, without the reward.) Since most teachers are under pressure to "maintain standards," relatively few high grades are given, creating a kind of competition that works against the sort of collaborative learning we've been advocating. Students who're competing for grades tend to feel uncomfortable about group or collaborative work, not wanting to share credit for what they do or be graded down because of someone else's failure to do enough work. But in almost all teaching situations, teachers are required to grade—to certify students' mastery of the work of classes and to do so in terms that rank students in relationship to one another.

Tests and quizzes allow teachers to rank quickly and easily, and they also provide a quick means for evaluating student learning. David observes that John introduces quizzes and tests to his students as an opportunity "to demonstrate your knowledge." But David wonders how much value such quizzes actually have. While they may provide a check on reading or of general familiarity with a set of terms, we need extended uses of language to see evidence of extended thinking. Janet, in Chapter 2, decided that the number of questions students asked or how involved they were in contributing to discussion might be a better indicator than a test for the sort of active thinking that she hoped to foster. And writing provides one of the best opportunities for students to expand and reflect in language.

To use writing effectively as an alternative to "objective" testing in assessing students' learning, teachers need to change "red pencil" habits of marking papers. They need to read papers for evidence of a student's developing thought about the work of the course. As they look at development and growth, they can invite their students to participate in the process of evaluation. And they can make explicit a new set of criteria for grading. When the primary work of the course is the writing itself, students and teacher together can consider answers to these questions:

1. Has the student done the writing?

The answer to this question provides an "objective and quantifiable" beginning — some common ground — and reinforces the assumption that writing, in a community of writers, is a large part of what's needed for learning.

2. Has the student made progress?

According to what criteria? For a basic writer who enters the classroom unable to write more than a few sentences, writing longer journal entries — moving toward fluency — can be a mark of significant progress. Students who keep journals in or out of class can see over the course of a term how much longer their entries are, how much more they are thinking about the work of the class. In Unit 2 we talked about writing development and suggested that readers analyze the writing of an individual student. The criteria a teacher uses to evaluate a student's writing progress should be made explicit, and students can use those criteria to evaluate their own development as writers. (The self-evaluation questions that Ellie asks her freshman writers to answer were included in Chapter 6.) Such a formal self-evaluation is, in itself, an effective teaching device. The questions suggest some of the things students should consider as they produce more formal pieces of writing. And they help students see that they can be responsible for, have control over, their own growth as writers. A student who has been receiving real responses to writing from a teacher and from peer response groups will develop a clear idea of where she's making progress and what she wants to work on next.

The teacher can respond to a student's self-evaluation in kind — not just with a grade, but with a written evaluation of progress in writing for that portion of the term or semester. The teacher's evaluation should:

1. Respond to the student's overall evaluation. ("You've written a good, thoughtful self-evaluation. I found it to be very accurate.")
2. Respond to specific concerns. ("I agree that you're writing longer

papers now." "Yes, it's important to begin to proofread more carefully." "I don't think that 'coming up with ideas' is as big a problem
in your writing as you think it is.")

3. Review overall patterns in the work. ("In all of these papers you
have done a good job of picking incidents that illustrate your larger
point.")

4. Indicate problems and what to do about them. ("You need now to
add some serious work on the surface of your writing — on the
words, sentences, spelling, punctuation, etc. First, I can't tell how
much of the problem is due to a sort of carelessness or inattention to
these details and how much comes from your not knowing the right
forms. I want you to start by going back over your finished drafts
very carefully, correcting with a different color any mistakes you
catch. Then I can see what you still really need to learn about.")

(The above examples are excerpts from Ellie's midsemester responses to
a self-evaluation done by Allison, whose writing about Anne Frank and
about her own experiences we looked at in Chapter 2.)

To measure progress, the teacher and student must be able to look
at a whole sequence of written work. Maintaining a folder of all of each
student's writing, to be reviewed periodically, is very important in
shifting attention from the individual paper to overall development.
And, for students, reviewing the work of a term or a semester can
provide a real sense of accomplishment.

3. Where does the student's writing fall in relationship to the next level of work required?

All students understand that they have to master any subject to a
particular level before they can go on to the next level of work in the
subject. Development in student writing takes a good deal of time, and
end-of-term grading schedules don't allow this sort of time. But, as
teachers help students discover and use what they know about writing,
they can recognize accomplishment in particular domains. If students
should be able to use evidence to support a main point by the end of the
year or term, teachers can note relative degrees of progress toward that
goal in successive writings.

When a subject involves mastery rather than memorization, there's
little point to grading each early effort in terms of the final goal.
Allison's class was asked to choose two earlier papers and submit
revisions, and also to write a midterm essay (and to turn in a folder of
all writing to that point) as part of the midsemester evaluation. These
papers were graded (the first grades of the term) in relation to Ellie's
midsemester goals of having students achieve more fluency, connect
general ideas with specific examples, and extend their thinking about

the ideas they focused on. Such grades are based on the best work that students are doing at the time grading is required, rather than on their earliest struggling. And writers dare to take more risks when each attempt is not averaged into a final grade. Where administrations demand that each piece of work be graded, or where students feel too insecure without daily and weekly grades, a final grade can still be based on final work. When students see that evaluation is based seriously on progress in writing, they soon stop dashing off assignments and hoping to get by, and they are less inclined to give up after an early unsuccessful effort.

The role of teacher — cothinker, questioner, respondent

The most important responsibilities that fall to the teacher in the new classroom community are not those of evaluator and grader. Chapter 2 explained how Vygotsky believed that the teacher could, through dialogue with the child, provide a scaffold for extending the child's thought and language, helping the child to discover new concepts and the words that name them. The teacher who listens carefully and responds seriously to students' words — written or spoken — supports learning in exactly these ways. We've already talked about how teachers can respond to student writing in ways that support and extend the writer's thinking, and the letter exchange between advanced and freshman students shows how such scaffolding can work in writing. When Socrates talks to his student Meno, his well-framed questions allow room for Meno's own thinking. The transformed teacher will not only allow students more time to develop their own ideas through talking in groups, but will work to change the larger patterns of classroom discourse.

1. Ask questions that provoke thought and tentative ideas and not just correct answers.

While *who* and *what* questions can be important in making sure that everyone agrees about what the text said or what the basic frame of knowledge under discussion is, they require only limited responses and invite students to sit back passively. Questions that ask *"Why* do you think Maya Angelou began to talk for Mrs. Flowers when she had been silent for so long?" or *"How* does Holden Caulfield's relationship with his sister Phoebe affect his actions?" require reflection and interpretation and finding ways to support ideas. And teachers who ask such questions can't respond with "right" or "wrong," but must think along with their students: "Let's see, when does Holden first mention Phoebe? I guess we know early on that he has a sister. And Bob says he had a sense that she was important right away. But I think I first really started to notice her when he buys that record for her."

2. Give more room for thought and allow more silence while students consider their responses.

This is always hard for teachers, who feel the burden of responsibility for what goes on in the classroom. It's much easier to keep performing and to fill in the silences than it is to wait quietly while students think. But classroom discourse studies show that increased waiting time significantly increases the involvement of all students in thinking about whatever question has been raised, even when the question has been directed to one student. One useful strategy for dealing with extended silence around a significant question is to have students pull out their journals or a piece of paper and write for five minutes about the question. Then all students will have something to say as the teacher asks them in quick succession to read what they've written.

3. Observe all aspects of students' responses.

When David observed the wise-guy behavior of students in the "difficult" reading group in John's class, he speculated that they were really scared, afraid to take risks, and that their behavior provided them with a kind of protection. Often students' misbehavior or poor performance is not really directed at the teacher but is driven by other forces in the student or the student's life. The teacher who can look, as a learner, to see what might be going on, rather than responding only as a disciplinarian or evaluator, can often find ways to change the learning experience of such students.

4. Make students' ideas part of the "official" shared knowledge of the classroom.

One of the easiest and most important ways to make students' comments part of the classroom "record" is to write those comments on the blackboard. Traditionally teachers use the blackboard to highlight the "right" answers, the "important" information that students should know. And though they elicit student responses first, they still write down only those responses that they see as correct. But where a teacher jots down quickly all of the ideas that students throw out, all student contributions are available for everyone to use. Here's how Margaret, a student teacher, creates a record of shared knowledge with her inner-city students:

> I finally got around to introducing Shakespeare. I did this by asking students anything and everything that they thought of when they thought of Shakespeare or England during Shakespeare's time. I wrote

all their called-out responses on the board. I then tried to incorporate all of the responses into the notes that I wanted them to have. I guess Ellie and Hepsie would call this "connecting what is known to what is unknown."

Where individual contributions become common and public knowledge, students can restructure their own understanding. They can ponder the responses as a set and categorize them and make sense of them. The teacher can step back and look at what has been recorded and think along with the students about what all of this might mean. (Full sentences and even handwriting aren't very important to such jottings. And having a student do the recording allows the teacher to use responses in this way without turning her back on the class.)

Student ideas become shared knowledge when written responses and written reports of investigations are collected and "published." And the teacher can contribute to such collections, or contribute an "afterword" in response to such a collection, formalizing the things that students have come to know.

5. Mediate between the students and the curriculum.

When the teacher becomes a mediator between students and the curriculum, he's approached Vygotsky's concept of the teacher's role; knowing what comes next, he provides support for students to move on to the next area of development. This doesn't mean that he knows all the answers, but he knows what kinds of questions might be asked, what sorts of things there might be to learn.

Of course, some part of "what there might be to learn" is already established—by school curriculum guidelines, by the textbooks that have been purchased by the school system (often with little or no teacher consultation), by what is available in the bookroom at a particular week of the term in sufficient quantities for all the students of a class. But whatever the constraints of the curriculum, the teacher's role must be to work out ways of accomplishing its goals while making it meaningful and accessible to students. Initially, it's pedagogy—how something is taught—rather than curriculum—what that something is—that matters the most for learners. The lists of decontextualized words in a standard vocabulary text can be contextualized and used to support writing when groups of students write stories using them all. A usage rule—"That song is *different from* the others on the album—That song is *different than* the others are"—can provide the basis for recording what people really say in conversations and for the discovery of rules of actual use in a particular context versus textbook rules. A "modern" short-story collection can generate discussion about what the editor's criteria for modern must have been, what the class's criteria would be, and it can be supplemented with a set of reviews by individuals of stories that they would suggest for a collection. We'll talk more about this sort of thing in Chapter 10, as we look at the larger framework of what schools demand and how teachers can respond. But at this point we'd like to affirm that there is no such thing as a teacher-proof curriculum, that it's the teacher who makes the curriculum learnable, and that the transformed teacher will conceive of his role in terms of student learning and how it can be supported rather than in terms of the mandated curriculum and how it can be covered.

CHAPTER 10

Reinventing the Curriculum

We've described the teacher as a mediator between the curriculum and the learner. A curriculum can be helpful, even necessary to teachers as they plan their work. But what is that curriculum? What is the student supposed to be learning in the English classroom?

A good curriculum establishes goals and guidelines, suggests lines of inquiry, implies a framework for the work of the class. But when curriculum is simply handed down to teachers and then handed out to students, when it's seen only as units of time and of study, it becomes a hindrance to learning rather than a support for it. The standard curriculum in place explicitly or implicitly in most American schools offers, in itself, little support for the sort of learning that we've been arguing for. To create new classroom communities, learners and teachers must question that curriculum and find ways to adapt it to the needs of individual classrooms and learners. Teachers and students can work productively with an established curricular plan, can mold it to suit their needs as writers and thinkers, and can thereby transform it into something vital rather than something static. But there are difficulties with such an undertaking. Most curricula are developed backwards: curriculum gets made from the top or the outside down and into the classroom. Imposed by a committee, a school board, a textbook approach, the curriculum is *responded to* rather than created by teachers and students in a classroom. This book has argued that any kind of transformation must begin within—must begin in the classroom with teachers observing what students know and what they need to know, and observing themselves as knowers and learners as well. In this chapter, we'll look at the standard curriculum and at the ways in which teachers have accommodated themselves to it or accommodated it to their needs. But we'll also explore how a pedagogy that's unquiet teaches us to reinvent curriculum, create new goals, build new structures for learning, and make new knowledge.

Standard curriculum

The 1983 "High School English Curriculum Objectives" for the Boston Public Schools illustrates the typical curricular plan. Its purpose is "to present clear objectives in English for all Boston high school students. The objectives state the skills students should have mastered by the end of each grade level" (i). The 185-page document includes a statement of philosophy and goals that's entirely congruent with our concerns in this book, one that stresses "the maximum development of students' language power—their ability to read, write, speak, study, listen to, and evaluate a wide variety of materials." It speaks of "development" and says:

> Our goal as educators should be to locate our students on the continuum [of developing language skills] and teach them in ways that bring about maximum individual growth.... English instruction should continually stress meaning. It should not allow mechanics to be the primary concern. Language skills are not developed for their own sake, but as paths to literacy. These skills are best learned in context. (x)

The statement lists a variety of general goals, like "developing students' abilities to evaluate written and spoken material, including their own." It then divides skills into twelve categories: variety of material read, literal comprehension, interpretive comprehension, evaluative comprehension, vocabulary building, variety of writing, writing—the process, writing—the craft, writing—mechanics and usage, language structure, speaking, and study skills. The rest of the document lists specific objectives under each topic for each grade level, and suggests questions teachers might ask to focus on those objectives.

A few examples will serve to illustrate how little the larger goals are embodied in an actual plan. The category of Interpretive Comprehension would seem to suggest that there is, in fact, room for the reader's interpretation in understanding texts. But the questions suggested under this category for grade nine are predominantly *what* questions that suggest just one right answer: "In example 2a, what is the writer's purpose?" Broad objectives, such as "Identifying and giving examples of the elements of works of fiction," are followed by suggestions for precise and limiting instructions: "After reading *Romeo and Juliet* by Shakespeare: a. Summarize the plot of the play, and b. Identify the major characters and classify them as protagonists or antagonists." Other examples are equally limited. Under "Identifying verbals and verbal phrases: gerund, participial, and infinitive," the student should "label the verbal and verbal phrase in this sentence (gerund, participial, or infinitive)—'Playing dramatist Lillian Hellman in *Julia*, Jane Fonda shared the screen with Vanessa Redgrave.'" And the "Composing effective paragraphs" objective gives no specific examples but suggests that such paragraphs be "assessed through focused holistic scoring."

What sort of guidance does a document like this give to the teacher who must implement curriculum objectives? Despite the sound philosophy, nowhere is there a coherent statement of how learners' language skills develop and how development might be supported in context. And the document itself belies its stated philosophy by ignoring context as an aspect of teaching and learning. All the objectives and examples are, by the very nature of the document's structure, decontextualized. The teacher sees one discrete example of a question to ask about the author's purpose, another discrete example of how to test for knowledge of a gerund. There's nothing to indicate that the author's purpose might not be so easily knowable, that readers might interpret it differently, that where deciding on the purpose is an appropriate goal, it might have to be approached differently in the context of different works. There's no discussion of why one might study gerunds and participals in isolation in a school system where the philosophy is that English instruction should "continually stress meaning," and that language skills "are best developed in context." There's no suggestion that some skills build on others and that there are meaningful sequences to activities. And, while the emphasis on writing (with three categories devoted to it) is laudable, the one covering statement about evaluation for all the objectives in all three categories — that writing will be assessed by holistic grading — is out of place in this otherwise detailed, prescriptive document, suggesting either that writing may be ignored in favor of other more "objectively" measurable outcomes, or that the drafters of these objectives really have no idea how to evaluate writing within such a framework.

One striking thing about this document is its lack of focus on any content. Among the general goals listed are "exposing students to a wide range of written and spoken material: narrative, expository, persuasive, lyric, dramatic, and procedural" and "developing students' awareness of multicultural diversity in written and spoken material." For grade nine over two hundred suggested works of fiction, poetry, drama, and nonfiction are listed, representing a wonderful range of multicultural perspectives. But there are no descriptions of the books, no basis for selection, no guidance about how any of this might be drawn on in a coherent way within a year's course of study. (This document was written just before a new superintendent went to the opposite extreme and ordered a system-wide basal-reading series for lower grades that offered no choice or flexibility or room for the teacher's development of a curriculum.) There's little relationship between the content and the behavioral objectives in a curriculum like this. And, despite a category labeled "Writing Process," there's little sense that the student's process of writing or learning has any bearing on what is learned or written.

Finally, the precisely detailed curriculum plan for the Boston Public Schools ignores the context in which it will be taught. It reflects nothing specific to those schools, no hint that teachers might draw on the resources of a culturally rich and diverse urban community. Its objectives provide a mere overlay on the implicit curriculum of most American high schools, where knowledge is divided up into bits of time and space, and where students move from subject to subject throughout the course of a day's work. Virtually all school systems have similar formal statements of curriculum, described in terms of content and objectives, and these statements are updated periodically to serve both political and administrative ends. But in any version they confirm rather than challenge the power of existing school categories and traditions.

In fact, the curriculum in place in high schools is oddly the same from one system to another. You can count on a student reading *Romeo and Juliet* in ninth grade, whether the student is in ninth grade in Massachusetts or North Carolina; you can place the learning of grammatical forms in ninth grade as well, no matter where the student goes to school. (And often those grammatical forms are learned by students today from the same textbook we used when we were in ninth grade.) There appears to be little real recognition of the individuality or diversity of students from place to place or from class to class or from year to year, despite the changes taking place in culture and in society and despite philosophical position statements from school administrations to the contrary. In his book *Horace's Compromise* (subtitled *The Dilemma of the American High School*), Theodore Sizer talks about the remarkable sameness of the curriculum throughout the U. S. high schools he studied, regardless of the varying contexts in which the teaching takes place: "We have One Best System — in spite of the irrepressible individuality of adolescents and of the sharply etched discrimination between rich and poor" (6–7).

Press most adults about what high school is for, and you hear these subjects listed. *High school? That's where you learn English and math and that sort of thing.* Ask students and you get the same answer. High school is to "teach" these "subjects."

What is often absent is any definition of these subjects or any rationale for them. They are just there, labels. Under those labels lie a multitude of things. A great deal of material is supposed to be "covered"; most of these courses are surveys, great sweeps of the stuff of their parent disciplines.

While there is often a sequence *within* subjects — algebra before trigonometry, "first-year" French before "second-year" French — there is rarely a coherent relationship or sequence across subjects. Even the most logically related matters — reading ability as a precondition for the reading of history books, and certain mathematical concepts or skills before the study of some of physics — are only loosely coordinated if at all. There is little demand for a synthesis of it all; English, mathematics, and the rest are discrete items, to be picked up individually. The incentive for picking them up is largely through tests and, with success in these, in credits earned.

Coverage within subjects is the key priority. (80–81)

The title of Sizer's book comes from the name of a high school English teacher, "Horace," who represents a composite portrait of the teacher that emerged from his five-year-long major study of U.S. high schools. Horace's classroom is much like most of those we've seen in this book. Horace is a veteran teacher who knows what is best for his students — he believes in the importance of writing, for example — but is "realistic" about the time he can spend on responses to student writing, on preparation, on working on the curriculum with his colleagues. And so his response is to compromise what he knows about student learning for what he can actually do.

Other teachers, fictional and real, have found their own compromises for working in the curriculum. Miss Brodie, whose Edinburgh girls' school curriculum is organized around similar units of subjects and years, with similar goals of coverage for tests, departs from tradition and blithely reinvents the curriculum in her own terms. She objects to teaching to a test, so she expects her students to master on their own the items that will be covered on their qualifying exam. She has her students prop their history books up on the desk in case the headmistress comes into the classroom and talks, instead, about her Italian journey. Her narrative is filled with a combination of cultural knowledge and her own experience:

> "We ought to be doing history at the moment according to the time-table. Get out your history books and prop them up in your hands. I shall tell you a little more about Italy. I met a young poet by a fountain. Here is a picture of Dante meeting Beatrice — it is pronounced Beatrichay in Italian which makes the name very beautiful — on the Ponte Vecchio. He fell in love with her at that moment. Mary, sit up and don't slouch. It was a sublime moment in a sublime love. By whom was the picture painted?"
>
> Nobody knew.
>
> "It was painted by Rossetti. Who was Rossetti, Jenny?"
>
> "A painter," said Jenny.
>
> Miss Brodie looked suspicious. (68–69)

Miss Brodie continues:

> "Next year," she said, "you will have the specialists to teach you history and mathematics and languages, a teacher for this and a teacher for that, a period of forty-five minutes for this and another for that. But in this your last year with me you will receive the fruits of my prime."

The fruits of Miss Brodie's prime serve as the curriculum for her students. They'll remember what she tells them because the information is wholly contextualized in stories of their teacher's life and experiences, but they won't necessarily have learned how to bring experiences from their own lives into the framework of subjects they study. And their learning goes only in one direction. They use the story of Dante and Beatrice to understand the frustrated love affair of Miss Brodie, whose lover died in the war. But they won't read Dante's account of how Beatrice became his divine muse in *La Vita Nuova*, and so Miss Brodie's experience won't become for them a route to understanding Dante or to understanding Rossetti's portrayal of the lovers. Miss Brodie rejects the standard curriculum, with its subject specialists who talk about "this and that" in forty-five-minute periods. But she offers her students only her accounts of her own life in its place.

Some of the more effective real-life teachers turn not to themselves but to their students, beginning by observing their behaviors and responses, seeing what they seek and what engages them. A number of the cooperating teachers who have worked with us define their teaching philosophy in terms of learners, and when asked by their student teachers, they talk in ways that show how much they pay attention to observing, interacting, and encouraging their students:

> Everything that happens in the classroom depends on who the learners are, on their group's personality, on what they know and are interested in, on what they are able and willing to do. John places a great emphasis on the teacher's learning, as the school year progresses, "who the kids are," and adapting teaching methods to suit, as best as possible, the learning styles of the students. For instance, John's fifth-period class has proven to be generally unresponsive as a group, and often completely silent. John is therefore more and more often having these students work in small groups, in the hope that the smaller groups will "enhance the students' interaction with each other," and will thus improve the levels of communication and learning in the class. Another example of adapting methods to suit the learning styles of the students can be seen in the third period class, ninth grade Basic English group. For this class, John always prepares at least two, and usually three, separate activities, since the class is generally "not able to sustain one task for an entire period." (David S)

David is impressed by the quality of John's interest in and interaction with the students, and how this works to elicit the students' cooperation even in unpleasant tasks like vocabulary or grammar review. He goes on:

> The idea of "accepting the students as they are" is a central point of John's teaching. When asked what one piece of advice he would give to prospective teachers, John responded, "You've got to understand that to really, really like kids, is essential to this job.... You've got to be able to get a kick sometimes out of kids being kids."

John's focus on learners helps keep them "on task," but it keeps his attention off the curriculum. David sees him as "a teacher with lots of experience who feels forced by the school administration to teach vocabulary this way [from a vocabulary text], and feels forced to make these exercises a major investment in class time." And David, as a beginning teacher, worries about such constraints, wondering "how much choice a teacher really has in avoiding tasks that are close to worthless." He finds himself focusing on the related concern:

> How do we get kids interested in what's going on in the classroom? How do we get them to care? It's no wonder that kids who are memorizing word lists and copying down a grammar outline into their notebooks feel that school is silly. What they're doing *is* silly. We need to make the reading and writing that goes on in class a meaningful act of communication somehow.

David sees a tension between John's attempts to implement new classroom practices, like writers' workshops, and the messages given by the curriculum that it is correctness, not communication, that finally counts. His concerns suggest that being genuinely interested in learners, while it's an important beginning, isn't enough. The formal curriculum does shape learning; it places value on learning certain things in certain ways, and where those things and those ways run counter to the ways in which learning really takes place—as when new grammatical constructions (which are learned effectively only through use in a meaningful context) are taught by having students copy an outline—it sends mixed messages to students. Although John "knows the theory," and teaches grammar only because it's mandated in the school curriculum, he doesn't really question that curriculum or its goals, doesn't let himself perceive the conflict between that curriculum and the learners he cares so much about. He institutes sound pedagogical practices, like writing workshops, but his students adapt them to what's implicitly valued in the rest of the curriculum and turn them into another version of a grammar lesson.

A student teacher in conflict with the curriculum

An experienced teacher like John may have developed ways of interacting with and responding to students that take away some of the bad taste of their daily doses of curriculum and keep them involved in the more meaningful work he's incorporating into his classroom. But for the beginning teacher, the standard curriculum with its implicit expectations and values and labeling of learners may offer a seemingly insurmountable roadblock to effective teaching. The student teacher or beginning teacher must plan her teaching within the constraints set by the intersecting demands for coverage of specific units of work, by the need to test, by administrative structures, and often by system-purchased textbooks.

Under this kind of pressure, it's easy for a new teacher's excitement and creativity to diminish, as the following excerpts from a student's journal demonstrate.

As a student teacher, Deb tries to mediate among the established curriculum, students' responses, and her own standards and expectations. Over the course of the semester represented in her journal, Deb taught one "low-level" or "general education" class (which is called C *block* in the journal) with a curriculum focused on grammar, vocabulary, and the reading of short stories, and to which she introduced journal writing. She also taught two college-prep sections (A and D *blocks* in the journal) with curriculum centered on grammar, vocabulary, and the reading of ancient literature from a Western Literature textbook. The journal excerpts show that Deb's ability to plan lessons to fit her own emerging educational philosophy is challenged by a maelstrom of different forces: the prevailing educational philosophy of the school and classroom, the definition of the curriculum by units and objectives, textbooks, tests, administrative structures, and the students' attitudes and responses to all of this.

Deb has been thinking about teaching and learning in the ways we've been discussing in this book. During her prepracticum she worked with Bruce Rettman, whose reflections on the Boston Writing Project we saw in the last chapter, and she now believes firmly that writing should be at the center of all activities in the English classroom. She sees the interrelationship among writing and reading, speaking, listening, and tries to integrate these activities. She wants to use what students already know and connect it to what they're learning, and to give students more control over their learning, and she uses response journals toward these ends. She builds in contact with different cultural perspectives and supports an individual student by drawing on her cross-cultural knowledge. She tries to pull together a coherent and integrated course of study for her students, developing their skills as readers and writers and creating links between the things they're reading and writing. She tries to avoid disconnected, fragmented activities such as the memorization of decontextualized vocabulary words. And she works to create tests that will allow students to use their developing language to express their expanding ideas.

Through her journal entries we see Deb begin with enthusiasm for her task:

> 2/11—For today, Mrs. Z asked me to plan out my overall weekly plans for when I start teaching after the vacation. I really found planning rather interesting, and I feel like I have many good ideas, mainly focused around writing, that I hope the students will find motivating and imaginative. When I presented my ideas to Mrs. Z, she thought they were okay, but had many suggestions on how I should develop more homework assignments and simply more *stuff* to fill my time.

She generates interesting lessons to draw students into their study of literature:

> 2/24 — Well, Ellie came today, and this was probably the best day I've ever had in my whole teaching experience. I had spent almost all night trying to come up with a creative, thought-provoking lesson to tie the students' interests into this unit on Greek mythology. Hepsie gave me some great suggestions, bringing kids in through the back door in order to stimulate their interest.... I created a Pandora's box which stimulated curiosity at all levels. But the best part of the lesson for me was listening to the myths I had my students write for me the night before. I thought that the myth I had written had done nothing for them, but I guess I had inspired them because *all* of the students wrote something and the something was GOOD! I also created a vocabulary worksheet, taken directly from contextual clues/sentences from the myths the kids are reading. I like this vocabulary (and its relevance) better than the workbook. But I must admit, the workbook comes in handy when my brain seems empty.

She successfully introduces journal writing:

> 3/1 — I just had another great journal entry with C block. I had the kids listen to an excerpt I read from the book *Night* by Elie Wiesel. I first explained a bit about the Holocaust, and then read aloud. The excerpt was about Elie's separation from his mother and sister. I had the kids write a reaction to this passage and/or about an experience of separation they might have felt. The entries were rather moving. Oh, I like this when it's like this.

She builds a multicultural perspective:

> 3/30 — Today was a major breakthrough for one of my students, a very shy girl from India. I asked her to give an oral report (for extra credit), about what life was like in India. She was a bit apprehensive at first, but she came to me with a report, a drawing of the Taj Mahal, and she allowed students to ask her questions. This was really exciting for both Tina and myself. And it was a nice way to talk about setting, since "A Bank Fraud"'s setting is in India.

However, Deb struggles to accomplish these things in the face of a curricular demand for coverage of prescribed units of work (particularly grammar), in established formats (exercises, drills, reviews, and tests), and within a rigid timetable (adverbs on Monday, the *Odyssey* in March). Interspersed entries show that it is difficult to keep students involved in their reading and writing.

> 2/26 — I thought I would try my hand at another writing assignment, since the myths went so well. Since we're starting the *Odyssey*, in a very abridged story version, I might add, I decided to have the kids write about a personal odyssey of their own that they have taken. Hopefully this will get them to search for a *meaning* in the story of Odysseus and his voyage. I have again written my own personal

Odyssey, which I read to the class. I also decided to make study guide
questions for the kids to use as references, since I'm not quite sure of
their capacity of reading. I emphasize *questions*, so that to use them,
they have to go to the text to find the answer. I hope this is a way of
inspiring the kids to read. I also hope to use these study guide
questions in some sort of group work, to help get kids in the text. But
D block looks to be trouble! The kids *did not* want to read aloud their
personal Odysseys. My disciplinary skills weren't up to par, and I
ended up sending two kids out! Yuk! I hate this part of teaching.

She finds herself increasingly thrown back on traditional tasks.

3/10—HELP! Most kids are *not* keeping up with these last chapters of
the *Odyssey*. I can't really believe it, since we're almost done, and the
book is so much more interesting now than in the beginning. I gave a
reading check in desperation (scare tactic), and the scores were horrible.
The main excuse, when I asked them about the scores, was that they
didn't *understand* the story. I find this rather hard to believe, but as a
remedy to this I'm making more vocabulary worksheets which come
directly from the text. I hope this will help, but I really think the kids
just need to read.

The journal writing Deb believes to be so important to her students'
learning isn't a part of this prescribed curriculum, and so her cooperating
teacher insists that it be followed with "massive doses of grammar and
vocabulary" to get the students "back on track." And the emphasis on
drill and testing finally drives all other work out of the classroom.

3/22—I *hate* doing the grammar and vocabulary. I can't tell you the
fear I have going through this unrelated stuff, that students are going
to ask me a question I can't answer. And I *know* they can sense my
apprehension toward these grammar lessons. And Mrs. Z doesn't help
much at all! She is constantly throwing these jabs at me. "Do you
know what gerunds are?" "Can you recognize this dangling modifier?"
I can't stand it! But I'm doing it because these kids have a final exam
and have to know *all* of the *rules* of grammar to pass. I don't know
how they are going to memorize all the rules, but I guess that is what
they end up doing. Today Mrs. Z took the reigns of grammar and
forced onward. She decided to review the parts of speech and found
that no one had remembered anything. So, I was summoned to the
back and watched her do the drilling. My journals are completely on
hold.

These kids have no closure with anything. They kept asking me if
we were going to do journals—so obviously the kids were interested!
But I had no answer for them because Mrs. Z gave me no sign of
positive reinforcement.

Some of these constraints in Deb's classroom are set by larger
curricular and administrative structures. Departmental divisions keep

grammar and vocabulary and reading (and occasional writing) as the province of the English department, while exploration of cultural perspectives would fall under social studies (if it fits in anywhere). The texts Deb must use suggest a concern with a broad cultural literacy; yet the abridged version of the *Odyssey* eliminates the richness of the original, to fit into a schedule full of "stuff." The schedule allows little time for background study or for reflection, and Deb's experience confirms a finding of Sizer's study—that the high school curriculum in general allows almost no time for the sort of reflection and repose that supports serious thought. The short-story text Deb must use has, as she complains, "no common thread," and no writing by women. The prescribed vocabulary text has no connection to the prescribed reading, though in this instance Deb has some leeway and is able to draw vocabulary items from the literature her students are reading. And the unavoidable grammar text contains no hint that the parts of speech whose definitions are being memorized are actually used in real ways, ways that create stylistic effects in the literature and in students' own writing.

Deb copes with all of this rather well, working both persistently and creatively to "make sure my lesson has the students engaged," to "get these kids thinking." But she's not, finally, able to reach all of them. And, ironically, the "D block" class that gives her the most trouble isn't the lower, "generals" group that she had been warned might "act up." In the generals class, with somewhat less pressure from a rigid timetable, she's able to experiment and introduce more activities, like writing to music, or pretending to be an advice columnist—and these activities keep the students engaged. But in the college-prep section, where sophomores must cover ancient literature this term while keeping up the pace of grammar study, she encounters trouble: the students have learned to step through all of the paces without thinking or feeling about any of them. These are not the highly motivated "Honors" or "Advanced Placement" students, and many of them may not, in fact, go to college. But they must be moved through this material, though they resist both the material and any attempt to deviate from it. Deb's experience with curriculum is clearly defined by the dominant administrative structure in American schools—the division of students into homogeneous groups, or "tracking."

Curricular constraints

There are several aspects of the formal structure of schooling that present constraints to responsive teaching practices—constraints that a student teacher like Deb must work within.

Units and objectives

The division of an English curriculum into content units often becomes rigid, preventing students and teachers from connecting the knowledge that gets made in a classroom. In Deb's classroom vocabulary, grammar, and literature (there's virtually no writing in the formal curriculum) have been defined as separate and testable bits of study in the class. Within each category are smaller, discrete units, equally rigid—a unit on the *Odyssey*, a class on adverbs.

The problem with all these categories within English studies is that their repetition makes the categories begin to seem *real* rather than what they are, idealized models. The category begins to live a life of its own as tradition makes it seem true and unchangeable rather than expedient and mutable and invented by human beings to describe and organize an aspect of their reality. "Is it all right to use argument in a comparison/ contrast essay?" "Does a personal narrative belong in an argument paper?" "May I use first person when I talk about the *Odyssey*?" These questions aren't simply naive uncertainties from inexperienced students. They proceed directly from a curriculum that stresses the rigid categorization and specialized application of knowledge.

The instruction that follows from this sort of curriculum also tends to focus on the application of standard forms—the funnel paragraph (the general to specific movement of ideas) or the five-paragraph essay. The separation of form from content (skill from subject) or the separation of elements within the English curriculum (grammar from vocabulary, writing from reading) continues in the curriculum of introductory college English courses, which are typically divided by content areas— into composition and literature—and typically focus on forms within those areas—rhetorical modes of comparison and contrast, or process analysis, and literary genres of narrative, poetry, drama. Such units are easy to define and memorize (the sonnet is fourteen lines of iambic pentameter, the comparison essay looks systematically at similarities and differences of two objects or ideas), and that's part of the reason for their continuing dominance in textbooks and curriculum plans. The authority of the curriculum, too often unquestioned, stands between teachers and students.

Deb's response is to try to break down the rigid categories of the English curriculum, integrating the study of vocabulary with reading, the writing of personal narrative with reading and writing about litera-ture. But her efforts to do so are defeated by the teacher's rigid definition of what's on or off track, and by the tests that give dominance to the "on track" rules of grammar.

Testing and evaluation

The pressure for testing doesn't originate with Deb's cooperating teacher. She's responding to larger external pressure from her department, school, and system, who've put curricula in place. As Deb has re-discovered, a lot of any curriculum is really test-driven, and this testing emphasizes forms and content. If a curriculum is driven by a test, there's a certain body of information that has to be memorized by students so that they can perform well on the test. Yet this emphasis works against everything we've said about the way learning works, about the process of knowing through reading and writing. A curriculum bound by the end rather than the means — the evaluation rather than the process — limits the teacher's ability to make imaginative connections between units of study, ideas, acts of reading and listening, because the pressure is always on "coverage" for the test.

The standardized test that's gained the most attention and concern in recent years has been the Scholastic Aptitude Test of the College Entrance Examination Board, and many high schools devote whole English courses to preparing students to take the exam, emulating the expensive prep courses that children of affluent families have been able to buy, and showing that the test is, at least in part, one of test-taking skills and experience rather than scholastic aptitude. But of far greater impact on school curriculum are tests of minimum competency, whether local, state, or national. Such tests define a particular level of skills or knowledge as the minimum level appropriate to an age or grade level. And it's easy to see how such tests go hand in hand with a competency-focused curricular plan like the one we examined from the Boston Public Schools. But most such tests tell us little about learning and development, and they encourage concentration on this minimum, rather than on a large, extended range of learning, as they break complex learning into measurable units — into small isolated bits.

Deb tries to respond to the pressure for testing by making up her own "good" tests — ones that are interesting and creative and involve "much writing." And her students perform well on these tests, which give them an opportunity to display more of their real learning, "to apply the knowledge they learn, not just spit memorized stuff back to me." She finds it more effective to engage students in reading and writing and to create tests that really draw on that reading and writing, rather than teach to a multiple-choice test.

Textbooks

Increasingly, the textbooks used in classrooms and purchased by school systems are shaped by the sort of testing and assessment of competency that we've been discussing. Textbooks are generally designed to mediate between what it is that students must learn and the teacher's responsibility for that learning. In fact, textbooks are largely designed to be "teacher-proof," to offer, in one package, the materials that students will read, the questions that teachers will ask, the assignments that students will be given (and in a separate package for the teacher, the correct answers and responses). With the "ideal" textbook, anyone can lead a class through a lesson on "Bartleby the Scrivener," asking "Who was Bartleby?" or "What is a scrivener?" or "What was Melville's purpose in writing this story?" or "What significance do you find in the subtitle 'A Story of Wall-Street'?"

With the recent emphasis on the reader's response to literature, some questions in current textbooks will suggest ways students might make a connection with a story: "If you were an employer with Bartleby on your hands, what would you do about him?" (Litzenger). But such questions still represent empty exercises when they don't come from an individual student's and teacher's own engagement with the text. They demand more effort than "What is a scrivener?" and students resent this effort when it's externally motivated. Despite occasional new emphases, textbooks, by their nature, present a reduced, rigidly structured introduction to a subject area. They represent distillations of the "facts" of a discipline. They don't raise questions about how knowledge gets made in the discipline, of what kinds of questions have been asked or what procedures have been used to arrive at these facts, and teachers who aren't encouraged to go beyond standard ways of thinking in curriculum or in textbooks will seldom think to bring these considerations before the class themselves.

The textbooks used in Deb's class are typical. The survey of ancient literature text offers only an abridged version of the *Odyssey*, with questions that are answered in the Teacher's Edition. The world-literature anthology is similarly structured, but without even a chronological order that offers some principle of relationship between works in the other textbook. Deb doesn't use the end-of-the-chapter questions; she uses writing to provoke student interest in reading through response journals, and her own exercises and activities to engage students' interest, setting aside the vocabulary text (though it's really the grammar book she wishes she could ignore).

Tracking

The curriculum Deb's students study, the textbooks they use, and what they're expected to do with them are determined by another constraint — their "track." The college-prep students mostly "cover" what they'll ultimately be tested on in their SATs and other exams. The general, "C block" students don't need to read ancient literature, though they'll be drilled even more to achieve levels of minimum competency in grammar.

We've talked about the failure of administrative imagination that makes the tracking of students the primary organizational tool for placing them in classes. But it's also a curricular failure and calls into question the assertion of American education that it provides equal educational opportunity to everybody. John Goodlad, the educational theorist whose focus on the tension between home and school culture we discussed in Chapter 4, ferreted out differences in high-level and low-level courses in math and English and discovered that the content, first of all, was different enough to "suggest virtually different subjects" (1983, 311). In English, high-track students read standard works of literature, engaged in expository writing, used grammar as they analyzed language, and prepared for the SAT. At least part of their learning time was spent in making judgments, drawing inferences, using symbolism. Teachers included in their goals for the class such things as creativity, self-direction, and critical thinking. Low-track classes followed the line that Goodlad describes as the majority approach to curriculum. They practiced basic reading skills and language mechanics, wrote simple narratives, learned to fill out forms. They spent more of their learning time listening to teachers than did their high-track counterparts, and rote learning (memorizing and repeating) dominated in question-and-answer formats. When teachers were asked about goals for this group they responded with items like "working quietly," "improving study habits," "obeying rules" (312).

In a frightening paradox, Goodlad noted that the teaching practices most conducive to learning were used in the high-track classes, while those most clearly associated with dissatisfaction and lack of achievement were confined to the low-track students. High-track teachers were more enthusiastic, specific in directions, supportive of individual difference, responsive to student work. Low-track teachers were more punitive, less inclined to tolerate individual difference, less enthusiastic, more didactic. But Deb found, to her delight, that "these kids aren't stupid." In fact, students who have been treated as less competent in traditional classrooms may respond with great enthusiasm to a teacher who doesn't think "you can't expect much from these kids; they're the stupid ones," but who respects the knowledge they bring from outside of the classroom and treats them as having real potential as learners inside the class as well.

Interestingly, Goodlad found that in the few classes he observed where students were in a mixed group, the curriculum took the higher road rather than the lower, which contradicts what supporters of tracking fear — that upper-group students will "sink down" to the level of the lower-group students. "The burden of proof is on tracking, not mixed grouping," Goodlad argues (312). Like Sizer and many others, he'd replace tracking with a common curriculum — one that's flexible enough to accommodate the varieties of knowledge and experience students bring to the classroom but that doesn't present radically different educational expectations, if not experiences, to students.

Reinventing the curriculum

In the introduction to Paulo Freire and Donaldo Macedo's book *Literacy*, Henry Giroux talks about Freire's pedagogy of knowing and how it's based on recognition by the learner of what's in the world around her and how it's represented, and on recognition by the teacher of what the learner knows. Such a pedagogy is based on reinvention. In Freire's terms, "reinventing requires from the reinventing subject a critical approach toward the practice and experience to be reinvented." In other words, teachers can reinvent the curriculum so that it follows from what they've come to understand about learners and about their own practices as both teachers and learners. But to reinvent, teachers must continue to see and resee learning and practice. A responsive curriculum, like a responsive pedagogy, can't remain fixed but must be continually reinterpreted within particular situations and contexts. The principles of Freire's pedagogy of knowing can inform the examination by other teachers of their own practices and their own contexts. But the curriculum he's developed within the contexts of third-word literacy programs cannot be transferred wholesale to American education. Reinventing the curriculum is something we must do ourselves, within our own schools and classrooms.

A beginning teacher making quiet change

The beginnings of a reinvented curriculum can lie in small changes. Matt's cooperating teacher, like Deb's, emphasized "digging in to the basics," drilling students on grammar and having them answer plot and character questions about literature. As a student teacher, Matt had to begin by working within the teacher's curricular and classroom struc-tures. But his curricular goals, though just developing, were quite different from hers. In his teaching journal we see him observing the students. On his first day at the school he sits in the library where "there is a constant din of many conversations, and I do not think most of the students come here to do research or to read — they come because it's a nice place to be." He talks about his concern about "handling student behavior," but he finds the students generally to be "sympathetic, tolerant," as he is with them. He starts to define his teaching in terms of his relationship with the students: "If I can think of my job as seeing to the maintenance and enhancement of thirty-one individual relationships and succeed in even small ways along these lines, I should do all right." He wants to teach classes that are "interesting to most of the students." And he objects to his cooperating teacher's limited expectations of her "basic" students.

Matt senses that most of the students he sees want comfortable surroundings, interesting studies, and sympathetic and tolerant human relationships, and these observations might provide the underpinnings for his educational goals. But he's also beginning to think that learners are shaped by what and how they've been taught before. When he looks at the overall curriculum of the classroom he must begin teaching in, he finds the combination of limited goals, limited pedagogy (drill, repetition, and testing), and limited curriculum that Goodlad found characterizing the education of students in lower tracks.

> Here's a list of the graded work done so far this year in the two courses I'm now teaching:
> 9/21 West Side Story worksheet (18 full sentence answers)
> 9/23 West Side Story class discussion ("fill in the answers as we speak")
> 9/25 Drama terms quiz (give definitions)
> 9/29 West Side Story homework questions (five short sentence answers)
> 10/5 Grammar exercise on fragments (from Warriner's) (no date) Sentence fragment test
> 10/29 Run-on sentence test
> 11/20 Quiz on Autobiography of Miss Jane Pittman (7 short sentence answers)
> 12/7 Discussion questions on Miss Jane Pitman (must answer in *complete* sentences)
> 1/8 Quiz on Miss Jane Pittman (fill in the blanks)
> 1/12 Test on Miss Jane Pittman (true false, matching, short answers, short answer in sentences — 50 questions in all, 10 answered in sentences)
> 1/25 Spelling test
> 2/2 Spelling test

This list of graded assignments exposes several important facets about the curriculum in Matt's class. The class seems to include no extended writing (or if there's any writing, it's not counted toward a grade). It includes the reading of only two works of literature in four months, and although one is a work of minority literature and the other would lend itself to a discussion of multicultural issues, there's no indication that class "discussions" in which students fill in answers on worksheets for a grade present a format that will allow real issues to emerge. About half the grades are for grammar and spelling or vocabulary (e.g., definitions of drama terms), and all the work on literature consists of questions to be answered in a sentence or less. Matt observes the consequences of such a curriculum:

> I have noticed that it is nearly impossible to pull more than 3 or 4 sentences out of these kids. I have distributed 3 sheets of discussion questions and have assigned two on-the-spot writing assignments. Each time I get no more than 4 sentences. It is their limit, apparently.

Looking over the assignments listed above might explain this: they simply have never been required to do more. Is this correct? Ought we not to challenge them? Should we just say "Look, these are basic kids"?

It's obvious, of course, that Matt doesn't think that teachers should say this. He begins to work, within the classroom structures, to extend students' speaking and writing and thinking, to bring the things they know into the classroom and build on them, to create a small community in which students can talk with one another and do interesting work and have a nice place to be.

This is Matt's plan for a lesson on *The Outsiders*. Notice how he remains with the question-and-answer format his cooperating teacher has established, while formulating those questions to make knowledge of the text shared and to make that knowledge part of students' own experience.

General Introduction

Purpose: To introduce the two groups in *The Outsiders* and to relate the social setting to the social setting of a local high school student. To determine the setting of the novel and to determine the correct pronunciation of *Socs*.

Questions:
1. (After writing *Socs* on the blackboard) How do you think you pronounce this word?
2. What is a Soc?
3. What is a Greaser?
4. Does anybody call anybody else a Soc or a Greaser in this community?
5. When does this story take place? Where?
6. Does anybody know what a collegiate is? A hitter? A juicer?
7. What are some of the group names in this school?
8. What are these groups like?
9. Does anybody know what a Barney is? (tell story of experience)

Introduction to *The Outsiders*

Purpose: To continue the discussion above but to bring the focus of it to the novel.

Questions:
1. Who is telling the story? (Name on board)
2. Is he a Soc? A Greaser?
3. What do we call the person who tells a story?
4. What is the first event of the novel?
5. What mistake did the narrator make to help bring about this event?
6. Who rescues him?
7. What are the names of his friends? (names on blackboard)
8. What are the names of his family? (names on blackboard)
9. What can you tell me about each of the characters on the blackboard?

Matt's lessons continue to move back and forth between the details of the story and the facts of life in this high school, between the world of *Socs* and *Greasers* and the world of *Barneys*. Students begin to write, and they write about their own experience:

> Like the Greasers and Socs, we all have a need to belong to a group. What group are *you* a part of? Describe your group and describe the positive and/or negative feelings you have about it.

They learn vocabulary as it arises in the context of the novel, beginning with what they think the word means, from the context, and then looking at the dictionary definition.

> *Menace* (p. 119) What you think it means_____
> Dictionary definition:——————— Part of Speech:_____
> Your sentence:_____.

They discuss the novel in groups, with questions that acknowledge their response as readers and that help them connect those responses to the words of the text.

> **Discussion Questions for Chapters 4, 5, and 6**
> 1. In this part of the novel we begin to get a closer look at Dally. Do you think that Dally is just hardened and mean, or do you think there is more to him than that? Refer to page 68 and page 80 for help.
> 2. On page 69 Ponyboy recites a poem by Robert Frost. Then he says to Johnny: "He meant more to it than I'm gettin', though." What do *you* think this poem is about?"

And so on.

All Matt's lessons respond to the formal curriculum of the classroom and to his cooperating teacher's expectations about texts and vocabulary, parts of speech, testing. But he *reinvents* this curriculum through his lessons, asking the detailed questions that will show that his students have understood the basic plot and elements of the story, but connecting these details with the events and people in their own world, and illuminating that real world as well as the world of the novel. He gives vocabulary worksheets and tests, but he shows students how they can make meaning from context and lets them see the relationship between that contextual meaning and the decontextualized dictionary definition. He gives tests (one, for example, in which students identify characters from passages in the novel), but those tests support larger understandings the students are developing through discussion and writing. He tests students' reading comprehension "informally," through discussion. And he evaluates the success of his lessons through observing a range of student responses: "by the expression on the kids' faces, by the number of kids responding, by the number of kids drifting off or yawning, by the amount of extra noise and disorder." "[The lesson] went well for both classes. Well over half of the students contributed to the discussion."

Matt's course curriculum includes not only the content mandated by the cooperating teacher, and not only the reconceiving of that content in ways that are relevant to his students' lives and learning. It also includes developing new patterns of learning and of interaction in the classroom. He's concerned, for example, about introducing group discussion in a class where the focus has been on individual seatwork, on carefully controlled responses to teacher's questions, on order and silence. For his first discussion group class, he states that his goals for this lesson are to "free up discussion of the novel a bit and set the stage for peer review of writing later on. This is an introduction to group work for this class — they have never done it before." So he decides that "tight control will be the key to success this first time. I hope it will not hinder easy discussion once the groups are formed." And he plans the logistics: "I will supervise the physical difficulties of moving desks around. I will introduce the idea to the class and distribute the questions the group will be responsible for. I will move from group to group for reinforcement purposes." And he will evaluate the success of this lesson not by the content of any group's answers, though those will be reviewed and discussed by the larger class, but by "a steady, medium volume noise level. I hope there will be no silent groups and no wild groups."

In reflecting on this group lesson, Matt says:

> I would spend more time clarifying the operational requirements of the groups, especially to myself. My idea that students should answer the questions individually after the group discussion was wrongheaded. This idea seemed to confuse everyone. Some students did what I thought I wanted — that is, they used the group as a forum and then went about answering the question themselves as individuals. Most of the groups formulated a group answer that was written down verbatim on each member's answer sheet. I suppose they were following a natural path here, and had I specified a group president and a group secretary and emphasized a group answer, I might have gotten better compliance. I could have done a better job circulating, reinforcing, and encouraging. Also I could have done a better job moving the chairs around. . . . The whole thing needs more practice, especially the movement of chairs, and the communication of group goals.

Matt plans lessons that he thinks will meet his goals, but he also observes his students and how they respond to those lessons. Although in the classroom of this cooperating teacher, there's no explicit negotiation about structures and procedures in the curriculum, there's no doubt that negotiation is taking place here — that Matt is shaping new ways of learning for the students, and that the students, through their responses, are reshaping the teacher's conceptions. The structure of group work, for example, is altered by the students' "natural path," though there was nothing natural to the students about this initial move into groups, and it had to be carefully orchestrated by the teacher.

Throughout his work, Freire talks about the process of naming as essential to the process of changing. In order to reinvent or transform something, people must first see it as it is and name it, and then recognize it (see again what's been named). Once that process begins, people can begin to see how the named object might be seen differently, how it might be reinvented. This is true for the peasants of Brazil or São Tomé who meet in a Cultural Circle and name the things that shape their lives — *planting, land, plantation* — recognize how their lives are determined by these names, and then begin to imagine how these things might be reinvented. And it's true for Matt, in a U.S. high school classroom, where, on his last day of student teaching, he must direct his students to memorize a list of pronouns in Warriner's *English Grammar and Composition*, which must then be listed on a quiz. "There will be about fifty, by my rough estimate. There will be no writing. There will be no paragraphs, no sentences, no phrases. The students will simply be asked to list the pronouns they were assigned to memorize." In an ironic aside, Matt decides that he had the perfect cooperating teacher. "I don't think anyone could have done a better job of convincing me of the uselessness and futility of this kind of exercise.... [Her] attitude toward her students is not at all stinting or mean. It is actually kindly and maternal. But still, this is bad medicine, I think." By naming his reality, as "bad medicine," Matt commits himself to a process of change. He's actually begun the process already in small but real ways within this classroom. But on this last day, as he renames what he has seen, he prepares himself to move beyond it: "I really do want to begin teaching my own classes and applying my own ideas." Matt continues a process he began with the students in his ninth-grade class. With his help, they too had begun to observe and name their reality — the social world of their high school.

Reinventing the curriculum can begin with taking a critical perspective on that curriculum. What Paulo Freire calls "conscientization" calls upon an awareness of process as well as product, context as well as content, and such critical skills must be learned by both teacher and student in reinventing curriculum. "Becoming critical," Ann Berthoff says, "developing a method, is the best way, I think, for teachers and students to learn from one another" (1981, 41). Berthoff establishes the method for dynamic curriculum here:

> If we are all continually discovering, recognizing what it is we are doing, we'll have many more ways of finding out how to do it. In other words criticism in the classroom could help us get rid of rigid

lesson plans so that we would be able to take advantage of what John Donne called "emergent occasions." (41)

Emergent occasions emerge only if teachers look. Berthoff argues that standard curriculum plans stymie the kind of looking that would allow for a living curriculum within a classroom and explains what taking advantage of the emergent occasion means for teachers:

> We could get rid of study questions, refusing to order textbooks that include them; refusing the Instructor's Manual that has the answers, asking for a refund of the money added onto the cost of the textbook so that the manual could be "provided free of charge." Out would go prefabricated units and tests and assignments. A ritual bonfire of those pink and yellow markers used to make pastel islands out of "important passages" would close this introductory phase of criticism in the classroom. We would then be free to undertake what I. A. Richards considered central to all learning, "the continuing audit of meaning." (41).

When teachers begin to see curriculum as a blueprint for action instead of a prescription to remedy illness or a recipe to be followed line by line, they begin to conduct the audit Richards and Berthoff argue for. They observe, test, experiment, and challenge curricula they use, and their tests of a curriculum are always evaluated by the most real of all tests: how it works. "What difference does it make to learning, to literacy, when I do it this way rather than some other?" teachers ask themselves, and in questioning, teachers become critical — and so do the curricula they remake.

The reinvented curriculum

While we've been talking about the kind of curriculum plans that get lodged in large three-ring binders and referred to as teachers make lesson plans and consult objectives, much of the standard school curriculum isn't written down or discussed but invisible — involving expectations about behavior and values. ("Silence is golden." "Know right from wrong." "Teacher knows best.") Some behaviors may be made explicit in curriculum guides and the plans that accompany them. (You may have practiced writing *behavioral objectives* sometime, especially if you've taken an education course, objectives that begin with the phrase "the student will" — write a paragraph on one topic, be able to recognize the adjective clause, read aloud without faltering, etc.) But the values that accompany such objectives for behaviors aren't spelled out. To change students' roles in learning, what has been implicit must be made explicit, and then held up for inquiry, examination, and renegotiation. The reinvented curriculum begins with the learner and teacher in negotiation and dialogue about what learning is, about how it comes about, about what is learned.

1. A reinvented curriculum will make explicit the subject of responsibility, authority, discipline, control of learning.

Too often curriculum is used as discipline within the classroom. Few teachers now make kids stay after school to write on the blackboard, a hundred times, "I will not speak out of turn in class." But many still give writing assignments or extra reading assignments as a form of punishment. (Matt's cooperating teacher tells him that "written assignments are effective tools in forcing students to do work.") More use curricular bribes — "If you do well on this grammar test we'll see a videotape tomorrow." And even more focus on material that can be studied through individual seat work — students who work individually in vocabulary workbooks can generally be expected to maintain total silence in the classroom — or through teacher "examination" — students who are asked limited questions that are answerable in a sentence are unlikely to raise others. Students may be passive in the classroom, but that passivity is perceived as discipline, as order, and is preferable to the chaos or unruliness that many teachers fear will result if student voices are heard.

Teachers are partly right in this fear. Students who have been through many years of limited, rigid schooling and whose passivity has been accepted and encouraged have had no opportunity to learn other, more effective learning behaviors. It's no wonder that they're likely to operate in only two modes: sullen silence while the teacher is present or noisy "misbehavior" if left on their own. For the beginning teacher, such students present real difficulties, because they'll test her limits constantly until they finally shape her into a replica of all the other teachers they've known. Then they can sit back and let school go by them again.

Students need the opportunity to learn how to be learners; they need to have their self-discipline and responsibility as learners become an explicit part of their activities in school — to have discipline as an aspect of curriculum replace curriculum used for discipline. All learners need structure, as well; they need to know what to expect. But teachers can make structures and the reasons for them both explicit and negotiable. "This is the purpose of this activity. Is it working O.K.? How could we do better?" Where the classroom becomes a community of learners, all members should have an opportunity to define their expectations of and responsibilities to that community, and to reflect on those expectations and responsibilities.

Deb makes this part of the curriculum explicit at several points. At one time she asks her students to write about why they haven't done the reading. Another time she steps into the unruly class of a substitute teacher and asks students to write about what they did to that teacher. Matt makes it explicit as he moves students into groups, reflects on how they function, and adapts group structure to student responses. In both instances, students are introduced to new ways of seeing their roles in the classroom. In helping groups to function well as small communities of learners, both Deb and Matt also help students extend their concept of discipline in the classroom. The term *discipline* means more than maintaining good behavior; it means self-ordered responsibility and intellectual order associated with study and inquiry.

2. A reinvented curriculum will make explicit the question of how knowledge gets made and what gets counted as knowledge.

As we've seen, the school curriculum has been defined primarily in terms of areas of knowledge and limited demonstrations of that knowledge. Students see knowledge as absolute, as existing "out there" in an unchanging realm of ideas, because it's most often taught that way. Rarely do students have the opportunity to consider *how* knowledge gets made by individuals and scholarly communities engaged in inquiry, or even *that* knowledge is made, as a human construct. The common view of knowledge leaves the learner relatively powerless — either you're good at remembering all that "stuff" that makes up the subjects you study, or you're not. Being "good at" chemistry or history means remembering the "stuff," the periodic table of the elements or the dates of the Spanish-American War. Being good at English means remembering the "stuff" about grammar and literature while using the standard discourse forms of school and the dominant class.

School curricula recognize that scientists "discover" knowledge, and most science courses offer laboratory sections in at least token acknowledgment that students should replicate the activities of scientists. But historians, too, "make" history as well as find it, by gathering certain kinds of data, asking certain kinds of questions. The knowledge of *any* field reflects the process of its making, and to really understand the knowledge it's necessary to understand the process, to participate in it, and to reflect on it. In English, teachers can ask what literary historians do, what linguists do, what writers do, inquiring into the nature and characteristics of categories and divisions — into the separation of expository and creative writing, into genres — and how they might be reconceived. Students can generate questions about the language they learn, about the literature they read — even about why some writing is designated as literature and other writing is not. "What makes *literature* and who decides?" is a valid subject of inquiry in the English classroom. While it's a large, abstract question, it can begin with a small step, with inquiry into students' own worlds of literature—the stories from family members, for example—and can use such steps to arrive at new criteria or new categories and to rethink those in place.

It's also important that teachers change their own relationship to knowledge. While students see knowledge as fixed, teachers tend to see knowledge as made by others—and therefore as something they simply pass on in the classroom. But both students and teachers must participate in the making of all of the knowledge of the English classroom, by asking questions that raise important issues, by making observations and interpretations that add to the common understanding. Knowledge doesn't reside only in school textbooks. Teachers and students who question the ways in which knowledge gets made and passed on soon move beyond the narrow vision and narrow boundaries of knowledge as textbooks describe it and make themselves participants in the discourse of the field they're studying.

When students get to participate in the making of knowledge—when they see how the knowledge of the subject gets made—the knowledge made by others becomes more understandable and meaningful to them (as well as more open to question). A student who reflects on her own considerations in turning a family episode into a "short story" will have a different perception of Eudora Welty's craft than a student who only reads "Petrified Man" and answers questions about setting and character. A student who's collected examples of people's actual language usage will have a different understanding about what usage rules are and how they get made than a student who's simply had to memorize those rules. This active making of knowledge reflects back onto the issue of responsibility in the classroom; it's authors who have authority, and students who participate in authoring their studies come to share in the responsibilities that go along with authority.

3. The reinvented curriculum will make explicit the sequencing and the structure of learning and inquiry in the classroom.

Any curriculum that really takes into account the process learners will go through to master what's in it must do more than specify units to be covered. In designing curriculum, teachers must consider rather how the learner comes to know, and the relationship between knowing and what is to be known. The teacher can consider sequence first by drawing on his own experience as a learner. (Part of his authority comes from that experience, the experience of his own more advanced study.) The teacher who's conducting research with students, writing with students, is encountering similar difficulties and questions, but he's developed a repertoire of strategies for responding to them. His strategies can provide guidelines for the process of others. "I've found that discovering your own questions about a topic before reading something else helps you to know what you really want to get out of what you're reading, helps you to decide what's important to remember and take notes on. That's why we're starting this way." As students gain experience, their experience can help to reshape this process. But a preliminary sequence can be structured to move through the process of inquiry, to move toward more cognitively complex tasks, to move from the known to the unknown.

Some principles for sequencing may emerge from students' reflections on their own learning. If a group decides it's had trouble figuring out how to get background information about Shakespeare's life, then strategies for gathering and using library information will find a place on the curricular agenda. The group that wants to figure out how to get background information needs to work on processes of data gathering, selection, sorting. But these skills are not enough; students need to consider *why* they want background information on Shakespeare's life, what larger purpose it'll serve. Then they can begin to decide what's relevant and irrelevant to whatever larger purpose they're trying to accomplish. Do controversies about who the real Shakespeare was matter for their purposes, or is it the dominant view that's most important? Students involved in making knowledge learn to observe, to describe, to work on categorization, comparison, and differentiation. They'll interpret, generalize, find implications, develop hypotheses, discover analogies. And the process of inquiry itself, from early questions to final focus, becomes the basis for the sequencing of course assignments.

Still other principles of sequencing derive from what we know about the larger process of learning. These principles underlie James Moffett's work:

> The most sensible strategy for determining a proper learning order in English, it seems to me, is to look for the main lines of child development and to assimilate to them, when fitting, the various formulations that scholars make about language and literature. This strategy is opposed to starting with some notions of structure derived from linguistics or literary criticism and trying to found a curriculum on them by negotiating a compromise between theory and the classroom facts of life. In other words, the sequence of psychological development should be the backbone of curriculum continuity, and logical formulations of the subject should serve only as an aid in describing this natural growth. Meshing learner and learned, in the case of a native language, is a matter of translating inner reality into the public terms of the subject. (1968, 15)

To examine their values, Moffett argues, learners must revise their old thinking, their old models of the world, and to do this they must see old abstractions from a larger perspective, a broader perspective than that from which the original abstraction was created. The assignments that led to Allison's writing about her own experience and about Anne Frank's were designed to help students build on what they knew from their own lives, to step back and see that experience in new ways, to link it to the experience of others, to see what was "significant" in an experience, what governed its retelling. Learners carry out this revision of understanding best in communication with others:

> Ideally, a student would spend his time in a language course of study abstracting a large amount of raw material into categories of experience and then into new propositions which finally he would combine so as to arrive at new propositions not evident at any of the lower stages. By discussing his productions in a workshop class, he could profit from other points of view, discover what part of his abstracting is peculiar to him and what he shared with a public, and see how the worth of his higher abstractions is determined by the worth of his lower ones. (28)

In Moffett's curriculum, which is outlined in *Teaching the Universe of Discourse* and detailed in *Student-Centered Language Arts and Reading, K-13*, there's a shift from abstraction for oneself to abstraction for others, who are increasingly distant, in moving from using language in reflection to conversation, to correspondence, to publication. (And classwork that involves journal writing, discussion groups, letter-writing exchanges, and publication of reports or collections gives students practice along this whole range.) The schema also suggests a movement through the genres of human discourse, from recording — the drama of what is happening — to reporting — the narrative of what has happened — to generalizing — the exposition of what happens — and finally to theorizing — the argumentation of what will or may happen.

There are many ways we can structure our study, many frames we can give to the knowledge and the ways of knowing represented in the discipline of English. But, within any of these frames, effective sequencing of work will grow out of discovering what learners know and helping them build on that knowledge, seeing and reseeing it from different perspectives, negotiating about it in dialogue with others, and representing it in different ways to different (and real) audiences. The point is that there should be a reason that one activity precedes and one follows another, that this reason should take into account the context of the classroom — the students, the teacher, the semester, the work to be accomplished. Students should see their work developing from task to task; they should see how one task helps them accomplish another, how work in groups affects individual work, how teacher comment and evaluation guide the process of assignments. In other words, students as well as teachers should understand the reasons for sequencing of activities. There's no better way to demonstrate belief in an integrated approach to knowledge than to model it in a sequenced curriculum. To have a rationale for the sequence, teachers must become theorists of their work; they must speculate about the ways in which their students learn most effectively and they must investigate approaches that test out their theories. In creating a well-founded curricular sequence, a teacher remakes the knowledge in her field.

4. The reinvented curriculum will draw on the social and cultural context of the learner.

James Britton, in *Prospect and Retrospect*, emphasizes the force of the social relationship and how it can affect curriculum. Like Moffett, he would focus on watching and listening to how children acquire language, but he emphasizes the cooperative, social nature of such learning:

> "Watching and listening"—It is only in more recent years that we have begun to realize how language behavior builds on earlier non-verbal behavior: how cooperative routines set up between infant and adult, mostly in the form of play, increasingly generate *meaning* for the infant; and how early language comes in to highlight meanings already established in this way. Thereafter, language has a crucial role to play, enriching and extending cooperative behavior, cumulatively reaping the harvest of earlier understandings, organizing memory into narrative form, vastly increasing in scope and accessibility the body of expectations with which the child will meet every new event. (202–203)

Britton argues that this social view of learning is crucial in multicultural classrooms, if teachers are to avoid pulling students away from their roots and their cultures. He calls for "cherishing and nourishing the speech of the home and the neighborhood by helping it to find the kind of expression, in story, poem, and play, which can communicate the spirit of the subculture to a multicultural audience" (203).

Britton doesn't attempt to define, as Moffett did, the curriculum that would follow from this understanding of how we learn in a social context, in a community and a culture. But we can articulate its principles and suggest some examples that have appeared in this book. A curriculum that considers the social and cultural context of the learner will build on what the learner brings to the school from that context, making explicit and conscious what learners know, how they go about learning new things, and drawing on the language in which they represent and extend that knowledge in their homes and communities. It would bring those ways of knowing and talking into the classroom, and it would make connections between those ways and school ways, between informal, personal knowing and formal, public knowing, between the different forms that formal, public knowing takes in different communities.

The first-grade classrooms Shirley Brice Heath described, in which young children looked for words they already knew on signs and cereal boxes and brought that knowledge into the classroom, the fifth-grade science students gathering local knowledge about planting and translating it into "science book" knowledge and terms, college freshmen gathering information about discourse patterns in their homes or workplaces and comparing these with the patterns of formal academic discourse — these suggest foundations for a sequencing of activities that can run through the school curriculum. Such activities move from focusing on what's near or familiar (home culture and language) to what's distant and less familiar (school culture and language). And, as multiple perspectives are brought together in the school setting (either because the learners bring them or the teacher supplements what they bring), learners move from comparing them to finding larger generalizations that can encompass them all. In this way Moffett's movement toward abstraction can come to be generated naturally within a multicultural framework, as students see and resee what they know from widening cultural perspectives.

5. The reinvented curriculum will include the world outside the school, the relationship between the world and the school, and will make explicit how school shapes and frames knowledge.

In most classrooms, the day's work goes on, covering the scheduled portion of the curriculum, as if the world outside of the classroom didn't exist. Students must leave immediate concerns about a family member addicted to drugs or alcohol at the door to the classroom; they must leave their concerns about the larger social context of these con-cerns — poverty, unemployment, homelessness, world affairs — outside as well. Where such issues do enter the curriculum, they're often part of enrichment courses for advanced students, while the students in basic courses, whose lives are at least equally affected by these concerns, continue with the standard curriculum. A student teacher described the curriculum of two classrooms she would be working with at an inner-city high school. One is a classroom for "basic" English:

> In our conversations, Mrs. J has stated that these students really only respond to repetition and drills, films and worksheets. There aren't enough books for the students to take reading homework home with them and because of their own low reading levels, all of the reading selections must be kept short. Instead of reading a story, Mrs. J will often show a film and then pass out follow-up questions. A great deal of time is devoted to vocabulary lists from a text and an elaborate system of worksheets which the students are to keep track of on an assignment sheet. (Diane)

The other is an advanced class.

> The seventh and last period of the day is a different story. Mrs. S teaches a level four English class comprised mostly of seniors. Carried

over from the last marking period is their continued work on research papers. Their topics range from apartheid to nearly any Latin American theme which the teacher okays. The curriculum circles around a Horace Mann grant concerning the civil rights movement, the women's movement, Hispanic issues, Irish political strife, and apartheid. After reading her proposal I can see that nearly any good idea that I might have that pertains to these topics would be welcomed.

When the curriculum is reinvented in the ways we've been describing, real-world issues can't remain an add-on for advanced students only. As all students bring their own language into the classroom, work together as a community of learners, ask questions, and search for answers, their work will lead them outside the individual classroom as they learn to question the relationship between their classroom and the outside world, and in turn to raise questions about the larger society in which their classrooms and schools are situated. For example, as students begin to study language in some of the ways we suggested in Chapter 5, and ask and answer questions about how people use language, they begin to perceive the disjunction between the values implicit in the school curriculum around language and those in the home and community, and they may then begin to ask questions about power, about class, about discrimination.

Ellie and her colleague Suzy Groden team-teach a freshman seminar they designed for students who enter the university lacking "academic skills"; hoping to break the cycle of repetition and drill in "basic" that most of these students had faced year after year, they involve students in the sorts of research and discovery that were usually reserved for advanced students. (In fact this seminar was modeled after the seminar for freshman honors students.) For several years (until the blackout of news from South Africa) the seminar focused on a study of language and power, and looked specifically at the case of South Africa—through writing that emerged from that context and through the news accounts published in the United States. Students followed and charted daily news coverage in U. S. newspapers and on television. They read essays, magazine articles, literature from South Africa. They observed and wrote about relationships of language and power in their own lives and interactions. And they became engaged (many for the first time) in their learning.

One student, Nancy, made it clear on the first day of class that her experience in the larger world would be important to her as a learner (although, in the typically brief text of a basic writer, she did not elaborate). She asserted that one of the things most important to her was "that I am hispanic which has a great deal to me. To be able to influence by another language and traditions."

Midway through the course, Nancy summarized (in a lengthy five-page review) what she had learned from the South Africa study. In her review, she makes clear how engaged she's become by the issues raised in this course, how they've fueled all her uses of language, including her "listening and conversational skills," how she's learned "to do research and gather data" in the context of this study, how from her exposure to new literature — "South African Black literature" — she's "developed an interest in it." She now appreciates the power of language in a new way, and she wants to use that power in her own writing. She has real questions about South Africa that will carry her beyond the end of the formal unit of study, and asks: "What is the history of apartheid in South Africa? Why don't the whites in South Africa change when they know they are wrong?" She sees how her study of South Africa can provide a model for studying other contexts and particularly that her own life as a Hispanic American has its roots in a political context that she can learn more about: "It is important to me to learn more about people who are exploited. For example, I would be very interested to find out more about the situation in Central America." And she asks the most important question of all — "How are we making a difference in knowing what we know?"

The questions that emerge from making connections between students' lives outside and inside school, between their personal lives and the larger world, must find a place in the curriculum. Only in this way can students gain a critical understanding of their lives, their society, and their roles as moral and responsible members of the larger community.

Strategies for change: what the individual teacher can do

Chapter 1 traced Mina Shaughnessy's stages of educating herself to work in new ways with the diverse learners who entered her English classroom via new open-admissions policies. She described her development from the asking of questions, to careful observations of her students and herself, to "diving in" and studying new disciplines in order to "remediate" herself. We argued that teachers who dive in will "learn how to look in more than one direction at once, at their students, their schools, their society, and themselves." Throughout this book we've been trying to look in these many directions, and, in the process, to create a coherent philosophy of what teaching English is all about. We've looked at learning as active discovery in a social context, we've looked at some of what we know about different home contexts and school contexts, we've looked at the classroom in the context of our larger multicultural society, we've looked at traditional subfields of English — language, reading, writing, literature — and explored ways of integrating these in relationship to how learners learn and use language, and we've considered how the work of learners and teachers might be reconceived within the classroom to fit with what we have come to understand of these complex relationships as seen from these multiple perspectives. Along the way we've seen many classrooms, heard many voices, drawn on many observations and insights, to suggest that an unquiet pedagogy, a transformed classroom and a reinvented curriculum, while based on all of these understandings, can't be prescribed but must evolve out of teachers' and learners' immediate settings. Here we'd like to summarize some of the things that teachers can do in their immediate situations, both within and outside their own classrooms.

Within the classroom

Teachers can reinvent the curriculum by:

1. *Adding* connections to the outside world through newspapers, TV, movies; drawing on students' home cultures, making connections with other classes and schools, and in general bringing the world to bear on the word in the classroom. Ellie's students who studied about South Africa, Hepsie's students who made the rhetoric of the 1988 presidential election the focus of their study for that semester drew on such connections.
2. *"Problematizing"* situations and concepts. Freire's term means questioning, posing problems, holding something up for examination and inquiry. A curriculum that asks students to gather examples of real language usage from family and friends *problematizes* the subject of usage rules, raising questions about what this term represents, the values it implies, its dominance in our curriculum.
3. *Redefining* so that student texts become literature, expository writing becomes creative, public discourse becomes personal. This, of course, opens to question the nature of existing categories and the purposes they serve.
4. *Sequencing* to be responsive to student inquiry, to the questions that get raised and the things that get discovered in classes, and to events going on in the world outside school.
5. *Formalizing* by making explicit the method and process as well as the content of all the study we engage in in the classroom, including those of classroom organization and structures for learning. Matt begins to do this for himself as he reflects on the working of groups. In his own classroom he'll be able to invite his students to join in explicit discussion of this concern.
6. *Combining* one element of the curriculum with another. We've seen how grammar and vocabulary can be combined with the study of literature. Combining any two elements of study (point of view and subordination/coordination; *Julius Caesar* and political responsibility

in the 1988 election) allows us to see those elements in the new ways, make new connections.

7. *Revising* by reseeing the old. We can revise the canon of works that we read, the place of oral texts coming from the community, the role of language study, the place of writing. We can, and must, revise the curriculum we create for our classrooms, reseeing it in the context of a new classroom/community culture with each new group of students.

Within the school

While teachers can use the variety of suggestions we've offered here to reinvent the curriculum and make it more responsive to learners and more supportive of learning — bringing in the real world and students' experiences, challenging students to question as well as to accept, integrating strands of knowledge into coherent patterns — we also want to argue that a more fundamental questioning/reseeing of that curriculum can, for us as teachers, release energy and foster significantly new understandings about the way a discipline gets learned or even how a discipline is defined. We've argued here that there's nothing necessary about the way the knowledge of the discipline has traditionally been structured and formed, and that reimagining those structures, by integrating traditionally separate elements, for example, allows teachers to be real learners/inventors again. Teachers begin a larger act of reinventing the curriculum by first perceiving the curricular plan as a model, not as reality.

One of the things that keeps teachers bound to existing models, curricula, ways of doing things is that they don't talk enough to people who see things from different perspectives and do things in different ways. Our disciplinary boundaries, by and large, keep us talking to people who've been trained like us and who think like us (even though those boundaries too are a model or construct that could just as easily be seen another way). Getting outside our classrooms to talk to and work with other teachers who represent different perspectives, or with parents, or with administrators, is one way to broaden our own perspective. English teachers can take several paths that lead to new ways of seeing:

1. *Writing across the curriculum.* Many schools have initiated writing-across-the-curriculum programs to bring together faculty from all departments so that they can share perspectives on how writing can be used to foster learning in all areas. We saw in Chapter 2 how Janet, a biology major, wants to integrate expressive as well as descriptive writing into her classroom, to help students find connections between their own questions and the things they are learning in biology, and connections between what they are learning about

biology and larger social issues like AIDS. A math teacher who participated in the prepractice class has begun using journals in which students record and reflect on their process in solving problems, so that they come to see their developing problem–solving strategies, and not just whether they got the right answer, as important. English teachers who've effectively integrated writing and learning in their own classrooms can provide valuable support for teachers in other areas, while learning in turn from the perspective those teachers offer.

2. *Team teaching and interdisciplinary programs.* These offer even better ways of trying on other perspectives. Working out goals, priorities, approaches that can satisfy the concerns of two or more teachers who are approaching the curriculum from different perspectives demands a significant reseeing of what you've always done. Developing an interdisciplinary curriculum that fully incorporates these perspectives demands even more new understanding and insight and supports imaginative and fresh responses. In working to design a team–taught interdisciplinary program with representatives of five disciplines, Ellie came to revise her own earlier notion (based on her own educational experience) of history as a set of facts to be memorized, and to understand from her colleagues how a historian practices history, how a sociologist does sociology, and how these ways of carrying out inquiry in these fields were both similar to and different from the methods of inquiry she used with her students. Peter Elbow, too, makes a strong case for interdisciplinary, or "nondisciplinary" courses that exceed the range of any one teacher, where "at most, [the teacher] can profess to bring special skills and experience to the basic process of wondering about something and deciding to do something about it. He must take on the role of collaborator" (1968, 11). The nondisciplinary course helps students and teachers create new categories, and releases learners from rigid curricular barriers that get in the way of learning.

3. *Collaboration with other teachers, with students, with parents, with administrators.* The immediate community is an important part of the context in which learning takes place. Collaboration with members of that community on any enterprise, whether it's getting new equipment for the gym, putting out a school newsletter, writing a funding proposal, deciding what to do about sex education or a school health clinic, can help the teacher achieve new perspectives on the school and the community that it's part of and can lead to a common reseeing and renegotiation of goals and methods. Both inside and outside the classroom, collaboration nurtures the expressing of ideas, the negotiating of meanings, the creation of understandings that extend beyond what an individual could see alone. As collaborators in teaching and writing, we know this to be true.

Beyond the school

Teachers need ways to get beyond the isolation of their classrooms *and* of the local cultures of their schools, to talk with other teachers and learners who are working in different contexts. We have talked about the Boston Writing Project and its teachers throughout this book, and participating in institutes offered at the many locations of branches of the National Writing Project is an important way teachers can become part of a larger community of writers and learners. Participating in university/school collaborations, working and talking and thinking with student teachers in the ways that cooperating teachers described in this book have done, can give a teacher new perspective on her teaching and her classroom. Subscribing to the *English Journal* or *The Teacher's Journal*, or other publications that stress the teaching and theory of writing, and writing for these as well, can give teachers a forum for exchanging experiences and ideas, for engaging in a larger discussion about teaching and learning. Teachers who begin to move back and forth between their personal, experiential knowledge about teaching and a more public, shared knowledge begin to find ways to help their students connect personal and public language and knowing as well.

A teacher's revision of the curriculum, like a student's engagement with learning about the world, is bound to raise new questions about society and the role schools play in them. After working on a national project to create an interdisciplinary school science curriculum focusing on what it means to be human, Jerome Bruner assessed that experience in his autobiographical essay *In Search of Mind*:

> I think the lesson of the curriculum reform movement is that you cannot accomplish the deeper ends of education by altering only the content and spirit of the courses you teach. Schools as now constituted are not so much the solution to the problem as they are part of the problem. If I had it all to do over again, and if I knew how, I would put my energies into reexamining how the schools express the agenda of the society and how that agenda is formulated and how translated by the schools. (197)

Curriculum is part of schools, which are part of society, and in reinventing curriculum, both schools and society have to be questioned and examined.

Both teachers and students need to reach out, then, into their communities, their society, and the larger world as well. In his many essays about learning, Ralph Waldo Emerson argued again and again that the life of the mind musn't be seen as separate from the life of the world, that the scholar and the teacher must be a part of the world. Books alone can't offer all that we must learn, he said, and it's experience that shapes what we read and write and understand. Emerson would have us learn our grammar by talking to ordinary people: "This is the way to learn grammar. Colleges and books only copy the language which the field and the work-yard made" (61). He would have us bring to our reading and writing our experience of the world, so that "the page of whatever book we read becomes luminous with manifold allusion" (58). He would have us see that "life is our dictionary" (60). He would have the American scholar turn attention to "the literature of the poor, the feelings of the child, the philosophy of the street, the meaning of the household life" (67). And, to the quiet life of scholarship, he would join the unquiet life of action:

> Action is with the scholar subordinate, but it is essential. Without it thought can never ripen into truth. Whilst the world hangs before the eye as a cloud of beauty, we cannot even see its beauty. Inaction is cowardice, but there can be no scholar without the heroic mind. The preamble of thought, the transition through which it passes from the unconscious to the conscious, is action. Only so much do I know as I have lived. (59)

The life of the mind and the life of experience join when a person becomes a critical thinker, when life itself becomes the book to interpret. The real thinker—student or teacher—never stops interpreting, never stops asking the question that matters. It's the question Nancy asked when she completed her study of South Africa: "How are we making a difference in knowing what we know?"

STRATEGIES FOR THE TEACHER AND LEARNER

Throughout this book we've tried to emphasize the interaction between theory and practice, between teaching and learning, between reading and writing. We've drawn on our own experiences and observations, on those of our students, on those of teachers in the community and in the literature of our field. And here we invite you, also, to participate in the process of reflection and observation.

This chapter draws on activities that have been useful to us and to the teachers and students we've worked with, that have enriched our discussions and our understandings. You'll find, in this section, several sorts of strategies; some are focused on personal memories, some on classroom observation, some on more formal inquiry — the ethnography or the case study — some on the planning of teaching units. Some activities we've conceived of as group activities — activities that we've found helpful in facilitating the collaborative thinking of groups of teachers and learners. Many of the activities are individual ones, designed for personal reflection. As Vygotsky says, all our thoughts are conversations, and all our conversations, including those we create through our writing, lead us to think better ourselves. Understanding is fostered by dialogue, by talk, be seeing what we've seen before from new perspectives, by sharing and trying on the perspectives of others.

We offer what follows as suggestions for your own inquiry. You may not want to work through them programmatically; you may just want to read through them, or they may suggest other questions you'll want to pursue and memories you'll want to draw on. Our intention with this chapter is to offer you some ways to further the sort of active reading and inquiry and reflection that supports all our learning as teachers. Some of these strategies deliberately build on one another, so that an ethnography might be composed of little pieces that reflect the discussions of Unit 1, a case study of little pieces connected with Unit 2. We've suggested these two larger, more formal inquiries because they represent the sort of research that teachers have been carrying out in their own classrooms — research that has been most important in creating the theoretical understandings that inform our teaching of

English. And such research can be important to all teachers engaged in making their own pedagogical theory.

Strategies for unit 1 — language, thought, and culture

The strategies for this unit are of two types. The *reflections* are intended to help you become conscious of your own experiences as a learner through remembering your past experiences and becoming more conscious of your present ones. These may help you understand the subjective base of the experience you bring to present and future classrooms and draw consciously on that experience as you inquire into the nature of language and learning and schools. The *ethnographic* activities ask you to engage in a more formal inquiry, using the methods of ethnographic observation to gain an understanding of the culture of a particular classroom. They assume you're currently a participant or observer in some classroom (and if you're not, arranging even a morning or two of such observations at a local school can give you a preliminary sense of the sorts of insights such inquiry brings). The movement back and forth between these two sorts of activities — exploring subjective interpretations and following a formal method of inquiry — can help you develop the sort of *disciplined inquiry* that Frederick Erickson calls for in our studies of classrooms.

Reflections

- Begin by remembering a classroom culture that you were part of as a student. Picture yourself in the class and level closest to the class you'll be working with — eleventh-grade English, for example, or freshman composition — and try to describe what was around you — where the teacher sat, how often the students talked, when you moved around, and how you felt in that classroom. What you'll notice first in the classroom you're observing or teaching in will be shaped by these experiences.
- Identify something you found problematic or troublesome in your experience with schools or classrooms. Write freely about it for ten or fifteen minutes, then pause and read back through what you've written. Where has your writing taken you in your thinking about this issue? Has it clarified anything?
- How do you define learning? Describe an instance in which you were engaged in learning. Did this learning take place in a school setting? What facilitated it? How might you apply your experience as a learner in this instance to your teaching in an English classroom?
- Try writing to solve a problem — a math or physics problem, a

problem of clarifying a concept in a sociology course or a troubling part of a literary text, or a life problem. Then reflect on this process and on the part that verbalizing your thinking played in moving it along.

- Try to remember your own earliest consciousness of the way you spoke. Can you recall a moment at which you were first conscious of the fact that you spoke or used the language differently from someone else? What did you see as the meaning or significance of that difference?
- Were you tracked in your schooling? If so, where were you tracked? What would you say about this now? How did this affect your educational experience?

Ethnographic inquiry

Working toward an ethnography of the classroom

Begin by making detailed notes on what you observe in the classroom you visit or teach in. If you're currently teaching, it can be particularly useful to visit a variety of other classes in your school and compare other classroom cultures with your own. Over several weeks, try to record as much as possible about:

- The larger environment outside the school, and outside the classroom, insofar as it might have some effect on the class.
- The physical environment of the classroom — its arrangements of time and space, its artifacts, or objects, and materials.
- The movements and interactions among the people in this environment — those among students as well as between students and teacher.
- Gestures, language, and forms of discourse.
- Anything else that catches your attention.

Many seemingly insignificant details can be important within the classroom culture, so while you recognize that your own subjective perspective influences what you see, try to record as much as you can, without prejudging what's important.

Because you're likely to be a participant as well as an observer in this classroom (and even prepractice students should participate as much as possible — joining in class discussions where that seems appropriate, sitting in on small-group sessions, or beginning work with individual students where the opportunity arises), you'll need to participate first, and take notes second, using moments before and after class, when students are writing, or at the end of the school day.

Begin as well to reflect, at the end of each day you spend in the classroom, on the things you observed that day and how they connect to the issues discussed in this book, jotting down your thoughts on teaching, learning, writing, reading. (A double-entry notebook, with observation notes on one side and reflections on the other, is a helpful format for this work.) Your reading of Unit 1 should help you focus on particular aspects of the school environment and the classroom culture, and suggest other activities that move toward creating the sort of *thick description* of this classroom that will highlight its patterns of meaning. Periodically, you should review your notes, seeing what patterns begin to emerge and what questions you have which you'll want to try to answer with further observations.

To begin, we suggest that you look closely at the classroom's arrangements, artifacts, and structures. The selections from students' journals and ethnographies that appeared in the Introduction can direct you toward the sorts of features you'll want to attend to, and you might want to look back at them at this point.

Observing and analyzing classroom discourse

As we saw in Chapter 3, a typical class is a speech event with its own structures, rules, and roles. The class period is divided into structural units that will probably include openings, closings, segments of instructions, lecturing, questions and answers, individual seat work, and so forth. Boundaries between these activities will be marked in some way. Individuals will play particular roles, and there will be commonly understood rules about who gets to speak, when, and for how long. The teacher generally controls classroom talk, and the most common pattern for formal interactions between teacher and students is the one in which the teacher initiates an interaction, the student responds, and the teacher evaluates that response.

When you're observing a class you'll want to record as many of the features of the talk in this classroom as possible. (Teachers might have their students record this information — a favorite research strategy of Dixie Goswami in her own classes). You might consider:

- The larger structural units of classroom discourse. What units of activities are included in a typical class period and how are their boundaries marked?
- Teacher talk. Approximately how much time does the teacher spend in communicating about a subject: informing, explaining, defining, questioning, correcting, checking or confirming understanding? How much time is spent in controlling class behavior: getting and keeping attention, prompting responses, requesting, or ordering? What other activities can you add to the list? (Encouraging students, extending their ideas?)
- Student talk. How much student talk is there in this classroom, and what is its function? Does it respond to the teacher's intention (answering questions)? Does it focus on thinking about the subject

(reflecting, questioning)? Does it focus on a common purpose, or does it pull away (asking irrelevant questions, disrupting) or deny that purpose (conversing with another student about unrelated issues)? How much time is spent in each sort of activity?

- Interaction between teacher and students. Is this interaction marked by enthusiasm and cooperation (e.g., expansive questioning and reflective response)? By routine and reluctance (limited questioning and limited response or silence)? In each cycle of student/teacher interaction, what's the relative length of each participant's turn? What's the overall ratio of teacher talk to student talk?

- Interaction among students. Do turns ever move from teacher to student to student, or does each formal exchange involve the teacher? Do students extend the discussion of the focal subject? Do they respond to points that other students make? Or are all such inter-actions about concerns not related to the subject? Where there is a complicated pattern of interaction in class discussions, a diagram sketching lines of interaction can make larger patterns evident.

There's much more to observe in classroom talk: levels of address — is the teacher Mr. or Ms., the student John or Susan or "buddy"; levels of politeness — are requests by the teacher made using the polite or indirect forms that characterize relationships between relative equals ("Please take out your books!" "Can you add to what you've just said?") or are they the direct orders of a boss to a subordinate ("Open your books!" "That's not a complete answer, keep going!")? Of course, tone of voice is as important here as the actual words spoken.

The positioning of the participants in this communicative act is also important. Is the teacher always at the front of the room, with some students off in the distant rear? Does the teacher always address the whole group (even when calling on an individual student to "perform"), or does the teacher walk around and exchange ideas with individuals? Are students encouraged to talk to one another, and do seating arrangements support or inhibit such interaction?

How would you finally characterize the talk in this classroom? Do the patterns of classroom discourse connect in identifiable ways to other aspects of classroom culture?

Specific ethnographic activities

- Think of yourself as a kind of archaeologist on a dig. Examine and list the artifacts in the classroom, the pictures and posters, books, plants, papers, notes, etc. Then speculate about what these artifacts reveal about cultural perspective in your classroom. You might also think about the tasks assigned, the texts of both reading and writing, as artifacts that give clues to the cultural perspective of the group.

- Observe the ways in which the blackboard is used in the classroom

you are observing, or the ways in which you as a teacher use the
blackboard. What gets written on the blackboard? Whose words are
recorded here? How are these words used in the developing lesson?

- Record an exchange of ideas in the classroom. Observe how an
individual develops a sequence of thoughts, and how the teacher
and other students add, expand, contribute. Can you follow the
building of thought, the negotiation of meaning? (Do the arrangements of time and space that you described earlier support this
activity?)
- Look at a week's assignments for the class. Describe their relationship
to one another. Do they build on one another to create a larger
understanding at end than at beginning? Is there a sense of movement? Of seeing and reseeing?
- Interview the teacher about her or his general teaching philosophy
(or, if you are the teacher, describe your own), including how he/she
defines learning, sees it as best supported in the classroom, responds
to cultural or other differences.
- Interview a student, or several students, to get their sense of what
this class is like, of what seems to be going on here for them.
(Teachers might ask their own students to pause near the end of
class and recount what they thought and how they felt about various
parts of the lesson.) Or ask how they feel about school and the
ways that time is spent there in general.
- Write a brief vignette, recounting a particular episode that seems to
characterize life in the classroom you're observing. To what degree
does this vignette demonstrate the teacher's stated philosophy?
- Make a list of texts included in the classroom you observe. Are
these texts all from the traditional canon of Western literature, or
does the list include lesser-known writers, writers from a variety
of ethnic and cultural backgrounds, and women? How is the list
determined — by a school or department curriculum, by teacher or
student interest, by what's in the book room? In what ways would
you refine the list for this class and why? How would you do so
within the particular constraints governing the curriculum of this
classroom?

Completing the ethnography

You've been working as an ethnographer, observing and participating
in a classroom culture, taking notes on what you learn, reflecting on
your observations and on yourself as an observer, looking for larger
patterns of meaning in the details you see. As a first step toward a final
ethnographic account of this classroom, read through all of your notes,
looking for patterns of behavior or thinking. Consider physical details
of the school and classroom as a way of talking about the culture of the
classroom group. Describe the students — how they interact with one

another and the teacher. Describe the teacher's movements and inter-actions. Describe the classroom discourse—the exchanges of students and teachers. Look now for the generalities as well as the particulars that will help your readers understand the environment you describe.

In the following fragment of an ethnography, Jennifer begins with a physical description of the town and the school. Notice that the de-scription is not objective, but instead clearly asserts Jennifer's opinion of the particular school and probably something about her own memories of school experiences as a student. Her connection of experience to observation will lead her to find patterns that link what she sees inside the classroom to what she sees outside it.

> Sara lives in a predominantly white, upper-midde-class community. Its entire area covers only one square mile—everyone knows each other. If someone is engaged, or pregnant, or is getting a divorce, chances are that the whole town will know about it before the ink dries on the weekly edition of the *Sun Transcript*. This kind of intimacy is seen by some as quaint, but sometimes it can be downright annoying.
>
> The high school is like a smaller version of the community at large. The same people, with the exception of a few minor changes, have taught in the system for years. Unfortunately, this means that the same problems exist in the system now as did fifteen years ago, the chief one being a lack of emphasis on academic performance in favor of financing athletics.
>
> The classroom has the traditional seating of five rows, each con-taining five seats. The teacher stands in front, going over assignments and presenting new ones. Students respond when called on, and most follow along with the teacher. But there are never any follow-up questions or discussion with the teacher about a particular response to an assignment. There is just a right or wrong answer, which is accepted by the entire class with no real exchanges between teacher and students or among students. Learning in this classroom is an individual, isolated process that is not shared with others.

As Jennifer continues her ethnography, and as she moves on, in her case study, to observe a particular student in this classroom, she will draw on the patterns that begin to emerge in this initial description.

Strategies for unit 2—literacy and the learner

The strategies for this unit are again of two types: *reflections* that focus on your past experiences of learning and literacy, on your present processes as a reader and writer, and on your responses to your ongoing observations of learners and their literacy behaviors in a classroom; and a *formal case study* of an individual learner. Reading and writing, studying language and literature, are ways of perceiving and representing and making sense of the world and of our relationships to it. And so these strategies ask you to observe yourself and other learners in these acts of meaning making.

Reflections

- Try to remember your own earliest experiences with literacy. How were reading and writing used in your home and community, by the adults around you? What kinds of activities around reading and writing were you involved in before you went to school? Do you remember a discrete moment when you actually "learned to read," or did you just somehow find yourself to be a reader? Did your school experiences complement and build on your home experiences with reading and writing, or did they depart radically from what you'd been doing before? (You might also want to ask family members about their memories.)

- What do you remember of the explicit instruction you received in grammar? Did this instruction take place only in school, or were rules about appropriate language use discussed in your home? What have you perceived as your worst grammatical problem? How did you learn about it? Did the explicit instruction you received help you to understand it? To change it? (Has it changed?) Do you see grammar and its teaching differently after reading Chapter 5?

- How is grammar treated in a classroom you're observing or teaching in? Is it a separate subject in the curriculum or is it integrated into other areas of language study — reading, writing, communicating? How is students' knowledge in this area measured? Why do you think grammar is approached in the way it is here, and how effective do you find this approach to be?

- Describe your writing process for a paper you're writing now or have written recently for any course. How do you begin? How much time do you take? Do you write notes? Talk to people? Begin to write paragraphs immediately? How long does it take you to make a draft, start to finish? How much do you revise? How do you do it? (To discover more about your process, you might either talk into a tape recorder as you write or make notes about what you've been doing immediately after you write.) Do you think your process varies significantly with the type of writing you're doing? With how involved you are in learning something through the writing?

- Note the ways in which writing is used in the classroom you're observing/teaching in. Look back through your earlier notes to see ongoing patterns, and then characterize the uses of writing and the principles you think inform such uses.

- Choose a few paragraphs from an article or book you're reading and closely monitor your reading process. Where do you pause, hesitate, circle back to earlier statements in the article? Do you land on particular words? Which? Where do other, related ideas come to mind? Are there points at which you find yourself standing outside the text and agreeing or disagreeing with it? Do you find yourself predicting what will come next? Are your expectations always met, or are you sometimes surprised? Did you ever make errors in your first, quick reading of a word? If so, at what point did you catch such a miscue? What was it and what led you to realize that you had misread? Do you think you are a fluent reader of these paragraphs? Then summarize what you've learned.
- Having looked closely at both your writing process and your reading process, do you see any parallels between the two?
- What kinds of discussions take place around reading in your classroom? How is shared knowledge established? What role does writing play in relationship to reading? In what ways are students encouraged to become active readers and interpreters of texts?
- Having re-created or observed your own writing process as you worked on a paper, what metaphor would you now use to represent that process? In Chapter 6, Tricia talks about her journal writing using a metaphor from Joan Didion—gathering "the pieces of the mind's strings too short to use." Valerie compares her process to swimming: ideas "float and drift" as she plans and revises. Having re-created or observed your writing process as you worked on a paper, find a metaphor of your own that explains something about the process you go through when you write. What does the metaphor help you see that you might not have seen without it? Here's a bit of one student's reflections on the metaphor she's found to describe her process:

> I've done this exercise in the past. Some of the metaphors I came up with before include my writing process as skiing or spring cleaning. I decided I would give it some thought and came up with a new one. Recently I gave a dinner party, and as I went through the process of planning, setting up, and executing, I realized I had found another metaphor for my writing process.
>
> The beginning stages of planning this party and especially the feelings that I had—thinking about it for awhile and then jotting down ideas—were a lot like what I do to write. But the main thing, even from the very beginning, was the hope that everything would be perfect, and what if it wasn't? I couldn't believe I was feeling the same type of anxieties for both activities. (Diane)

- Try Ann Berthoff's exercise of observing and describing an object for ten minutes each day over the period of a week. How does the repetition of this act of seeing change what you see?

Case study

We suggest you focus on a particular student in the classroom in which you've been teaching or observing and participating. Make notes in your journal as you observe the student in interactions with peers, with you, or with a cooperating teacher, and as you observe the student's reading and writing behaviors. Think about questions you'll want to ask her about her composing and reading processes. And collect samples of her writing. Take time to form your own picture of this student as a learner before discussing her with other teachers or a cooperating teacher.

While the case study focuses in closely on one learner rather than taking the broad view of the ethnography, the picture you gain from this one representative of this classroom world will help you understand more about that world. And, in turn, what you've learned about a classroom culture will help you see the ways in which the individual student is shaped by it as well as how she shapes it.

Working toward the case study

Once you've chosen a student, reflect on why you chose that particular learner — what attracted your attention, and what, in your own experience, might have made this student interesting to you. Again, it's important to consider how your own subjective perspective shapes what you see.

The student you choose is an individual learner who brings his own background and expectations to this classroom. But he's also a participant in the classroom context which you've already described. And so he'll have particular ways of responding to that context that will both illuminate things you've described about it and tell you, insofar as his ways are different from those of other learners, more about him. And, to the extent that you begin to see the world of the classroom through his eyes, you'll come to see your own teaching, or that of a cooperating teacher, from a new perspective.

Jennifer begins her case study of an eleventh-grade English student by placing her within the context of her ethnographic observations of the town and the school.

> Sara, like most of the people in the town, has lived there all of her life. She is in her junior year at the high school. Her mother works for the local congressman, as Sara will tell anyone with a great deal of pride. Her sister goes to college in California.
>
> Sara does fairly well in school. In addition to her classes, she is a member of the varsity basketball team. She is also starting a new part time job at a clothing store in Boston. After high school, Sara hopes to go to Springfield College, where she can study to become a physical therapist.
>
> English is Sara's first class of the day. She sits in the exact center of the classroom, which has the traditional seating of five rows, each

containing five seats. Although she sits directly in front of the teacher, I've only seen Sara speak to her on a few rare occasions. At times she seems restless, periodically shifting positions in her seat. Sara does, however, make frequent eye contact with the teacher, a sign that perhaps there is more going on behind her eyes than in front of mine.

Jennifer goes on to observe Sara's classroom behavior and to study examples of her reflexive and extensive writing. Throughout Jennifer's discussion of Sara's learning, she emphasizes Sara's underlying competence, a competence that is not fully demonstrated in the classroom, where she tends to remain silent except for a one-time occasion of collaboration with her peers in the library. The theoretical framework established by Emig's study of the compositing process gives Jennifer a way of reinterpreting what she sees in the work of this successful but quiet student. Emig's distinction between reflexive or self-sponsored writing and extensive or school-sponsored writing suggests, to Jennifer, that she should discover more about Sara's nonschool writing practices as well as about her reading. What Jennifer discovers is that the quiet, seemingly passive learner in the classroom is much more active outside, not only writing on her own, but taking risks with her writing that she doesn't take in writing or speaking in shcool.

Specific case-study activities
- Look at a sample of your case-study student's writing. What is your initial response to this piece of writing? What rhetorical strengths does he have? What systematic assumptions about grammar, style, usage, conventions of written texts can you see in this piece of writing? Do you recognize features of his spoken language in this written text? Features of standard school discourse? As a teacher, are there new understandings about language that you'd want to work on with this student, based on what you see here?
- Interview your case-study student about her reading and writing processes. What picture of her as a reader, writer, learner do you get from this interview? How does this picture compare to the picture you've gotten from observing and working with her in the classroom? From looking at her writing?
- Compare what you've observed/learned about your case-study student as a writer and as a reader. Are there common pattern to how he approaches these two activities? How would you use reading and writing to support this student's overall development as a learner?
- Have you had an opportunity to observed this student in imaginative, problem-solving activities? If so, what sorts of strategies does she use to try to see things in new ways? Does she talk or write toward new understandings? Does she compare situations or compare per-

spectives? Does she keep reseeing and seeing? Does she play with forms, with words? Does she invent new possibilities?

Completing the case study
Each learner who comes into the classroom can be seen from a number of the perspectives of this unit — as a speaker, a reader, a writer, a listener, a member of a classroom community and a larger community. Complete your case study of a student, drawing on your observations, your study of the student's writing, your interview with the student, discussions with another teacher or counselor — on all of the data you've been able to collect in the last several weeks. How would you characterize this student as a learner? What leads you to make this characterization? What circumstances seem to foster this student's active engagement and best work? How would you further support this student's learning? What would you do next, and why?

Strategies for unit 3 — theory into practice

As we move in this unit into the practical implications of what we've been exploring in the first two units, we move as well into strategies that will involve readers as group members as well as individuals. The strategies for this unit again include *reflections* — this time on aspects of classroom structure and teaching practice — and a *more formal activity* — the design of a blueprint for teaching. But this time they include as well a set of *group activities* that are designed to help readers who are engaged in learning with others to try out some of the collaborative learning that this unit recommends. The group activities that conclude this set of strategies are taken from ideas that have come from all the chapters in the book. Of course, group work can be a provocative way to challenge your thinking in any of the reflections and responses you may have been writing. But the activities singled out here for group work are ones we've used with groups in our own classes to establish and support a community of learners.

Reflections

- Write about a time that you felt you really took responsibility for your own learning. How did you proceed? What did you learn about yourself as a learner? What might be the implications for your own classroom?
- Look back on your own experience as a student, and think of one teacher who provides a model for your own teaching. What do you most remember about this teacher? What aspects of this modeling would you draw on, what would you reject? What do you think this teacher's philosophy of teaching would have been, and how

was that reflected in the classes you remember? How would you describe the teacher's role? Hepsie remembers one such teacher:

> My teacher in eleventh-grade English, Martha Ellison, was a listener. When a student talked, Mrs. Ellison not only heard the student through but found a way to connect it to her own thinking. Everybody wanted to talk in that class because they knew their ideas somehow mattered. And we wanted to hear her stories. She answered questions about racism in terms of her husband's high school football team, composed of black and white players who won because they worked together. When we read *Great Expectations* she'd tell us about her little town in western Kentucky and how she felt as a teenager when she came to the big city of Louisville and had to lose "my country ways." Our class made sense out of what we read in our own terms. In Mrs. Ellison's class, we diagrammed sentences, we read aloud, we memorized and recited poems — all sort of old-fashioned activities, even then, none of them in themselves very innovative or interactive. We also wrote nearly every day, met in groups, conducted research, took trips. And always we talked, and she listened. We laughed a lot. Mrs. Ellison's philosophy, as I infer it now, was to make students feel valued. Now, years beyond eleventh grade, I realize that I model my teaching and learning after her. I learned from her that it's not activities that determine the teacher's role in the classroom, it's the stance toward learning and the learner that can make any activity meaningful. And it's knowing how to laugh.

Ellie remembers another:

> My eleventh-grade English teacher was seen as a tyrant by many of his students. As he wandered up and down the aisles of the classroom, roaring at them and spraying spittle into their faces, and as he carried on to the whole class about who had done well on a recent essay or test and who had not, he seemed to embody the worst of what a teacher could be. As he dictated rules of grammar and usage and definitions of terms like "tautology" for us to copy into notebooks, his methods seemed, even then, designed to destroy any interest in learning. He taught to the test — in this case the English Achievement section of the College Board Exam — and our scores on that exam, which we were all required to take in the spring of our junior year, provided his whole measure of our learning, his whole basis for evaluating his own success as a teacher. Those of us who scored well became his elite — a terrible fate that evoked the rest of the school's loud and public disdain of "brains." Those who did not were disdained in the classroom by the teacher. The lucky students whose scores fell in the middle could relax — they would be ignored both in the school and in the classroom.
>
> But "Dirty John," as he was known to generations of students, made us write. Each day, when we entered the classroom, we would write for ten minutes or so in response to a quotation or

question or thought for the day. Each evening we would write a
short essay in response to a reading assignment. Each week we
would write a long formal paper about literature. "The characters
in Thomas Hardy's novels are 'characters of conceptual origin'—
prove or disprove." And each week he would read the best and
worst of these papers to the class. "Brains" got to do even more
writing, because the only way to keep from being harassed by the
other students was to take on writing their out-of-class papers as
well—but with just the right sorts of problems or errors or
omissions to earn the undistinguished "C."

For my first college essay I was to write about a high school
teacher, and I chose "Dirty John." We had studied *A Tale of Two
Cities* with him, and I began by saying that "He was the best of
teachers. He was the worst of teachers." My college instructor
found that "trite." But this teacher had been both the worst and
the best in many of the violent and contradictory ways that
Dickens' words could suggest. And I came away convinced that
you don't learn about tautology by memorizing a definition, but
that you learn about writing by writing.

- Most lessons are like first drafts of a piece of writing. Even
where a teacher has taught the same subject many times, it will be
different with this group of learners. In Chapter 9, one experienced
teacher, John, talks of trying "to always feel like a first-year teacher,"
trying things out for the first time. Describe one lesson you have
observed or taught recently. What was the teacher's role? Why do
you think the teacher chose to teach this lesson in this way in this
classroom context? What other approaches might the teacher have
used? What revisions would you make in the lesson to teach it over
again with these particular students?
- Describe the curriculum (both explicit, if it's been stated in documents
or by the teacher, and implicit) of your school system or the classroom
you've been observing. If it were entirely up to you, what would
you choose to maintain and what would you change about this
curriculum and why? Where would you shift emphasis? Would you
make changes because you disagree with the curricular goals or
because you see other ways to accomplish these goals?
- Reflect on one of your own teaching plans in relation to the goal of
reinventing the curriculum. What would you see as the goals of a
reinvented curriculum? How might your lesson work toward those
goals? How could you alter it to have it do so more explicitly?

Group activities

The first activity serves as a good (and fun) introduction to group
process and helps to shape group dynamics. Such exercises can prepare
students to work together constructively. And reflecting on group
dynamics can help groups use and alter those dynamics—to draw on

the talents of a natural spokesperson or to rotate recording responsibilities so that everyone will take a turn. Mystery solving can then serve as a model for many other tasks, particularly for group research projects in which students ask questions about things they don't understand, search out and collect "clues" or data, and pull that data together to discover patterns and come up with findings to present to the class.

221 Baker Street

In this game, players emulate the famous Sherlock Holmes, trying to solve a mystery from a set of clues. One such mystery is "The Adventure of Silver Patch":

> Yesterday morning, the famous thoroughbred horse, Silver Patch, and his trainer, Oscar Swift, were found dead in the horse's stall at the Cosgrove Stables.
>
> The horse had been poisoned; and the trainer had been hit over the head and stabbed repeatedly with a sharp object.
>
> Silver Patch, so named for the patch of silver hair on his mane, was owned by Sir Reginald Cosgrove, a breeder who also owns four other horses.
>
> Persons routinely questioned by Inspector Gregson of Scotland Yard include Sir Reginald Cosgrove and his petite wife, Madame Hilda Cosgrove; the Cosgroves' cook, Mrs. Maggie Doan; Mrs. Doan's husband, house painter Henry Doan; and rival horse breeder Sir Archibald Baxter. Scotland Yard is also looking for one Bobby Jansen, a stable boy who left the Cosgroves' employ unhappily about a month ago.
>
> The only clues discovered at the scene of the crime were some broken pieces of glass from the bottom of an ale bottle, and a pawn-broker's ticket.
>
> Unable to develop a solid lead, Inspector Gregson has come to 221 Baker Street to consult with the master sleuth. Gregson wants to know
>
> a) who killed the horse and the trainer,
> b) the weapon used to kill the trainer,
> c) the motive.

To begin to solve this mystery, form new groups (not familiar ones that you've been working in all semester). Then distribute the following clues randomly to group members.

Clues:
1. The floor of Silver Patch's stall contained some fresh black paint.
2. Sir Reginald Cosgrove had a large insurance policy on his prize horse, Silver Patch.
3. Weapon Clue — Part III
      Rhymes with throttle.
4. Killer Clue — Part II
      An arrangement of fruit trees.

5. Some fresh silver paint was found on the stall floor of Night Dancer, another of Sir Reginald's horses.
6. Motive Clue — Part II
   Another word for positive or certain.
7. Motive Clue — Part I
   The opposite of out.
8. Motive Clue — Part III
   Creatures that love picnics.
9. Killer Clue — Part I
   Something that produces an effect.
10. The pawnbroker's ticket at the scene of the crime belonged to Sir Reginald Cosgrove.
11. Footprints at the stables show that the killer wore a size 12 shoe.
12. Weapon Clue — Part I
    When you have no money, you're flat——.
13. Weapon Clue — Part II
    The alphabet letter after M.
14. Bobby Jansen is not working at the locksmith shop.
15. Sir Reginald would never kill his prize horse, Silver Patch.

Each member of the group must hold on to the clues and read them aloud to other group members. (The point is to solve the mystery through group talk, to which all must contribute, rather than by passing all of the clues to one person.)

When you've solved the mystery, reflect back on your group process. How did you work together to find a solution? What roles did individuals take in contributing to the solution? How did members of the group arrive at consensus?

Trivial literacy — a new game
The popularity of Hirsch's "literacy list" reminds us of Mr. Gradgrind, the head of the school in Charles Dickens' novel *Hard Times*, who valued facts above everything else. The aim of this game is to illustrate something about facts — in fact, the crucial thing about them, which is how facts get shared and valued.

In your small group, find a group of terms or words from Hirsch's literacy list, or from the dictionary, or from a health book, or from a standard high school vocabulary book — any list of terms or concepts will do. (*The Greywolf Annual Five: Multicultural Literacy* is a list that provides an alternative to Hirsch, with terms drawn from lots of strands of various cultures.) Now read through the list and mark every word you don't know the meaning of. In your group, read your list aloud and try to discover the meanings of the words you don't know from other members of the group. Finally, talk with other groups in the class and try to find the meanings for words your group has not recognized. Agree on the meanings for the words that remain (if there are any).

You'll have put into action the process of making knowledge. It occurs informally, in conversation, collaboratively, in context, and with clues and cues to guide it. In your journal, comment on the process of sharing knowledge that you participated in with this exercise. Include such points as:

how we move from not knowing to knowing
how the group negotiates with one another
how individual modifies response
how individual and group responses build upon associations of group

What kind of list would you come up with of things you think all culturally literate people should know? Would the list be really long or really short? For just one letter in the alphabet, try to make a list with a classroom group.

Build your vocabulary, and amaze your friends
Find a word you know is esoteric (maybe esoteric is a good one). Deliberately use it in a group of friends of varying degrees of intimacy to you. Watch what happens. How many will look the word up in the dictionary? How many will ask you? one another? How many will try to figure out the word from context? How many later use the word themselves?

Parts-of-speech scramble
Cut up sentences into individual words, scramble them, and distribute them to groups. (Ellie uses the cardboard tiles from her daughter's Sentence Scrabble for Juniors game.) These sets of words can be used to make real sentences or nonsense sentences (with scores for the number of sentences generated or the number of words used). And seeing which words can substitute for others in particular slots allows you to establish categories of words according to their functions, generating a functional picture of parts of speech.

Read and respond
Read and discuss the following student paper:

> In this paper I will compare and contrast two cities, Boston and Los Angeles in weather, historical and in a sports sense. First will be the city of Boston.
> The weather in Boston is unique, for it is made up of four different seasons. The first I will talk about is summer, which are long hot humid days.
> Then comes the fall, which shows off the foliage and natural beauty

of Boston. Fall has warm days and cool nights. During the fall season
we have many hot and humid days and cool night which we call
Indian Summer. This can occur anytime up and including September
to December. One year we had warm days just before Christmas.

The next season that happens is winter, which has short cold days
and nights and usually a lot of rain, sleet, ice and snowy days during
this season of winter.

Last but not least is the spring which have mild days and cool
nights. Spring is the time our trees start to bud and our flower start to
pop their heads out of the ground.

Next the City of Boston in historical sense. Boston is the birthplace
of Independence of the United States, the place of the Boston Tea
Party, where Bostonians dumped tons of English tea into Boston
Harbor to protest the tax on tea. We have the oldest ship in the U.S.
Navy, called Old-Ironside U.S.S. Constitution. Also the historic Boston
Garden, where many great thing happen other than in a sports sense.

Finally the City of Boston in a sports sense. We start first with the
greatest sports dynasty in the World, the Boston Celtics, which best
emphasis the Boston working class in that they accomplish all their
feats by hard work. This team has been called a blue collar team just
like the working class of Boston.

Next is the Boston Bruins who are just like the Celtics in their
work ethic and another good example of Bostons' work like society.

Now I will talk about the City of Los Angeles. The weather which
is always consistently warm, drier days and cool nights with the
temperature in the 70's to 80's and because of this combination there is
a smog problem in Los Angeles. The rainfall is 10 inches or less a year.
Hardly any snow around this area.

The City of Los Angeles in a historical view has the oldest mission
in the United States. Also it is where many of the famous classic
movies were made, like Gone with the Wind, and the Wizard of Oz.
This was the focus of the Spanish American War when the United
States wanted to extend it's boundaries to the Pacific Ocean. Another
historical event was during World War II the putting of Japanese-
Americans into interment camps.

Finally the City of Los Angeles in a sports sense You would have
to start with probably the second greatest basketball franchise in the
history of basketball, the L.A. Lakers, whose style is fitted perfectly
for the style of the people of Los Angeles. The Lakers image is that of
glamour and everything they do is like it's a show rather than playing
the game the way it should be played.

They played it like there laid-back and there seems to be an atmosphere of no concern. Their teams play just like the fans or the working
class out in Los Angeles.

So this is my compare and contrast paper of two cities, Boston and
Los Angeles.

Are there any places where this writing begins to come alive, to become
more than the plodding, step-by-step filling out of the form? If you

could free this student from the three points per city format and support him in finding meaningful (to him) differences between the two cities — differences that might lead him toward a larger understanding — what would you suggest that he do next?

Read and respond to the following teaching strategy:

This lesson is designed for an advanced ESL class at the high school level. It serves as the third and concluding part of a short unit on assimilation. This unit could be part of a larger curricular unit on the history of immigration in the United States. It would tie in current issues for immigrants with an examination of past immigrant experiences.

The first lesson of this unit will present excerpts from *Hunger of Memory* by Richard Rodriguez. This is a well-known autobiographical work by an immigrant who believes in the importance of assimilating into the mainstream culture. The second lesson will present a short story in which the author expresses the view that becoming part of the mainstream means "selling out" and denying one's own culture. The final lesson will examine a variety of other views on assimilation and conclude the unit.

My goals are to have students realize that assimilation is and always has been an issue for many immigrants. They may have been consciously or unconsciously grappling with the issue themselves and may be able to relate to some of the experiences of other immigrants they read about. They will be able to pinpoint and discuss the different conflicts and consequences involved and be aware of where they stand on the issue (for now). They will also increase their vocabulary, reading comprehension, and ability to express themselves in English.

I will first hand out the sheet entitled "To melt or not to melt" and elicit information about the significance of the title and the idea of America as melting pot. We will then look at the line graph which has "complete assimilation" at one end, and "complete maintenance of culture" at the other end. We will determine where the readings covered in the two previous lessons might fall on the spectrum, and discuss where they think most immigrants might fall on the spectrum.

The students will then write down what they think the possible consequences (advantages, disadvantages, or otherwise) of the viewpoints at both ends of the graph might be. I will emphasize at this point that we are examining the issue as two opposing viewpoints for the purposes of comparison, and that we will later discuss the "middle ground." The class will then share what they have written.

The class will then be asked to read a series of five autobiographical excerpts that represent a variety of experiences and opinions on assimilation. After reading each one, they will be asked to note down what the areas of concern/conflict were for each person. We will then discuss each case as a class, deciding a) what the concerns or conflicts were, b) how they decided to deal with these concerns or conflicts, and c) where we might place them on the graph.

This lesson will allow for practice in reading, writing, and speaking skills. A relevant issue such as this will lead to interested reading, meaningful writing, and active participation in discussion. Having students write down some of what will be later shared with the class will make class participation easier for the more timid students. The graph and the listing of the two opposing viewpoints will clarify the issues in a concrete manner, while the autobiographical sketches will show that individual experiences differ greatly, and the middle ground is very wide.

The success of the lesson will be evaluated by the discussion in class, and the students' reaction to the readings and the follow up assignment. The students will be evaluated by their oral participation and by their written work.

The next lesson (or assignment) would be to write an autobiographical piece of their own experiences relating to assimilation. After the revision process (and with their permission) these would then be typed up and used as a text for reading and discussion. (Tracey)

The lesson is contained within a three-part curricular sequence. What principles of sequencing do you find represented here? What else would you want to know if you were going to teach this particular lesson? What parts of the plan do you particularly like and why? What parts might you change and why?

Ideas in motion: blueprints for the classroom

Think of a sequence of connected teaching/learning events focusing on language, reading, and writing organically connected by your developing ideas of how to foster literacy. The design you come up with will be a plan—a blueprint for action—in your classroom.

As you plan to put your ideas into action in this blueprint, keep in mind the principles we've been discussing in this book—nurturing active learning, integrating reading and writing (and speaking and listening), connecting the known to the unknown (eliciting and building shared knowledge), using language in meaningful contexts. And keep in mind that a blueprint is only a suggestion, a dynamic rather than static plan—one that gets altered and refined by clientele and environmental conditions.

In making this blueprint for a lesson in a classroom you might be working in, what aspects of that classroom and curricular context must you consider? What constraints of coverage, of textbooks, of tests, of tracks, and of present classroom practices determine the nature of this lesson, and how does your lesson work within them or try to move beyond them? In preparing a lesson for the teaching seminar or pre-practice class, where you're able to invent a larger curricular context and create a lesson within it, what is that context and how does it allow you to proceed differently?

Here are some questions to think about as you design your teaching plan. (These questions could provide a formal for a formal lesson plan if such a plan is required of you where you teach.)

1. Where would this lesson fit in the larger curriculum and course goals? (You should identify the group — year and background — for whom the lesson is intended. And describe briefly the larger curricular unit that it might fit into, as well as the intersecting pieces of this particular set of lessons.)
2. What are your goals for this lesson?
3. How will you meet these goals in the lesson? (What will you do?)
4. Why will you do it this way?
5. How will you evaluate the success of the lesson? The progress of the students?
6. What would you do next and why?

If you have the opportunity to teach this lesson to a class, reflect back on that experience, considering both the ways in which you feel it was successful, and the ways in which you would alter it if you were to teach it again to a similar group.

We offer the following general suggestions based on our past experience with such blueprints for lessons and their realization in the classroom.

1. Plan a lesson that you feel reasonably comfortable with. We all have particular personal characteristics we bring into the classroom, and we have to work within them to some degree (though we can expand our repertoire over time). In what circumstances do you feel most comfortable, effective, open to others? To what extent can you create these circumstances with your lesson?
2. Your plan will be logically organized, and you should be able to move through it logically. But the learners are also participants in this lesson, and they'll help to shape it as well. Try to leave room for student connections, associations, that you couldn't have anticipated beforehand.
3. Ask real questions that push students' thinking, not just those that elicit a one- or two-word, fill-in-the-blank response. It's all right to admit your own ignorance and to learn with your students. And some silence, in which people are thinking, supports learning.
4. You'll have decided, in your blueprint, how this lesson fits with what has gone before and what will come after. But the students need these connections as well. Remind them of where today's work fits in the larger context of their ongoing work, and help them to activate the "schemata" that they carry from previous lessons so they can build on them here.

5. Remember that you want your students to find their own authority as they read and write and speak. Use your authority as a teacher to help them to build theirs.

Designing blueprints for teaching can often be done most effectively in groups, collaboratively, or in team teaching. Working in groups, consider ways to structure students' learning from one activity or area of study to another. Each of you, as teachers, will have different styles and personas. From what you know of your own style, of the ways in which you're most comfortable doing things and elicit the most interest and cooperation from others, how will you approach your teaching? How can you structure your lesson to take into account both your own personality and ways of interacting easily, and your students' need to share responsibility and be constructively engaged in the lesson?

Finally, consider how the lesson might begin to work to reinvent curriculum in the school where you teach or observe. Does it bring in larger issues, problematize them, help students see them in new ways? Can it lead to interdisciplinary and collaborative efforts? Might it begin to move the members of this class toward critical thought and action?

BIBLIOGRAPHY

Angelou, Maya. *I Know Why the Caged Bird Sings.* 1970. New York: Bantam, 1971.

Applebee, Arthur. *Writing in the Secondary School: English and the Content Areas.* NCTE Research Report 21. Urbana, IL: National Council of Teachers of English, 1981.

Aristotle. *The Rhetoric.* Trans. W. Rhys Roberts and Ingram Bywater. New York: Modern Library—Random House, 1954.

Ashton-Warner, Sylvia. *Teacher.* New York: Bantam, 1963.

Atwell, Nancy. *In the Middle: Writing, Reading, and Learning with Adolescents.* Portsmouth, NH: Boynton/Cook, 1987.

Bartholomae, David, and Anthony Petrosky, eds. *Facts, Artifacts and Counterfacts: Theory and Method for a Reading and Writing Course.* Portsmouth, NH: Boynton/Cook, 1986.

Belenky, Mary Field, Blythe McVicker Clinchy, Nancy Rule Goldberger, and Jill Mattuck Tarule. *Women's Ways of Knowing: The Development of Self, Voice, and Mind.* New York: Basic Books, 1986.

Bereiter, Carl, and Siegfried Englemann. *Teaching Disadvantaged Children in the Preschool.* Englewood Cliffs, NJ: Prentice Hall, 1966.

Bernstein, Basil. "Language and Social Class." *British Journal of Sociology* 11 (1960). 271–276.

———. "Social Class, Language, and Socialization." *Language and Social Context.* Ed. Pier P. Giglioli. New York: Penguin, 1972.

———. "A Sociolinguistic Approach to Socialization: With Some Reference to Educability." *Language and Poverty: Perspectives of a Theme.* Ed. Frederick Williams. Madison, WI: Institute for Research on Policy, 1970. 25–61.

Berthoff, Ann E. *Forming/Thinking/Writing: The Composing Imagination.* 1978. Portsmouth, NH: Boynton/Cook, 1982.

——— *The Making of Meaning: Metaphors, Models, and Maxims for Writing Teachers.* Portsmouth, NH: Boynton/Cook, 1981.

———, ed. *Reclaiming the Imagination: Philosophical Perspective for Writers and Teachers of Writing.* Portsmouth, NH: Boynton/Cook, 1984.

Boynton, Percy. *Principles of Composition.* Boston: Athenaeum, 1915.

Britton, James. *Language and Learning.* Miami, OH: University of Miami Press. 1970.

———. *Prospect and Retrospect: Selected Essays.* Ed. Gordon M. Pradl. Portsmouth, NH: Heinemann, 1982.

Britton, James, Tony Burgess, Nancy Martin, Alex McLeod, and Harold Rosen. *The Development of Writing Abilities (11–18).* London: Macmillan Education, 1975.

Bronowski, Jacob. *The Origins of Knowledge and the Imagination.* Silliman Lecture Series. New Haven: Yale University Press, 1978.

Bruffee, Kenneth. "Collaboration and the Conversation of Mankind." *College English* 46 (November 1984). 635–652.

Bruner, Jerome. *Actual Minds, Possible Worlds.* Cambridge: Harvard University Press, 1986.

———. *In Search of Mind.* New York: Harper & Row, 1983.

———. *On Knowing: Essays for the Left Hand.* Cambridge: Harvard University Press, 1979.

———. *The Process of Education.* Cambridge: Harvard University Press. 1965.

———. "State of the Child." *New York Review of Books* 27 October 1983. 84–89.

Burke, Kenneth. *Counter-Statement.* 1931. Berkeley: University of California Press, 1968.

Carnegie Forum on Education and the Economy. *A Nation Prepared: Teachers for the 21st Century.* New York: Carnegie Commission, 1986.

Carroll, Joyce. "Reader Response and a Pedagogy That Informs Reading and Teaching Practice." Thesis. UMass/Boston, 1989.

Cazden, Courtney B. *Classroom Discourse: The Language of Teaching and Learning,* Portsmouth, NH: Heinemann, 1988.

Chall, Jeanne S. *Learning to Read: The Great Debate.* New York: McGraw-Hill, 1970.

Chomsky, Noam. *Knowledge of Language: Its Nature, Origin and Use.* New York: Praeger, 1986.

Coleridge, Samuel Taylor. *Biographia Literaria.* Ed. J. Shawcross. Oxford: Clarendon, 1907.

Conroy, Pat. *The Water Is Wide.* 1972. New York: Bantam, 1987.

Dellinger, Dixie. *Out of the Heart: How to Design Writing Assignments for High School Courses.* Berkeley: The National Writing Project, 1982.

Delpit, Lisa. "Skills and Other Dilemmas of a Progressive Black Educator." *Harvard Education Review* 56 (November 1986). 379–385.

Dennison, George. *The Lives of Children.* New York: Random House, 1970.

Dewey, John. *Experience and Nature.* New York: Dover, 1958.

Dickens, Charles. *Hard Times.* New York, Signet, 1961.

Duckworth, Eleanor, *The Having of Wonderful Ideas and Other Essays on Teaching and Learning.* New York: Teachers College Press, 1987.

Elbow, Peter. *Embracing Contraries: Explorations in Learning and Teaching.* New York: Oxford University Press, 1986.

———. *Writing with Power.* New York: Oxford University Press, 1981.

Emerson, Ralph Waldo. "The American Scholar." *Collected Works.* Ed. Robert Spiller. Cambridge: Harvard University Press, 1971.

Emig, Janet. *The Composing Processes of Twelfth Graders.* Urbana, IL: National Council of Teachers of English, 1971.

———. *The Web of Meaning: Essays on Writing, Teaching, Learning, and Thinking.*

Ed. Dixie Goswami and Maureen Butler. Portsmouth, NH: Boynton/ Cook, 1983.

Erickson, Frederick. "What Makes School Ethnography 'Ethnographic'?" *Anthropology and Education Quarterly* 15 (1984). 51–66.

Farb, Peter. *Word Play: What Happens When People Talk.* New York: Knopf, 1974.

Farrell, Thomas. "IQ and Standard English." *College Composition and Communication* 34 (December 1983). 470–484.

Finn, Chester E., and Diane Ravitch. *What Do Our 17 Year Olds Know?* New York: Harper & Row, 1987.

Fish, Stanley. *Is There a Text in This Class? The Authority of Interpretive Communities.* Cambridge: Harvard University Press, 1980.

Fishman, Andrea. *Amish Literacy: What and How It Means.* Portsmouth, NH: Heinemann, 1988.

Freire, Paulo. *Education for Critical Consciousness.* Trans. Myra B. Ramos. New York: Seabury, 1973.

———. *Pedagogy of the Oppressed.* Trans. Myra B. Ramos. New York: Continuum, 1969.

———. *The Politics of Education: Culture, Power, and Liberation.* South Hadley, MA: Bergin & Garvey, 1985.

Freire, Paulo, and Donaldo Macedo. *Literacy: Reading the Word and the World.* South Hadley, MA: Bergin & Garvey, 1988.

Frye, Northrop. *Anatomy of Criticism: Four Essays.* Princeton, NJ: Princeton University Press, 1957.

Gardner, Howard. *Art, Mind, and Brain: A Cognitive Approach to Creativity.* New York: Basic Books, 1982.

Geertz, Clifford. *Local Knowledge: Further Essays in Interpretive Anthropology.* New York. Basic Books, 1983.

Gelfant, Blanche. "Mingling and Sharing in American Literature: Teaching Ethnic Fiction." *College English* 43 (December 1981). 763–772.

Giroux, Henry A. Introduction. Freire, *Literacy.* N. pag.

———. Introduction. Freire. *The Politics of Education.* xi–xxv.

Goodlad, John. "Individuality, Commonality and Curricular Practice." *Individual Difference and the Common Curriculum.* Chicago: University of Chicago Press. 1983. 300–318.

———. *A Place Called School: Prospects for the Future.* New York: McGraw-Hill, 1984.

Goody, Jack, and Ian Watt. "The Consequences of Literacy." *Literacy in Traditional Societies.* Ed. Jack Goody. Cambridge: Cambridge University Press, 1968. 27–68.

Goswami, Dixie, and Peter Stillman, eds. *Reclaiming the Classroom: Teacher Research as an Agency for Change.* Portsmouth, NH: Boynton/Cook, 1987.

Graves, Donald H. *Writing: Teachers and Children at Work.* Portsmouth, NH: Heinemann, 1983.

Groden, Suzy, Eleanor Kutz, and Vivian Zamel. "Students as Ethnographers: Investigating Language Use as a Way to Learn to Use the Language." *The Writing Instructor* 6 (May 1987). 132–140.

Hakuta, Kenji. *Mirror of Language: The Debate on Bilingualism*. New York: Basic Books, 1987.

Hamilton, Edith, and Huntington Cairns, eds. *The Collected Dialogues of Plato*. Princeton: Princeton University Press, 1963.

Hartwell, Patrick. "Grammar, Grammars and the Teaching of Grammar." *College English* 47 (February 1985). 105–127.

———. "Creating a Literate Environment in Freshman English: Why and How." *Rhetoric Review* 6 (Fall 1987). 4–19.

Heath, Shirley Brice. *Ways with Words: Language, Life and Work in Communities and Classrooms*. Cambridge: Cambridge University Press, 1983.

"High School English Curriculum Objectives," Boston Public Schools, 1983.

Hillocks, George: *Research on Written Composition: New Directions for Teaching*. Urbana, IL: National Conference on Research in English, 1986.

Hirsch, E. D., Jr. *Cultural Literacy: What Every American Needs to Know*. Boston: Houghton Mifflin, 1987.

Iser, Wolfgang. *The Act of Reading*. Baltimore: Hopkins University Press, 1978.

Jackson, Jesse. "Common Sense and Common Ground." 1988 Democratic National Convention. Published in *Vital Speeches*, September 1989.

Kinneavy, James. *A Theory of Discourse*. Englewood Cliffs, NJ: Prentice-Hall, 1971.

Knoblauch, C. H., and Lil Brannon. *Rhetorical Traditions and the Teaching of Writing*. Portsmouth, NH: Boynton/Cook, 1984.

Koch, Kenneth. *Wishes, Lies and Dreams*. New York: Random House, 1970.

Kozol, Jonathan. *Death at an Early Age: The Destruction of the Hearts and Minds of Negro Children in the Boston Public Schools*. Boston: Houghton Mifflin, 1967.

Kutz, Eleanor. "Students' Language and Academic Discourse: Interlanguage as Middle Ground." *College English* 48 (April 1986). 385–396.

Labov, William. "Competing Value Systems for Students in Inner City Schools." *Children In and Out of School*. Ed. Perry Gilmore and Allen Glatthorn. Washington: Center for Applied Linguistics, 1982.

———. *Language in the Inner City: Studies in the Black English Vernacular*. Includes "The Logic of Nonstandard English." Philadelphia: University of Pennsylvania Press, 1972.

Lakoff, George, and Mark Johnson. *Metaphors We Live By*. Chicago: University of Chicago Press, 1980.

Langer, Susanne K. *Philosophy in a New Key: A Study in the Symbolism of Reason, Rite, and Art*. 3d ed. Cambridge: Harvard University Press, 1957.

Lederer, Richard. *Anguished English*. 1987. New York. Dell. 1989.

Litzinger, Boyd, and Joyce Carol Oates. *Story: Fiction Past and Present*. Lexington, MA: DC Heath, 1985.

Lourie, Dick, and Mark Pawlak, eds. *Smart Like Me: High School Age Writing from the Sixties to Now.* New York: Hanging Loose Press, 1989.

Luria, Alexander. *Cognitive Development: Its Cultural and Social Foundations.* Trans. Martin Lopez-Morillas and Lynn Solotaroff. Cambridge: Harvard University Press, 1976.

Macrorie, Ken. *Telling Writing.* New York: Hayden, 1970.

———. *Uptaught.* New York: Hayden, 1970.

Malcolm X. *The Autobiography of Malcolm X.* New York: Ballantine, 1973.

Marshall Paule. "Poets in the Kitchen." *The Borzoi College Reader.* Ed. Charles Muscatine and Marlene Griffith. New York: McGraw-Hill, 1988. 133–140.

Michaels, Sarah. "Sharing Time: Children's Narrative Styles and Differential Access to Literacy." *Language in Society* 10 (1981). 423–434.

Miller, George A., and Patricia Gildea. "How Children Learn Words." *Scientific American* 257.3 (1987). 94–99.

Moffett, James. *Student-Centered Language Arts and Reading, K–13.* Boston: Houghton Mifflin, 1983.

———. *Teaching the Universe of Discourse.* Boston: Houghton Mifflin, 1968.

Momaday, Scott. *The House Made of Dawn.* New York: Harper & Row, 1968.

Morrison, Toni. *Sula.* New York: Knopf, 1974.

Murray, Donald M. *A Writer Teaches Writing: A Practical Method of Teaching Composition.* Boston: Houghton Mifflin, 1968.

——— "Writing as Process: How Writing Finds Its Own Meaning." *Eight Approaches to Teaching Composition.* Ed. Timothy Donovan and Ben McClelland. Urbana, IL: National Council of Teachers of English, 1980.

Ogbu, John. "Literacy and Schooling in Subordinate Cultures: The Case of Black Americans." *Literacy in Historical Perspective.* Ed. Daniel P. Resnick. Washington: Library of Congress, 1983. 129–170.

Ohmann, Richard. *English in America: A Radical View of the Profession.* Oxford: Oxford University Press, 1976.

Oliver, Eileen. "An Afrocentric Approach to Literature: Putting the Pieces Back Together." *English Journal* 77 (September 1988). 49–53.

Perl, Sondra. "The Composing Processes of Unskilled College Writers." *Research in the Teaching of English* 13 (December 1979). 317–336.

Perl, Sondra, and Nancy Wilson. *Through Teachers' Eyes: Portraits of Writing Teachers at Work.* Portsmouth, NH: Heinemann, 1986.

Piaget, Jean. *The Language and Thought of the Child.* London: Routledge and Kegan Paul, 1959.

Ponsot, Marie, and Rosemary Deen. *Beat Not the Poor Desk.* Portsmouth, NH: Boynton/Cook, 1982.

Rettman, Bruce. "Growing in a Community of Writers." *Boston Writing Project Newsletter* 4 (November 1986). 1–5

Richards, I. A. *The Philosophy of Rhetoric.* New York: Oxford University Press, 1936.

Rodriguez, Richard. *The Hunger of Memory.* Boston: Godine, 1982.

Roemer, Marjorie. "Which Reader's Response?" *College English* 49 (December 1989). 911–921.

Rose, Mike. *Lives on the Boundary*. 1988. New York: Penguin, 1989.

———. *Writer's Block: The Cognitive Dimension*. Carbondale: Southern Illinois University Press, 1984.

Rosenblatt, Louise. *The Reader, the Text, the Poem*. Carbondale: Southern Illinois University Press, 1978.

Roskelly, Hephzibah. "A Marriage of Convenience: Reading and Writing in School." *Farther Along: Transforming Dichotomies in Rhetoric and Composition*. Ed. Kate Ronald and Hephzibah Roskelly. Portsmouth, NH: Boynton/Cook, 1990. 137–148.

Rubin, Louis, ed. *An Apple for My Teacher: Twelve Authors Tell About Teachers Who Made the Difference*. Chapel Hill, NC: Algonguin, 1987.

Salinger, J. D. *The Catcher in the Rye*. 1951. New York: Bantam, 1984.

Scollon, Ronald, and Suzanne Scollon. *Narrative, Literacy and Face in Interethnic Communication*. Norwood, NJ: Ablex, 1981.

Scribner, Sylvia, and Michael Cole. "The Cognitive Consequences of Formal and Informal Education." *Science* 182 (1973). 553–559.

———. *The Psychology of Literacy*. Cambridge: Harvard University Press, 1981.

Shaughnessy, Mina. "Diving In: An Introduction to Basic Writing." Goswami and Stillman. 68–75.

———. *Errors and Expectations: A Guide for the Teacher of Basic Writing*. New York: Oxford University Press, 1977.

Shuy, Roger. "Teacher Training and Urban Language Problems." *Black American English*. Ed. Paul Stoller. New York: Dell, 1975.

Simonson, Rick, and Scott Walker, eds. *The Greywolf Annual Five: Multicultural Literacy*. St. Paul: Greywolf Press, 1988.

Sizer, Theodore. *Horace's Compromise: The Dilemma of the American High School*. Boston: Houghton Mifflin, 1984.

Smith, Frank. *Understanding Reading*. 4th ed. Hillsdale, NJ: Laurence Erlbaum, 1988.

Smitherman, Geneva. *Talkin' and Testifyin': The Language of Black America*. Boston: Houghton Mifflin, 1977.

Sommers, Nancy. "Responding to Student Writing." *Composing in a Second Language*. Ed. Sandra McKay. Rowley, MA: Newberry, 1984. Also in *College Composition and Communication* 33 (May 1982). 148–156.

———. "Revision Strategies of Student Writers and Experienced Adult Writers." *College Composition and Communication* 31 (December 1980). 378–388.

Sontag, Susan. *Against Interpretation*. New York: Farrar, Straus and Giroux, 1966.

———. *Illness as Metaphor*. New York: Farrar, Straus and Giroux, 1979.

Spark, Muriel. *The Prime of Miss Jean Brodie*. Philadelphia: Lippincott, 1962.

Strom, Margot, and William Parsons. *Facing History and Ourselves*. Brookline, MA: The Facing History and Ourselves National Foundation, 1980.

United States Department of Education. National Commission on Excellence in Education. *A Nation at Risk: The Imperative for Educational Reform.* Washington: GPO, 1983.

Vygotsky, Lev S. *Thought and Language.* Ed. and trans. Eugene Hanfamann, and Gertrude Vakar. Cambridge: MIT Press, 1962.

Welty, Eudora. *One Writer's Beginnings.* Cambridge: Harvard University Press, 1984.

Whitehead, Alfred North. *The Aims of Education.* New York: Macmillan, 1957.

Zamel, Vivian. "The Composing Processes of Advanced ESL Students: Six Case Studies." *TESOL Quarterly* 17 (June 1983). 165–187.

Zemelman, Steven, and Harvey Daniels. *A Community of Writers: Teaching Writing in the Junior and Senior High School.* Portsmouth, NH: Heinemann, 1988.

INDEX

Ability grouping. *See* Tracking
Abstract thinking, 49, 59, 313–14.
   See also Logical reasoning
Allison's writing, 40–44, 49–50, 119,
   171–72, 243, 281
Amish, 78, 97, 102
Angelou, Maya, 40, 53–54, 104–5,
   145, 148
Applebee, Arthur, 160–61, 173
Aristotle, 149, 163
   the topoi, 163
Ashton-Warner, Sylvia, 201
Athabaskans, 51–52, 68

Basic Writing, 24–25, 100, 126, 159,
   217
Belenky, Mary, et al., 52
Bell, Terrell, 90, 103
Bereiter, Carl, and Siegfried
   Englemann, 65, 71
Bernstein, Basil, 59–61
Berthoff, Ann
   on composing process, 179–80
   on critical method, 307–8
   on double-entry notebook, 30–31,
     235
   on form and forming, 155, 240
   on heuristics, 168
   on imagination, 221
   using metaphor, 230
Black English Vernacular (BEV), 59,
   66
Blake, William, 228–29
Boynton, Percy, 164, 166
Boston Writing Project, 102, 204, 271
Britton, James, 19, 165, 170–71, 180,
   239, 314
Bronowski, Jacob, 224–25
Bruffee, Kenneth, 258
Bruner, Jerome, 40, 45, 52, 73, 225,
   321
Burke, Kenneth, 236

Carnegie Commission Report,
   91–92, 95
Carroll, Lewis, 61, 136–37
Categorization, 36, 46–67, 79, 227,
   231
Case study, 332–34
Cazden, Courtney, 74
Chall, Jeanne, 194–95
Chomsky, Noam, 62–63
Classroom discourse. *See* Discourse:
   classroom
Codes, restricted and elaborated,
   59–61, 65–66, 71
Coleridge, Samuel Taylor, 165, 221,
   224
Collaboration
   activities for, 336–38
   through groups, 259–67
   in learning, 258
   in reading, 260–61
   in school community, 320
   in writing, 76–77, 264–65
Competence
   linguistic, 62–63
   communicative, 64
Composing. *See* Writing: process
Conroy, Pat, 22–23, 53–55, 59,
   82–83, 105–8, 200
Conscientization, 112, 307
Culture
   circle, 307
   definition of, 14
Curriculum
   English, 117
   reinvented, 308–317
   standard, 94, 98, 101–2, 284,
     287–93, 298

Delpit, Lisa, 184–85
Dewey, John, 96–97, 102–13
Dialect, 69–71, 131, 145
Diary of Anne Frank, 40–41, 43, 114,